PEANUTS COLLECTOR SERIES #8

Could You Be More Pacific?

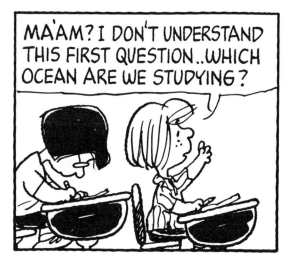

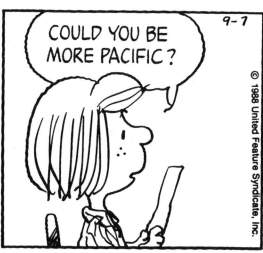

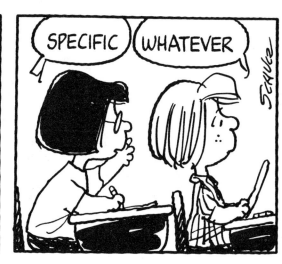

MA'AM? I DON'T UNDERSTAND THIS FIRST QUESTION..WHICH OCEAN ARE WE STUDYING?
COULD YOU BE MORE PACIFIC?
9-7
© 1988 United Feature Syndicate, Inc.
SPECIFIC
WHATEVER
SCHULZ

Charles M. Schulz

Ha HaHa!

TOPPER BOOKS
AN IMPRINT OF PHAROS BOOKS • A SCRIPPS HOWARD COMPANY
NEW YORK

PEANUTS® Comic Strips : © 1988
United Feature Syndicate, Inc.

Library of Congress Cataloging-in-Publication Data

Schulz. Charles M.
    [Peanuts. Selections]
    Could you be more pacific? / Charles M. Schulz.
        p.   cm. – (Peanuts collector series : #8)
    Selections from the comic strip Peanuts.
    ISBN 0-88687-627-3 : $6.95
    I. Peanuts.   II. Title.   III. Series: Schulz. Charles M.   Peanuts
  collector series : #8.
PN6728.P4S284   1991
741.5'973 – dc20   91-6894
                                                              CIP

Pharos ISBN: 0-88687-627-3

TOPPER BOOKS
An Imprint of Pharos Books
A Scripps Howard Company
200 Park Avenue
New York, NY 10166

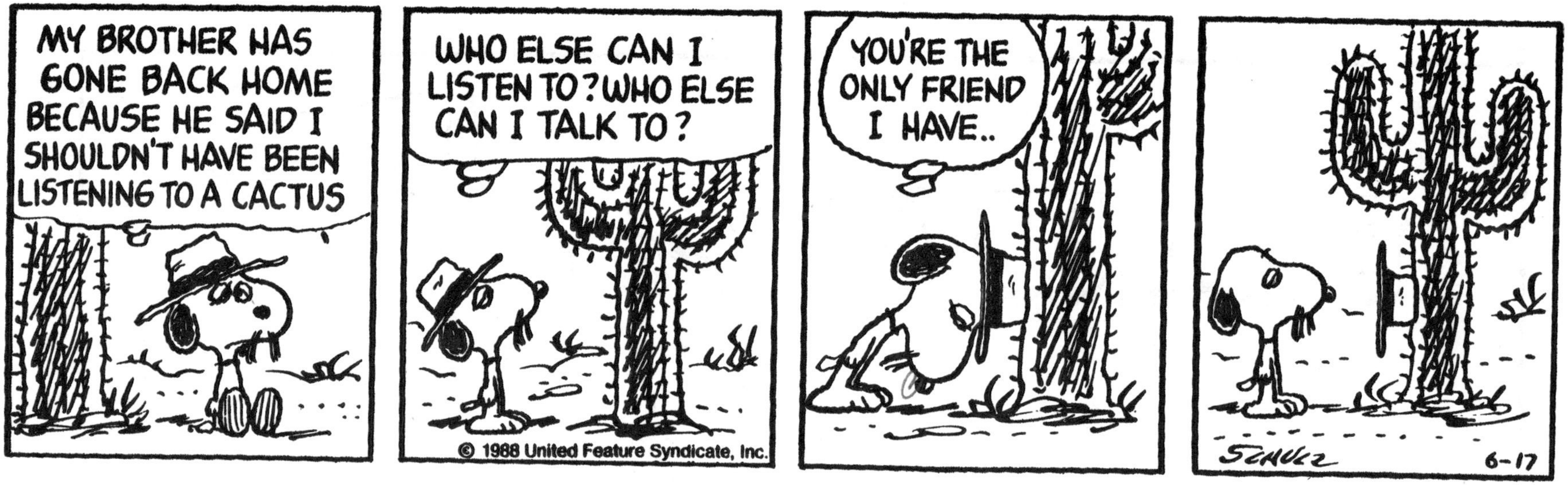
MY BROTHER HAS GONE BACK HOME BECAUSE HE SAID I SHOULDN'T HAVE BEEN LISTENING TO A CACTUS
WHO ELSE CAN I LISTEN TO? WHO ELSE CAN I TALK TO?
© 1988 United Feature Syndicate, Inc.
YOU'RE THE ONLY FRIEND I HAVE..
SCHULZ
6-17

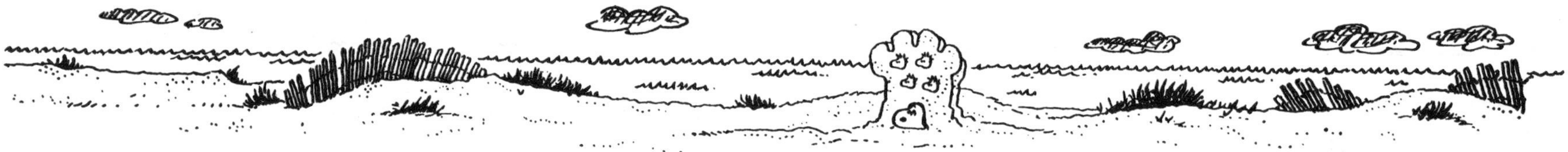

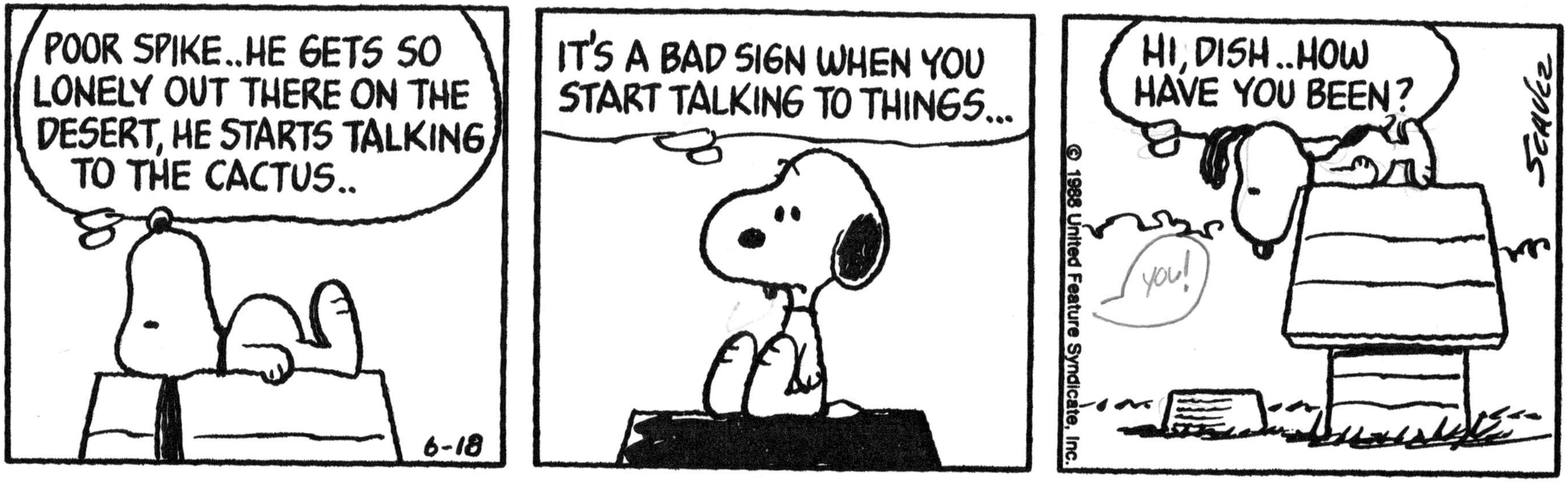
POOR SPIKE..HE GETS SO LONELY OUT THERE ON THE DESERT, HE STARTS TALKING TO THE CACTUS..
6-18
IT'S A BAD SIGN WHEN YOU START TALKING TO THINGS...
HI, DISH..HOW HAVE YOU BEEN?
© 1988 United Feature Syndicate, Inc.
SCHULZ

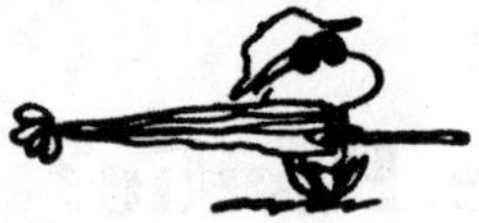

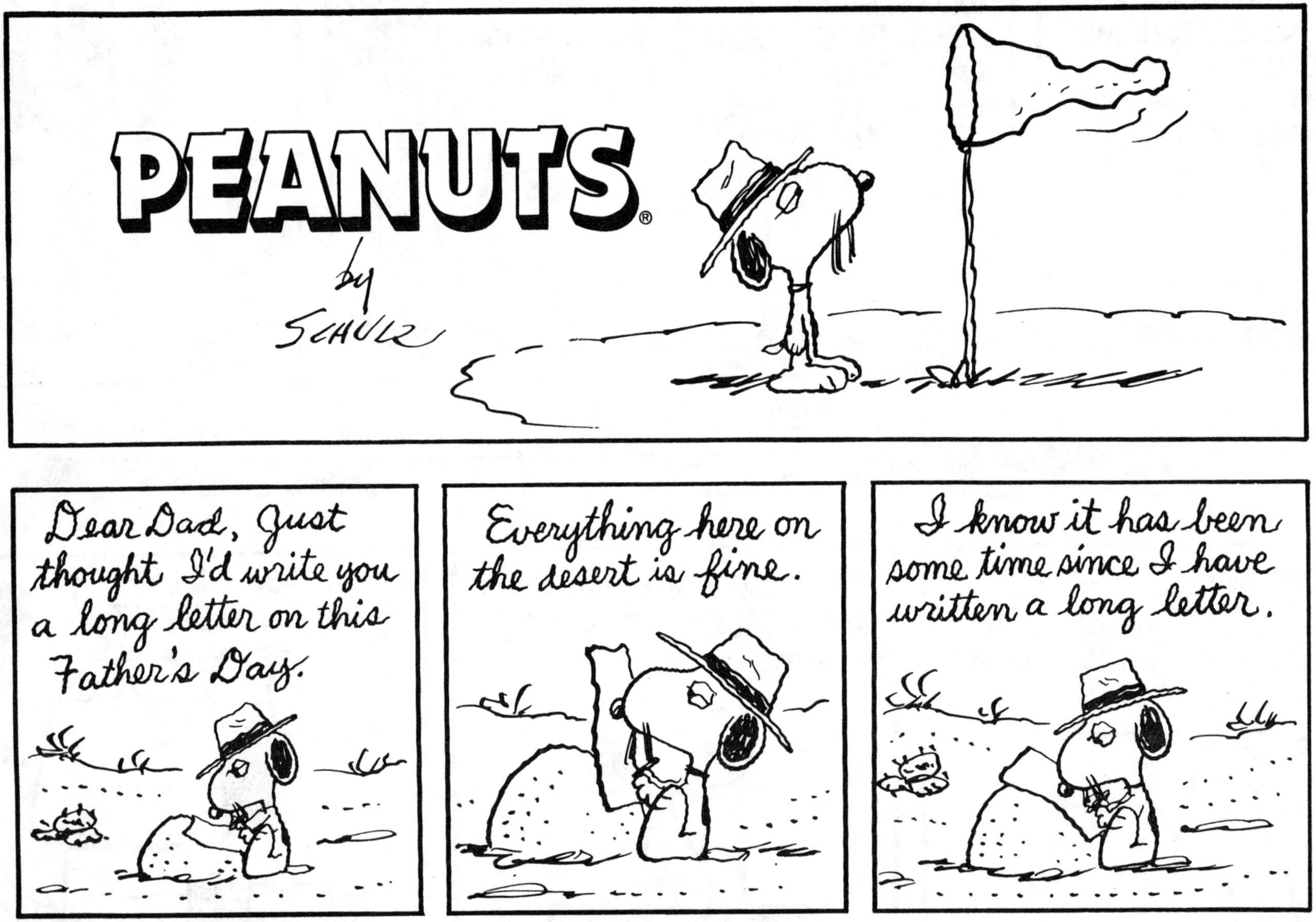
PEANUTS®
by SCHULZ
Dear Dad, Just thought I'd write you a long letter on this Father's Day.
Everything here on the desert is fine.
I know it has been some time since I have written a long letter.

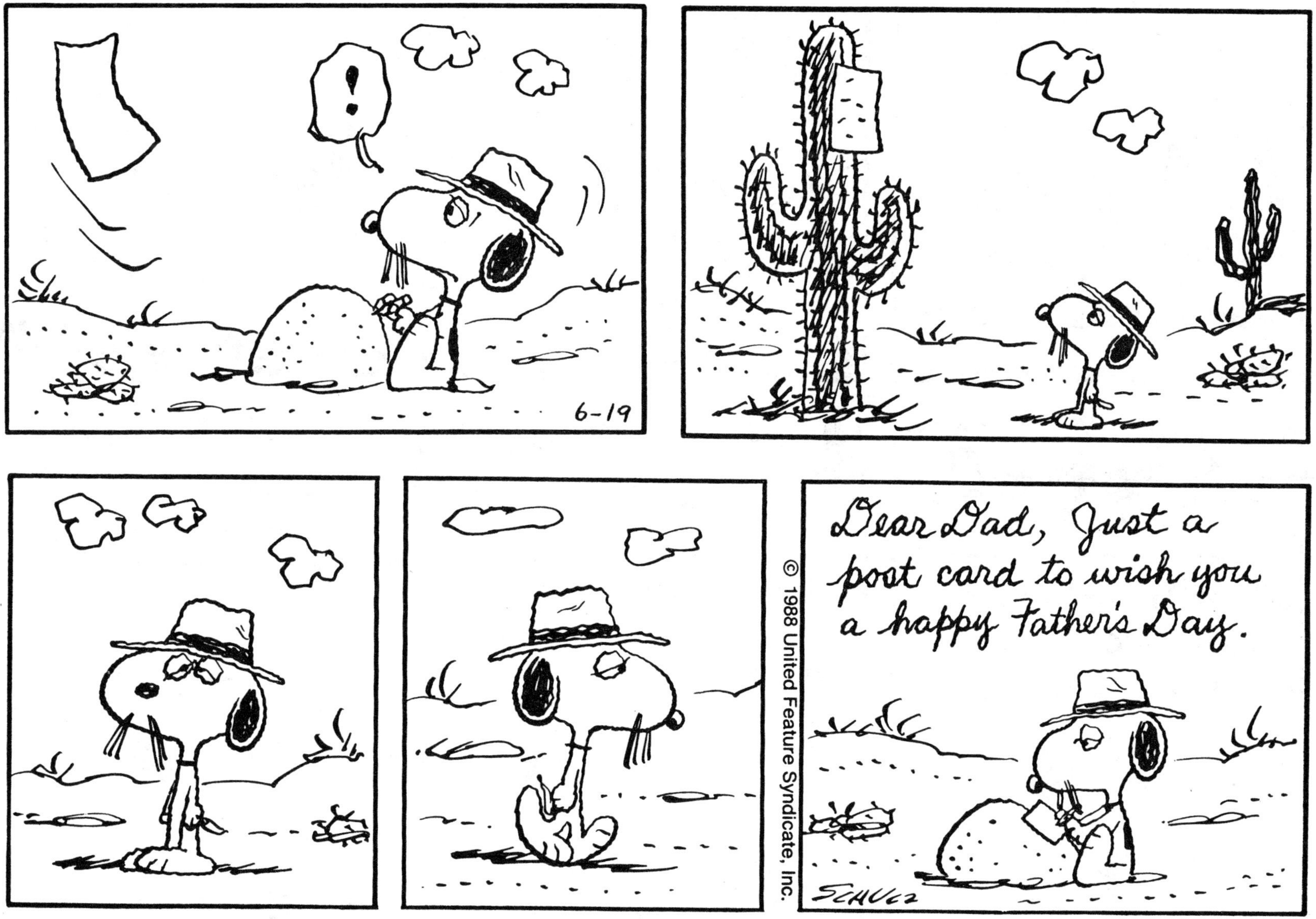
!
6-19
Dear Dad, Just a post card to wish you a happy Father's Day.
© 1988 United Feature Syndicate, Inc.
SCHULZ

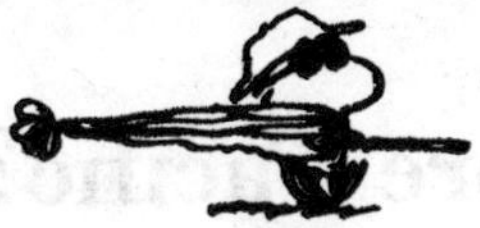

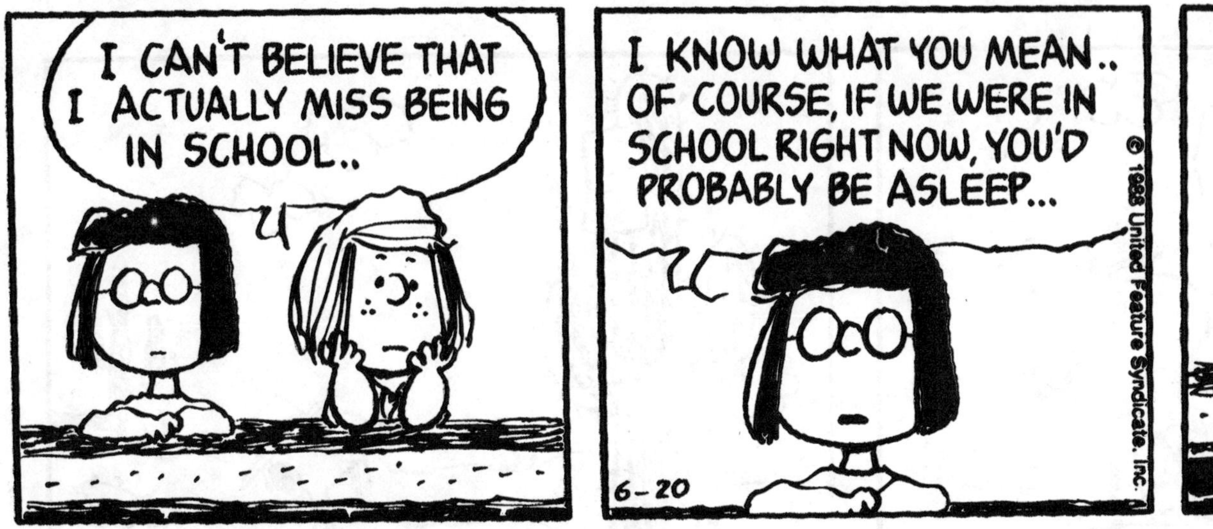
I CAN'T BELIEVE THAT I ACTUALLY MISS BEING IN SCHOOL..
I KNOW WHAT YOU MEAN.. OF COURSE, IF WE WERE IN SCHOOL RIGHT NOW, YOU'D PROBABLY BE ASLEEP...
6-20
© 1988 United Feature Syndicate, Inc.
Z
SCHULZ

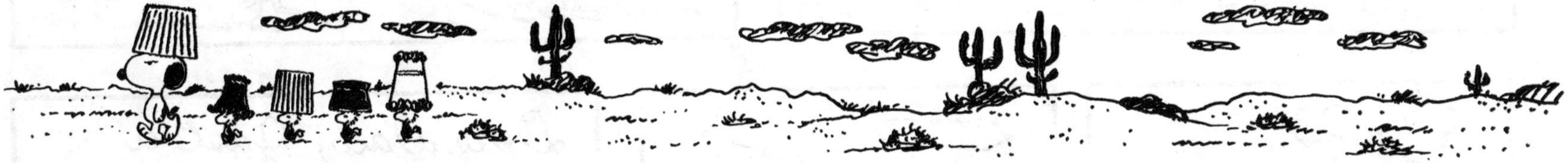

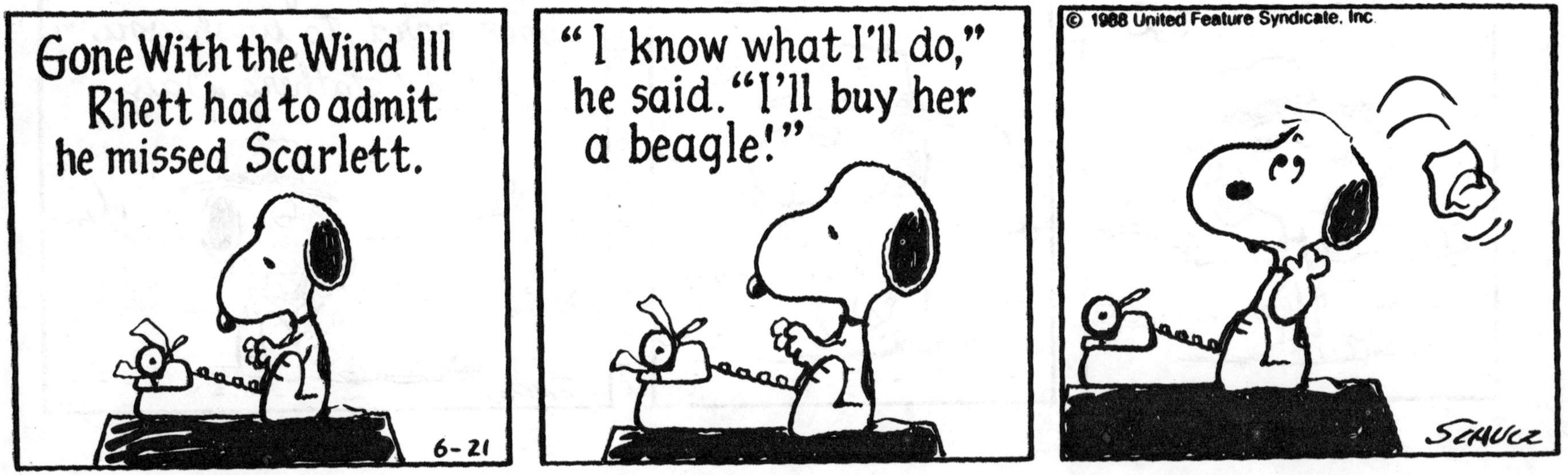
Gone With the Wind III
Rhett had to admit he missed Scarlett.
6-21
"I know what I'll do," he said. "I'll buy her a beagle!"
© 1988 United Feature Syndicate, Inc.
SCHULZ

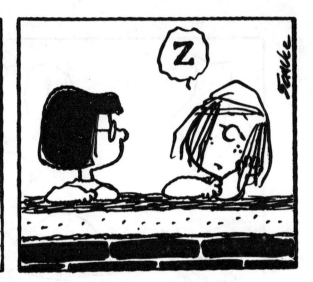

Could You Be More Pacific?

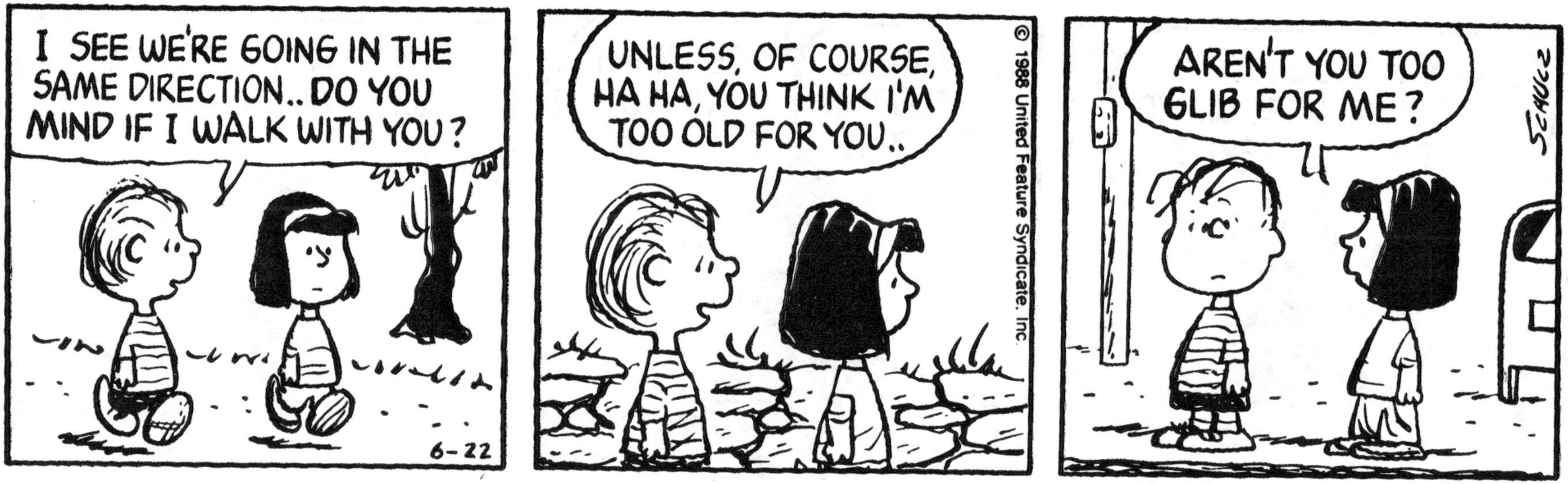
I SEE WE'RE GOING IN THE SAME DIRECTION.. DO YOU MIND IF I WALK WITH YOU?
6-22
UNLESS, OF COURSE, HA HA, YOU THINK I'M TOO OLD FOR YOU..
© 1988 United Feature Syndicate, Inc.
AREN'T YOU TOO GLIB FOR ME?
SCHULZ

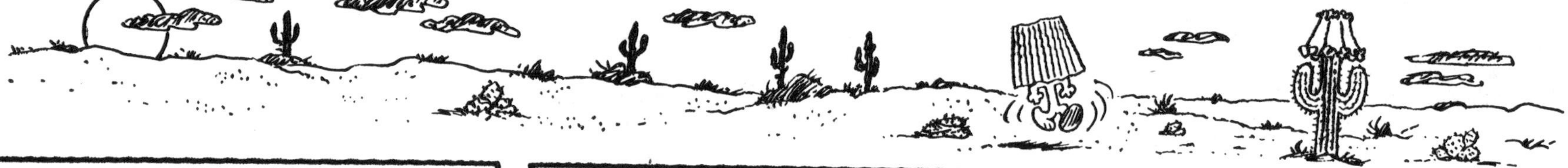

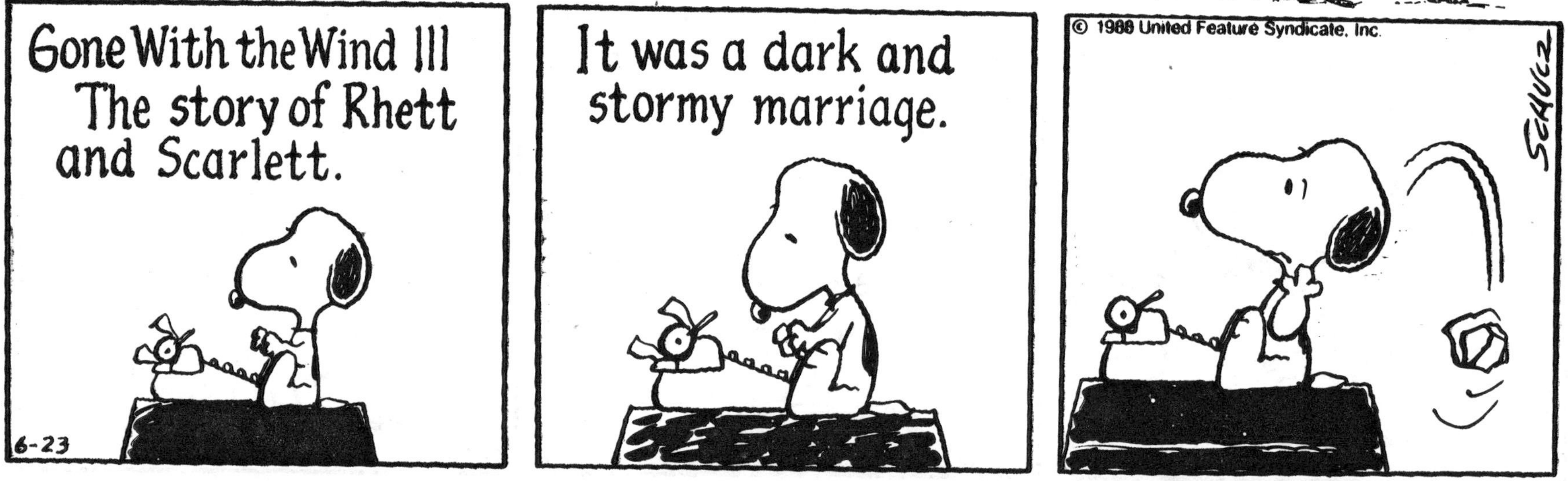
Gone With the Wind III
The story of Rhett and Scarlett.
6-23
It was a dark and stormy marriage.
© 1988 United Feature Syndicate, Inc.
SCHULZ

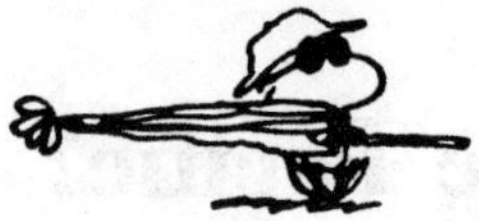

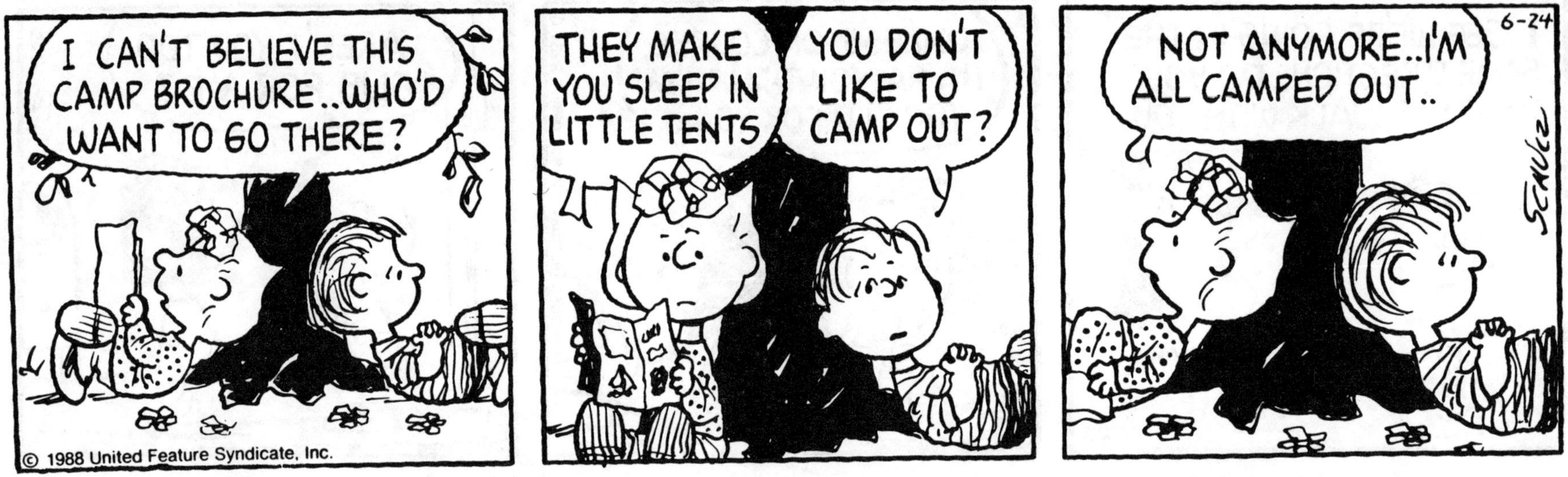
6-24
I CAN'T BELIEVE THIS CAMP BROCHURE..WHO'D WANT TO GO THERE?
THEY MAKE YOU SLEEP IN LITTLE TENTS
YOU DON'T LIKE TO CAMP OUT?
NOT ANYMORE..I'M ALL CAMPED OUT..
SCHULZ
© 1988 United Feature Syndicate, Inc.

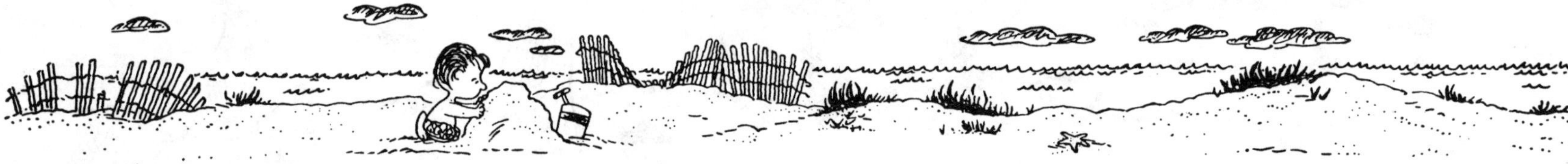

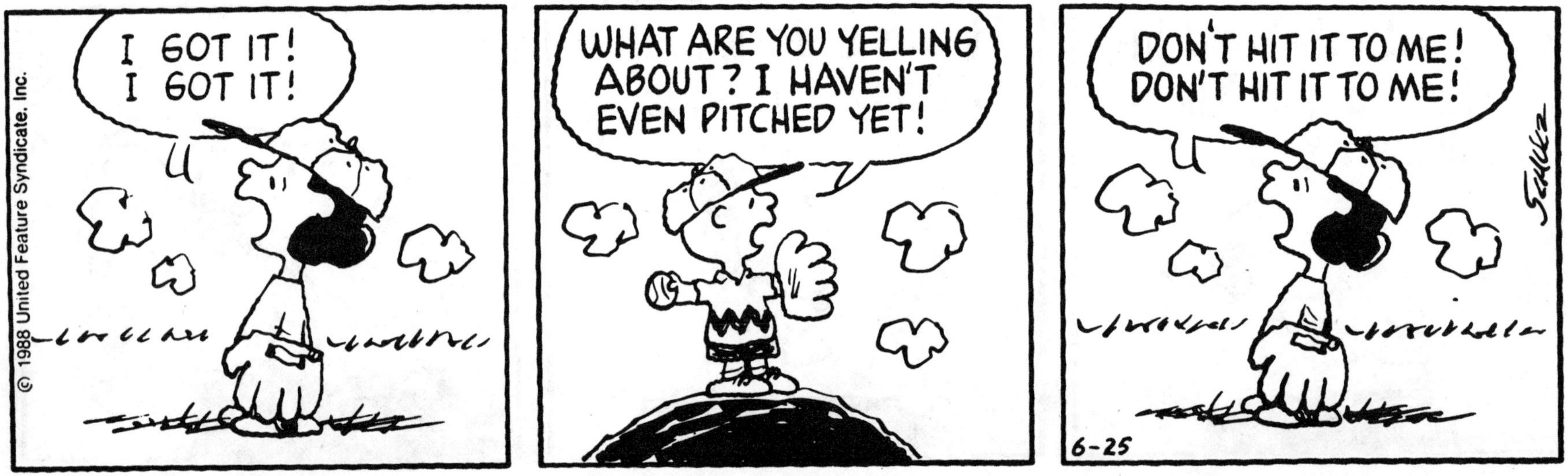
© 1988 United Feature Syndicate, Inc.
I GOT IT! I GOT IT!
WHAT ARE YOU YELLING ABOUT? I HAVEN'T EVEN PITCHED YET!
DON'T HIT IT TO ME! DON'T HIT IT TO ME!
SCHULZ
6-25

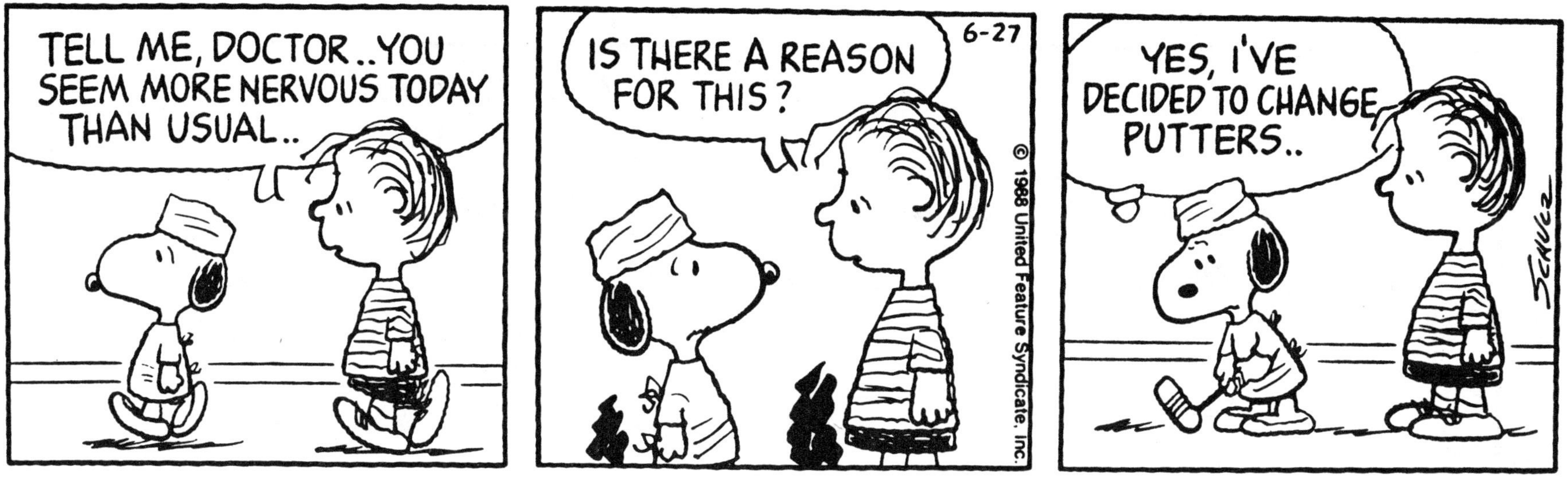
TELL ME, DOCTOR..YOU SEEM MORE NERVOUS TODAY THAN USUAL..
IS THERE A REASON FOR THIS?
6-27
© 1988 United Feature Syndicate, Inc.
YES, I'VE DECIDED TO CHANGE PUTTERS..
SCHULZ

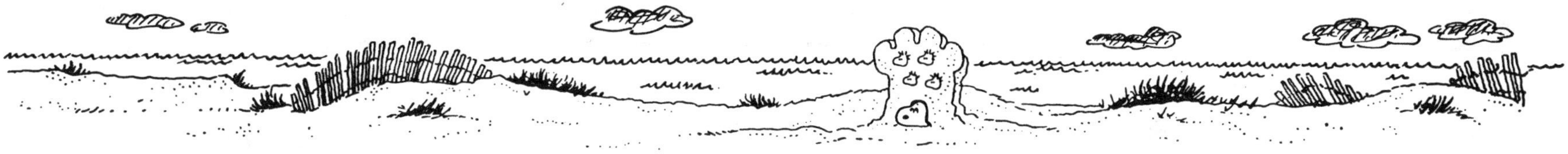

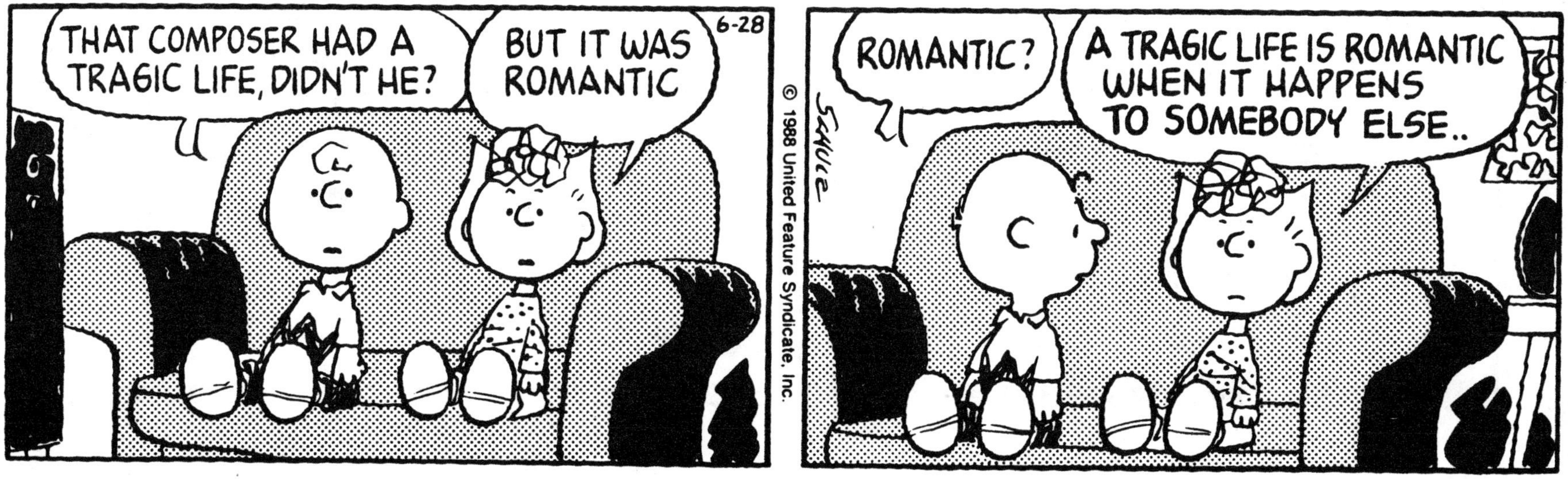
THAT COMPOSER HAD A TRAGIC LIFE, DIDN'T HE?
BUT IT WAS ROMANTIC
6-28
© 1988 United Feature Syndicate, Inc.
SCHULZ
ROMANTIC?
A TRAGIC LIFE IS ROMANTIC WHEN IT HAPPENS TO SOMEBODY ELSE..

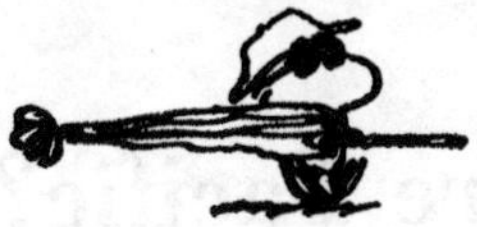

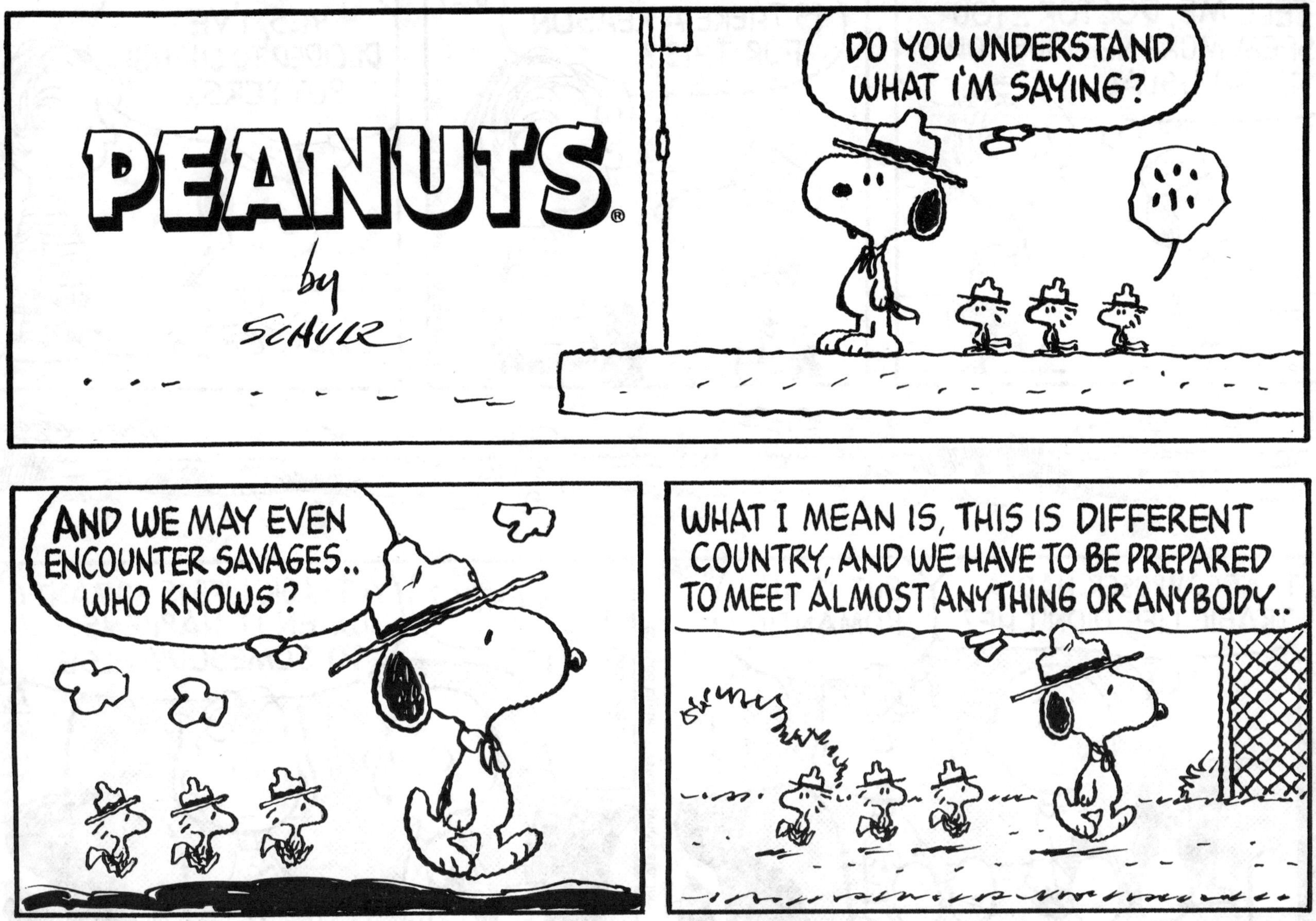
PEANUTS®
by SCHULZ
DO YOU UNDERSTAND WHAT I'M SAYING?
AND WE MAY EVEN ENCOUNTER SAVAGES.. WHO KNOWS?
WHAT I MEAN IS, THIS IS DIFFERENT COUNTRY, AND WE HAVE TO BE PREPARED TO MEET ALMOST ANYTHING OR ANYBODY..

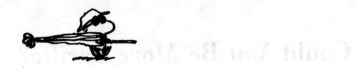

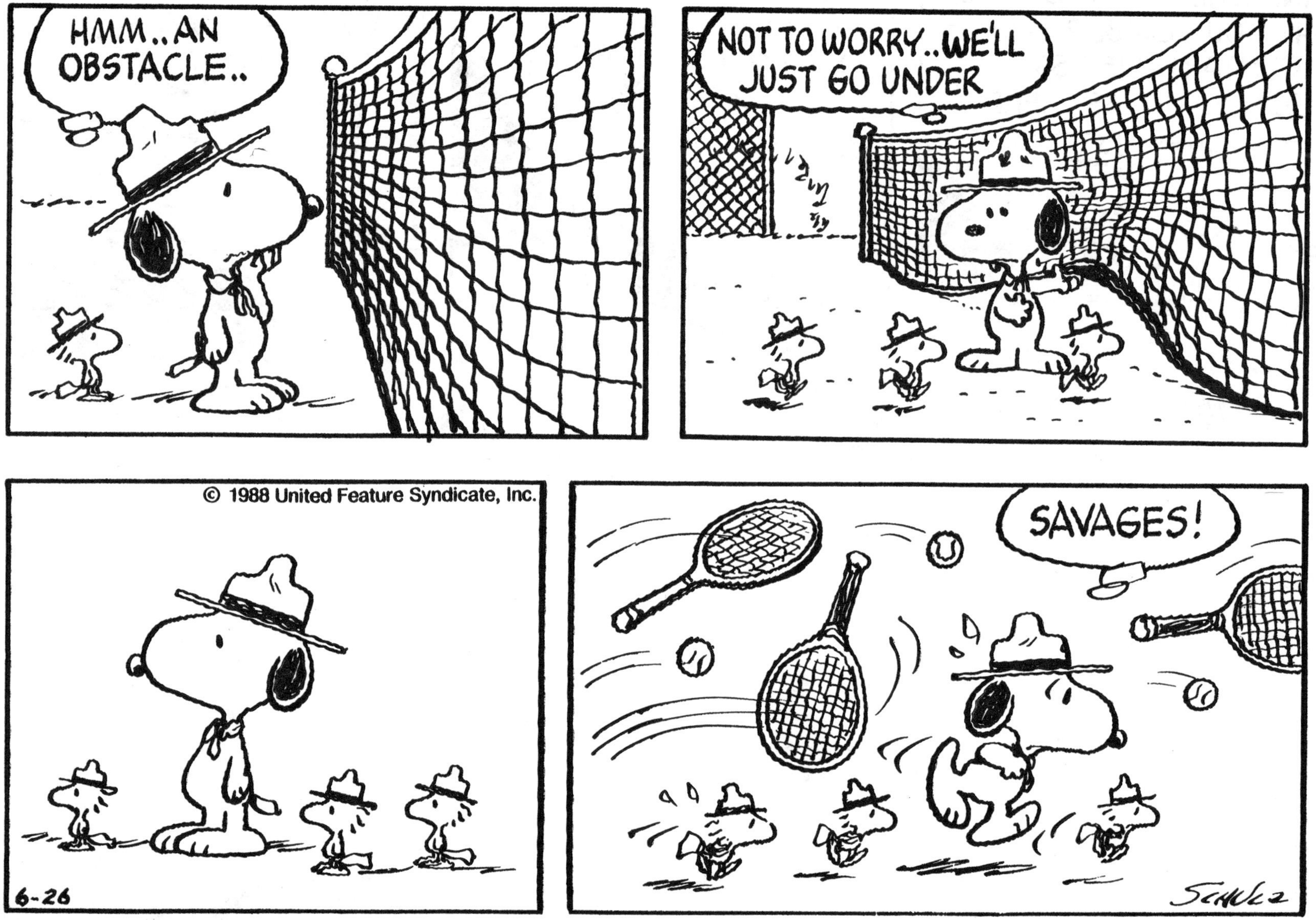
HMM..AN OBSTACLE..
NOT TO WORRY..WE'LL JUST GO UNDER
© 1988 United Feature Syndicate, Inc.
6-26
SAVAGES!
SCHULZ

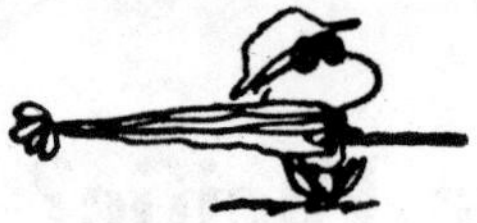

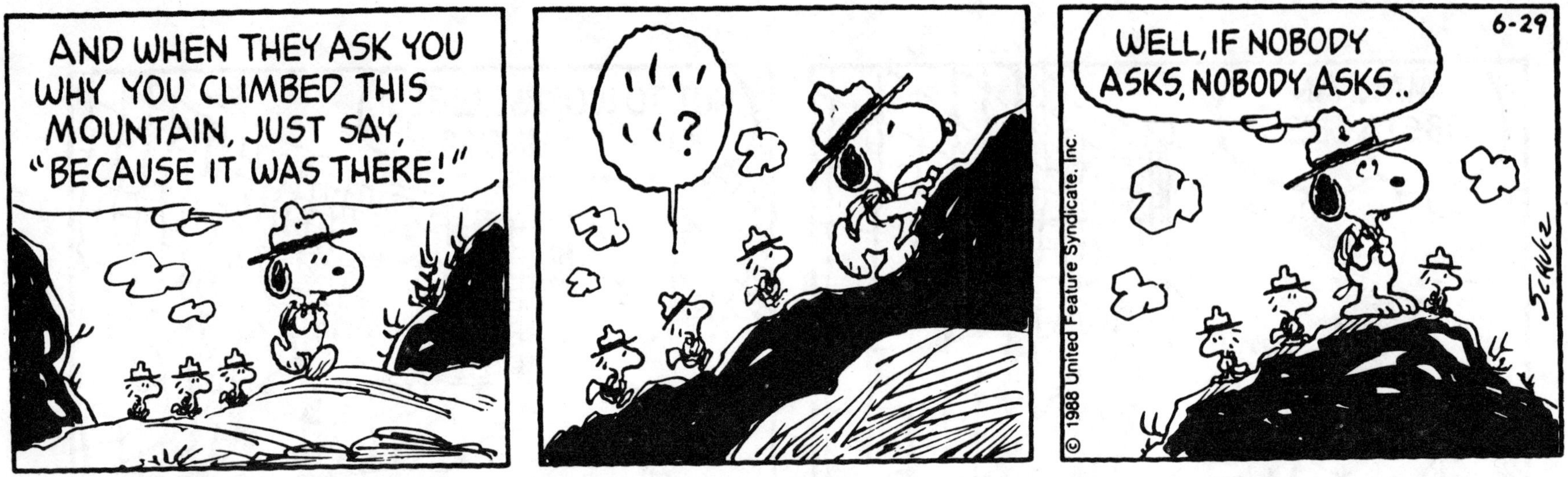
6-29
AND WHEN THEY ASK YOU WHY YOU CLIMBED THIS MOUNTAIN, JUST SAY, "BECAUSE IT WAS THERE!"
?
WELL, IF NOBODY ASKS, NOBODY ASKS..
© 1988 United Feature Syndicate, Inc.
SCHULZ

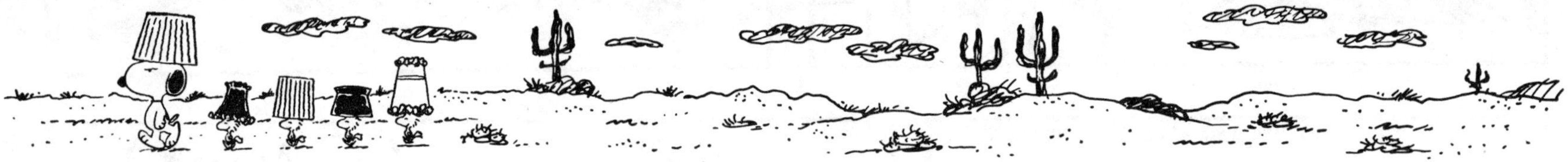

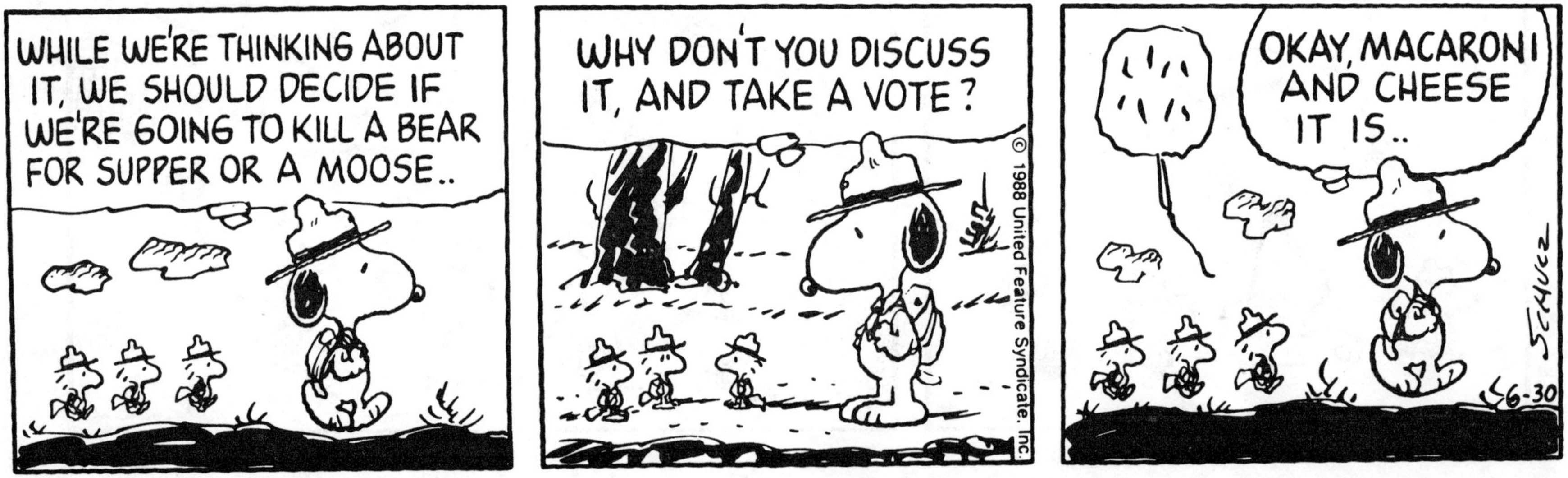
WHILE WE'RE THINKING ABOUT IT, WE SHOULD DECIDE IF WE'RE GOING TO KILL A BEAR FOR SUPPER OR A MOOSE..
WHY DON'T YOU DISCUSS IT, AND TAKE A VOTE?
© 1988 United Feature Syndicate, Inc.
OKAY, MACARONI AND CHEESE IT IS..
SCHULZ
6-30

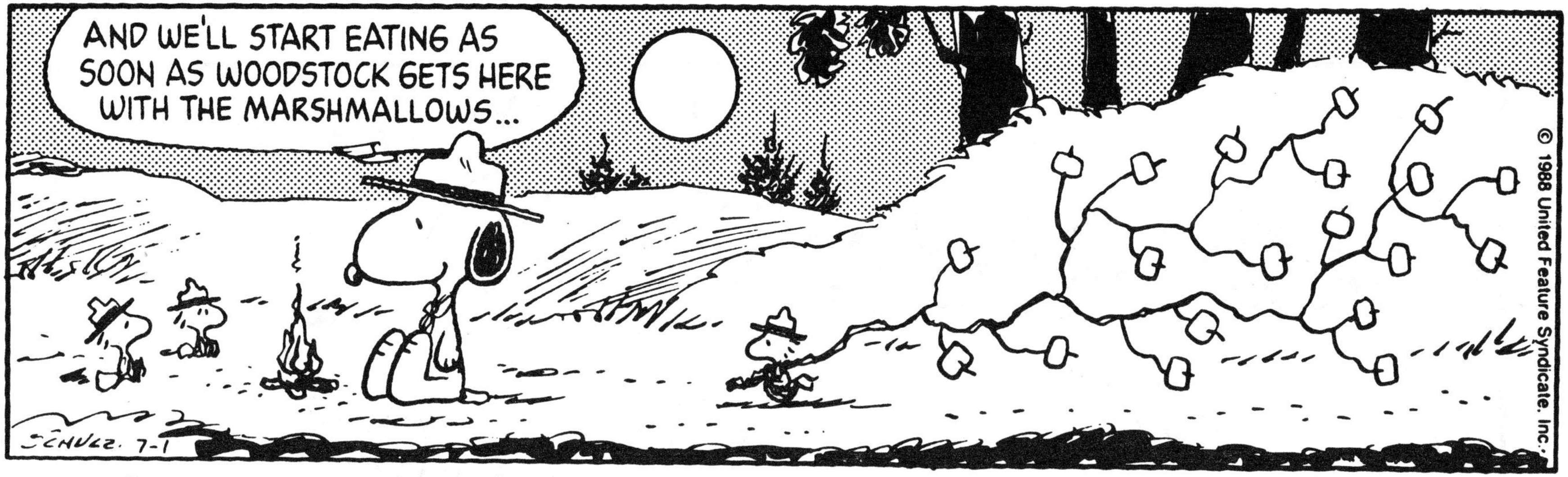
AND WE'LL START EATING AS SOON AS WOODSTOCK GETS HERE WITH THE MARSHMALLOWS...
SCHULZ 7-1
© 1988 United Feature Syndicate, Inc.

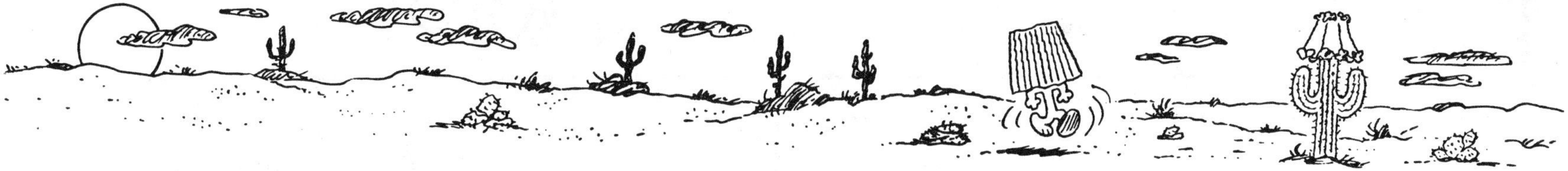

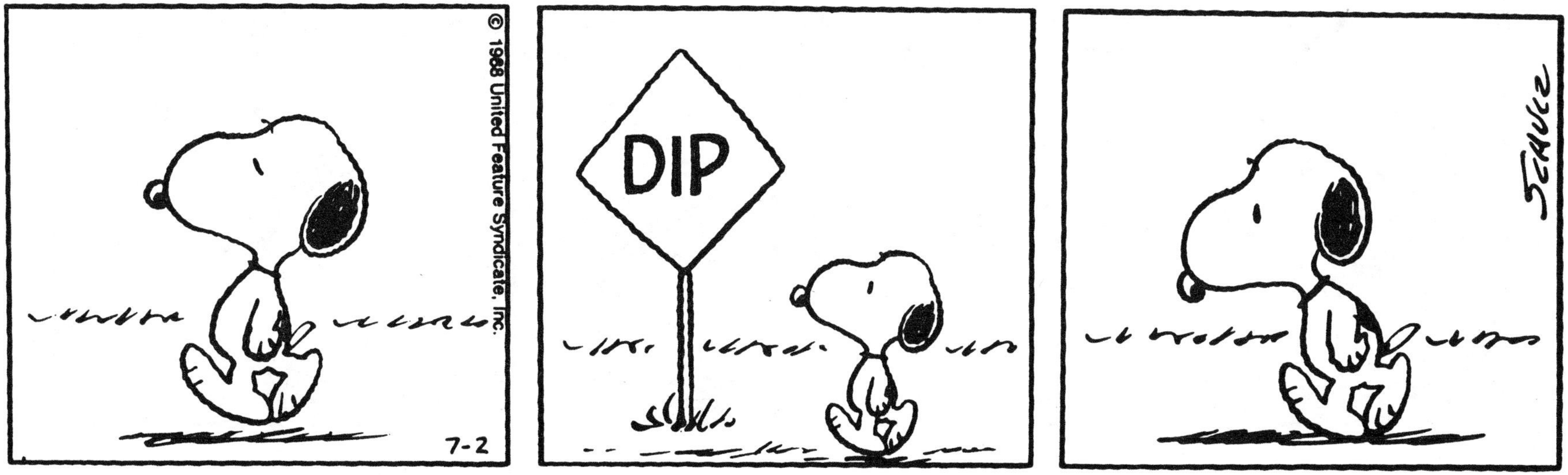
© 1988 United Feature Syndicate, Inc.
7-2
DIP
SCHULZ

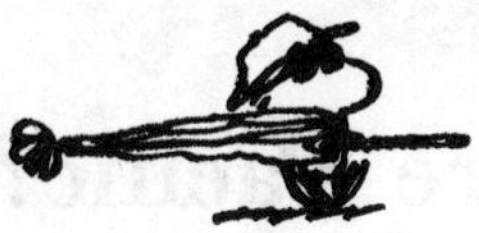

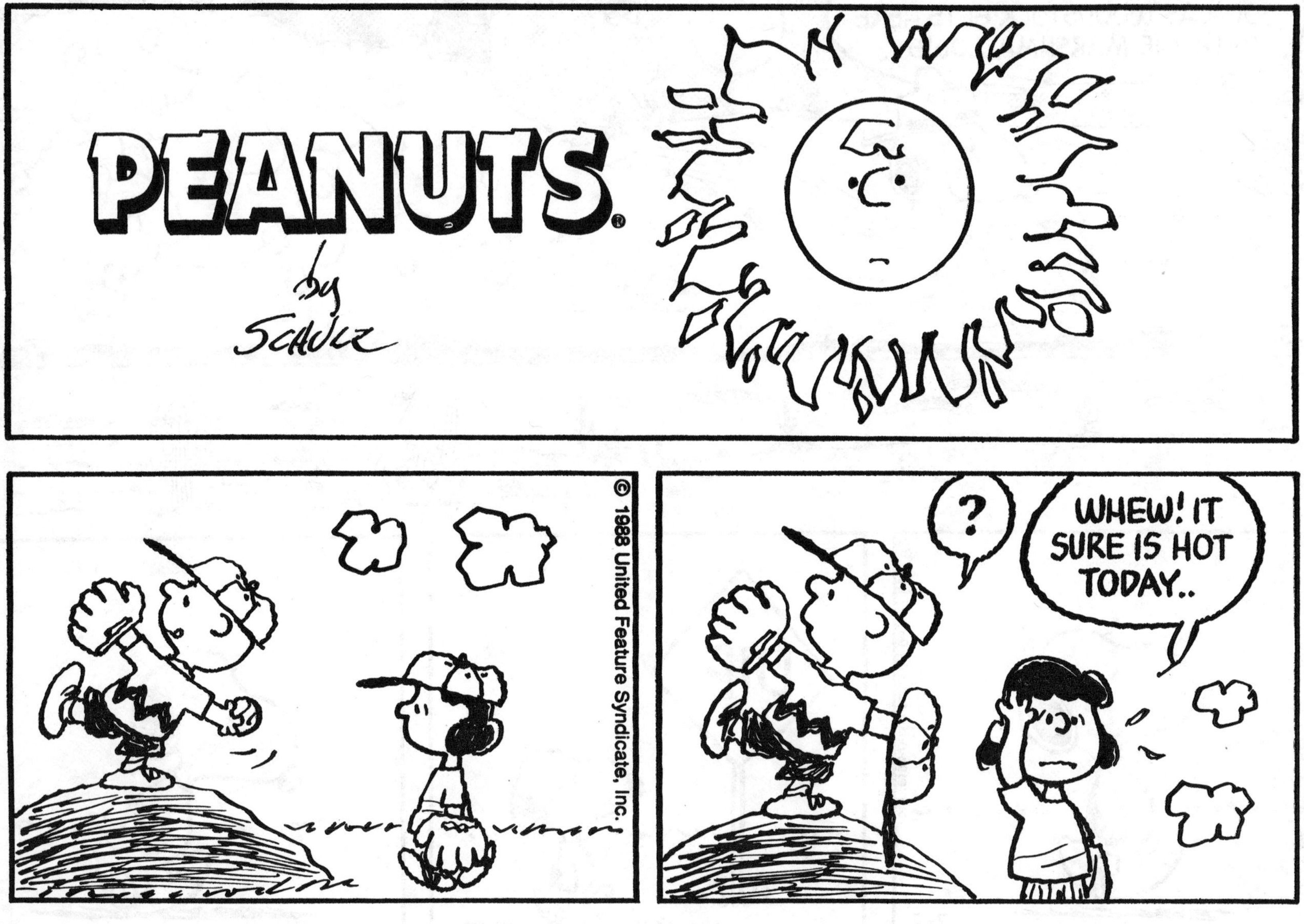
PEANUTS®
by SCHULZ
© 1988 United Feature Syndicate, Inc.
?
WHEW! IT SURE IS HOT TODAY..

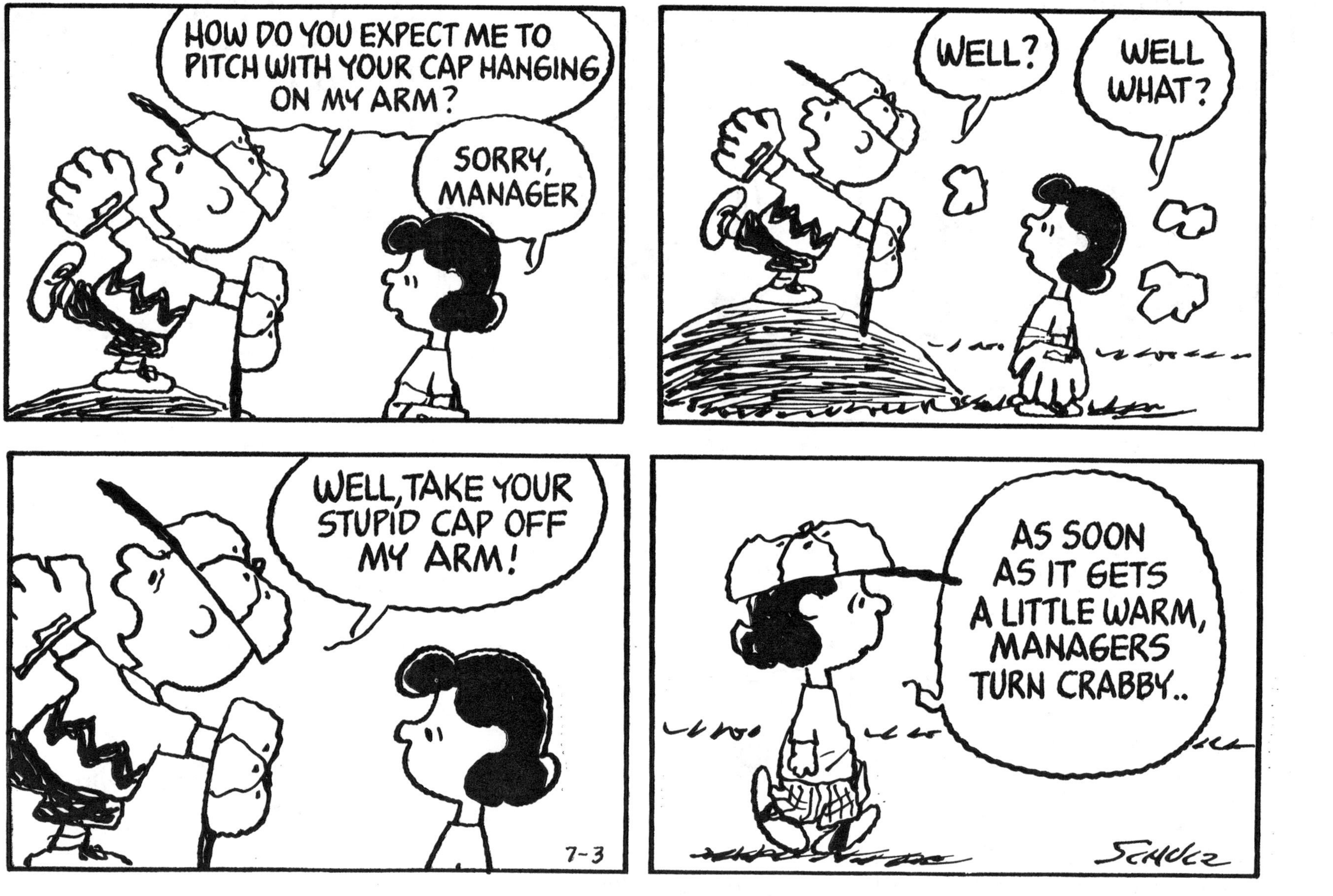
HOW DO YOU EXPECT ME TO PITCH WITH YOUR CAP HANGING ON MY ARM?
SORRY, MANAGER
WELL?
WELL WHAT?
WELL, TAKE YOUR STUPID CAP OFF MY ARM!
7-3
AS SOON AS IT GETS A LITTLE WARM, MANAGERS TURN CRABBY..
SCHULZ

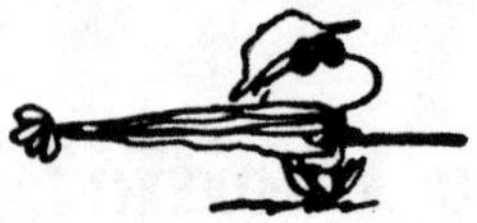

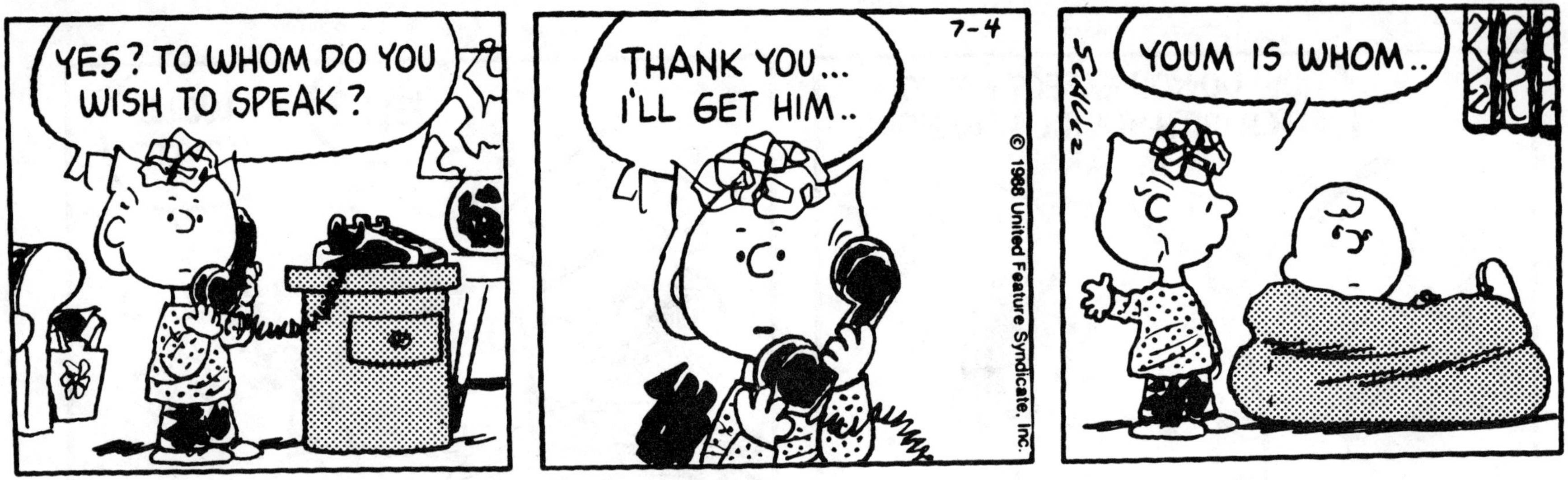
YES? TO WHOM DO YOU WISH TO SPEAK?
THANK YOU... I'LL GET HIM..
7-4
© 1988 United Feature Syndicate, Inc.
SCHULZ
YOUM IS WHOM..

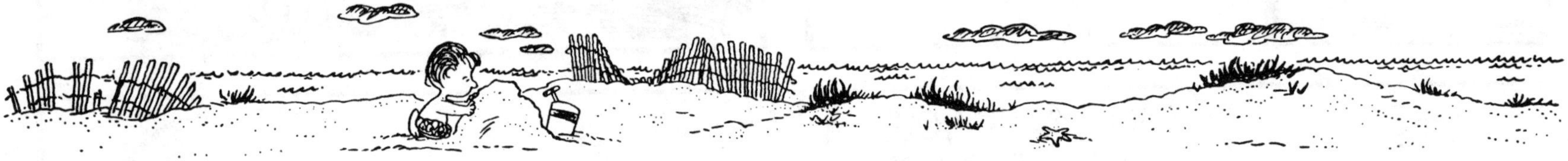

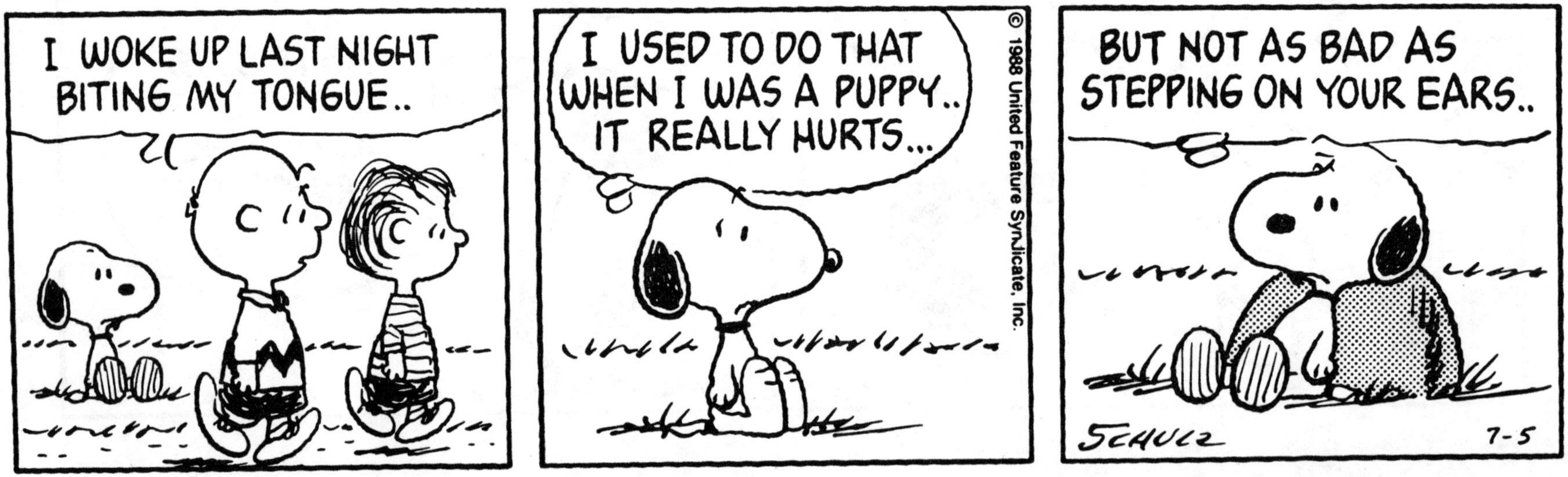
I WOKE UP LAST NIGHT BITING MY TONGUE..
I USED TO DO THAT WHEN I WAS A PUPPY.. IT REALLY HURTS...
© 1988 United Feature Syndicate, Inc.
BUT NOT AS BAD AS STEPPING ON YOUR EARS..
SCHULZ
7-5

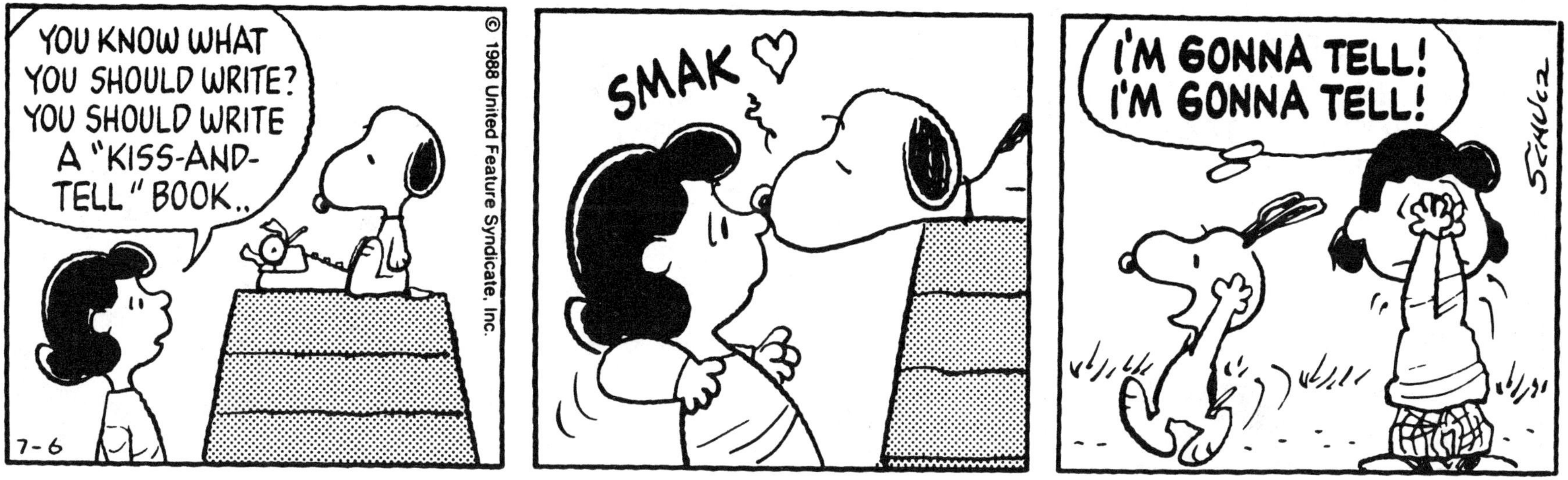
YOU KNOW WHAT YOU SHOULD WRITE? YOU SHOULD WRITE A "KISS-AND-TELL" BOOK..
© 1988 United Feature Syndicate, Inc.
7-6
SMAK
I'M GONNA TELL! I'M GONNA TELL!
SCHULZ

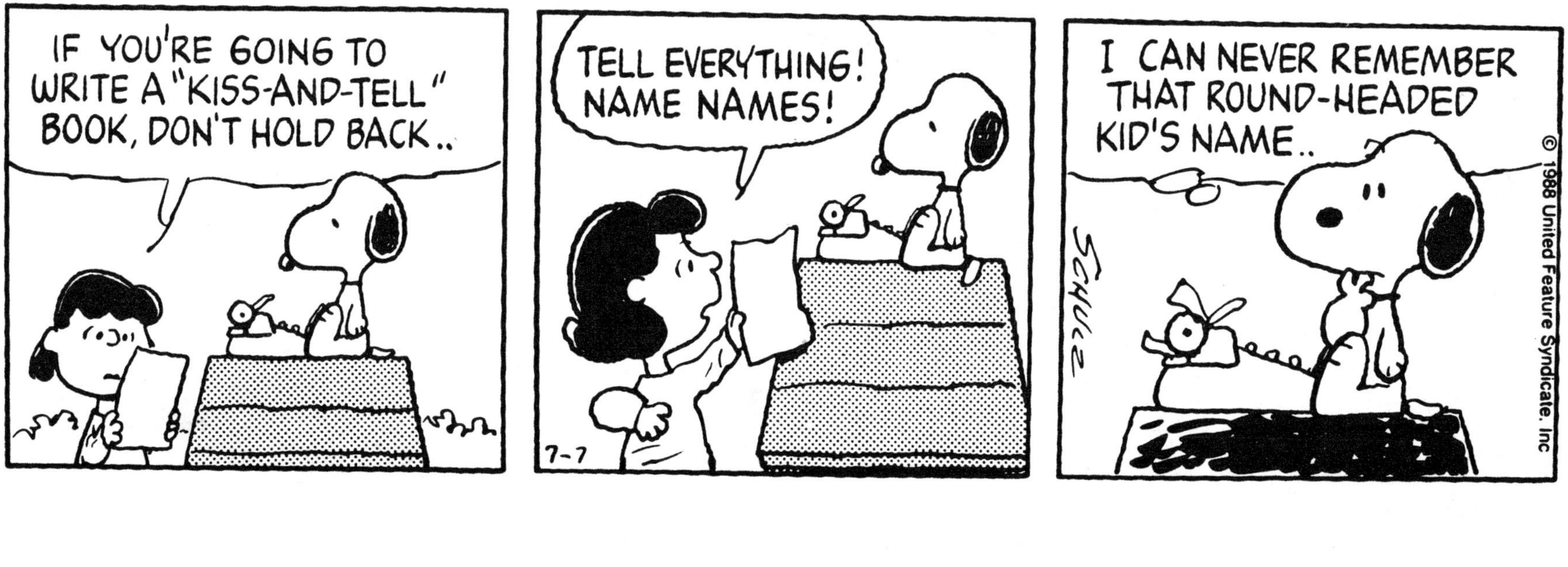
IF YOU'RE GOING TO WRITE A "KISS-AND-TELL" BOOK, DON'T HOLD BACK..
TELL EVERYTHING! NAME NAMES!
7-7
I CAN NEVER REMEMBER THAT ROUND-HEADED KID'S NAME..
SCHULZ
© 1988 United Feature Syndicate, Inc

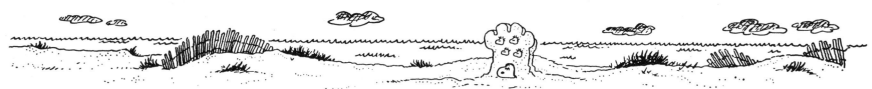

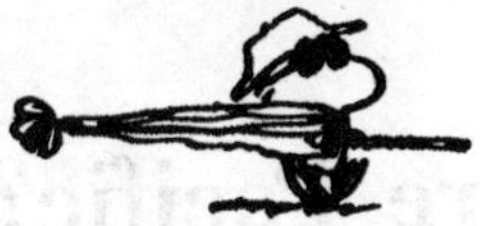

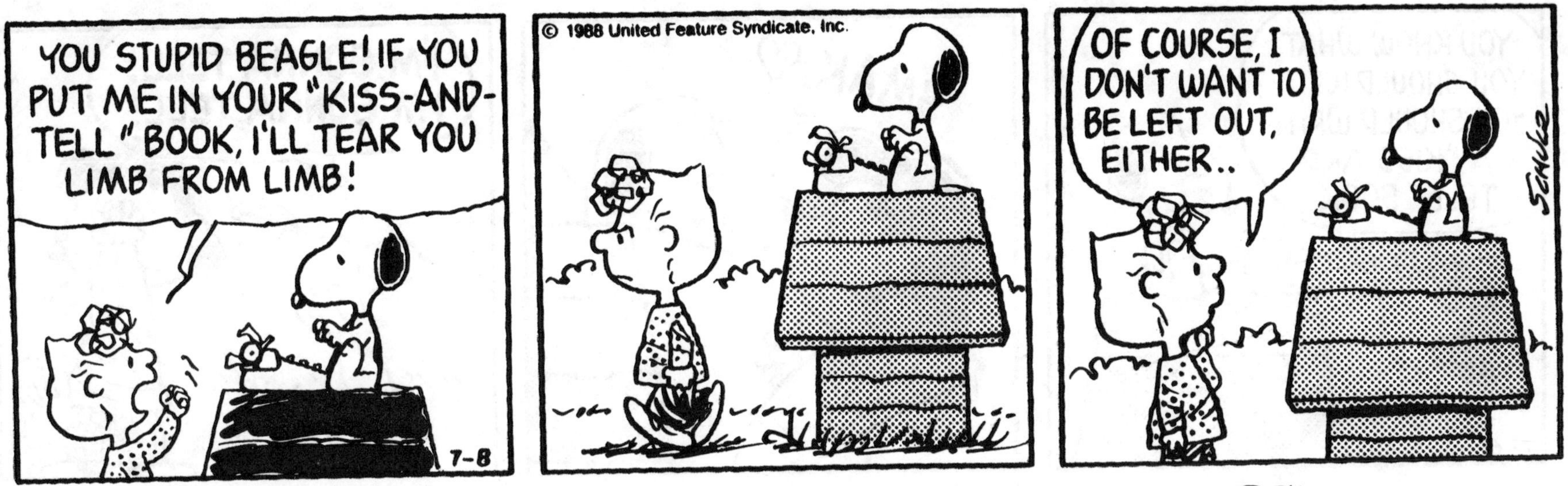

YOU STUPID BEAGLE! IF YOU PUT ME IN YOUR "KISS-AND-TELL" BOOK, I'LL TEAR YOU LIMB FROM LIMB!
7-8
© 1988 United Feature Syndicate, Inc.
OF COURSE, I DON'T WANT TO BE LEFT OUT, EITHER..
SCHULZ

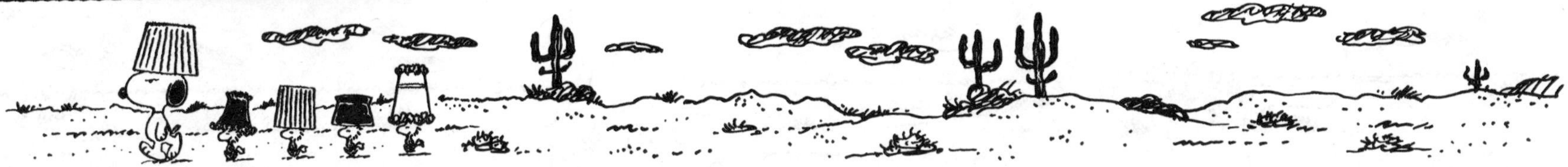

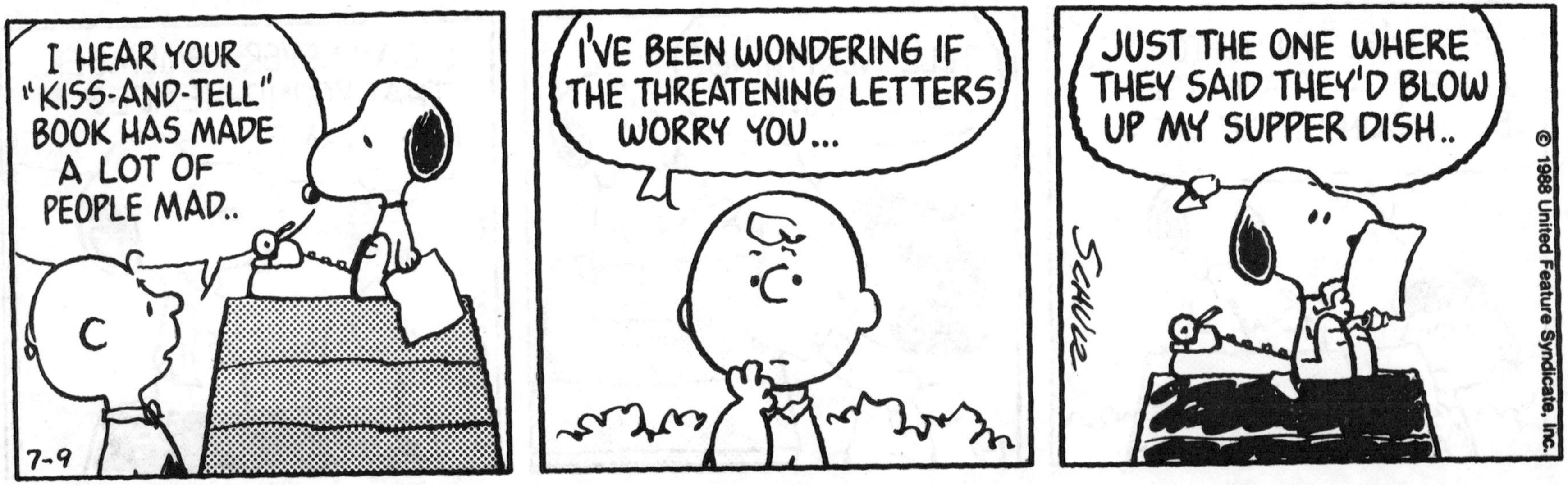

I HEAR YOUR "KISS-AND-TELL" BOOK HAS MADE A LOT OF PEOPLE MAD..
7-9
I'VE BEEN WONDERING IF THE THREATENING LETTERS WORRY YOU...
JUST THE ONE WHERE THEY SAID THEY'D BLOW UP MY SUPPER DISH..
SCHULZ
© 1988 United Feature Syndicate, Inc.

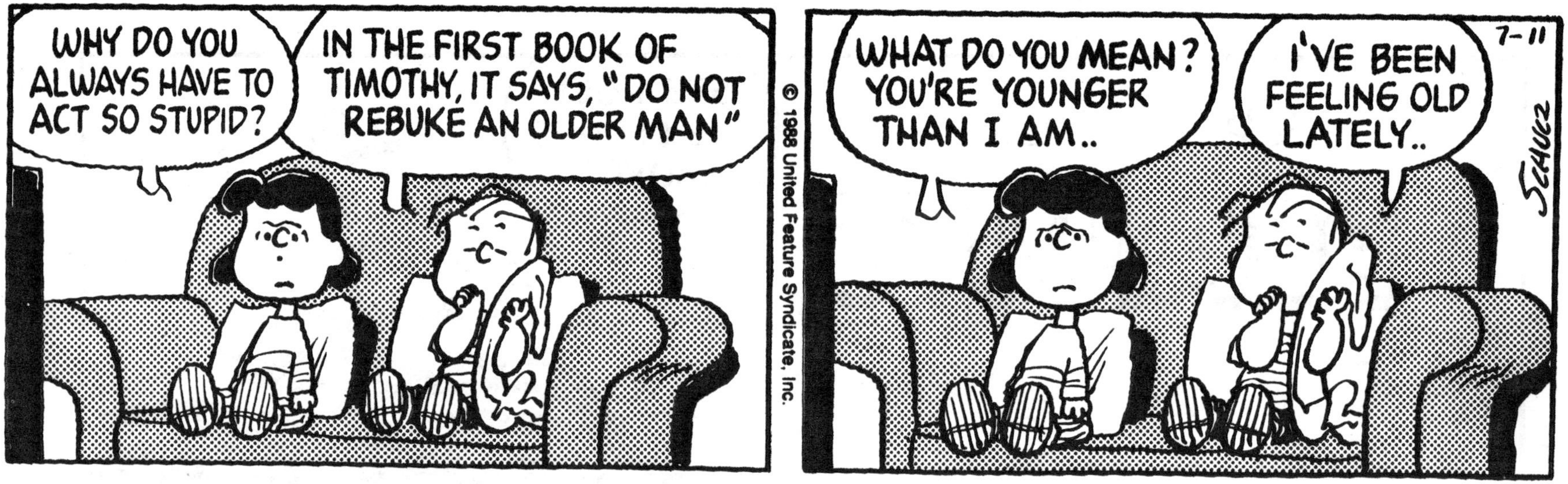
WHY DO YOU ALWAYS HAVE TO ACT SO STUPID?
IN THE FIRST BOOK OF TIMOTHY, IT SAYS, "DO NOT REBUKE AN OLDER MAN"
© 1988 United Feature Syndicate, Inc.
WHAT DO YOU MEAN? YOU'RE YOUNGER THAN I AM..
I'VE BEEN FEELING OLD LATELY..
7-11
SCHULZ

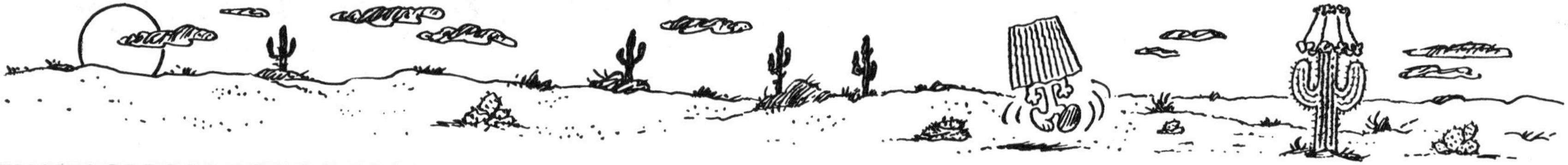

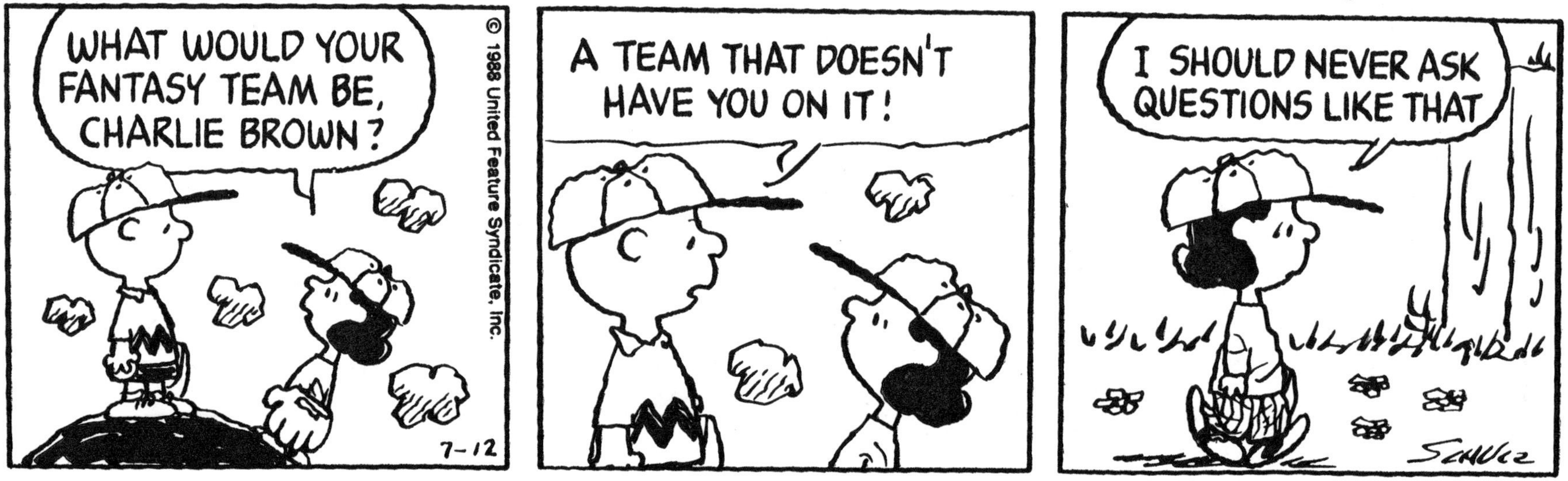
WHAT WOULD YOUR FANTASY TEAM BE, CHARLIE BROWN?
© 1988 United Feature Syndicate, Inc.
7-12
A TEAM THAT DOESN'T HAVE YOU ON IT!
I SHOULD NEVER ASK QUESTIONS LIKE THAT
SCHULZ

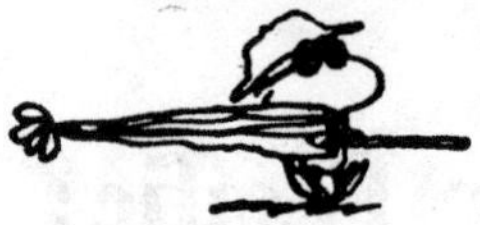

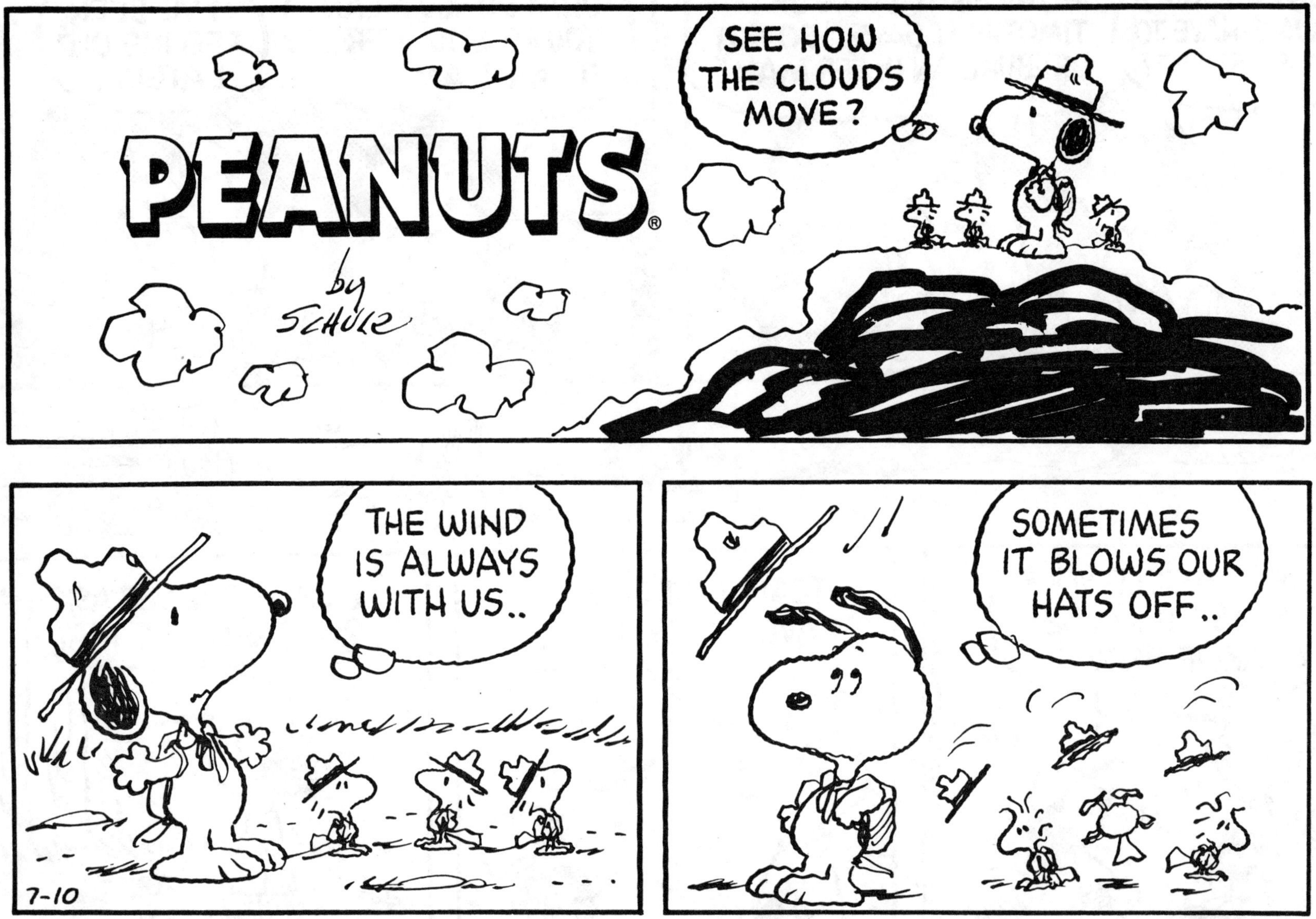

PEANUTS®
by SCHULZ
SEE HOW THE CLOUDS MOVE?
THE WIND IS ALWAYS WITH US..
7-10
SOMETIMES IT BLOWS OUR HATS OFF..

Could You Be More Pacific?

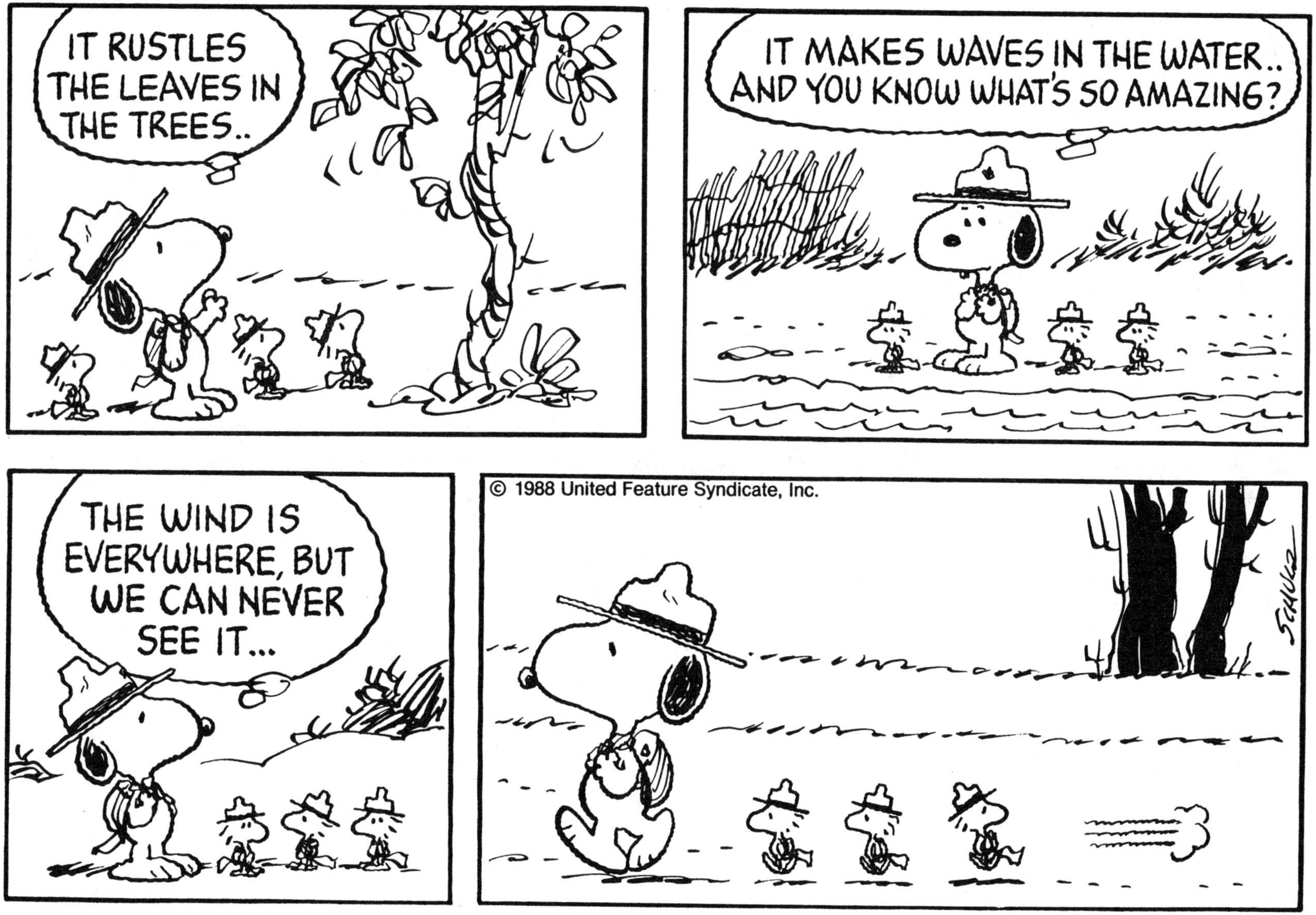

IT RUSTLES THE LEAVES IN THE TREES..
IT MAKES WAVES IN THE WATER.. AND YOU KNOW WHAT'S SO AMAZING?
THE WIND IS EVERYWHERE, BUT WE CAN NEVER SEE IT...
© 1988 United Feature Syndicate, Inc.
SCHULZ

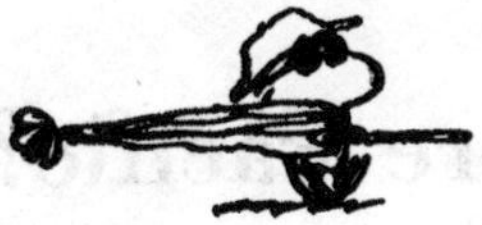

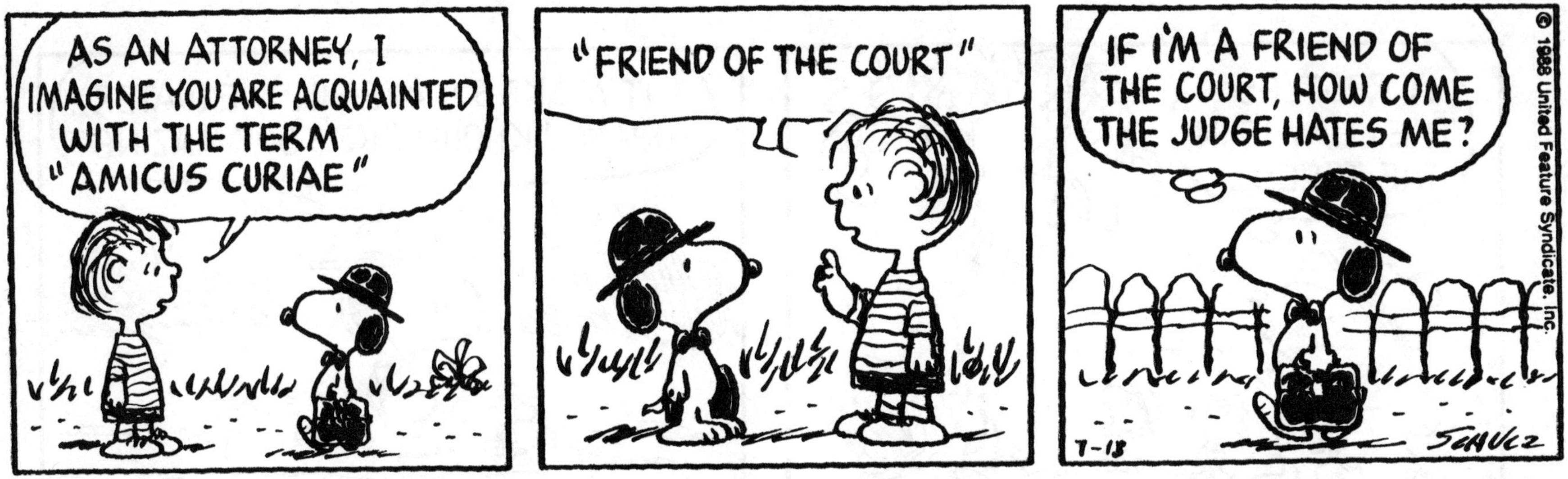

AS AN ATTORNEY, I IMAGINE YOU ARE ACQUAINTED WITH THE TERM "AMICUS CURIAE"
"FRIEND OF THE COURT"
IF I'M A FRIEND OF THE COURT, HOW COME THE JUDGE HATES ME?
© 1988 United Feature Syndicate, Inc.
7-13
SCHULZ

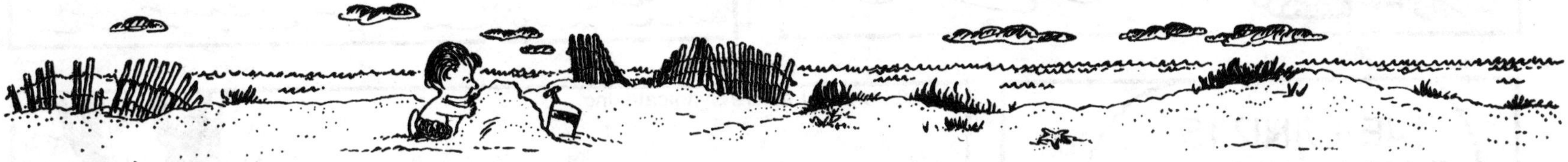

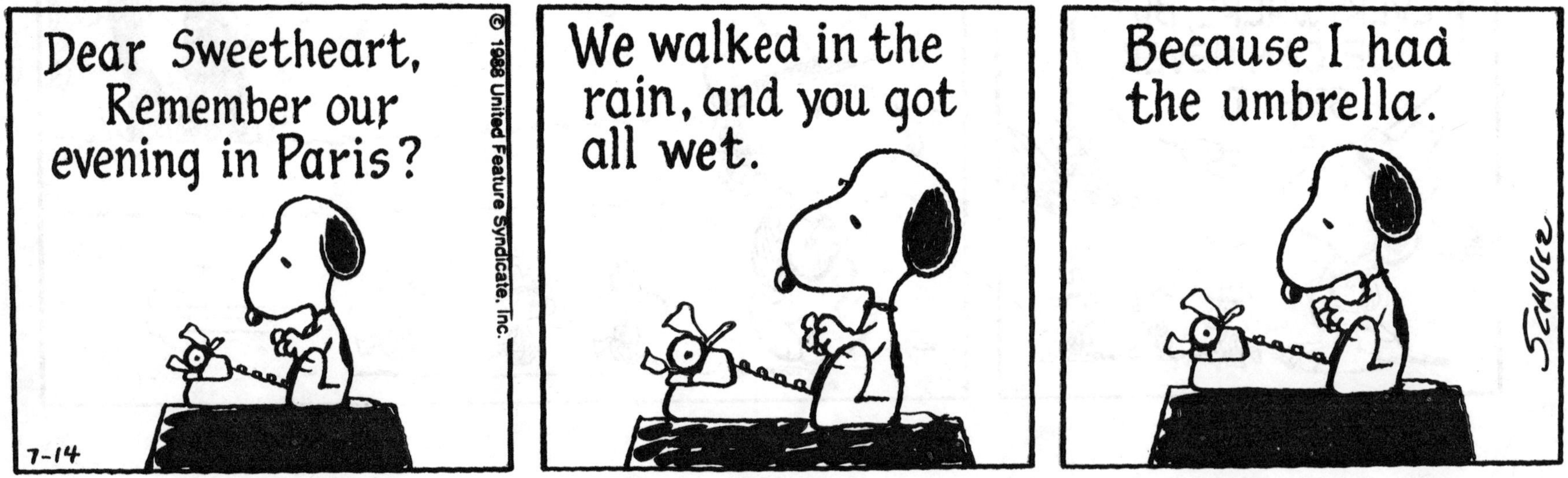

Dear Sweetheart, Remember our evening in Paris?
© 1988 United Feature Syndicate, Inc.
7-14
We walked in the rain, and you got all wet.
Because I had the umbrella.
SCHULZ

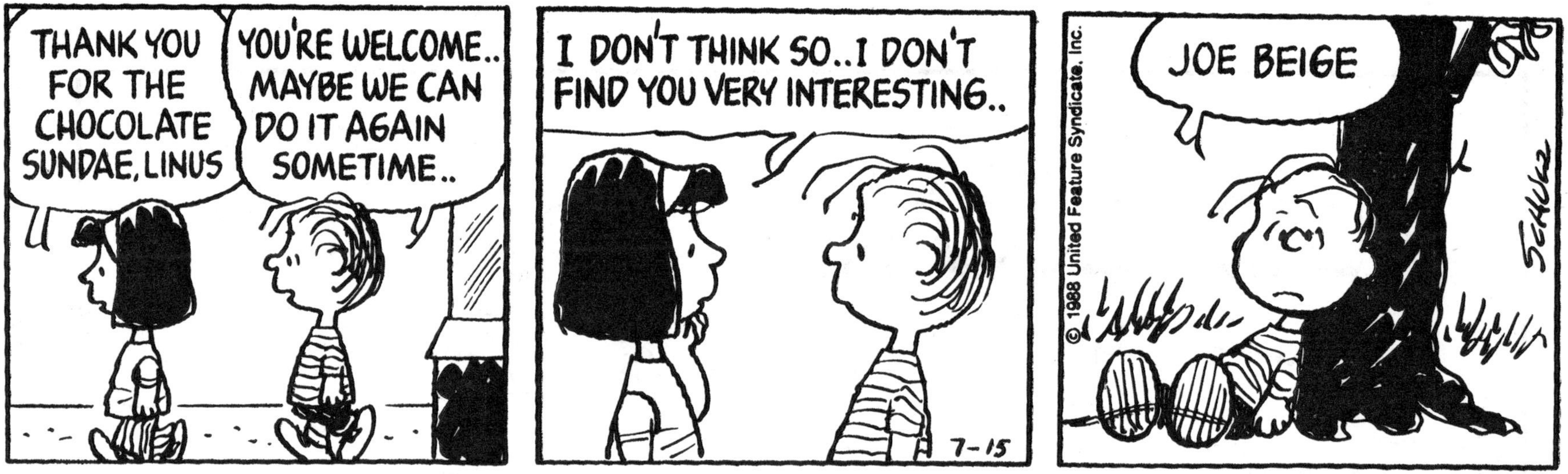
THANK YOU FOR THE CHOCOLATE SUNDAE, LINUS
YOU'RE WELCOME.. MAYBE WE CAN DO IT AGAIN SOMETIME..
I DON'T THINK SO..I DON'T FIND YOU VERY INTERESTING..
7-15
© 1988 United Feature Syndicate, Inc.
JOE BEIGE
SCHULZ

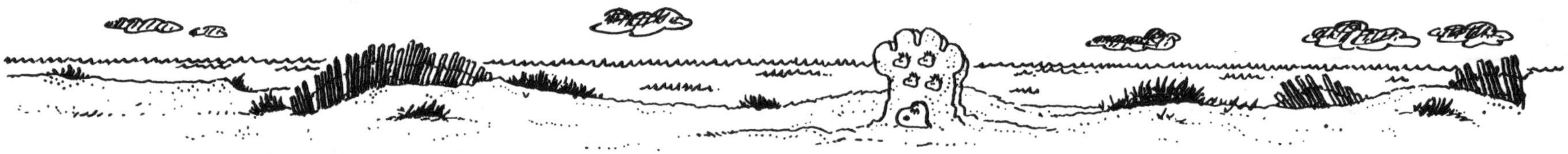

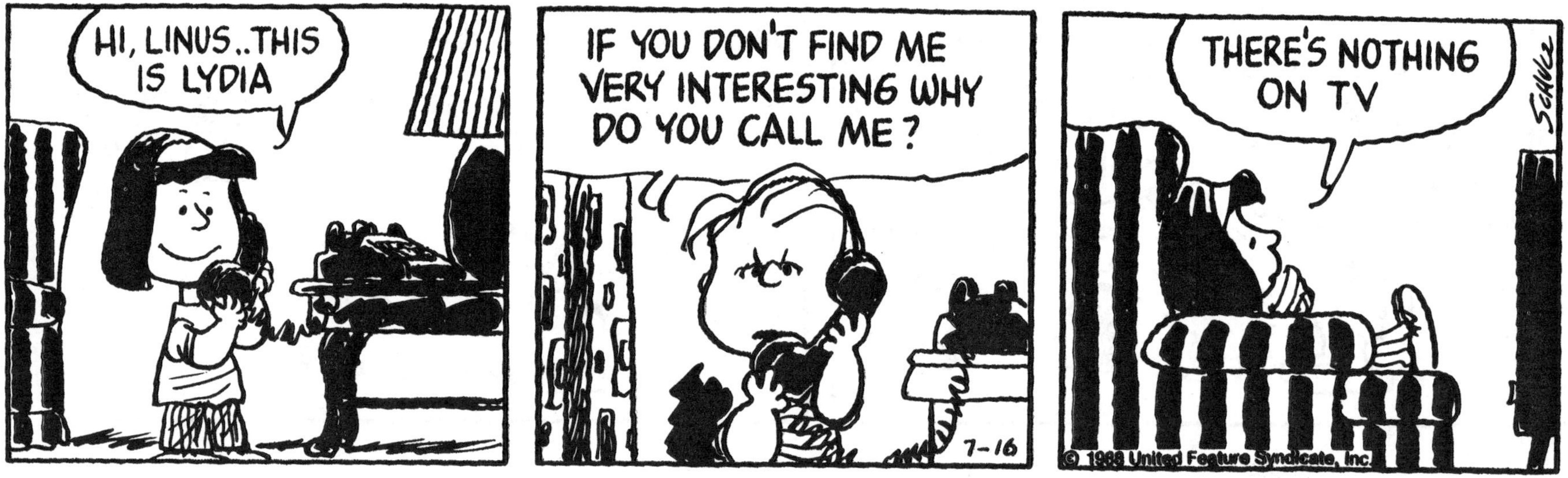
HI, LINUS..THIS IS LYDIA
IF YOU DON'T FIND ME VERY INTERESTING WHY DO YOU CALL ME?
7-16
THERE'S NOTHING ON TV
SCHULZ
© 1988 United Feature Syndicate, Inc.

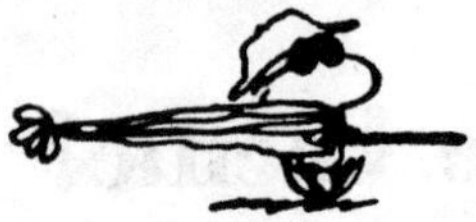

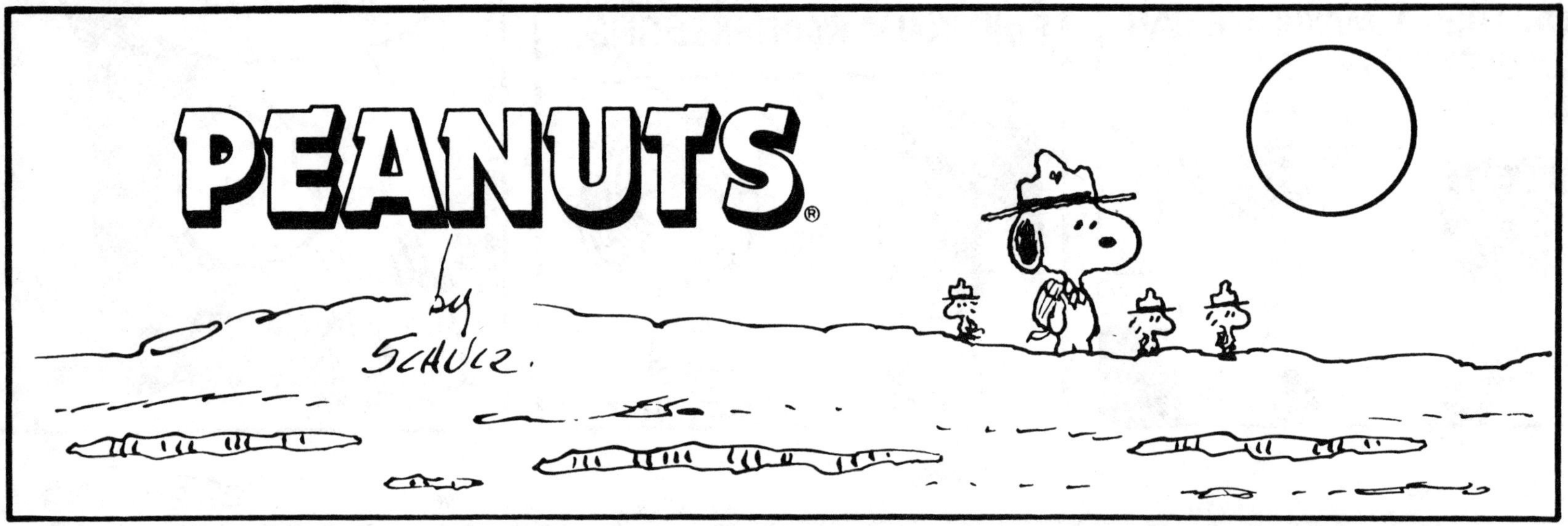
PEANUTS®
by SCHULZ

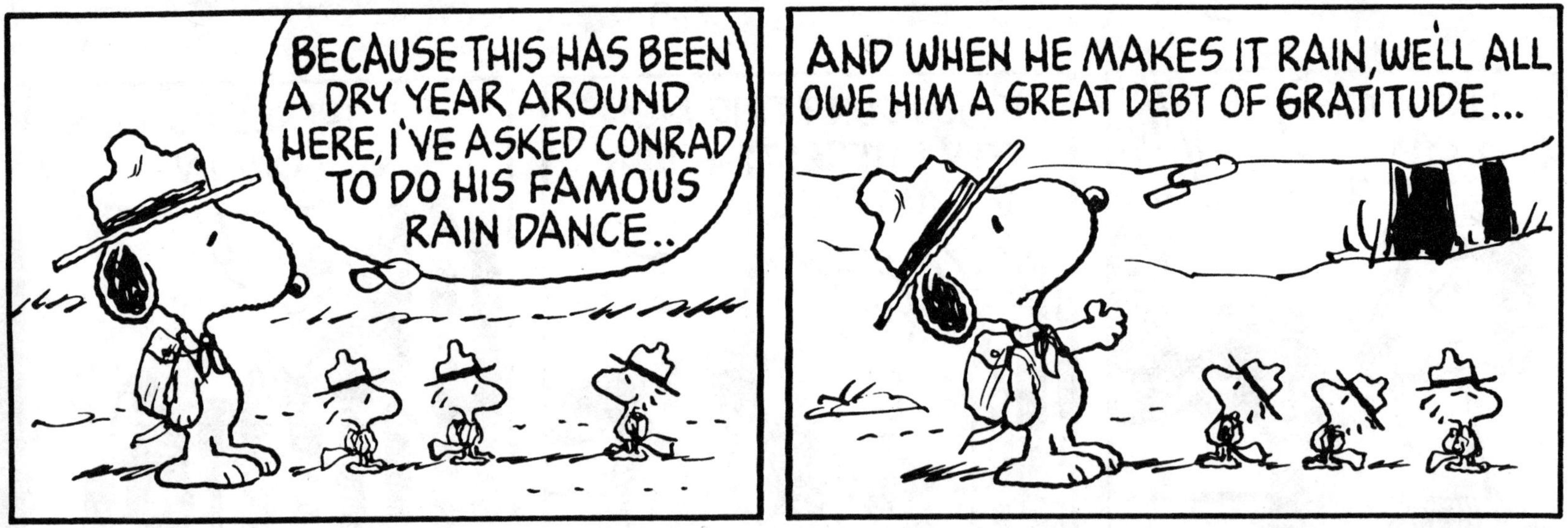
BECAUSE THIS HAS BEEN A DRY YEAR AROUND HERE, I'VE ASKED CONRAD TO DO HIS FAMOUS RAIN DANCE..
AND WHEN HE MAKES IT RAIN, WE'LL ALL OWE HIM A GREAT DEBT OF GRATITUDE...

Could You Be More Pacific?

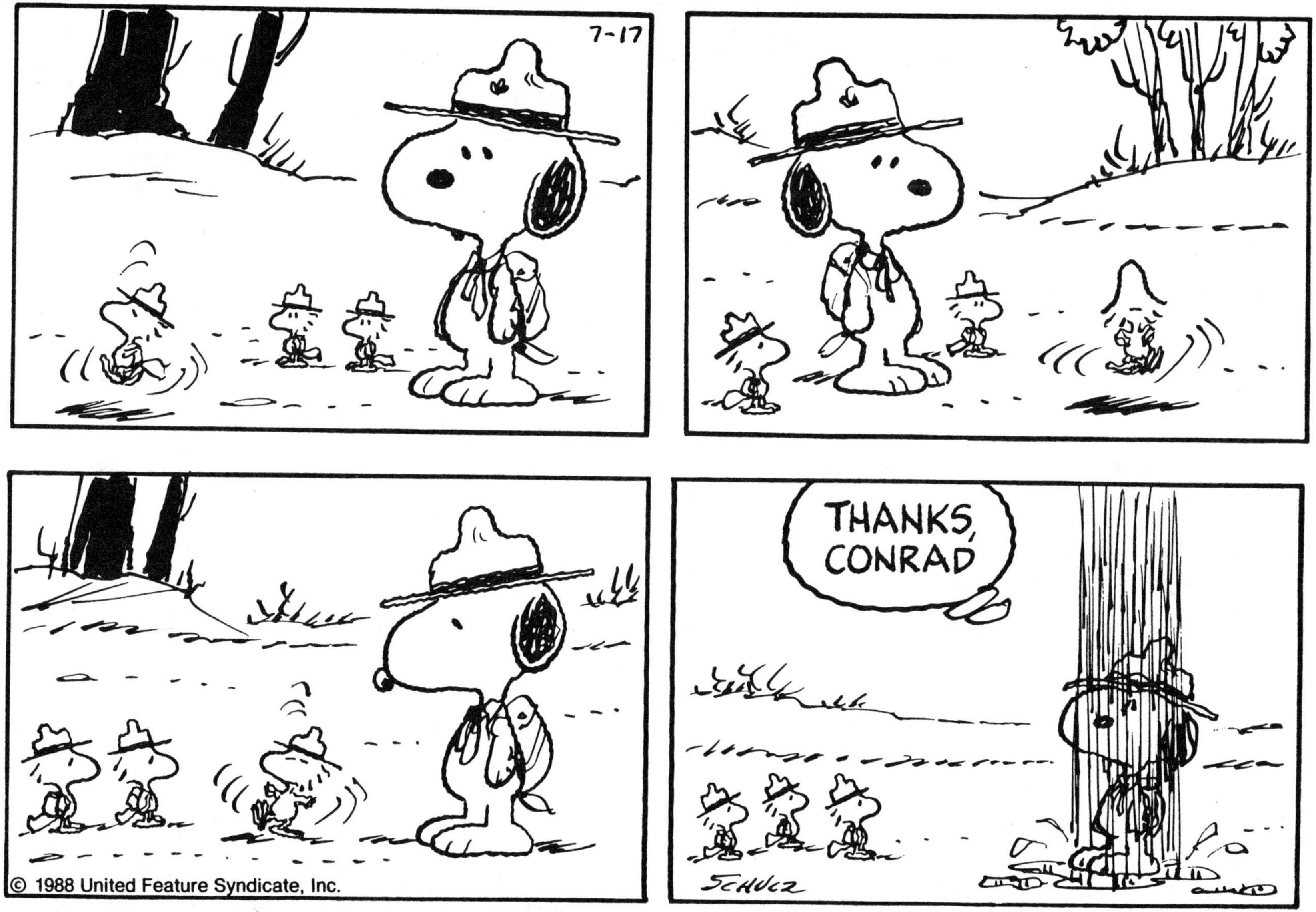
7-17
THANKS, CONRAD
SCHULZ

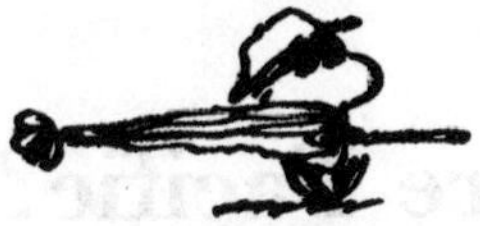

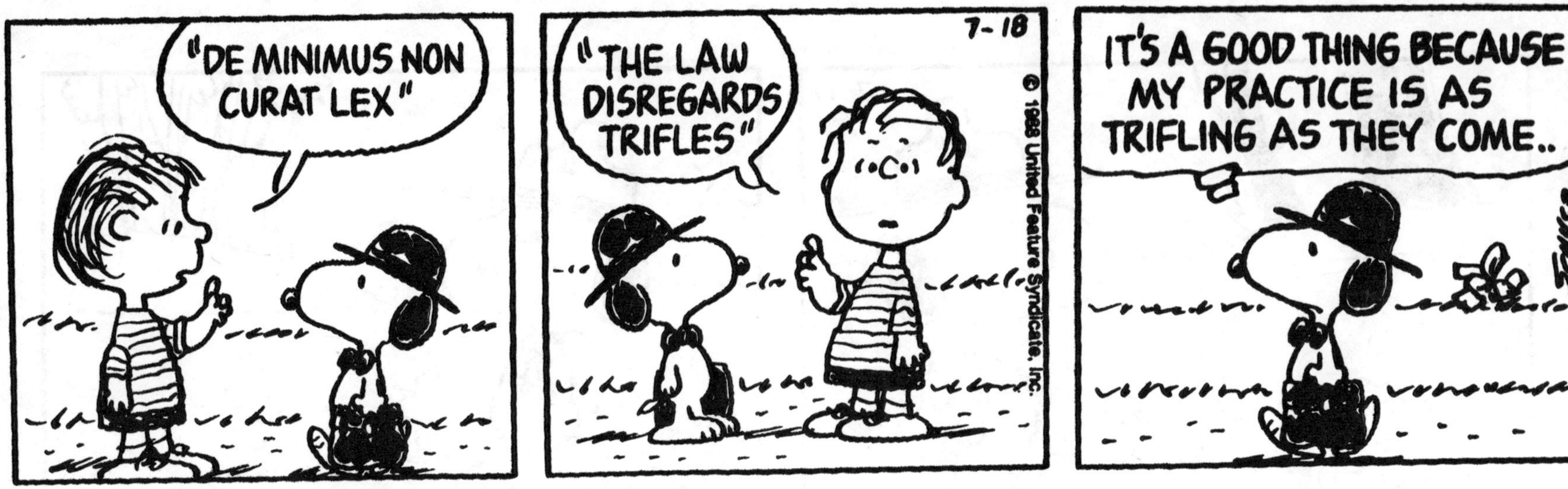
"DE MINIMUS NON CURAT LEX"
"THE LAW DISREGARDS TRIFLES"
7-18
© 1988 United Feature Syndicate, Inc.
IT'S A GOOD THING BECAUSE MY PRACTICE IS AS TRIFLING AS THEY COME..

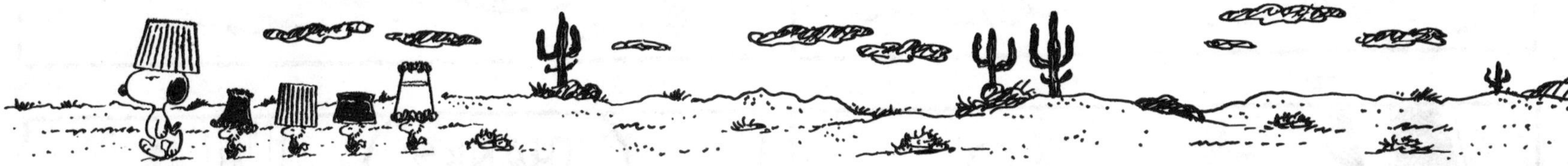

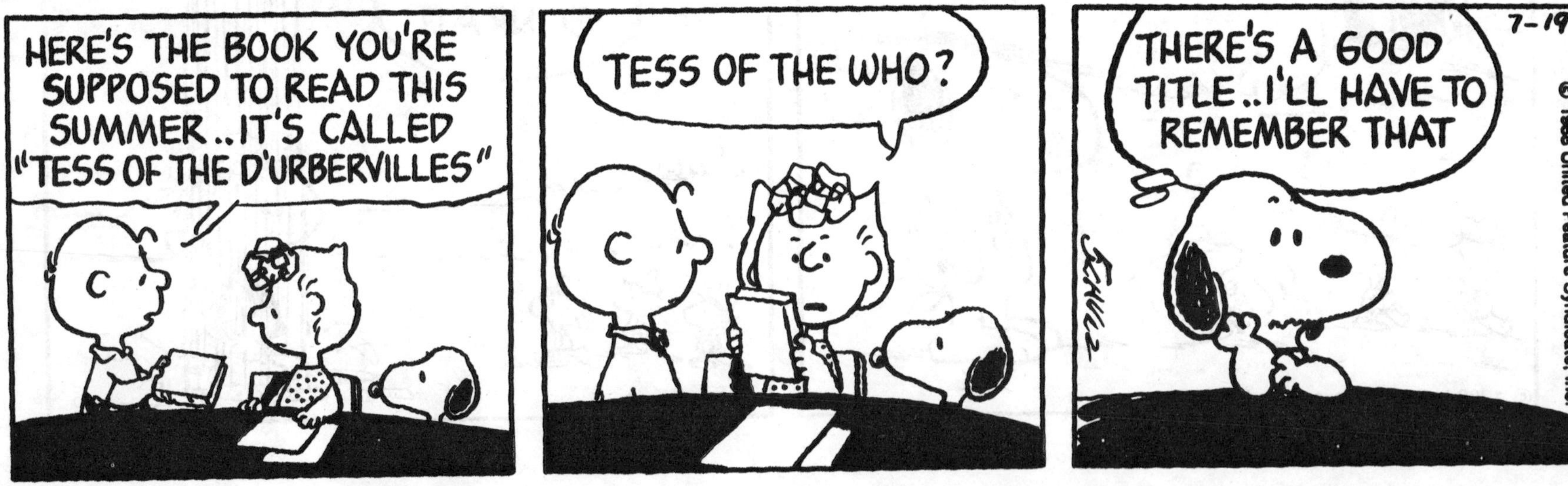
HERE'S THE BOOK YOU'RE SUPPOSED TO READ THIS SUMMER..IT'S CALLED "TESS OF THE D'URBERVILLES"
TESS OF THE WHO?
7-19
© 1988 United Feature Syndicate, Inc.
THERE'S A GOOD TITLE..I'LL HAVE TO REMEMBER THAT

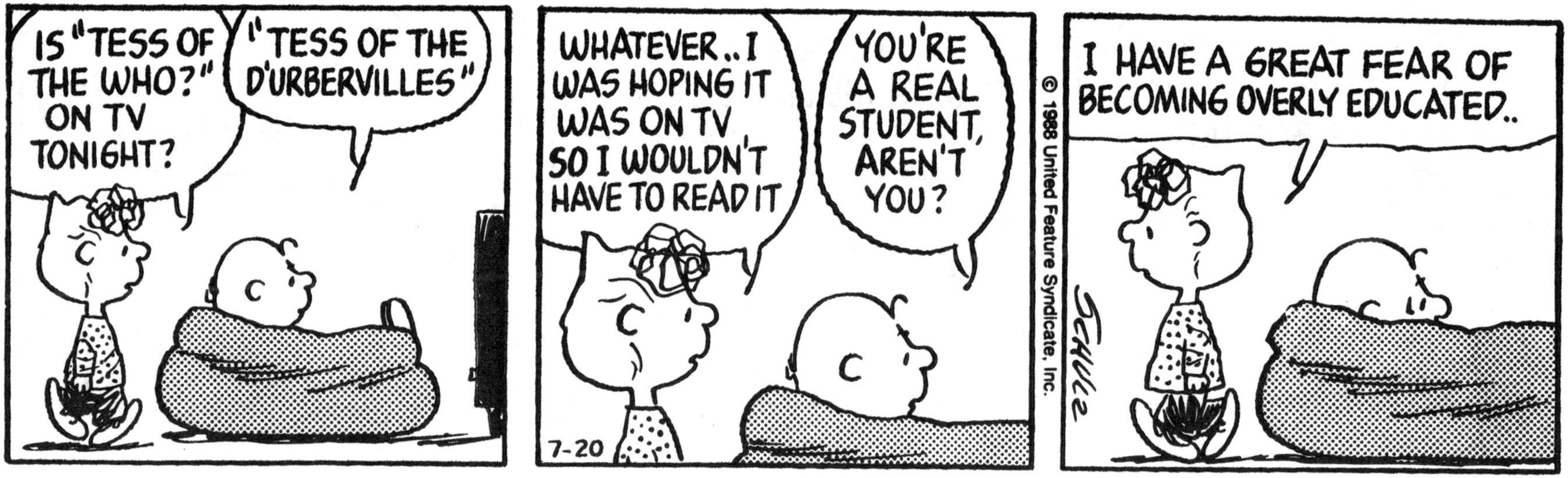
IS "TESS OF THE WHO?" ON TV TONIGHT?
"TESS OF THE D'URBERVILLES"
WHATEVER.. I WAS HOPING IT WAS ON TV SO I WOULDN'T HAVE TO READ IT
YOU'RE A REAL STUDENT, AREN'T YOU?
I HAVE A GREAT FEAR OF BECOMING OVERLY EDUCATED..
7-20
© 1988 United Feature Syndicate, Inc.
SCHULZ

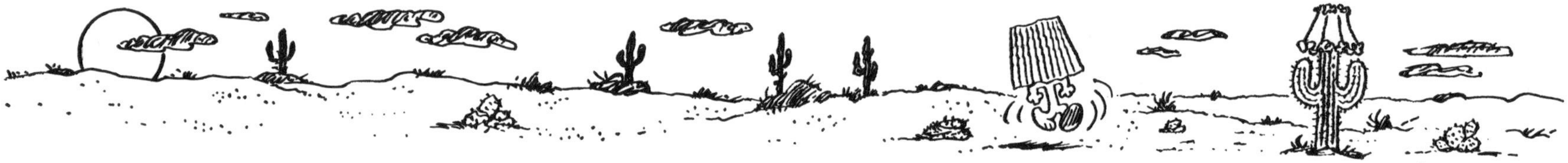

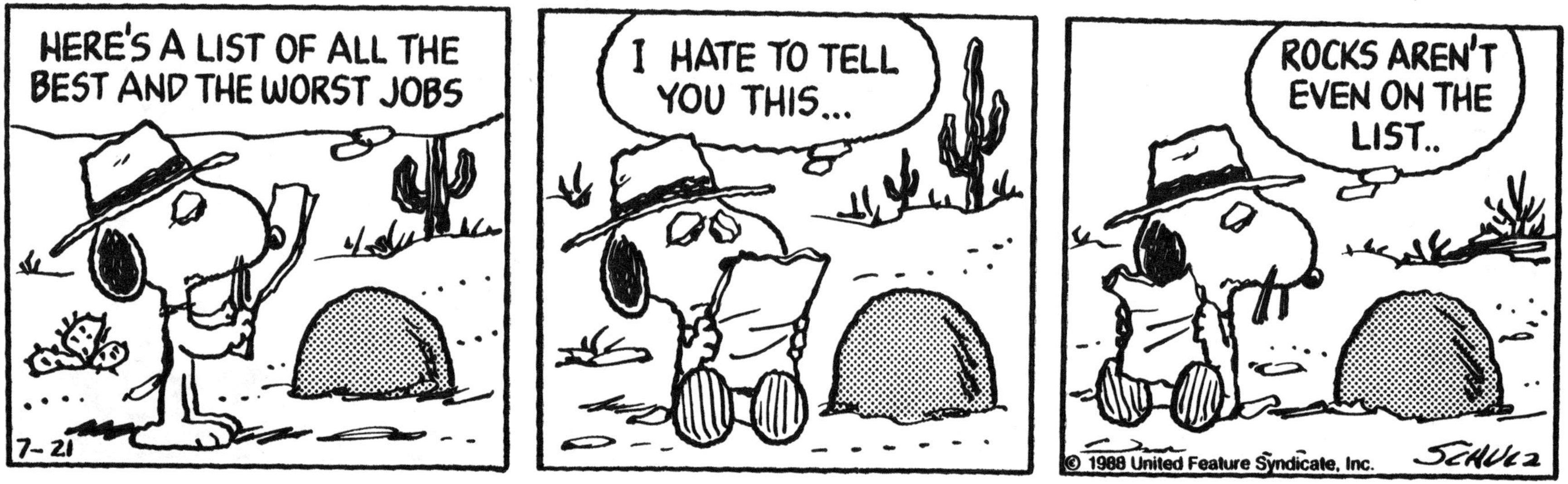
HERE'S A LIST OF ALL THE BEST AND THE WORST JOBS
I HATE TO TELL YOU THIS...
ROCKS AREN'T EVEN ON THE LIST..
7-21
© 1988 United Feature Syndicate, Inc.
SCHULZ

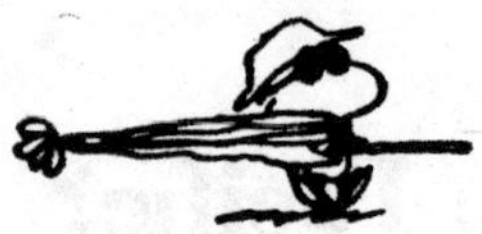

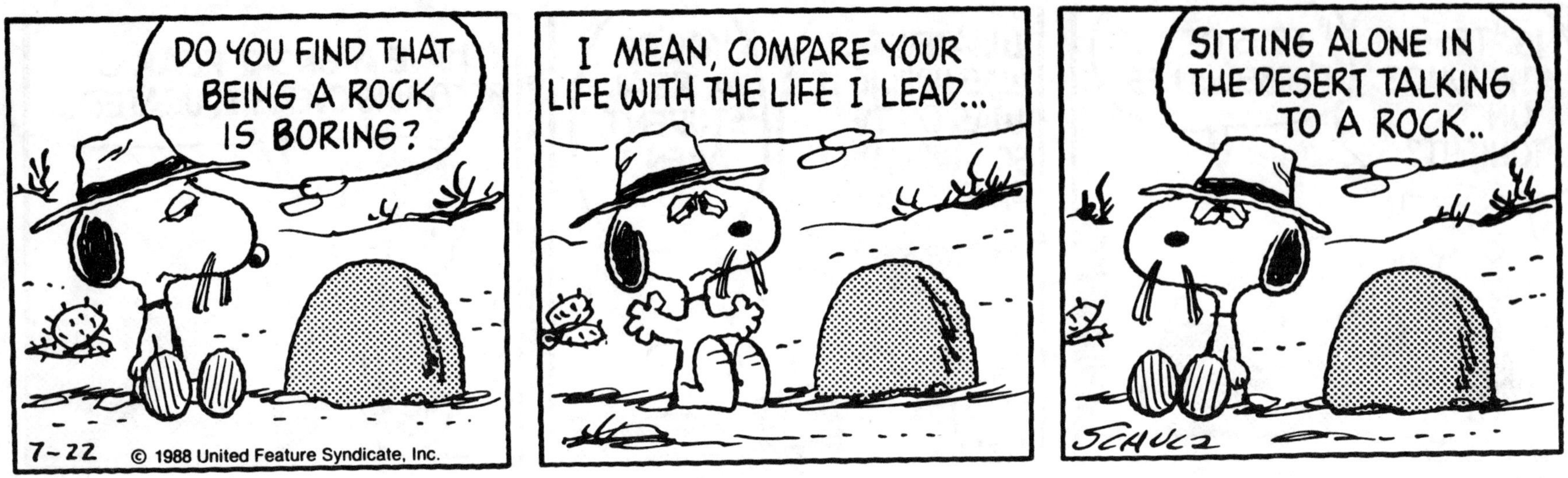
DO YOU FIND THAT BEING A ROCK IS BORING?
7-22 © 1988 United Feature Syndicate, Inc.
I MEAN, COMPARE YOUR LIFE WITH THE LIFE I LEAD...
SITTING ALONE IN THE DESERT TALKING TO A ROCK..
SCHULZ

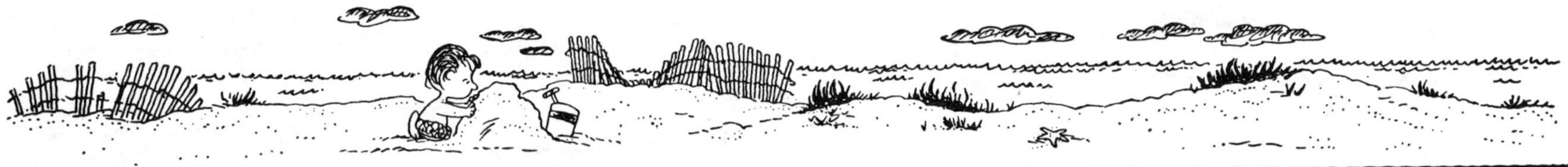

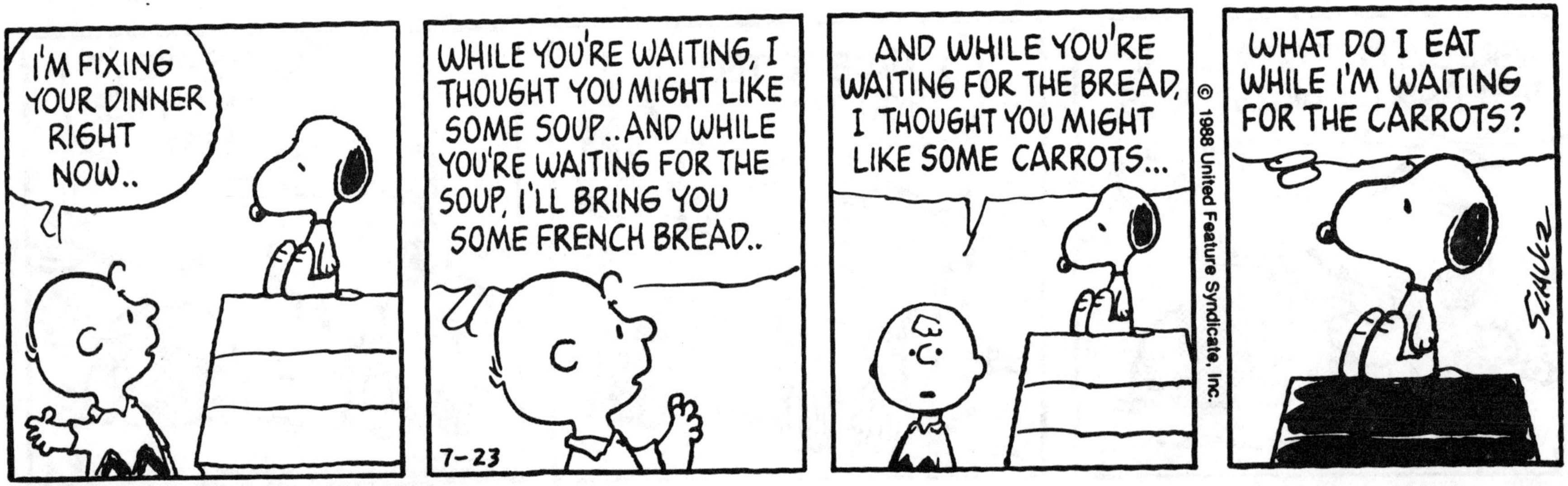
I'M FIXING YOUR DINNER RIGHT NOW..
WHILE YOU'RE WAITING, I THOUGHT YOU MIGHT LIKE SOME SOUP..AND WHILE YOU'RE WAITING FOR THE SOUP, I'LL BRING YOU SOME FRENCH BREAD..
7-23
AND WHILE YOU'RE WAITING FOR THE BREAD, I THOUGHT YOU MIGHT LIKE SOME CARROTS...
© 1988 United Feature Syndicate, Inc.
WHAT DO I EAT WHILE I'M WAITING FOR THE CARROTS?
SCHULZ

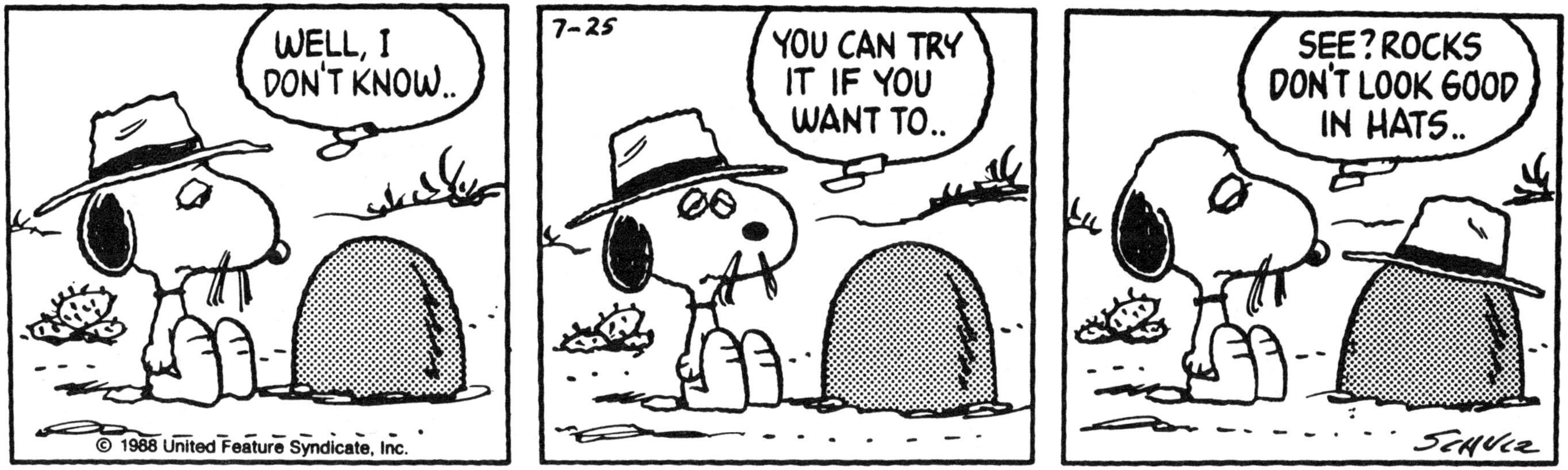
WELL, I DON'T KNOW..
7-25
YOU CAN TRY IT IF YOU WANT TO..
SEE? ROCKS DON'T LOOK GOOD IN HATS..
© 1988 United Feature Syndicate, Inc.
SCHULZ

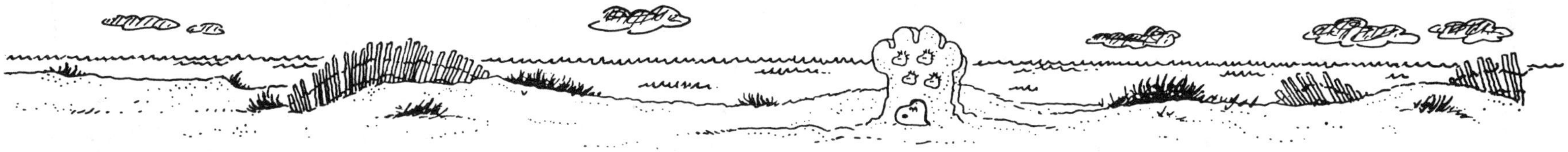

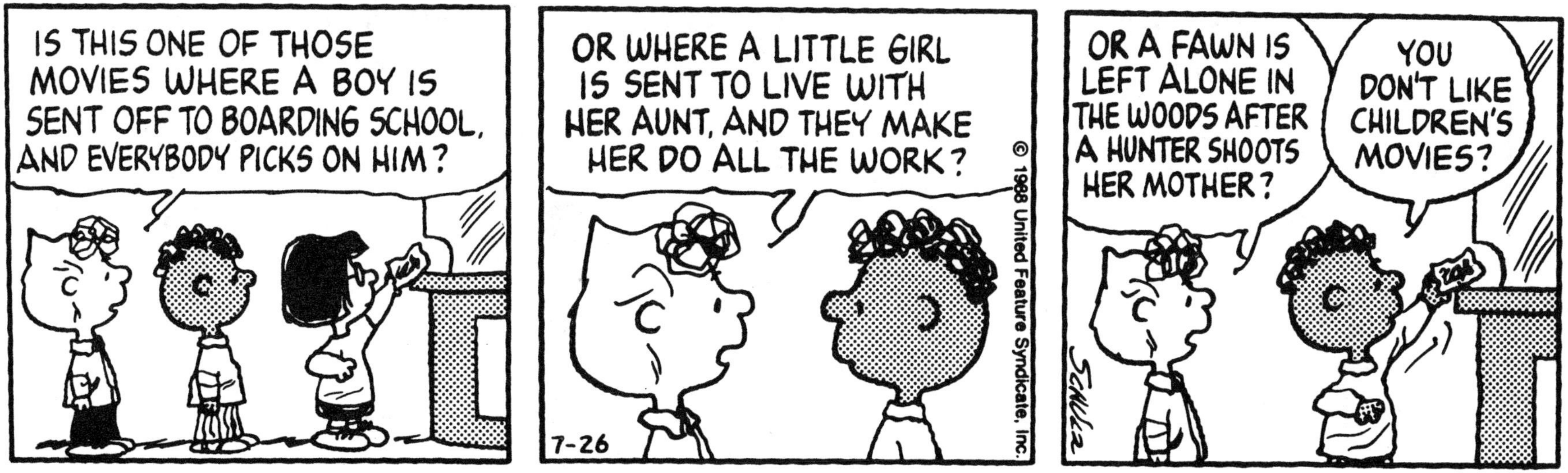
IS THIS ONE OF THOSE MOVIES WHERE A BOY IS SENT OFF TO BOARDING SCHOOL, AND EVERYBODY PICKS ON HIM?
OR WHERE A LITTLE GIRL IS SENT TO LIVE WITH HER AUNT, AND THEY MAKE HER DO ALL THE WORK?
7-26
© 1988 United Feature Syndicate, Inc.
OR A FAWN IS LEFT ALONE IN THE WOODS AFTER A HUNTER SHOOTS HER MOTHER?
YOU DON'T LIKE CHILDREN'S MOVIES?
SCHULZ

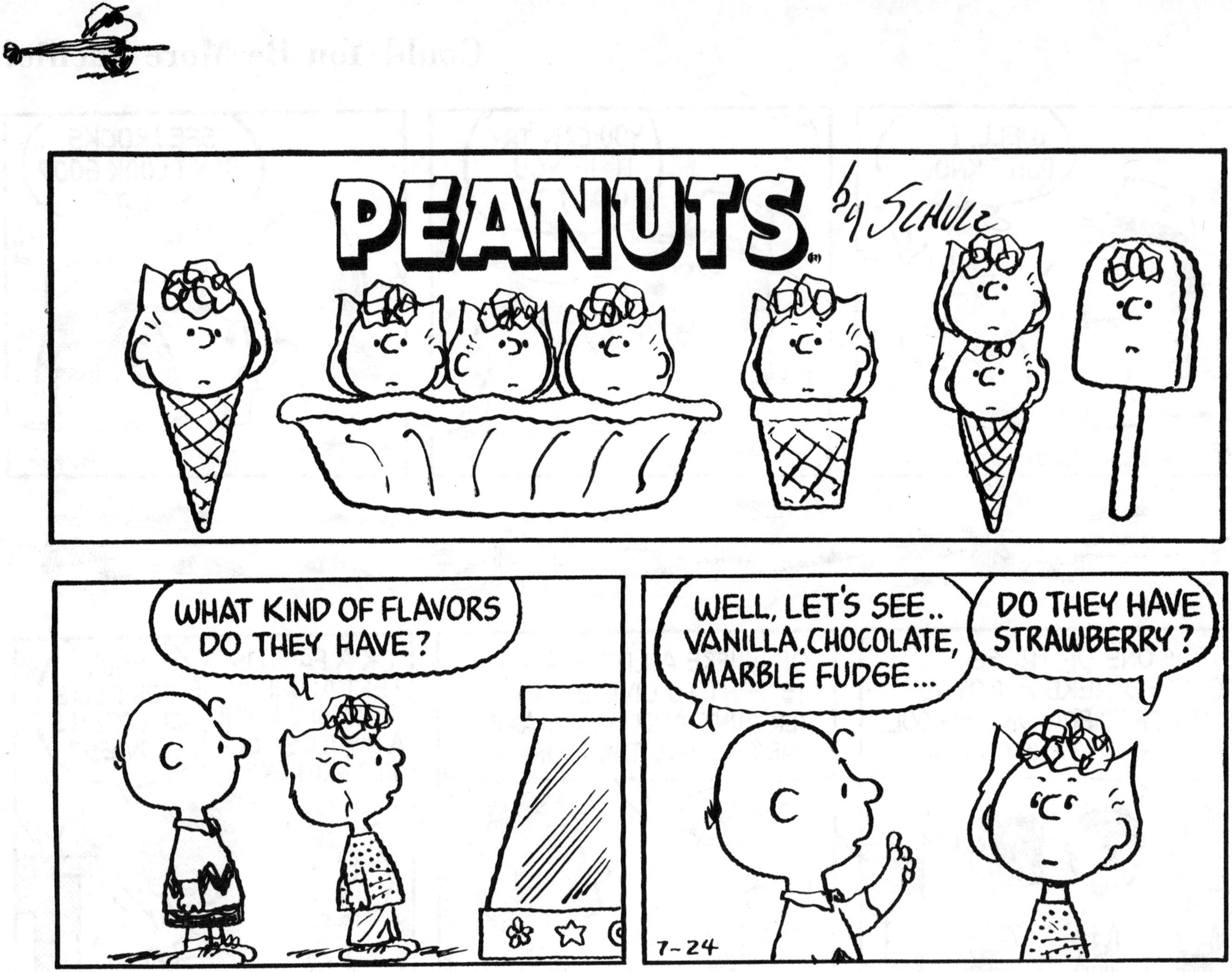
PEANUTS
by SCHULZ
WHAT KIND OF FLAVORS DO THEY HAVE?
WELL, LET'S SEE.. VANILLA, CHOCOLATE, MARBLE FUDGE...
DO THEY HAVE STRAWBERRY?
7-24

Could You Be More Pacific?

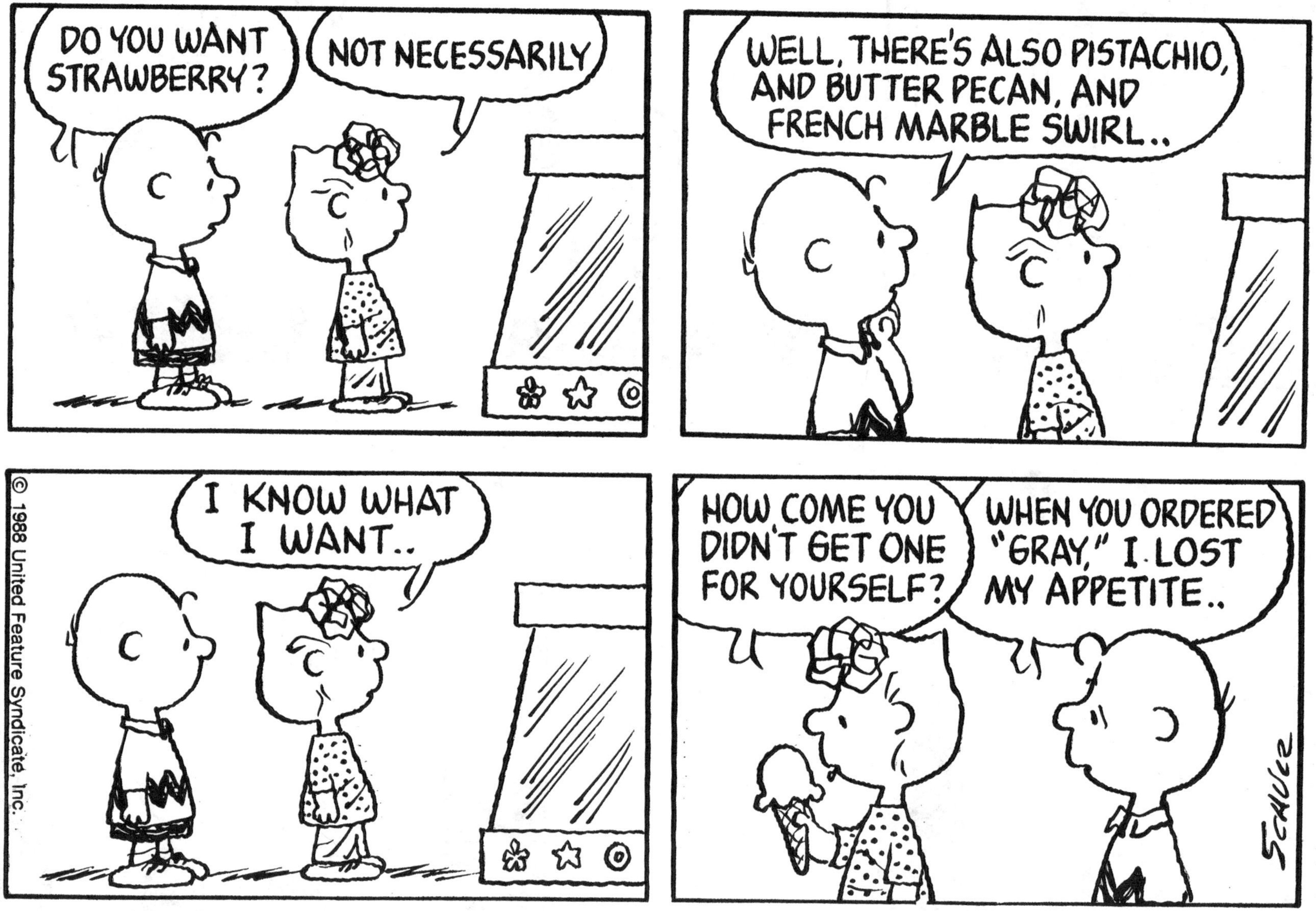
DO YOU WANT STRAWBERRY?
NOT NECESSARILY
WELL, THERE'S ALSO PISTACHIO, AND BUTTER PECAN, AND FRENCH MARBLE SWIRL..
I KNOW WHAT I WANT..
HOW COME YOU DIDN'T GET ONE FOR YOURSELF?
WHEN YOU ORDERED "GRAY," I LOST MY APPETITE..
SCHULZ
© 1988 United Feature Syndicate, Inc.

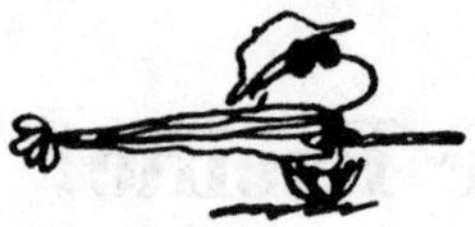

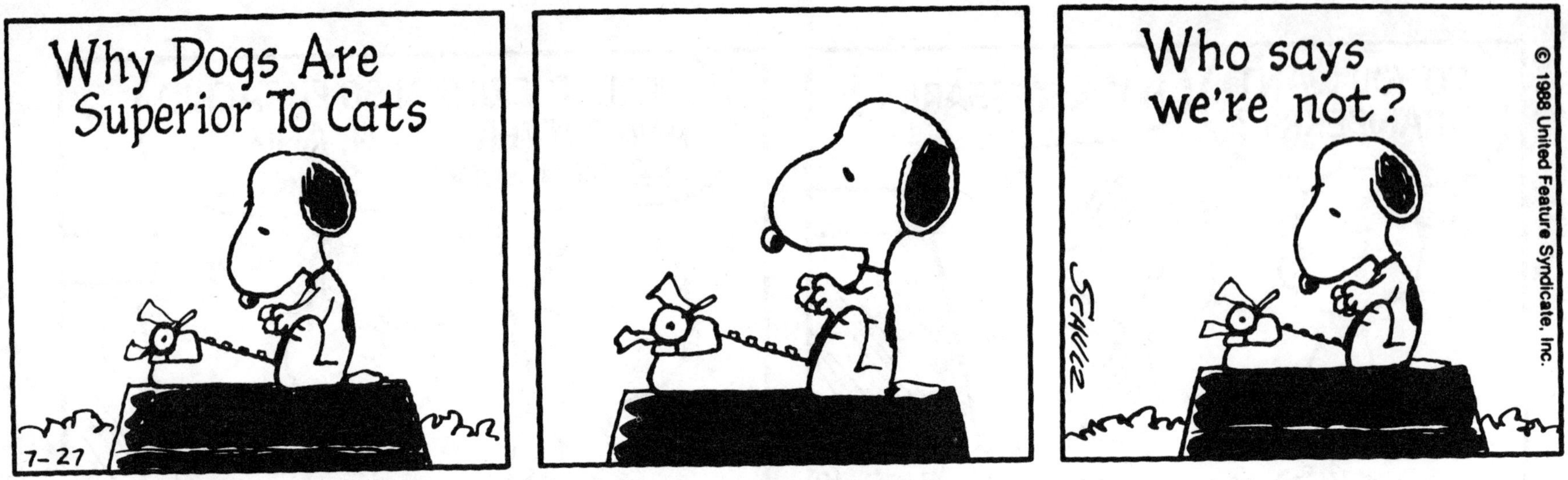
Why Dogs Are Superior To Cats
7-27
Who says we're not?
SCHULZ
© 1988 United Feature Syndicate, Inc.

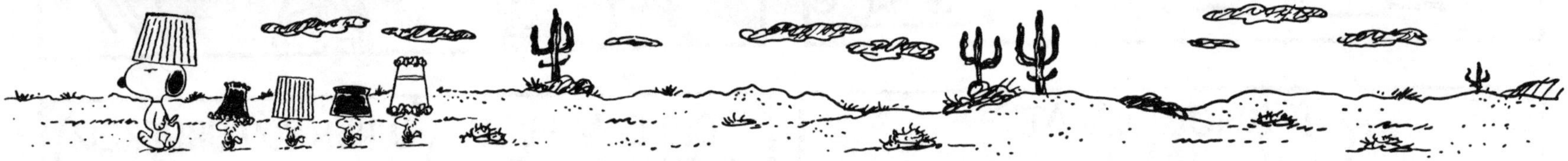

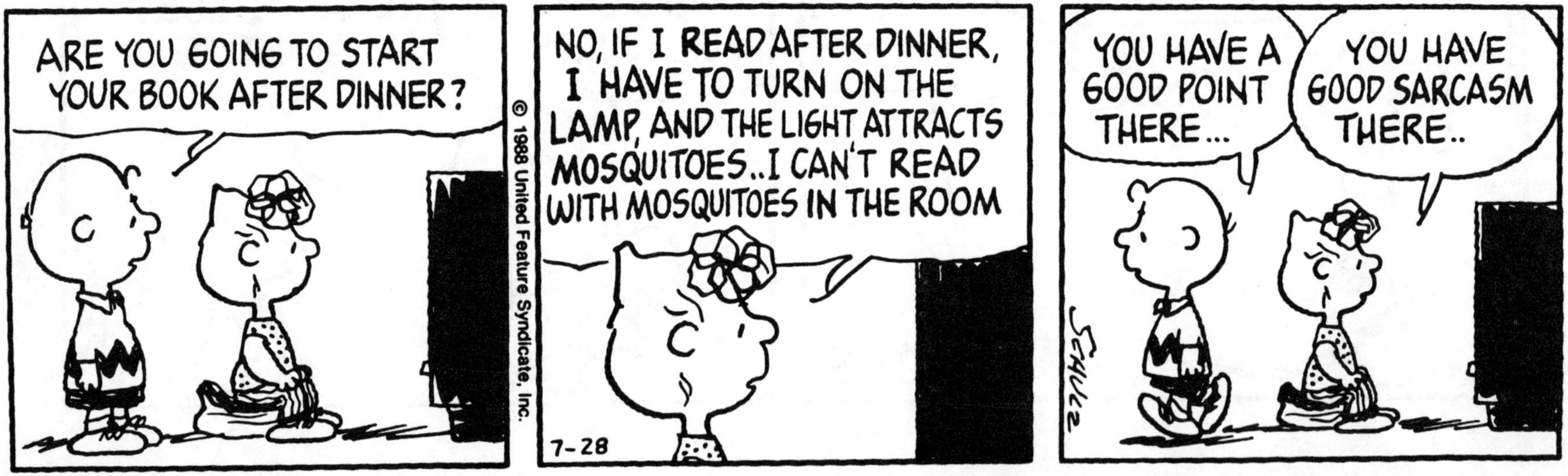
ARE YOU GOING TO START YOUR BOOK AFTER DINNER?
© 1988 United Feature Syndicate, Inc.
NO, IF I READ AFTER DINNER, I HAVE TO TURN ON THE LAMP, AND THE LIGHT ATTRACTS MOSQUITOES..I CAN'T READ WITH MOSQUITOES IN THE ROOM
7-28
YOU HAVE A GOOD POINT THERE...
YOU HAVE GOOD SARCASM THERE..
SCHULZ

Could You Be More Pacific?

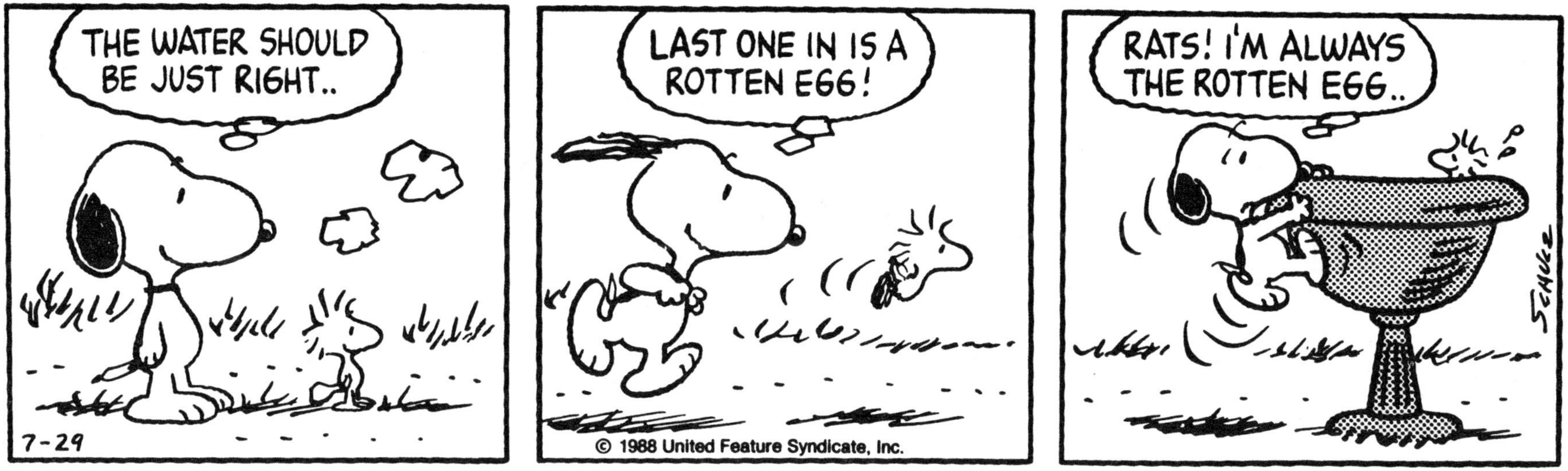
THE WATER SHOULD BE JUST RIGHT..
7-29
LAST ONE IN IS A ROTTEN EGG!
© 1988 United Feature Syndicate, Inc.
RATS! I'M ALWAYS THE ROTTEN EGG..
SCHULZ

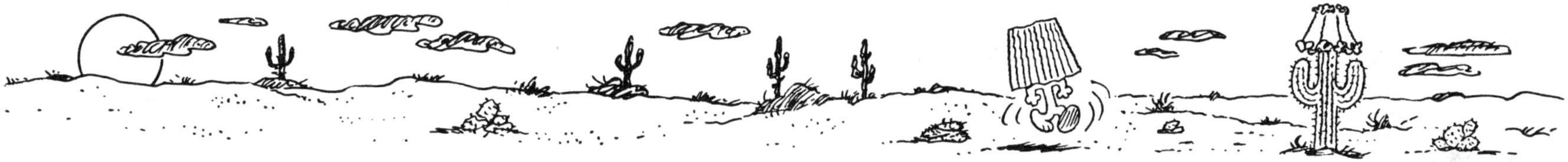

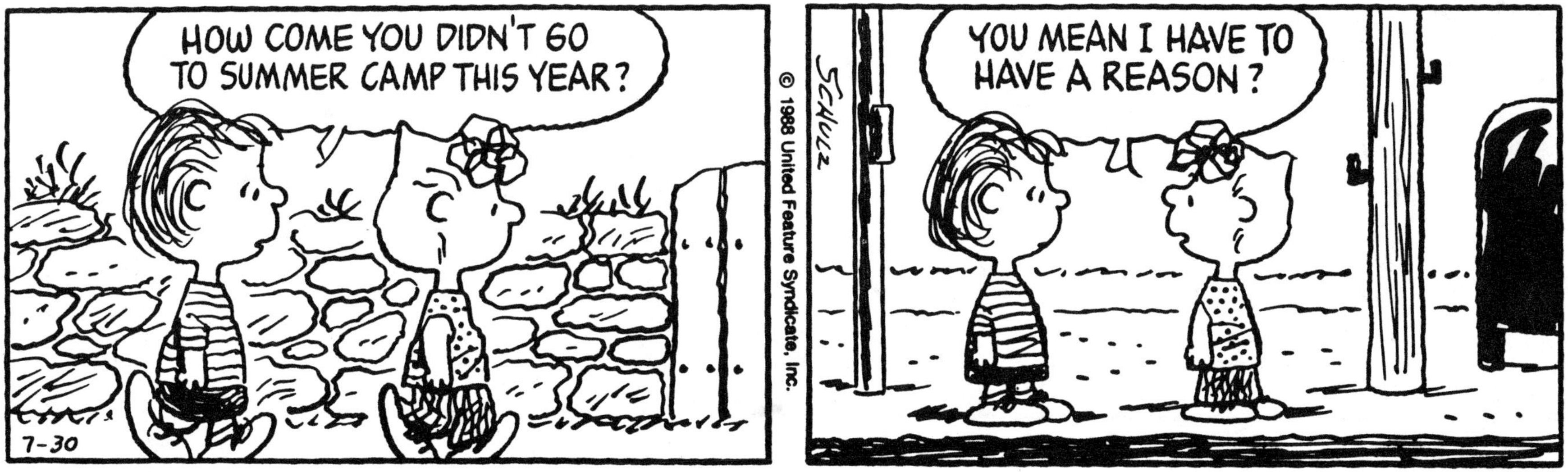
HOW COME YOU DIDN'T GO TO SUMMER CAMP THIS YEAR?
7-30
© 1988 United Feature Syndicate, Inc.
SCHULZ
YOU MEAN I HAVE TO HAVE A REASON?

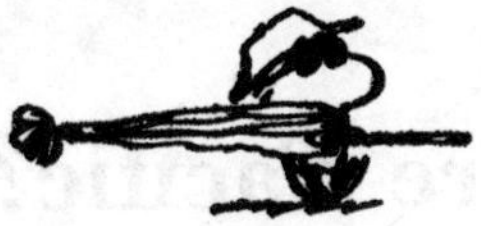

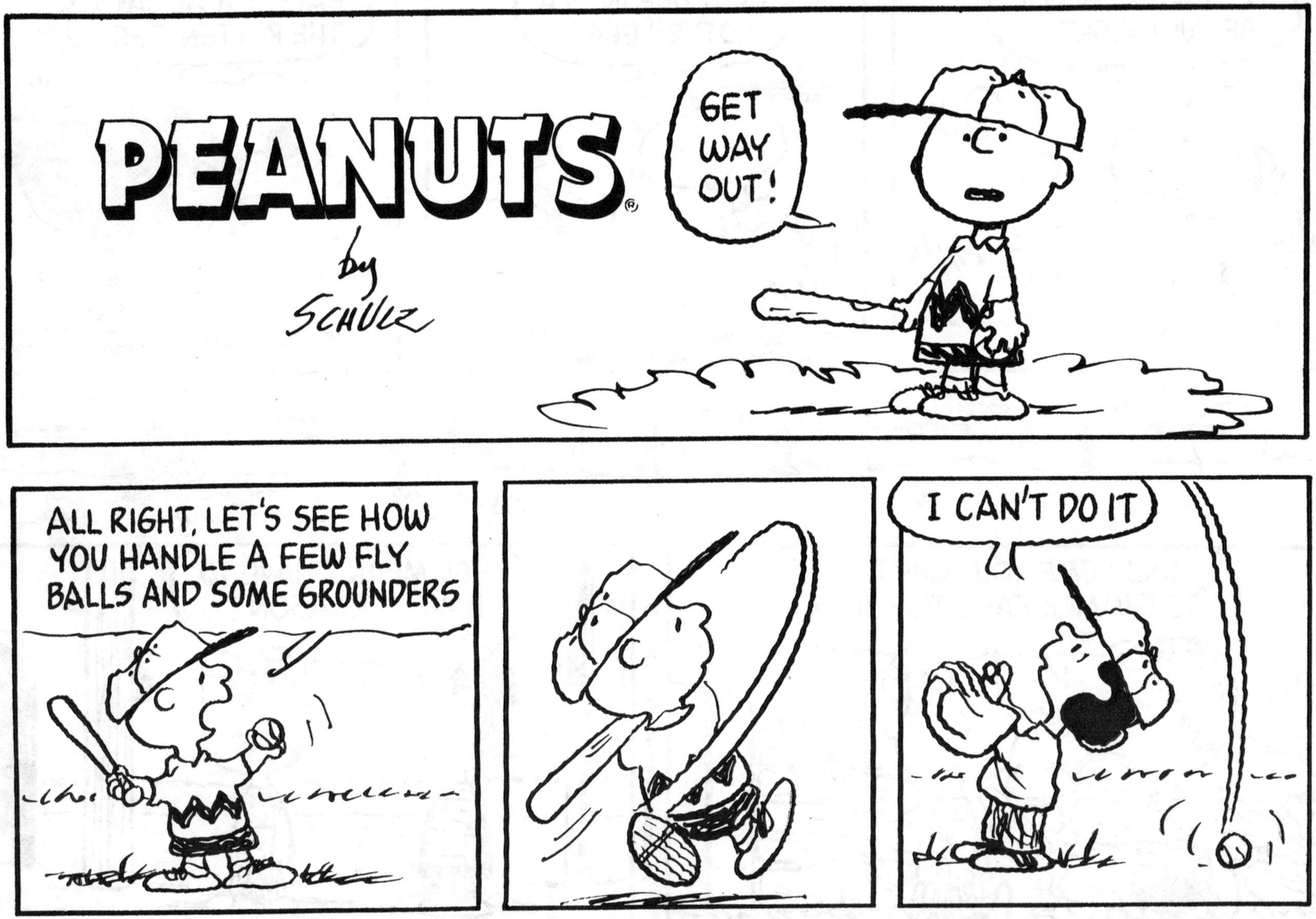

PEANUTS®
by SCHULZ
GET WAY OUT!
ALL RIGHT, LET'S SEE HOW YOU HANDLE A FEW FLY BALLS AND SOME GROUNDERS
I CAN'T DO IT

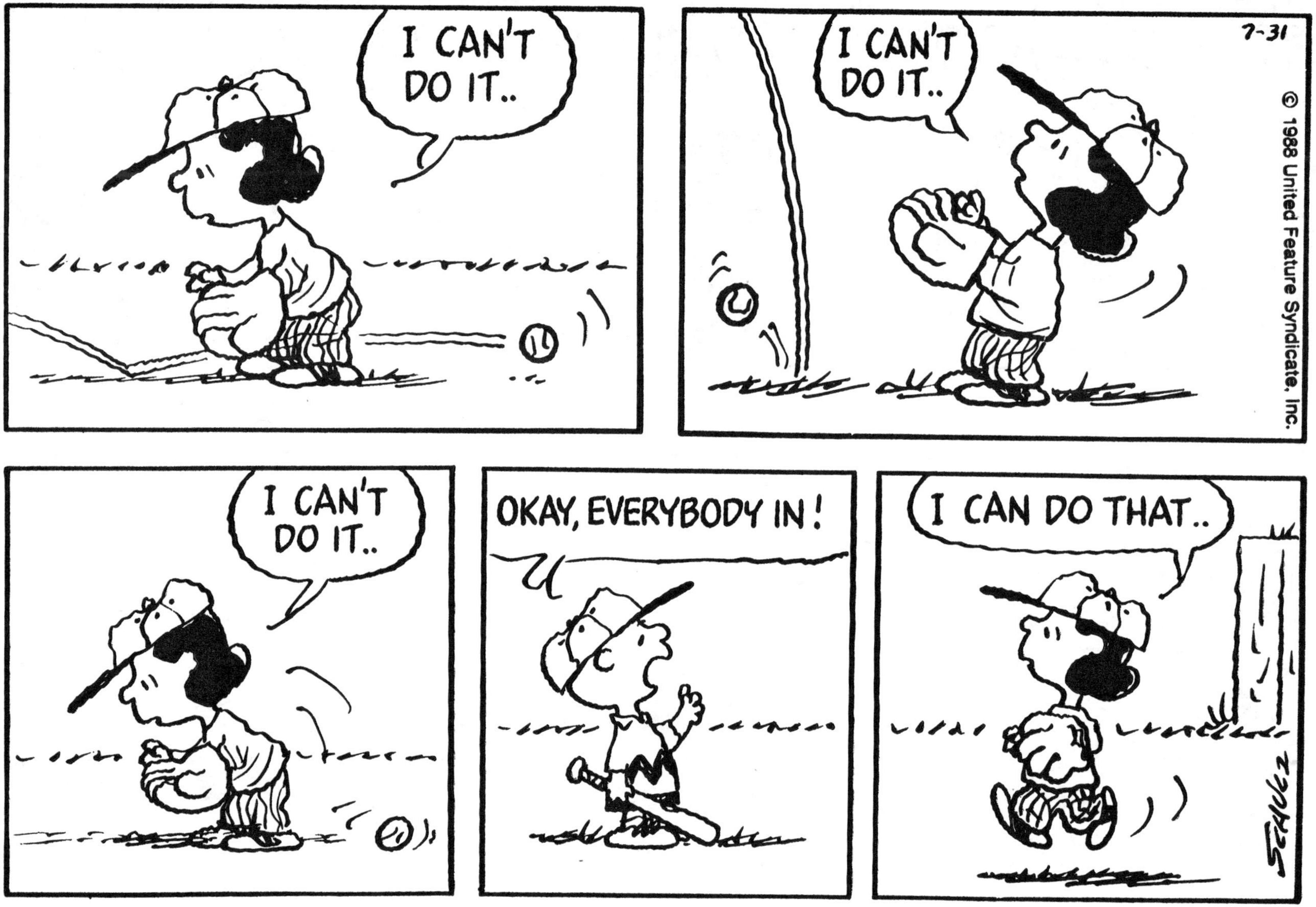
I CAN'T DO IT..
I CAN'T DO IT..
7-31
© 1988 United Feature Syndicate, Inc.
I CAN'T DO IT..
OKAY, EVERYBODY IN!
I CAN DO THAT..
SCHULZ

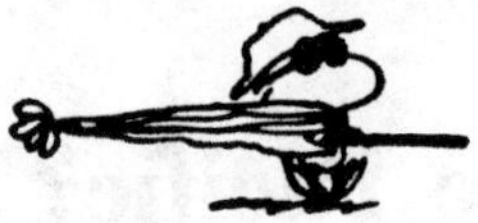

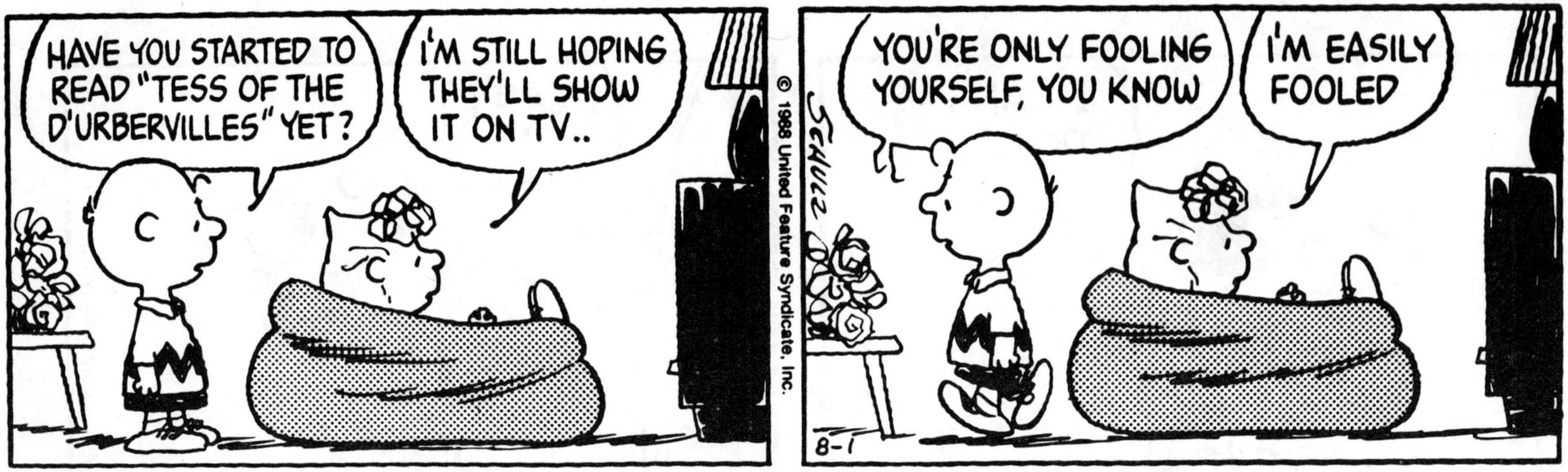
HAVE YOU STARTED TO READ "TESS OF THE D'URBERVILLES" YET?
I'M STILL HOPING THEY'LL SHOW IT ON TV..
© 1988 United Feature Syndicate, Inc.
SCHULZ
YOU'RE ONLY FOOLING YOURSELF, YOU KNOW
I'M EASILY FOOLED
8-1

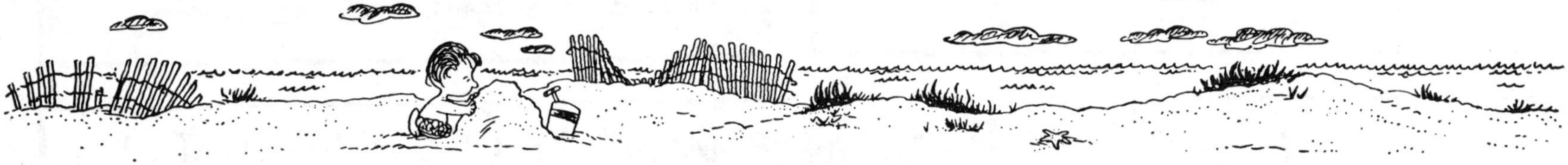

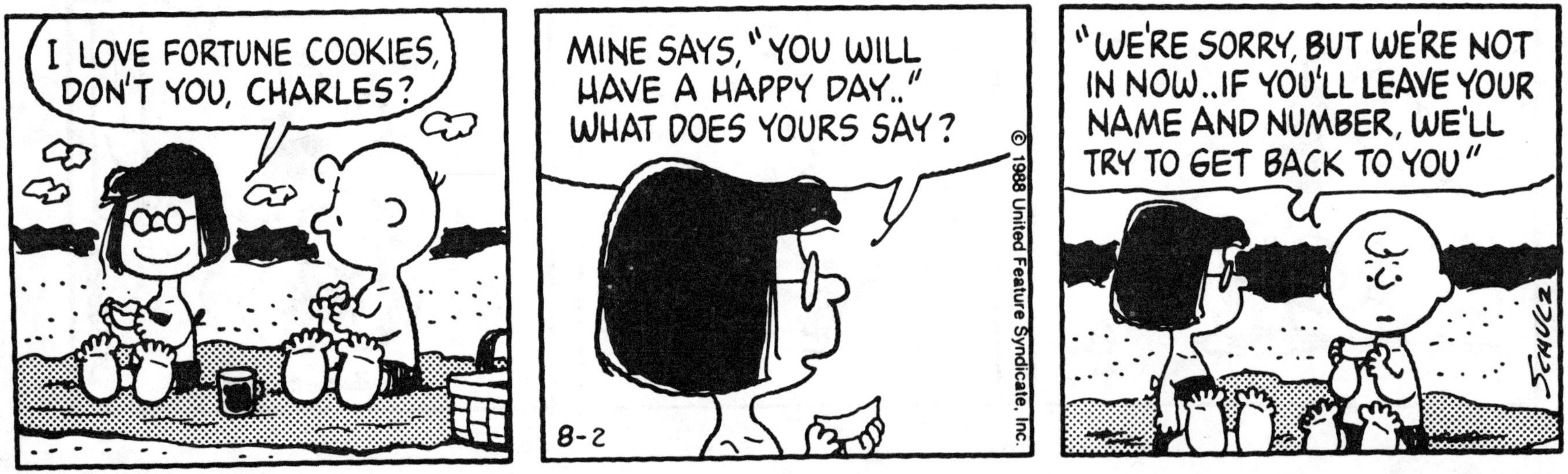
I LOVE FORTUNE COOKIES, DON'T YOU, CHARLES?
MINE SAYS, "YOU WILL HAVE A HAPPY DAY.." WHAT DOES YOURS SAY?
8-2
© 1988 United Feature Syndicate, Inc.
"WE'RE SORRY, BUT WE'RE NOT IN NOW..IF YOU'LL LEAVE YOUR NAME AND NUMBER, WE'LL TRY TO GET BACK TO YOU"
SCHULZ

Could You Be More Pacific?

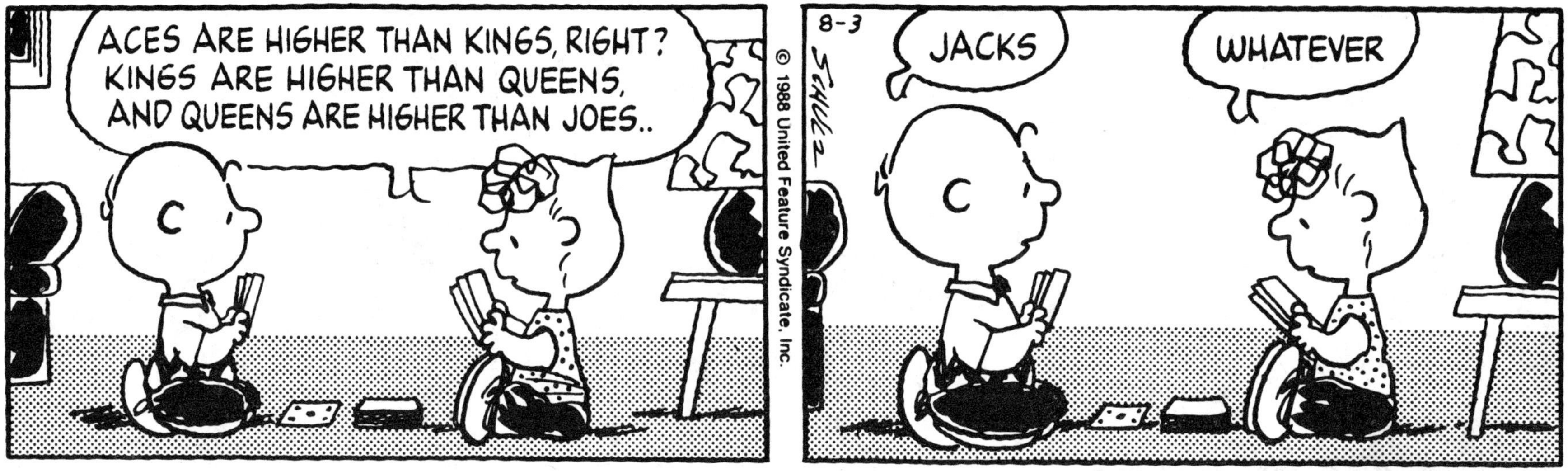

ACES ARE HIGHER THAN KINGS, RIGHT? KINGS ARE HIGHER THAN QUEENS, AND QUEENS ARE HIGHER THAN JOES..
© 1988 United Feature Syndicate, Inc.
8-3
JACKS
WHATEVER

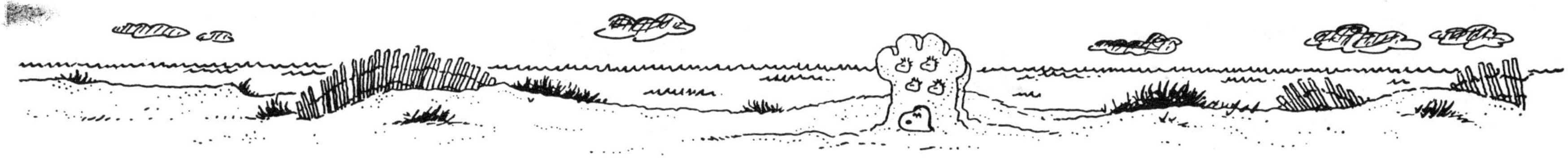

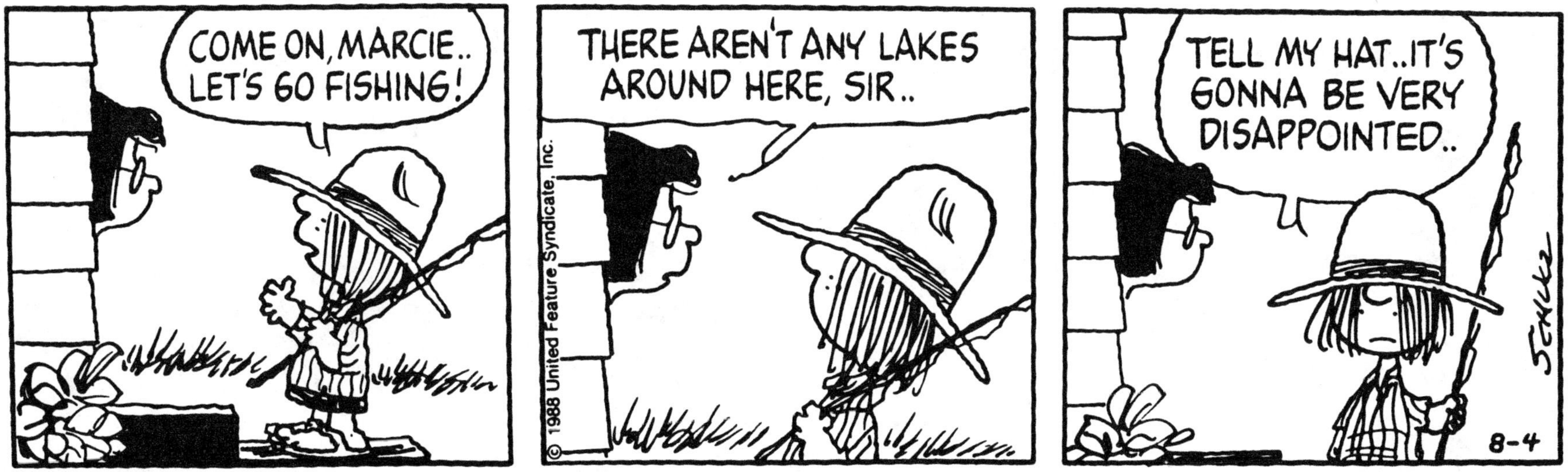

COME ON, MARCIE.. LET'S GO FISHING!
THERE AREN'T ANY LAKES AROUND HERE, SIR..
© 1988 United Feature Syndicate, Inc.
TELL MY HAT..IT'S GONNA BE VERY DISAPPOINTED..
8-4

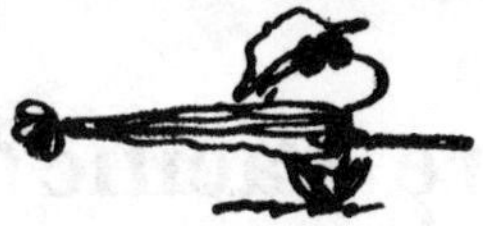

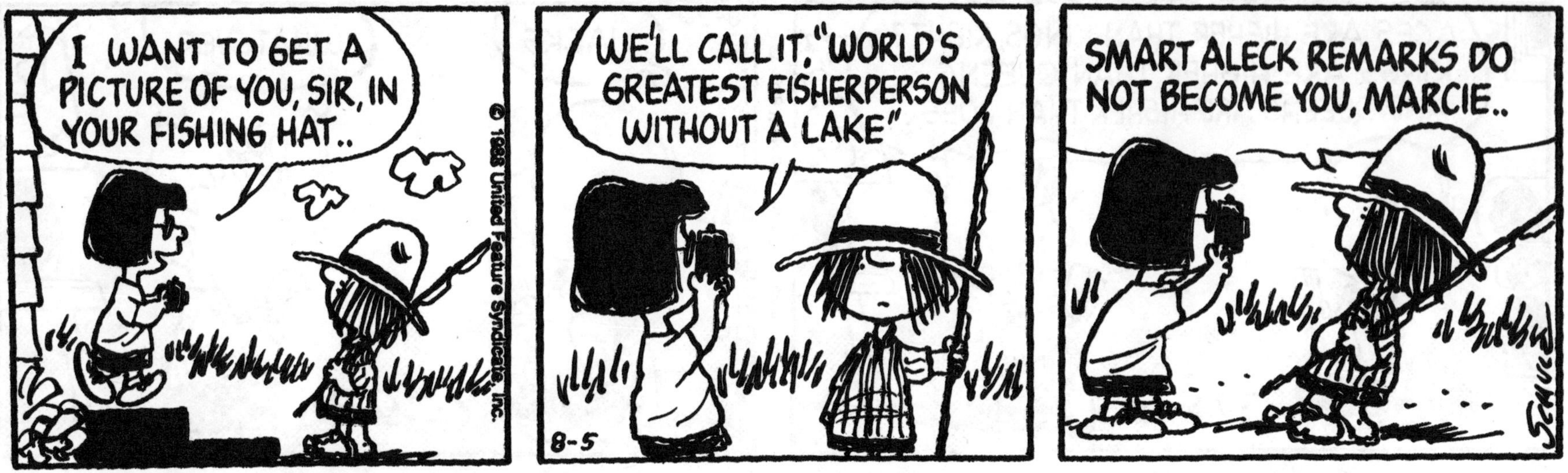

I WANT TO GET A PICTURE OF YOU, SIR, IN YOUR FISHING HAT..
© 1988 United Feature Syndicate, Inc.
WE'LL CALL IT, "WORLD'S GREATEST FISHERPERSON WITHOUT A LAKE"
8-5
SMART ALECK REMARKS DO NOT BECOME YOU, MARCIE..
SCHULZ

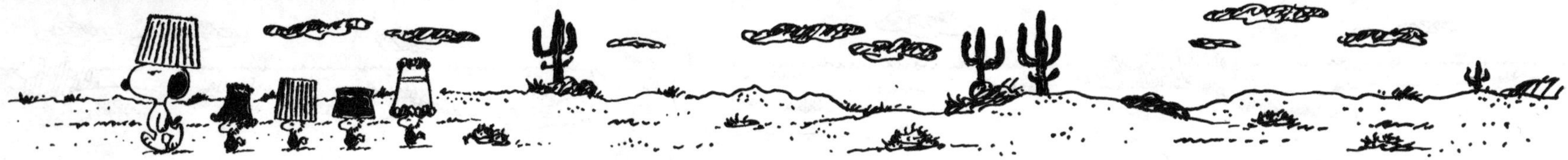

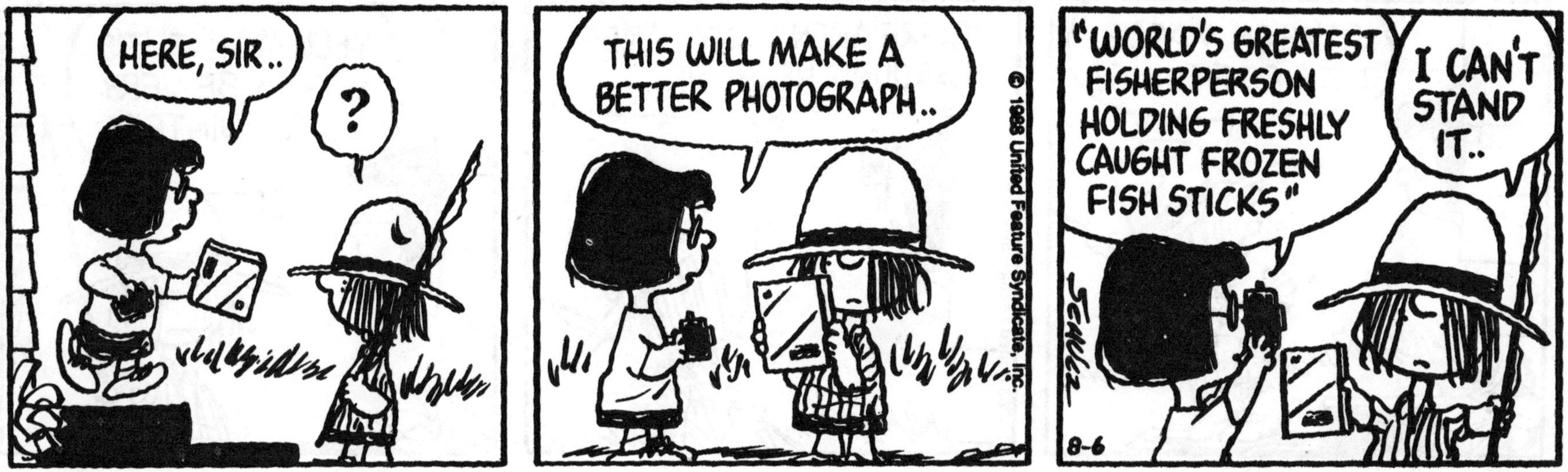

HERE, SIR..
?
THIS WILL MAKE A BETTER PHOTOGRAPH..
© 1988 United Feature Syndicate, Inc.
"WORLD'S GREATEST FISHERPERSON HOLDING FRESHLY CAUGHT FROZEN FISH STICKS"
I CAN'T STAND IT..
SCHULZ
8-6

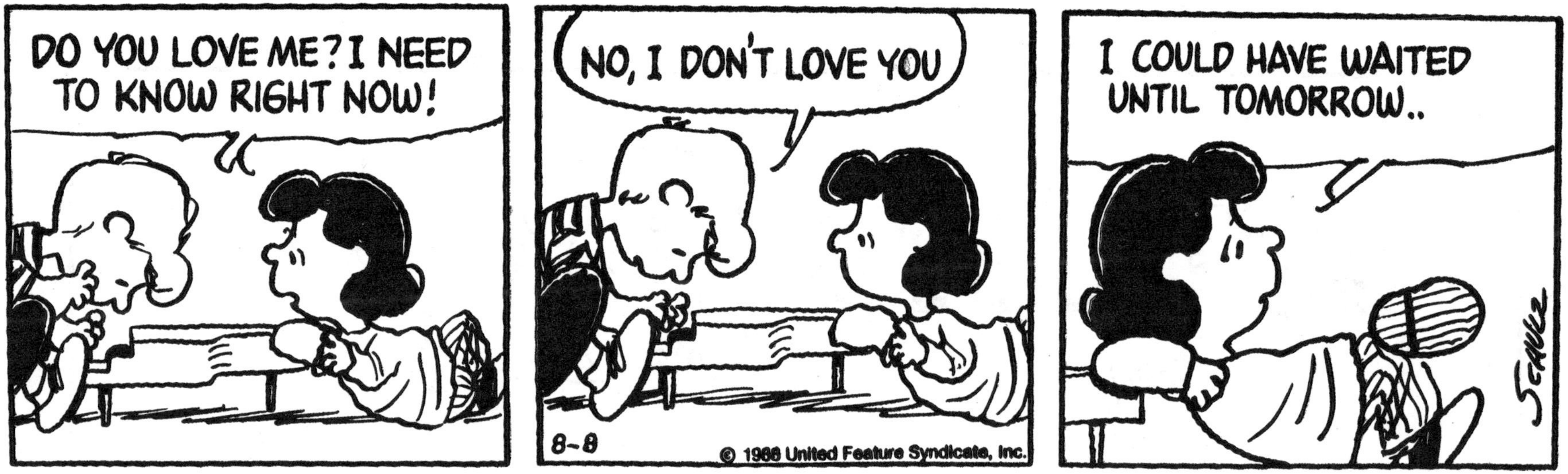
DO YOU LOVE ME? I NEED TO KNOW RIGHT NOW!
NO, I DON'T LOVE YOU
I COULD HAVE WAITED UNTIL TOMORROW..
8-8
© 1988 United Feature Syndicate, Inc.
SCHULZ

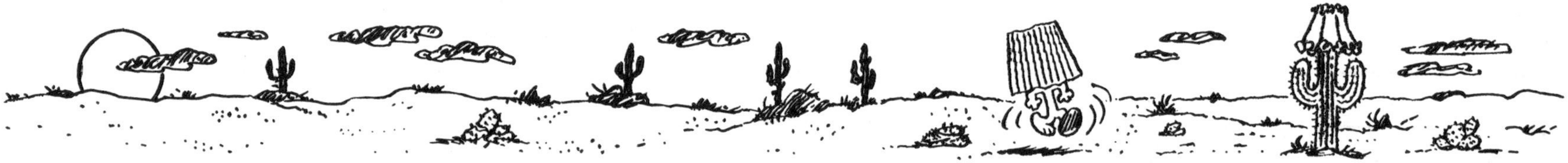

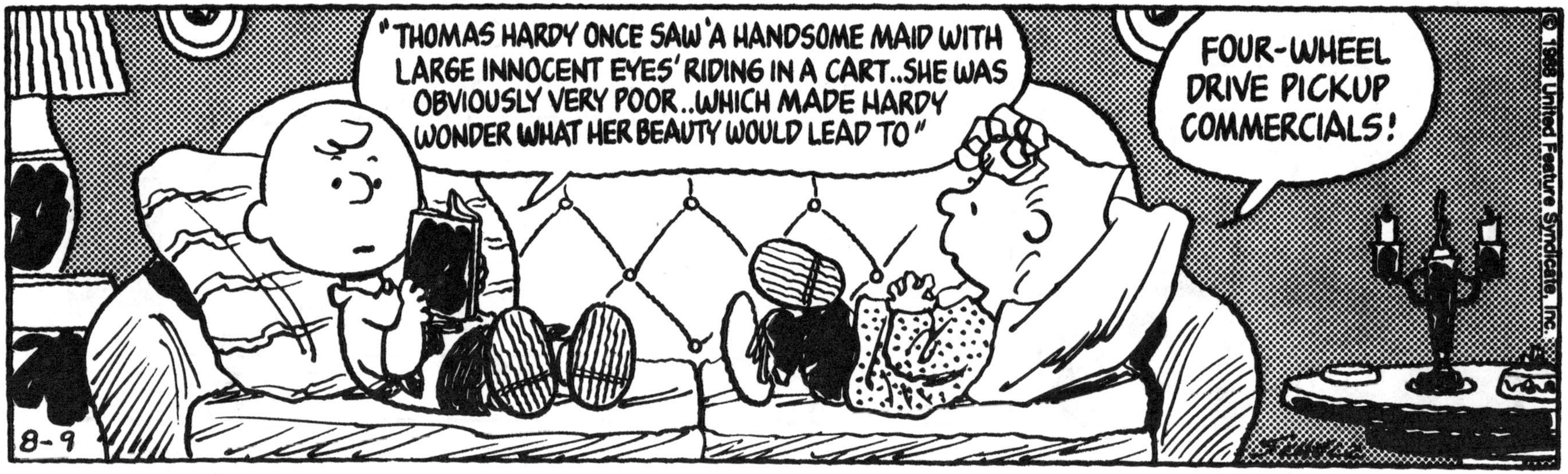
"THOMAS HARDY ONCE SAW 'A HANDSOME MAID WITH LARGE INNOCENT EYES' RIDING IN A CART..SHE WAS OBVIOUSLY VERY POOR..WHICH MADE HARDY WONDER WHAT HER BEAUTY WOULD LEAD TO"
FOUR-WHEEL DRIVE PICKUP COMMERCIALS!
© 1988 United Feature Syndicate, Inc.
8-9

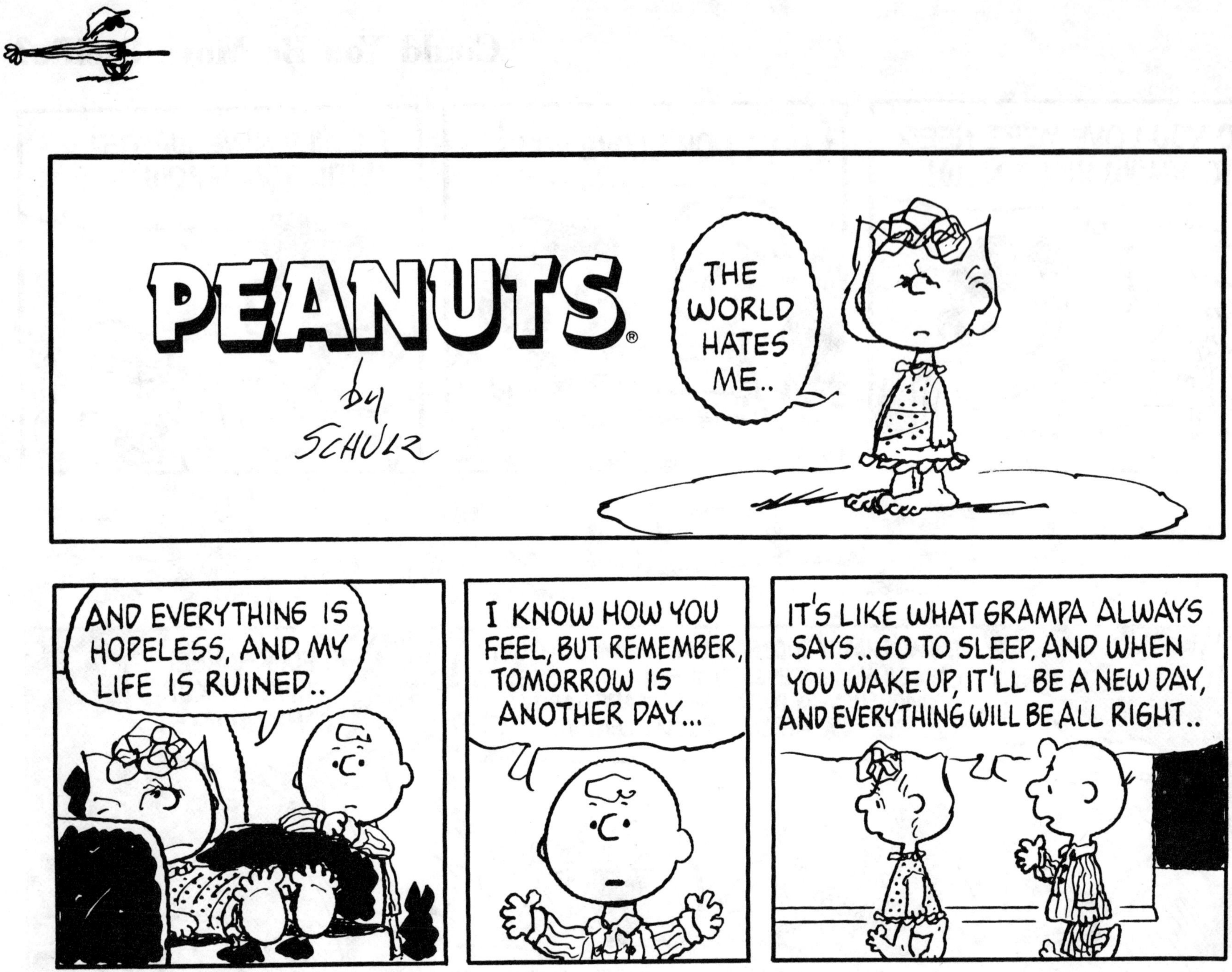
PEANUTS
by SCHULZ
THE WORLD HATES ME..
AND EVERYTHING IS HOPELESS, AND MY LIFE IS RUINED..
I KNOW HOW YOU FEEL, BUT REMEMBER, TOMORROW IS ANOTHER DAY...
IT'S LIKE WHAT GRAMPA ALWAYS SAYS..GO TO SLEEP, AND WHEN YOU WAKE UP, IT'LL BE A NEW DAY, AND EVERYTHING WILL BE ALL RIGHT..

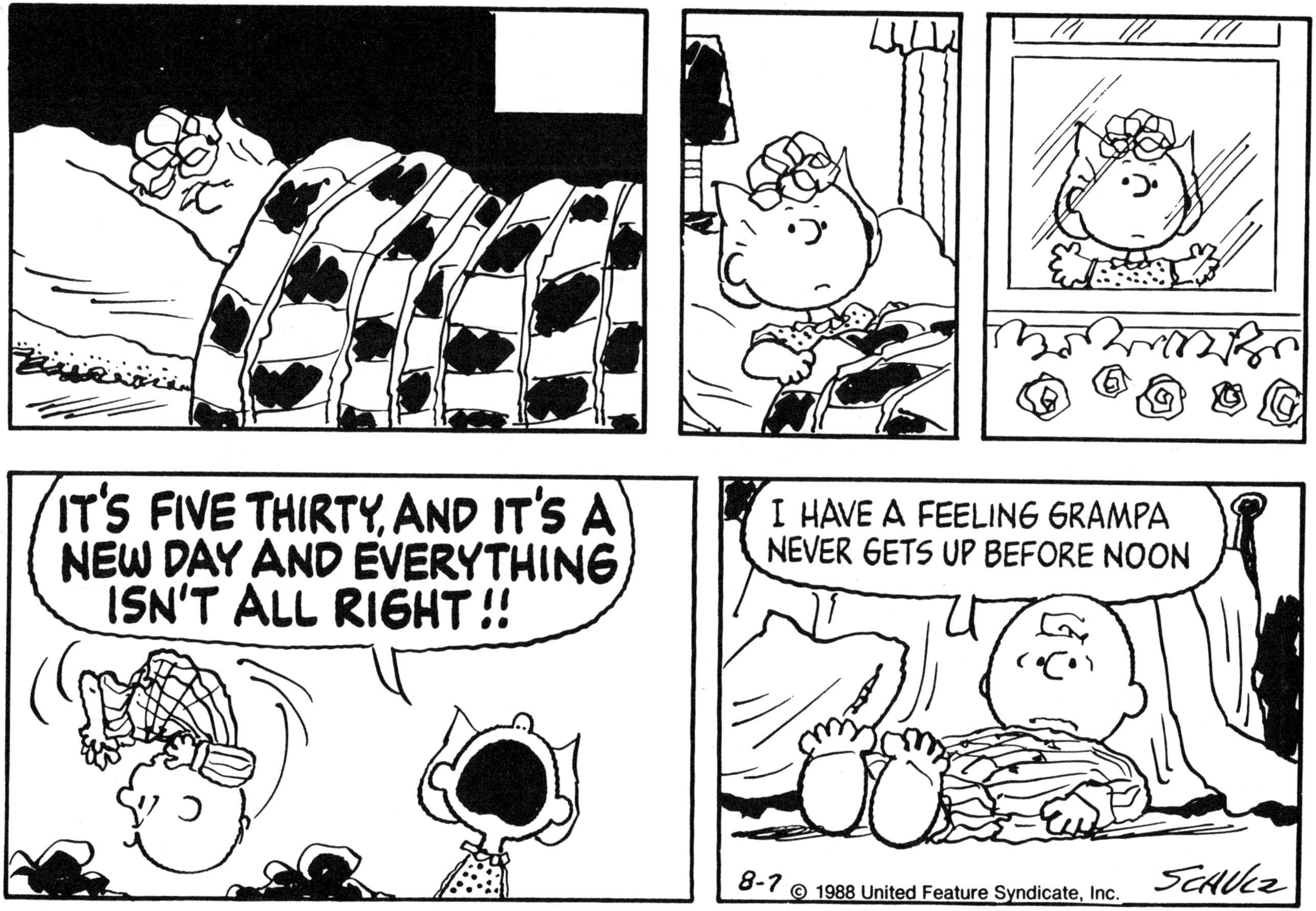
IT'S FIVE THIRTY, AND IT'S A NEW DAY AND EVERYTHING ISN'T ALL RIGHT!!
I HAVE A FEELING GRAMPA NEVER GETS UP BEFORE NOON
8-7
© 1988 United Feature Syndicate, Inc.
SCHULZ

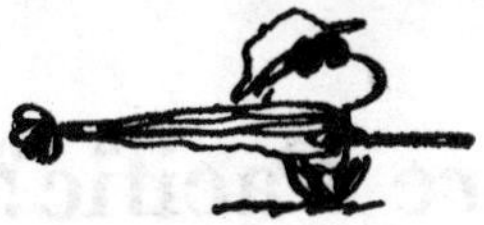

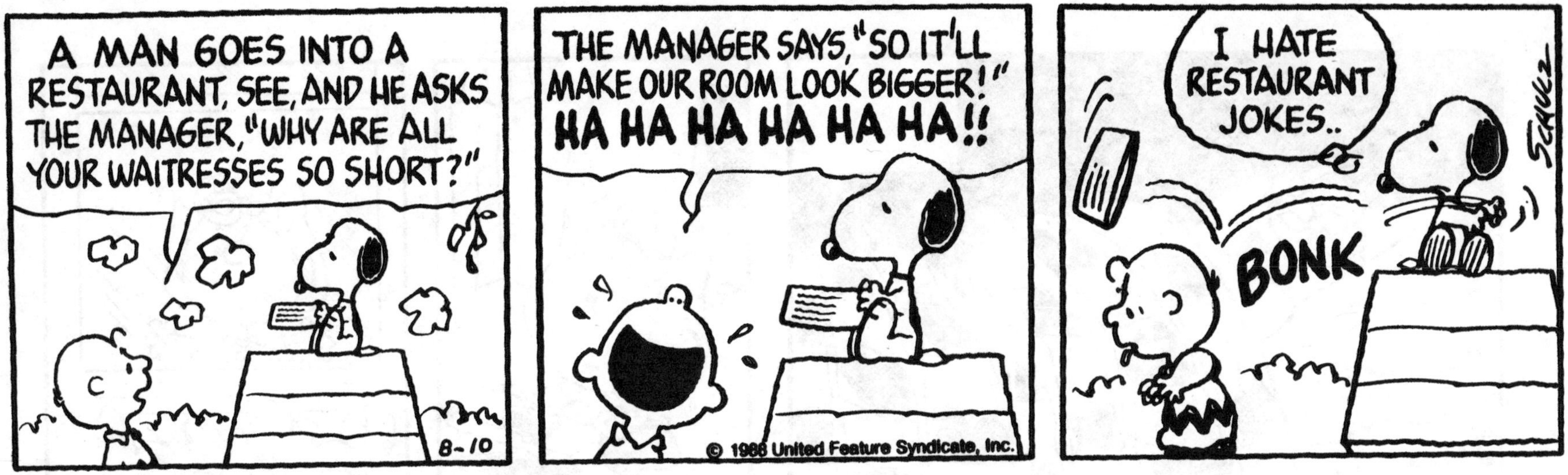
A MAN GOES INTO A RESTAURANT, SEE, AND HE ASKS THE MANAGER, "WHY ARE ALL YOUR WAITRESSES SO SHORT?"
8-10
THE MANAGER SAYS, "SO IT'LL MAKE OUR ROOM LOOK BIGGER!"
HA HA HA HA HA HA!!
© 1988 United Feature Syndicate, Inc.
I HATE RESTAURANT JOKES..
BONK
SCHULZ

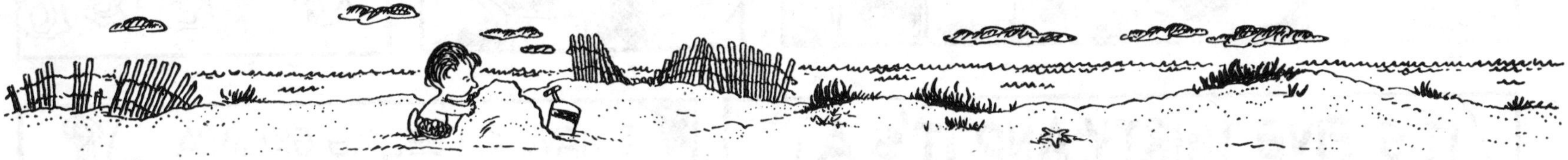

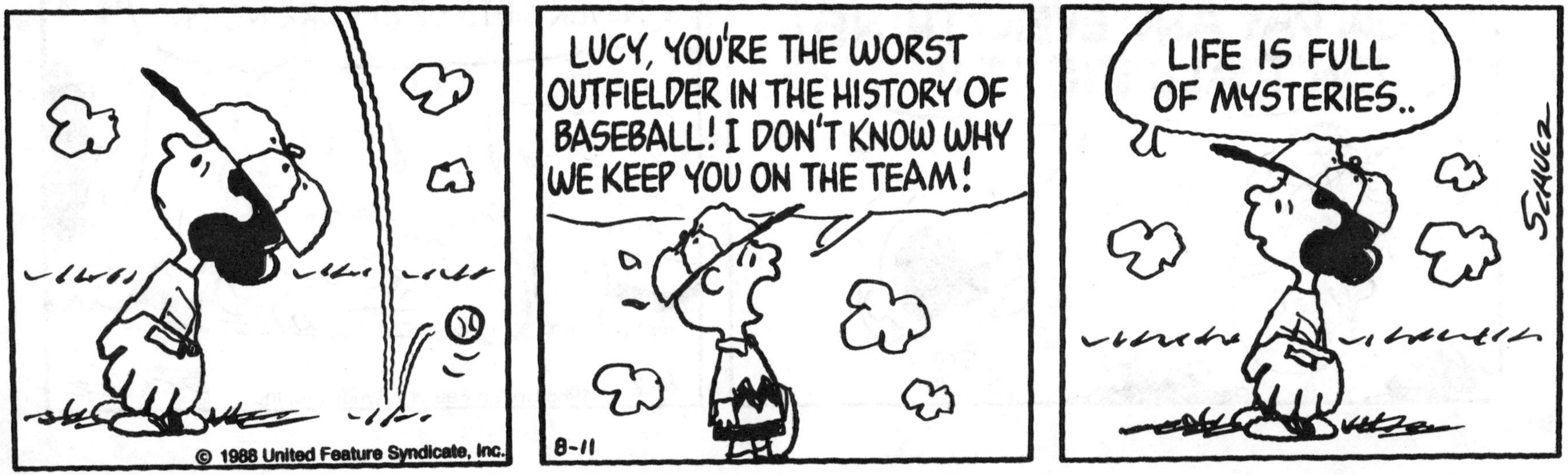
© 1988 United Feature Syndicate, Inc.
LUCY, YOU'RE THE WORST OUTFIELDER IN THE HISTORY OF BASEBALL! I DON'T KNOW WHY WE KEEP YOU ON THE TEAM!
8-11
LIFE IS FULL OF MYSTERIES..
SCHULZ

Could You Be More Pacific?

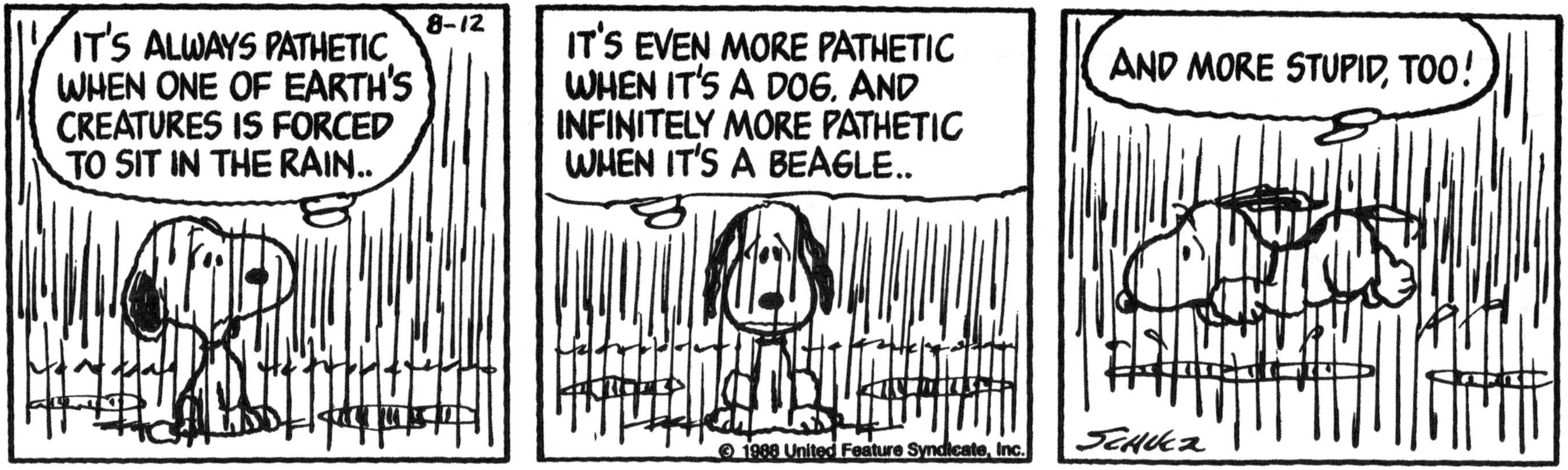
8-12
IT'S ALWAYS PATHETIC WHEN ONE OF EARTH'S CREATURES IS FORCED TO SIT IN THE RAIN..
IT'S EVEN MORE PATHETIC WHEN IT'S A DOG, AND INFINITELY MORE PATHETIC WHEN IT'S A BEAGLE..
© 1988 United Feature Syndicate, Inc.
AND MORE STUPID, TOO!
SCHULZ

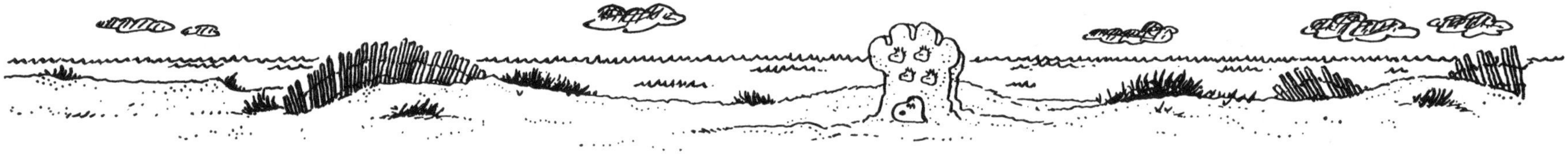

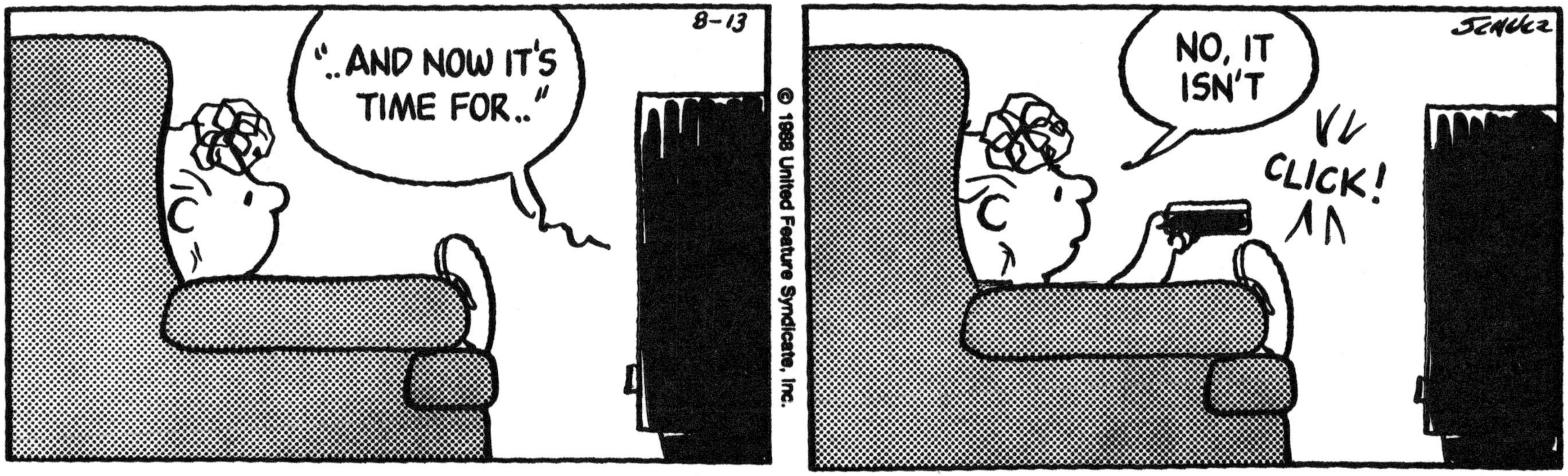
8-13
"..AND NOW IT'S TIME FOR.."
© 1988 United Feature Syndicate, Inc.
SCHULZ
NO, IT ISN'T
CLICK!

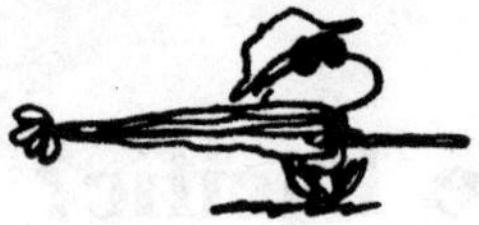

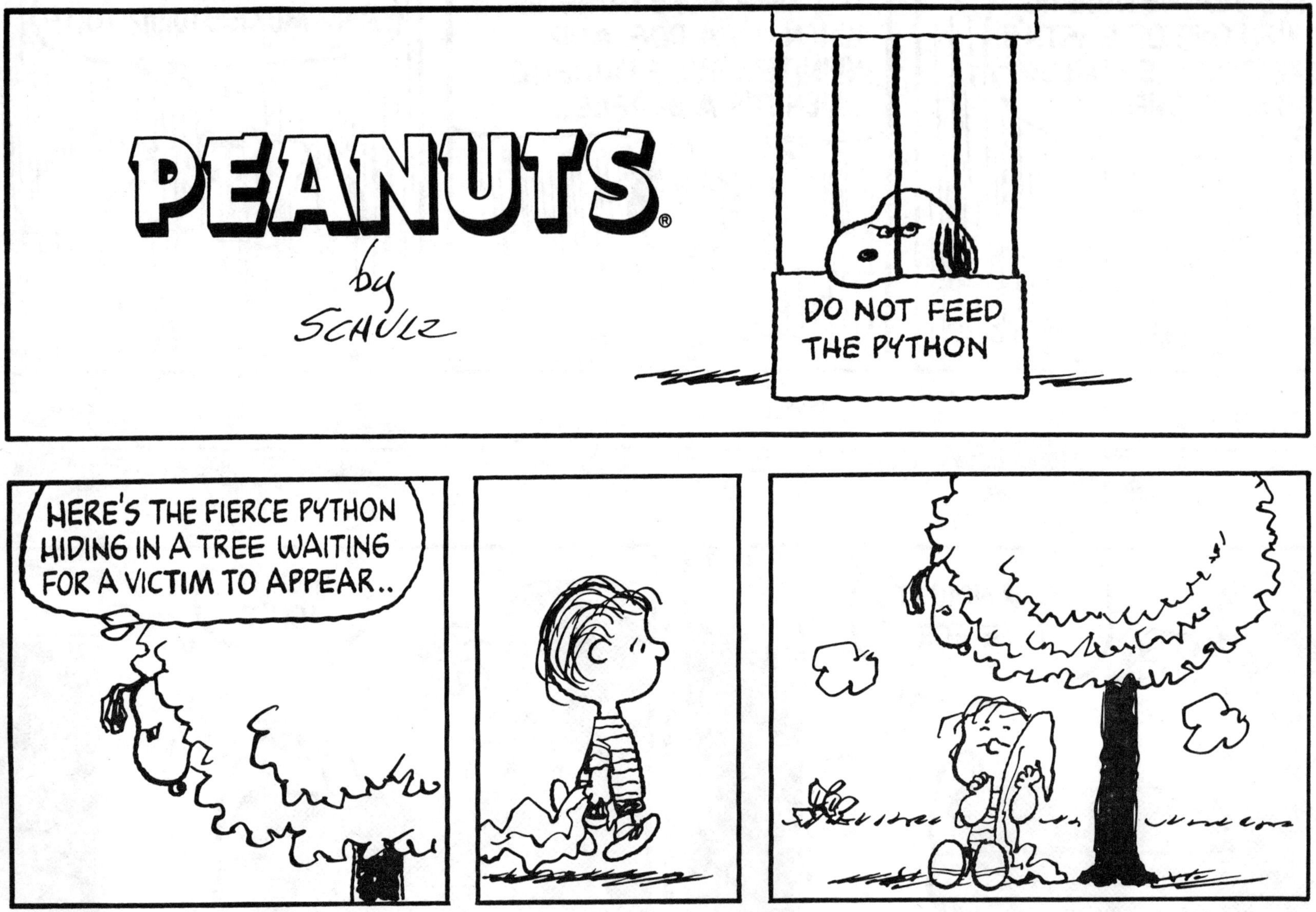
PEANUTS®
by SCHULZ
DO NOT FEED THE PYTHON
HERE'S THE FIERCE PYTHON HIDING IN A TREE WAITING FOR A VICTIM TO APPEAR..

Could You Be More Pacific?

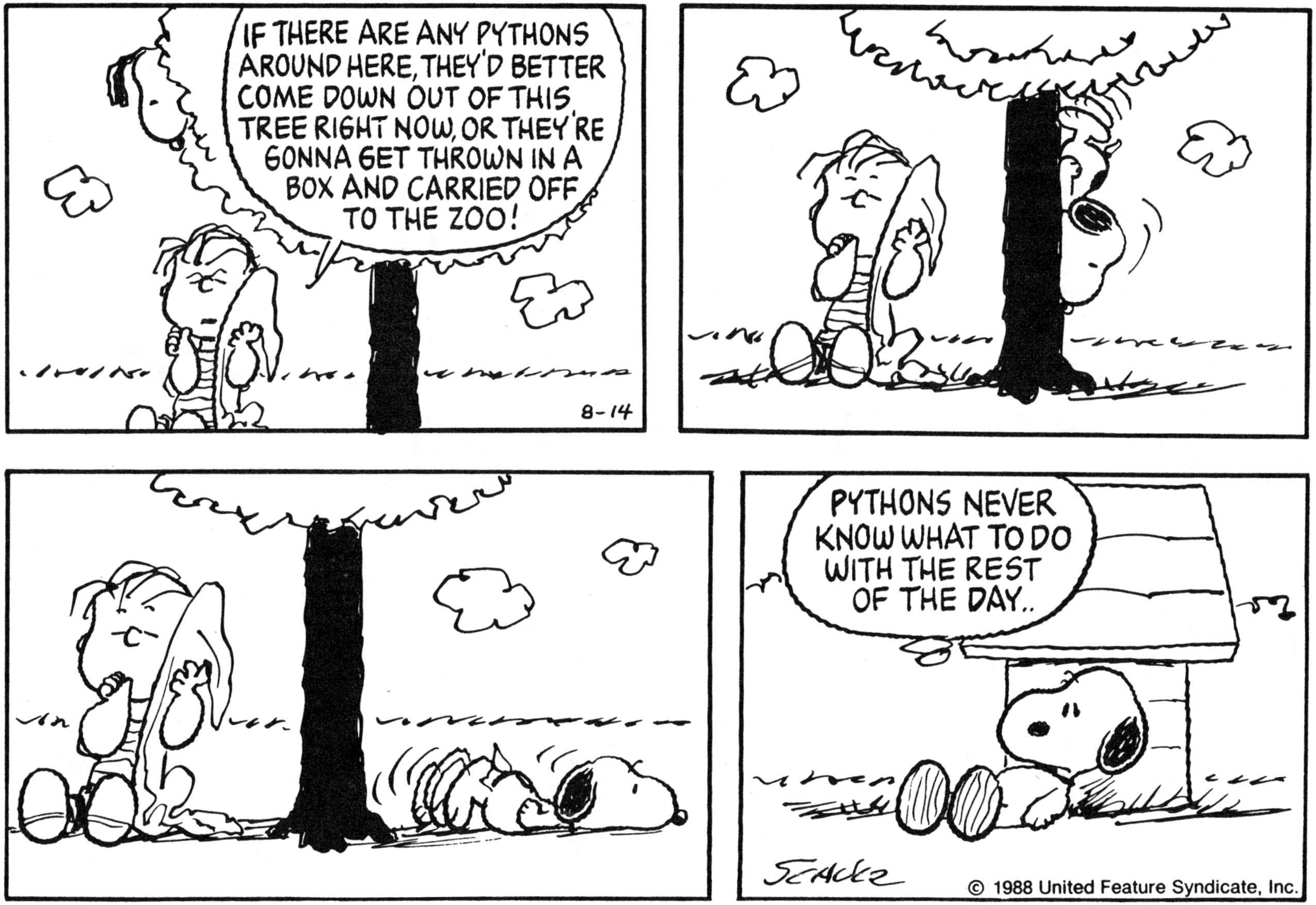
IF THERE ARE ANY PYTHONS AROUND HERE, THEY'D BETTER COME DOWN OUT OF THIS TREE RIGHT NOW, OR THEY'RE GONNA GET THROWN IN A BOX AND CARRIED OFF TO THE ZOO!
8-14
PYTHONS NEVER KNOW WHAT TO DO WITH THE REST OF THE DAY..
SCHULZ
© 1988 United Feature Syndicate, Inc.

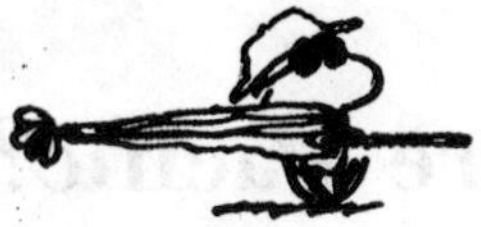

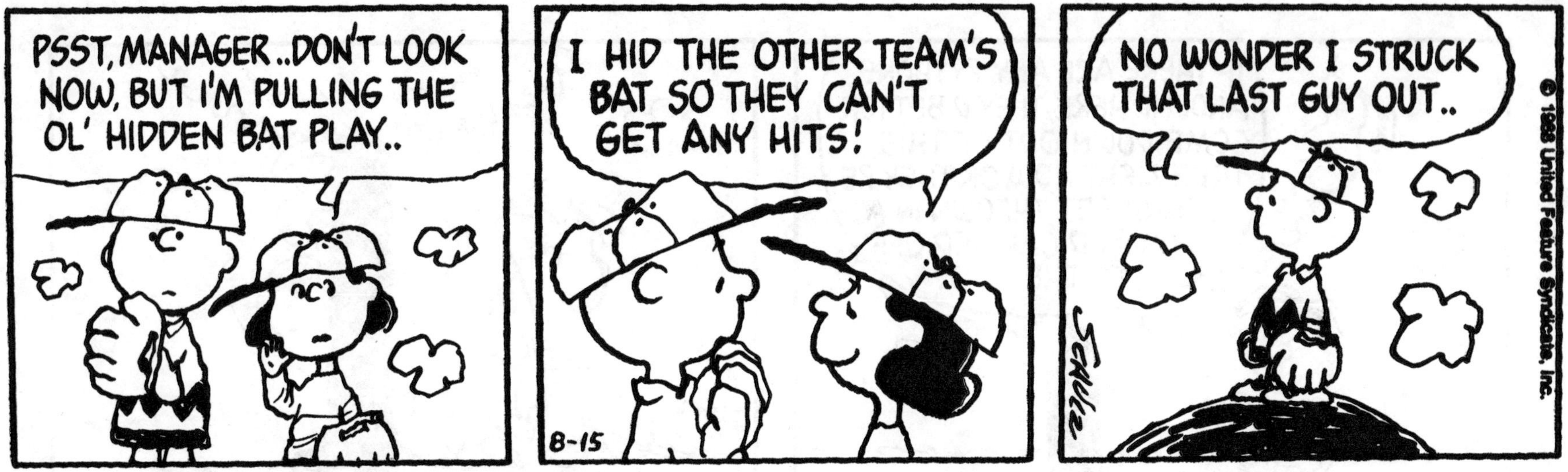
PSST, MANAGER..DON'T LOOK NOW, BUT I'M PULLING THE OL' HIDDEN BAT PLAY..
I HID THE OTHER TEAM'S BAT SO THEY CAN'T GET ANY HITS!
8-15
NO WONDER I STRUCK THAT LAST GUY OUT..
© 1988 United Feature Syndicate, Inc.
SCHULZ

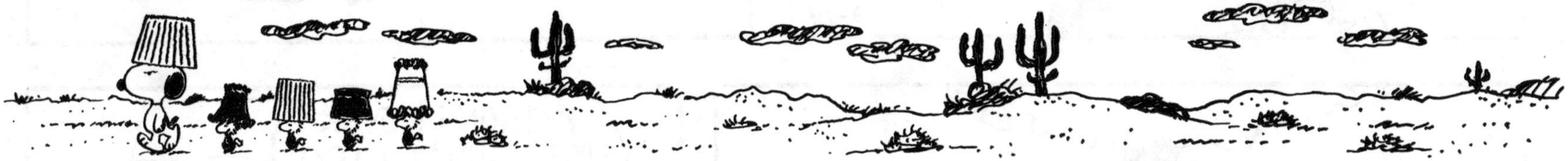

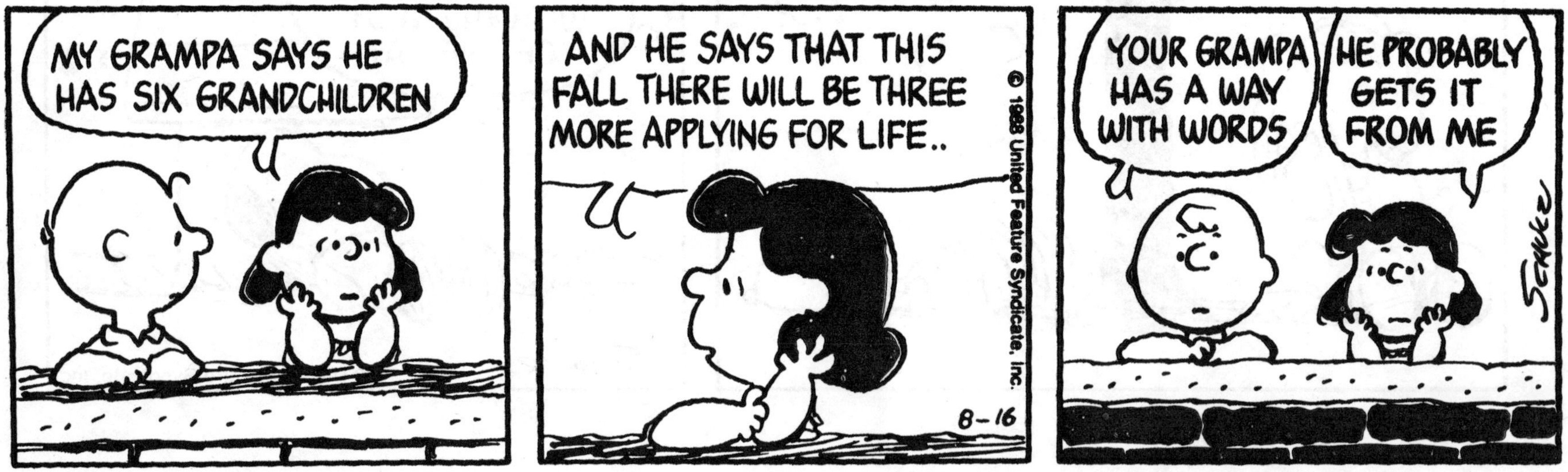
MY GRAMPA SAYS HE HAS SIX GRANDCHILDREN
AND HE SAYS THAT THIS FALL THERE WILL BE THREE MORE APPLYING FOR LIFE..
© 1988 United Feature Syndicate, Inc.
8-16
YOUR GRAMPA HAS A WAY WITH WORDS
HE PROBABLY GETS IT FROM ME
SCHULZ

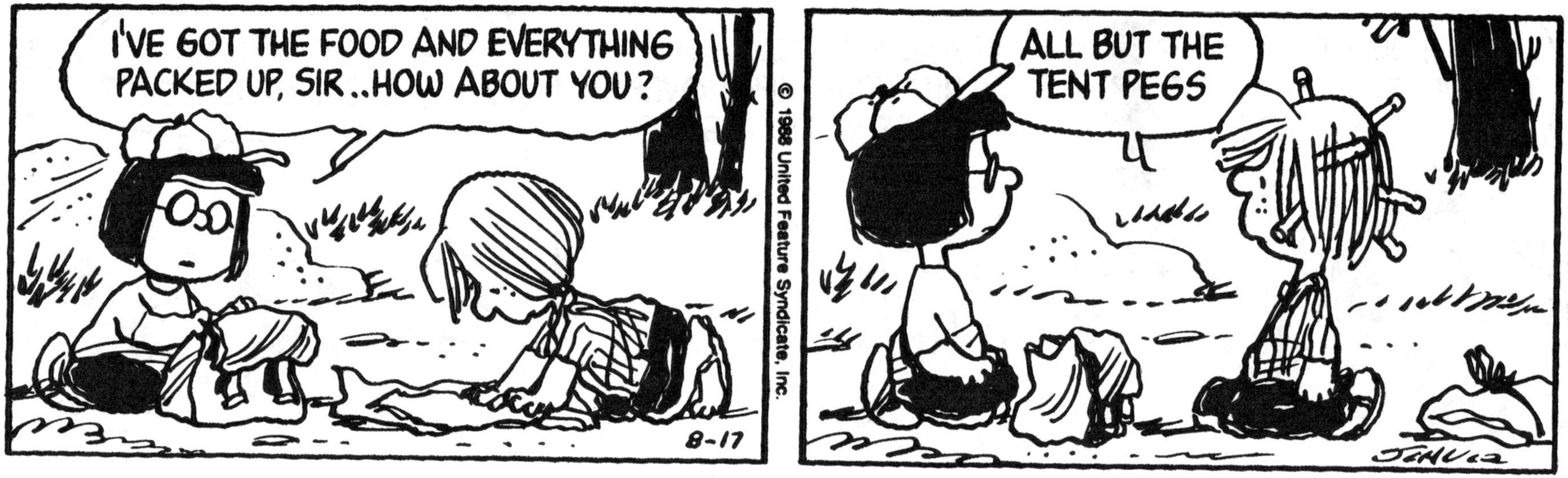
I'VE GOT THE FOOD AND EVERYTHING PACKED UP, SIR..HOW ABOUT YOU?
© 1988 United Feature Syndicate, Inc.
8-17
ALL BUT THE TENT PEGS
SCHULZ

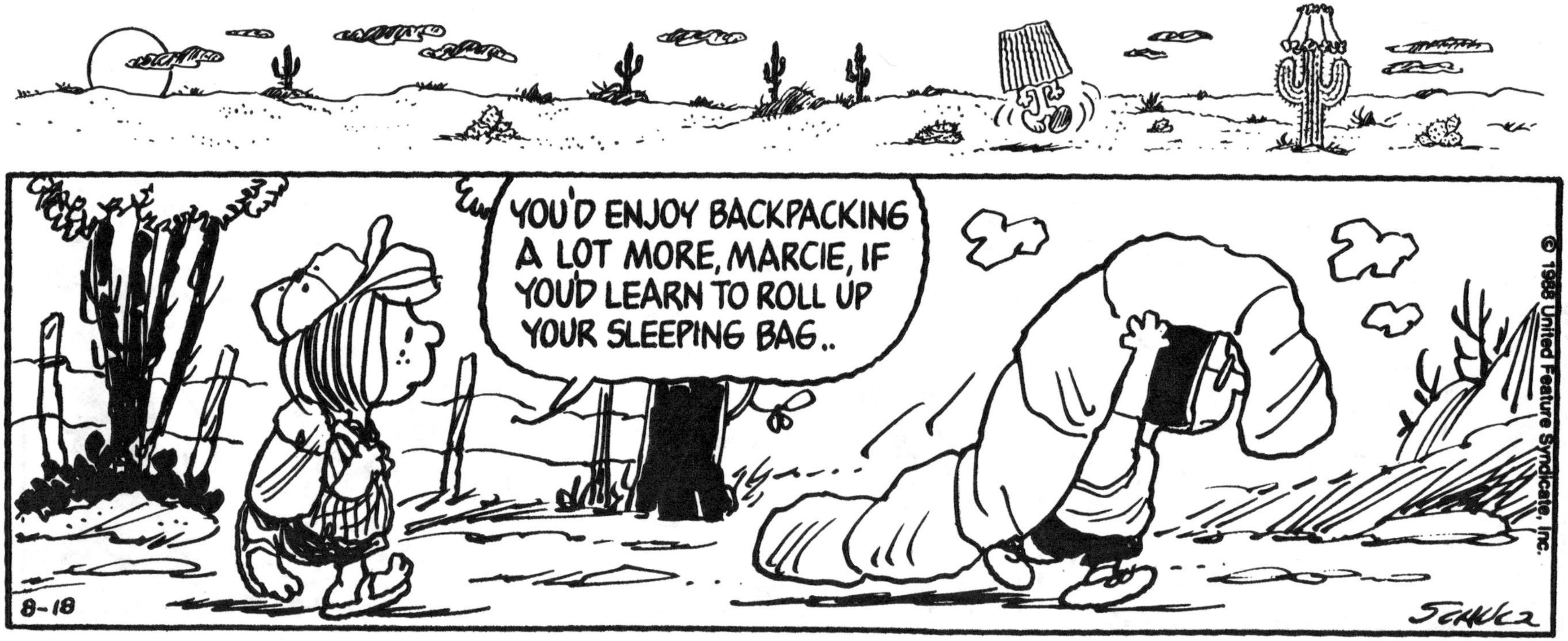
YOU'D ENJOY BACKPACKING A LOT MORE, MARCIE, IF YOU'D LEARN TO ROLL UP YOUR SLEEPING BAG..
© 1988 United Feature Syndicate, Inc.
8-18
SCHULZ

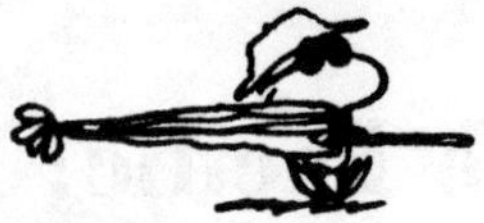

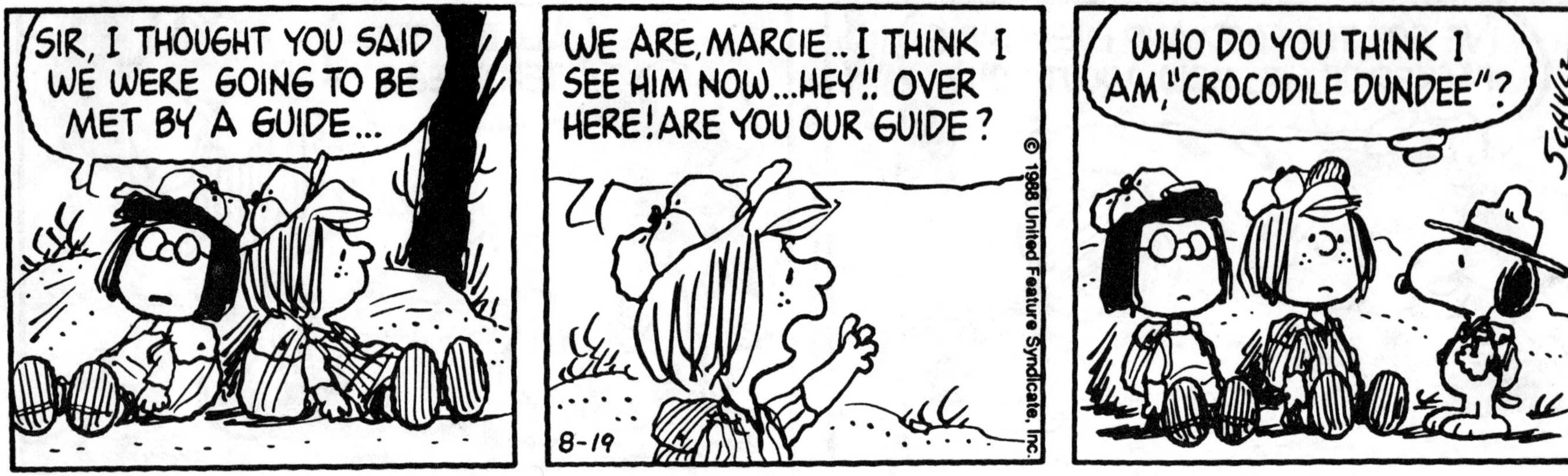
SIR, I THOUGHT YOU SAID WE WERE GOING TO BE MET BY A GUIDE...
WE ARE, MARCIE.. I THINK I SEE HIM NOW...HEY!! OVER HERE! ARE YOU OUR GUIDE?
© 1988 United Feature Syndicate, Inc.
8-19
WHO DO YOU THINK I AM, "CROCODILE DUNDEE"?
SCHULZ

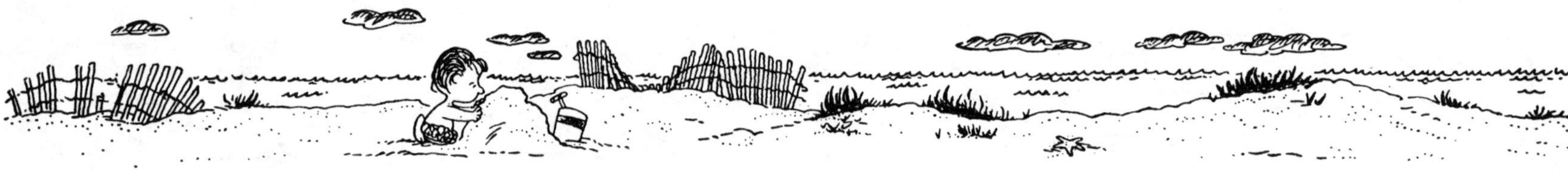

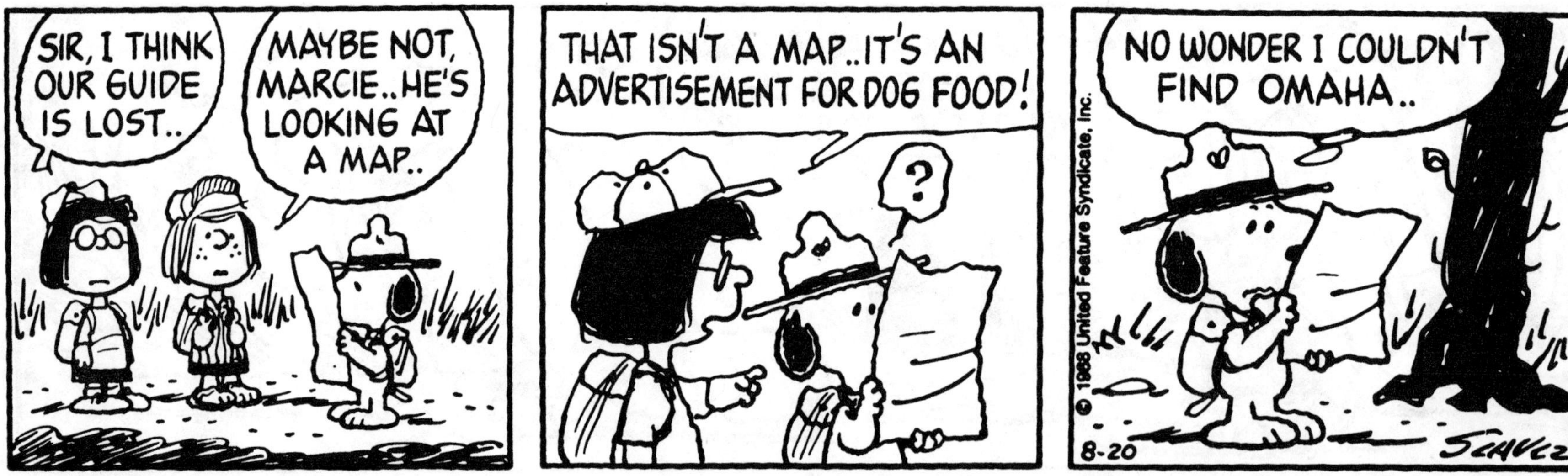
SIR, I THINK OUR GUIDE IS LOST..
MAYBE NOT, MARCIE..HE'S LOOKING AT A MAP..
THAT ISN'T A MAP..IT'S AN ADVERTISEMENT FOR DOG FOOD!
?
NO WONDER I COULDN'T FIND OMAHA..
© 1988 United Feature Syndicate, Inc.
8-20
SCHULZ

Could You Be More Pacific?

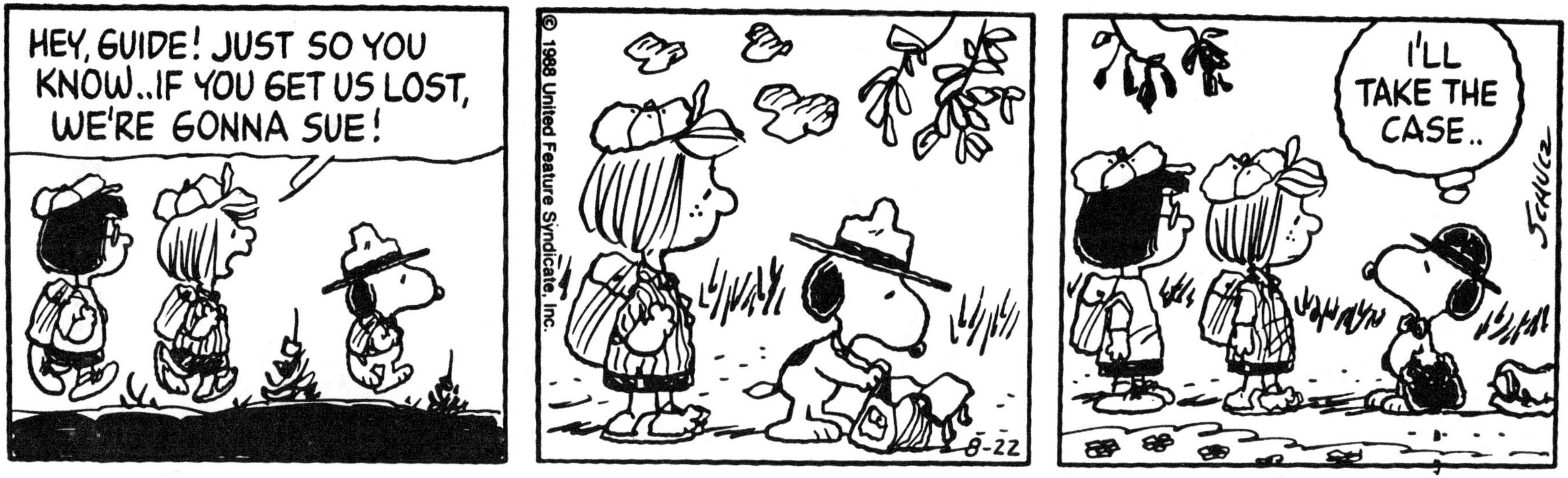
HEY, GUIDE! JUST SO YOU KNOW..IF YOU GET US LOST, WE'RE GONNA SUE!
© 1988 United Feature Syndicate, Inc.
8-22
I'LL TAKE THE CASE..
SCHULZ

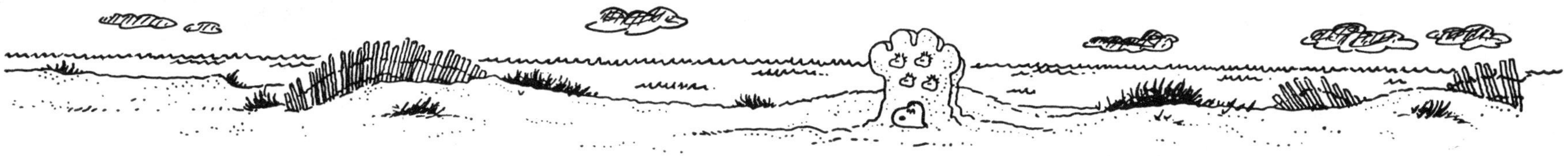

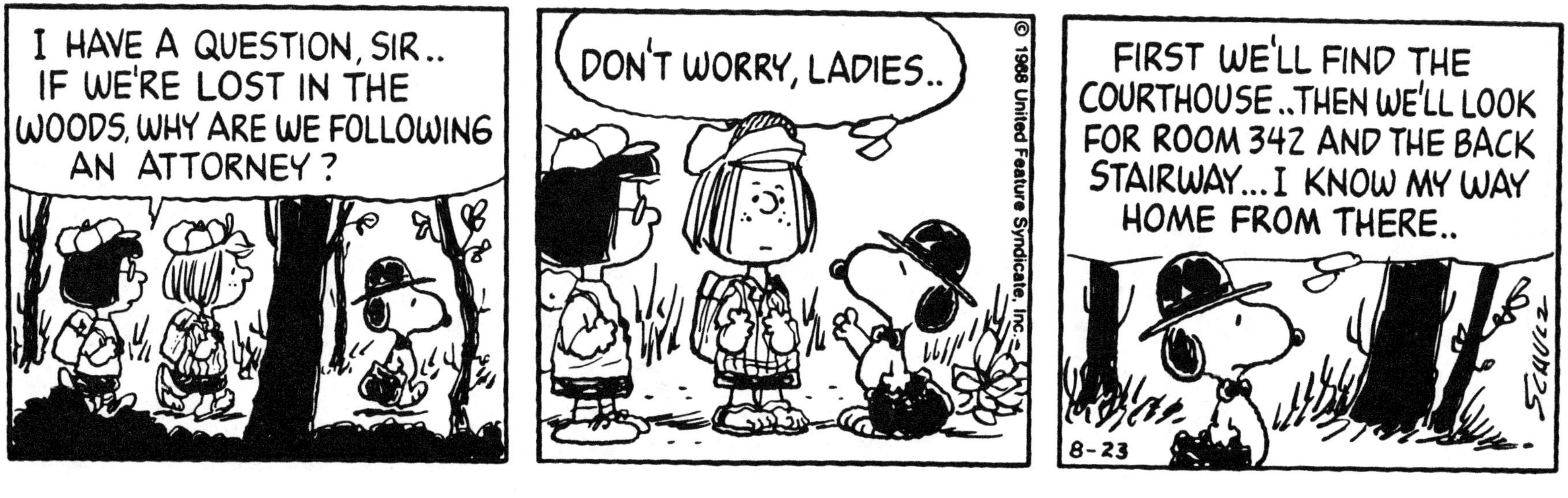
I HAVE A QUESTION, SIR.. IF WE'RE LOST IN THE WOODS, WHY ARE WE FOLLOWING AN ATTORNEY?
DON'T WORRY, LADIES..
© 1988 United Feature Syndicate, Inc.
FIRST WE'LL FIND THE COURTHOUSE..THEN WE'LL LOOK FOR ROOM 342 AND THE BACK STAIRWAY... I KNOW MY WAY HOME FROM THERE..
SCHULZ
8-23

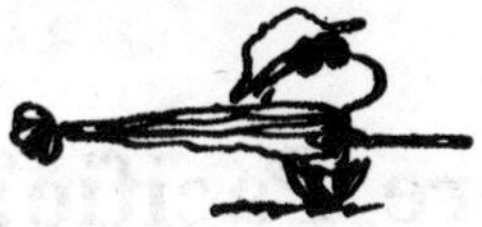

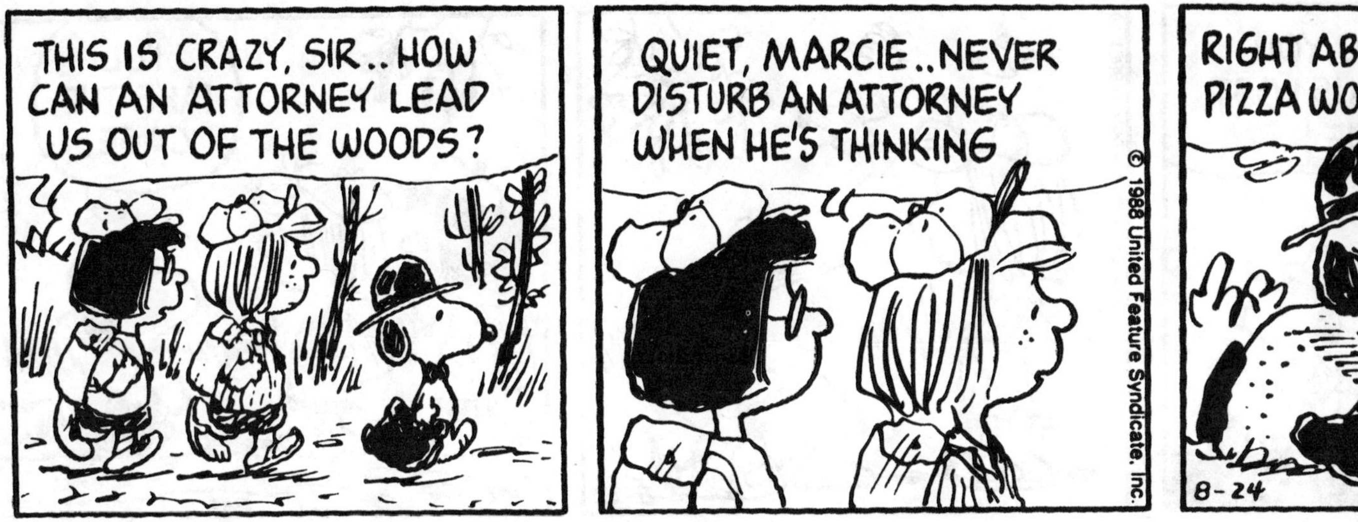
THIS IS CRAZY, SIR.. HOW CAN AN ATTORNEY LEAD US OUT OF THE WOODS?
QUIET, MARCIE.. NEVER DISTURB AN ATTORNEY WHEN HE'S THINKING
© 1988 United Feature Syndicate, Inc.
RIGHT ABOUT NOW IS WHEN A PIZZA WOULD TASTE GOOD..
8-24
SCHULZ

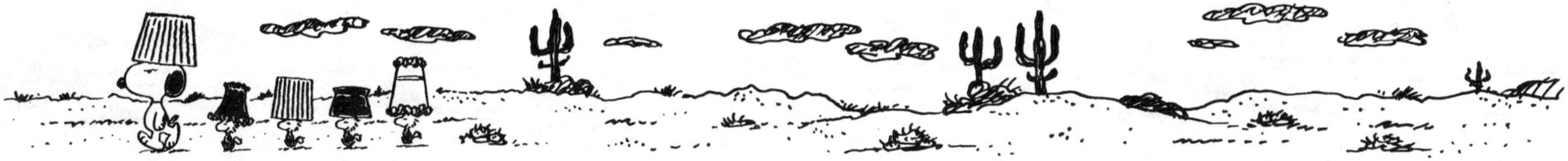

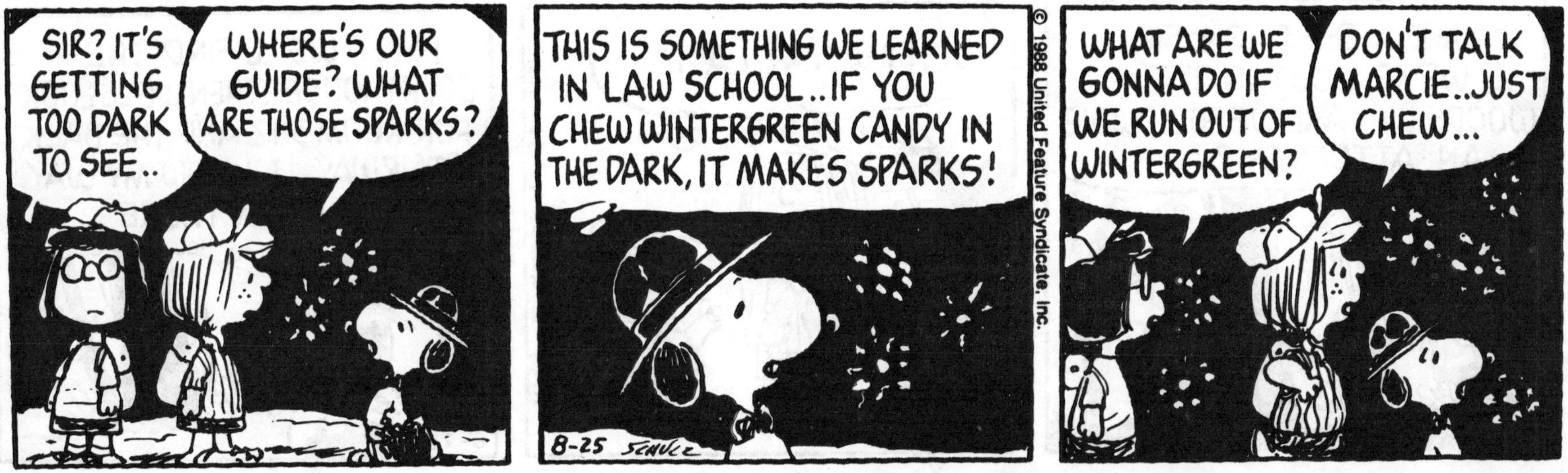
SIR? IT'S GETTING TOO DARK TO SEE..
WHERE'S OUR GUIDE? WHAT ARE THOSE SPARKS?
THIS IS SOMETHING WE LEARNED IN LAW SCHOOL.. IF YOU CHEW WINTERGREEN CANDY IN THE DARK, IT MAKES SPARKS!
8-25 SCHULZ
© 1988 United Feature Syndicate, Inc.
WHAT ARE WE GONNA DO IF WE RUN OUT OF WINTERGREEN?
DON'T TALK MARCIE.. JUST CHEW...

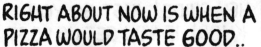

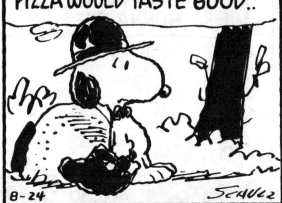

Could You Be More Pacific?

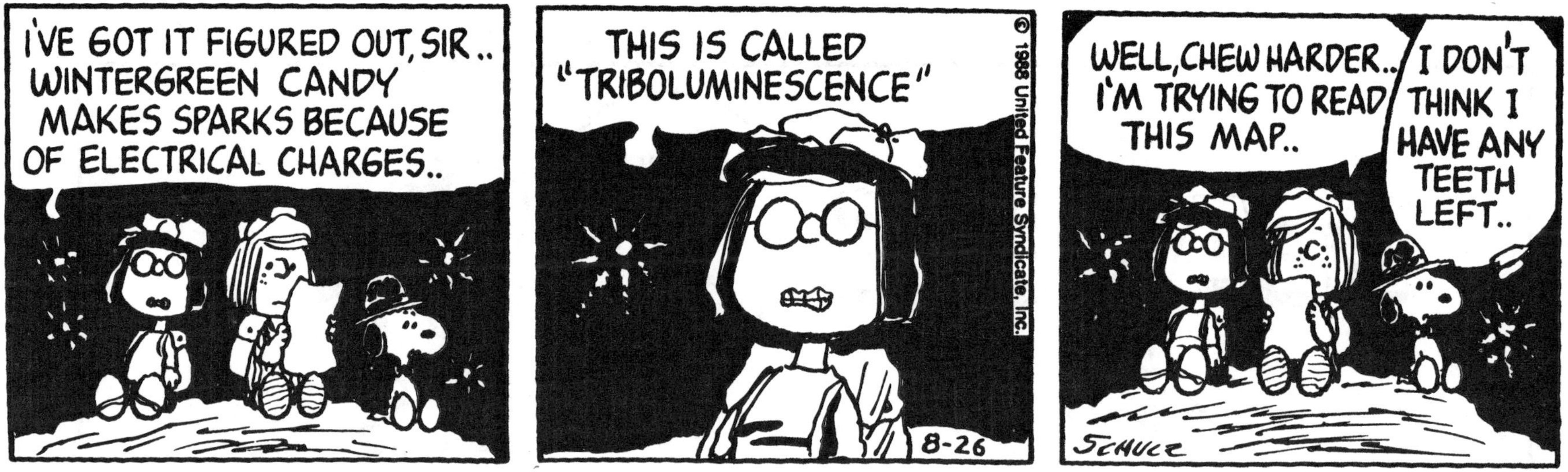

I'VE GOT IT FIGURED OUT, SIR.. WINTERGREEN CANDY MAKES SPARKS BECAUSE OF ELECTRICAL CHARGES..
THIS IS CALLED "TRIBOLUMINESCENCE"
© 1988 United Feature Syndicate, Inc.
8-26
WELL, CHEW HARDER.. I'M TRYING TO READ THIS MAP..
I DON'T THINK I HAVE ANY TEETH LEFT..
SCHULZ

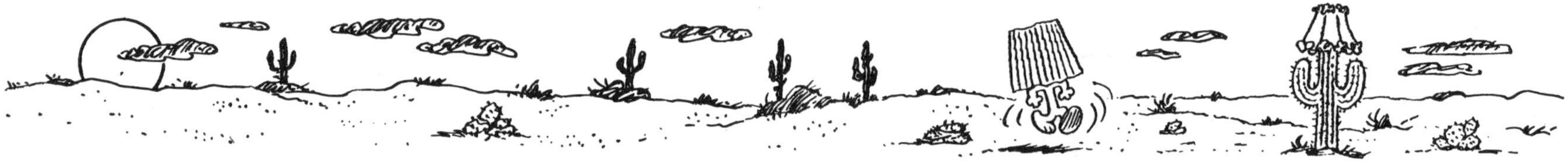

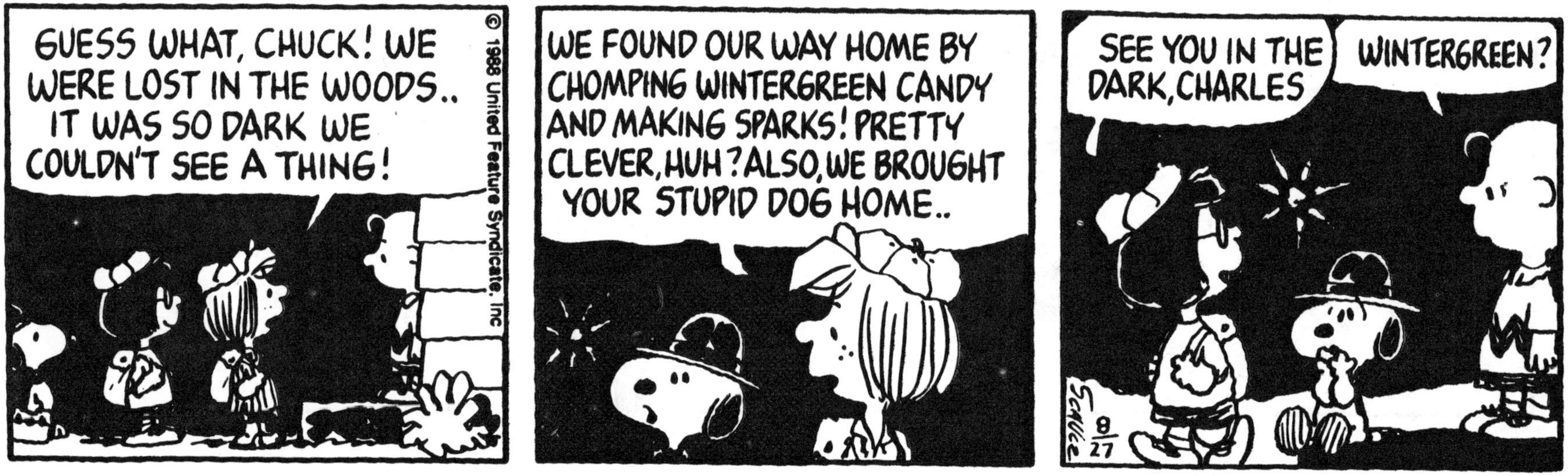

GUESS WHAT, CHUCK! WE WERE LOST IN THE WOODS.. IT WAS SO DARK WE COULDN'T SEE A THING!
© 1988 United Feature Syndicate, Inc
WE FOUND OUR WAY HOME BY CHOMPING WINTERGREEN CANDY AND MAKING SPARKS! PRETTY CLEVER, HUH? ALSO, WE BROUGHT YOUR STUPID DOG HOME..
SEE YOU IN THE DARK, CHARLES
WINTERGREEN?
SCHULZ
8/27

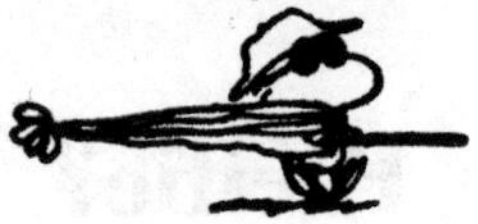

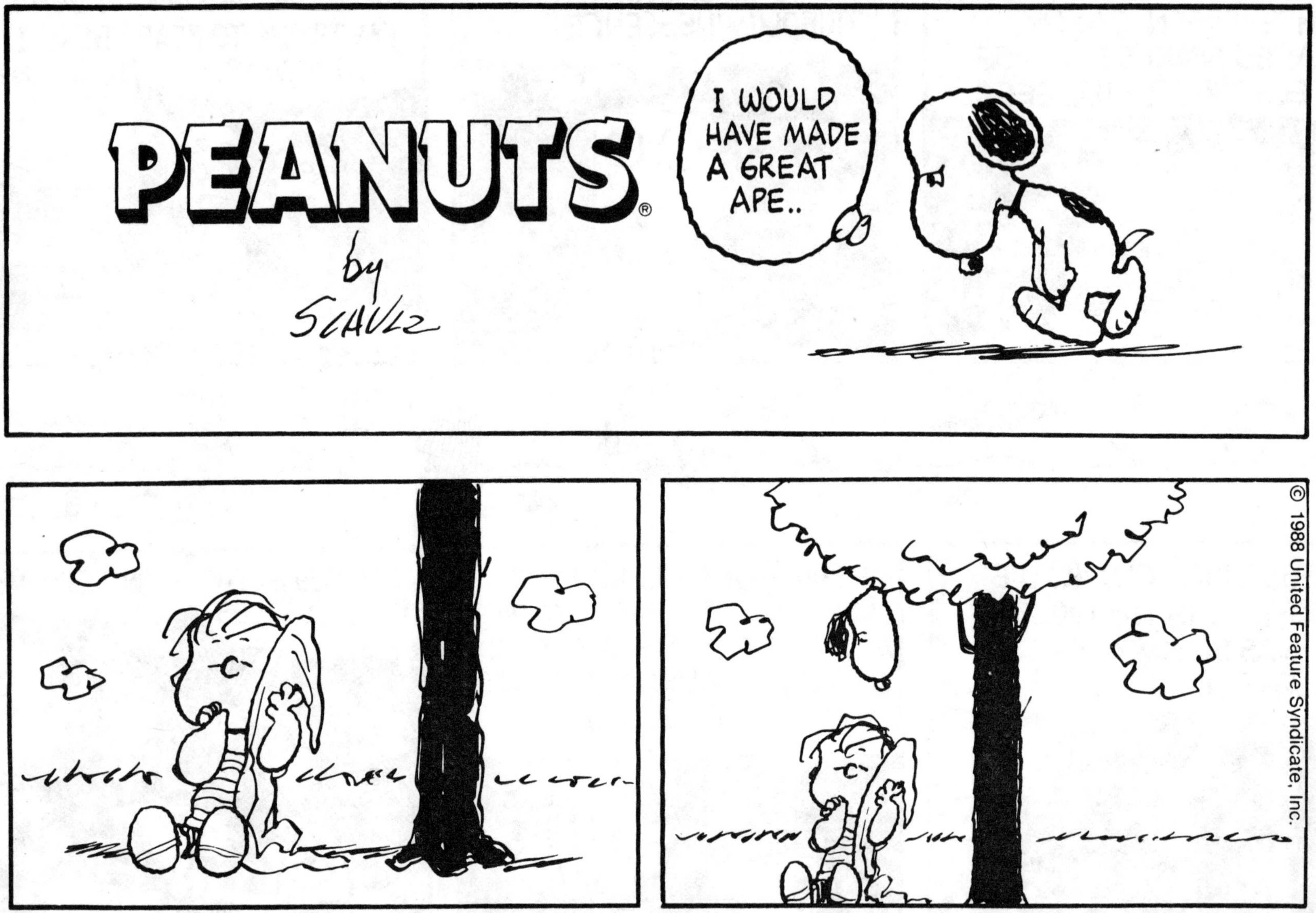
PEANUTS®
by SCHULZ
I WOULD HAVE MADE A GREAT APE..
© 1988 United Feature Syndicate, Inc.

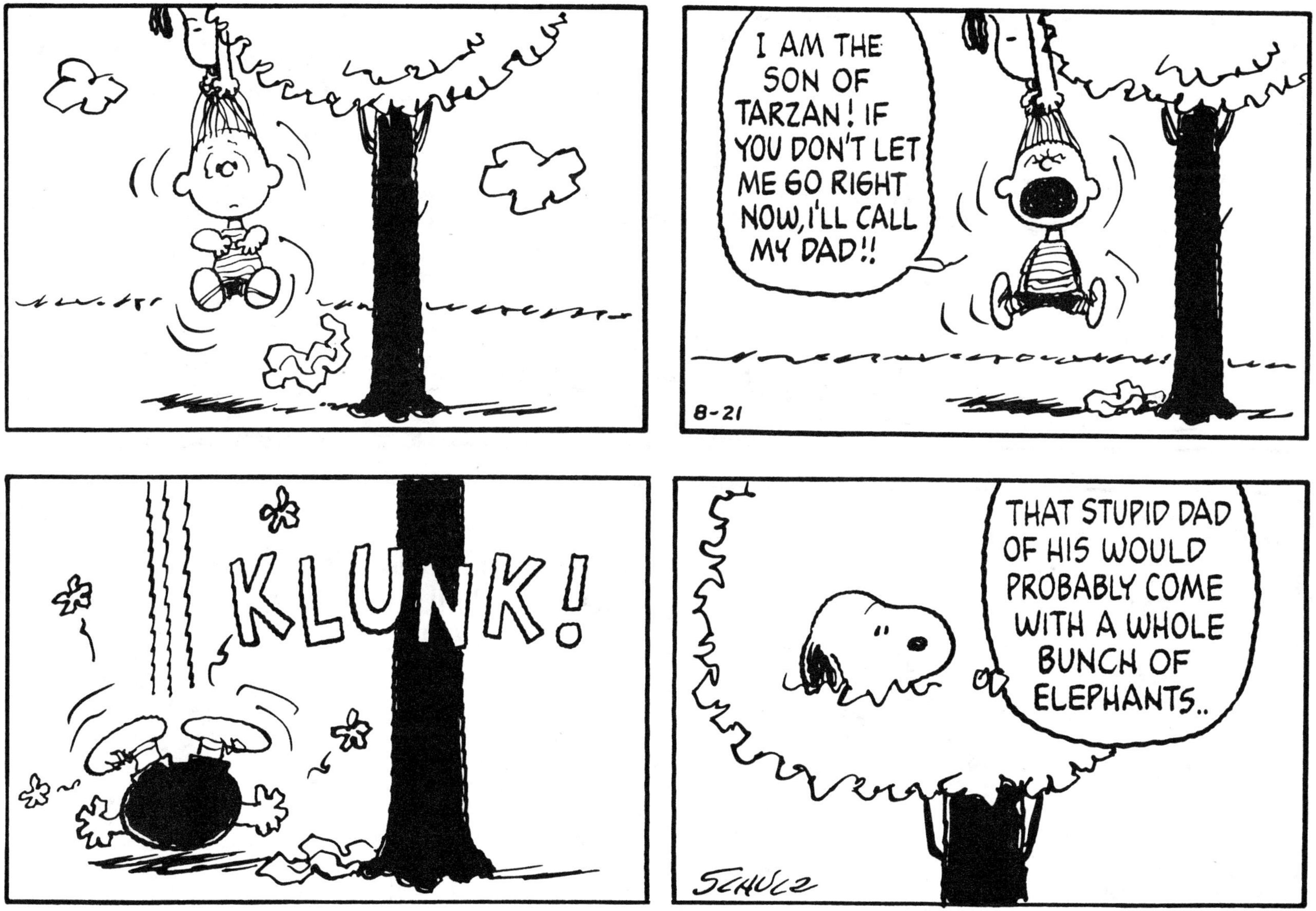
I AM THE SON OF TARZAN! IF YOU DON'T LET ME GO RIGHT NOW, I'LL CALL MY DAD!!
8-21
KLUNK!
THAT STUPID DAD OF HIS WOULD PROBABLY COME WITH A WHOLE BUNCH OF ELEPHANTS..
SCHULZ

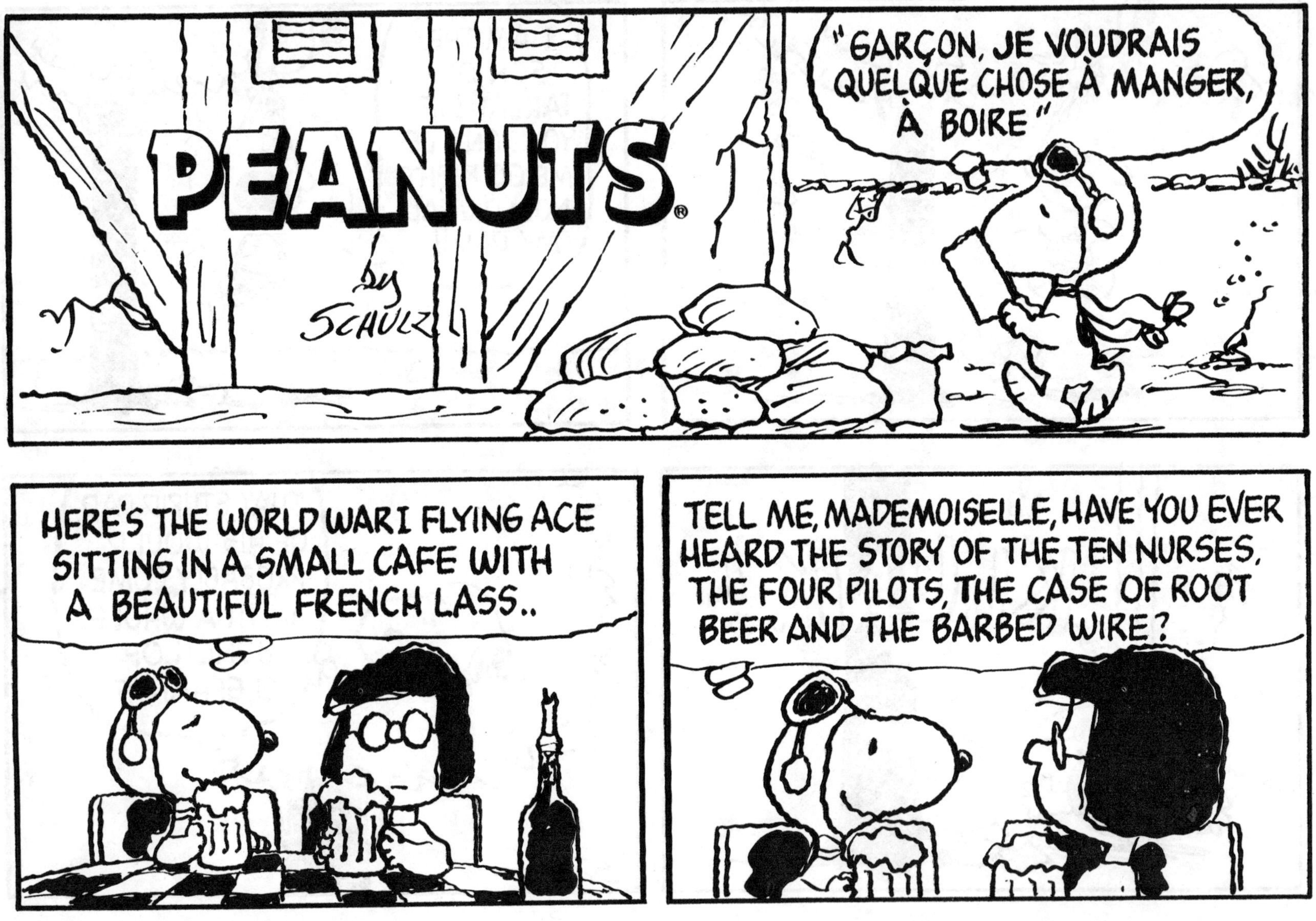
PEANUTS®
by SCHULZ
"GARÇON, JE VOUDRAIS QUELQUE CHOSE À MANGER, À BOIRE"
HERE'S THE WORLD WAR I FLYING ACE SITTING IN A SMALL CAFE WITH A BEAUTIFUL FRENCH LASS..
TELL ME, MADEMOISELLE, HAVE YOU EVER HEARD THE STORY OF THE TEN NURSES, THE FOUR PILOTS, THE CASE OF ROOT BEER AND THE BARBED WIRE?

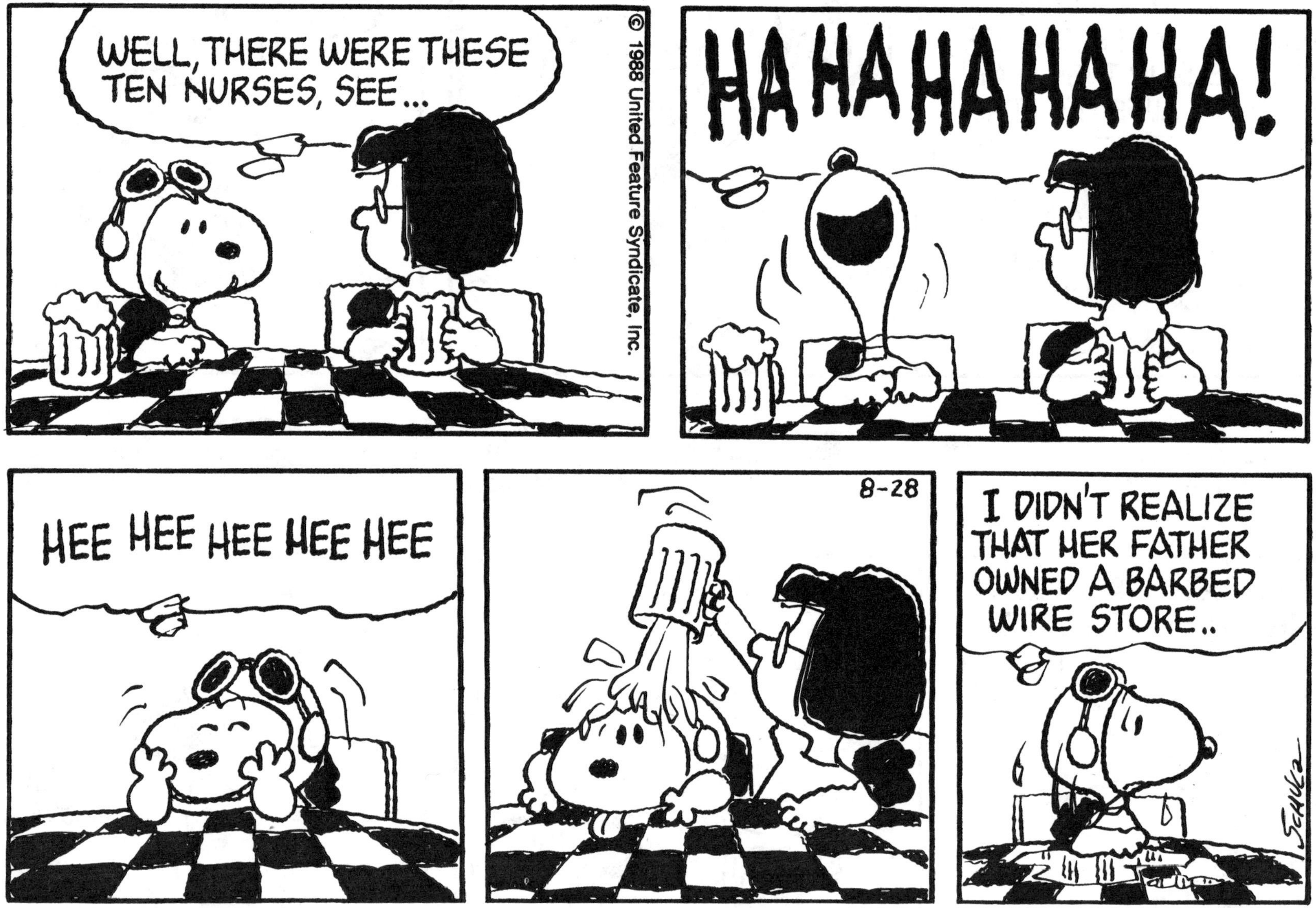
WELL, THERE WERE THESE TEN NURSES, SEE...
© 1988 United Feature Syndicate, Inc.
HAHAHAHAHAHA!
HEE HEE HEE HEE HEE
8-28
I DIDN'T REALIZE THAT HER FATHER OWNED A BARBED WIRE STORE..
SCHULZ

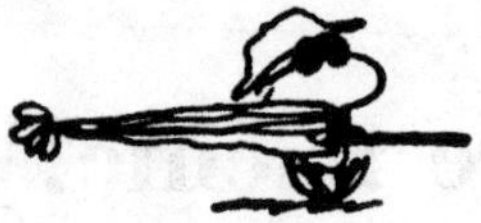

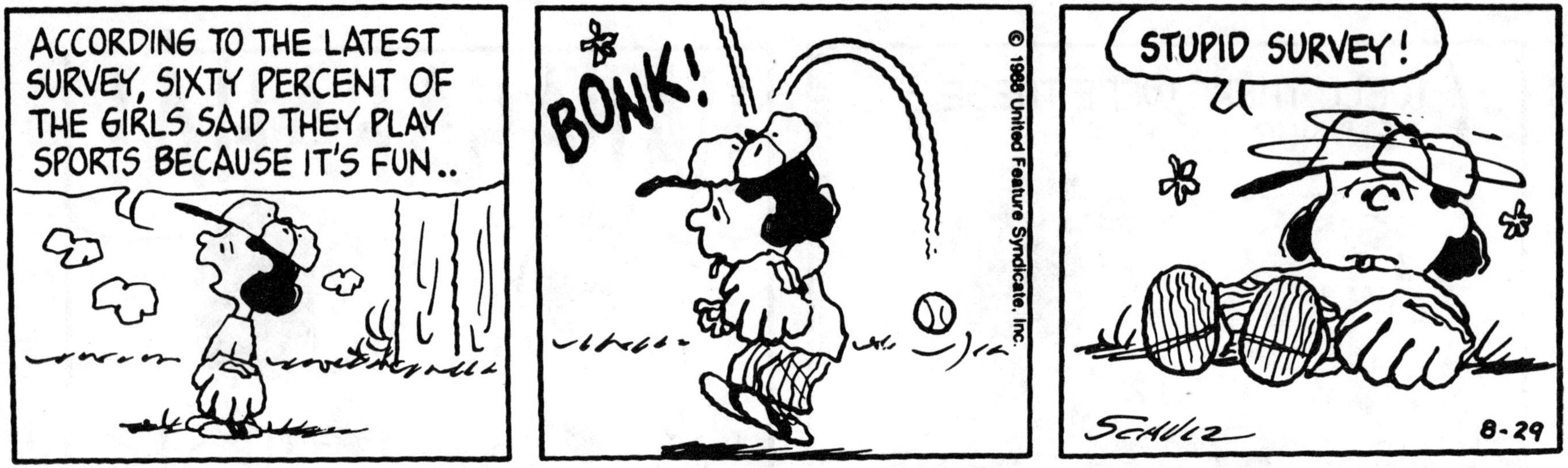
ACCORDING TO THE LATEST SURVEY, SIXTY PERCENT OF THE GIRLS SAID THEY PLAY SPORTS BECAUSE IT'S FUN..
BONK!
© 1988 United Feature Syndicate, Inc.
STUPID SURVEY!
SCHULZ
8-29

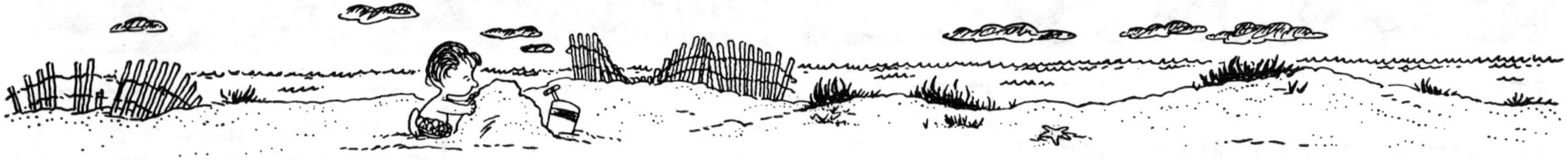

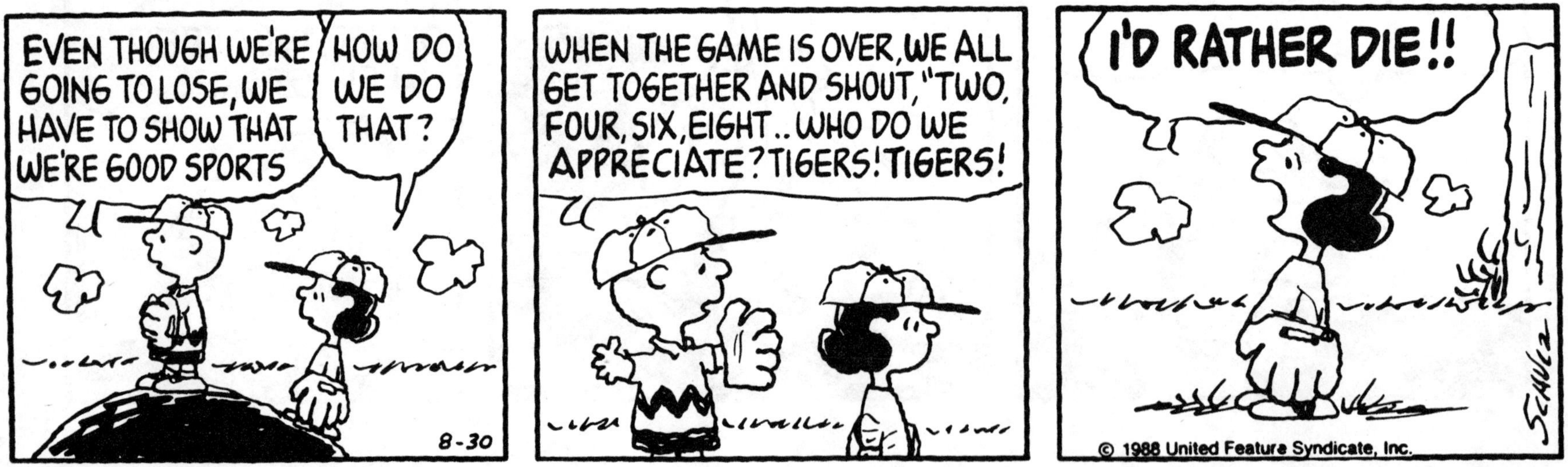
EVEN THOUGH WE'RE GOING TO LOSE, WE HAVE TO SHOW THAT WE'RE GOOD SPORTS
HOW DO WE DO THAT?
8-30
WHEN THE GAME IS OVER, WE ALL GET TOGETHER AND SHOUT, "TWO, FOUR, SIX, EIGHT.. WHO DO WE APPRECIATE? TIGERS! TIGERS!
I'D RATHER DIE!!
SCHULZ
© 1988 United Feature Syndicate, Inc.

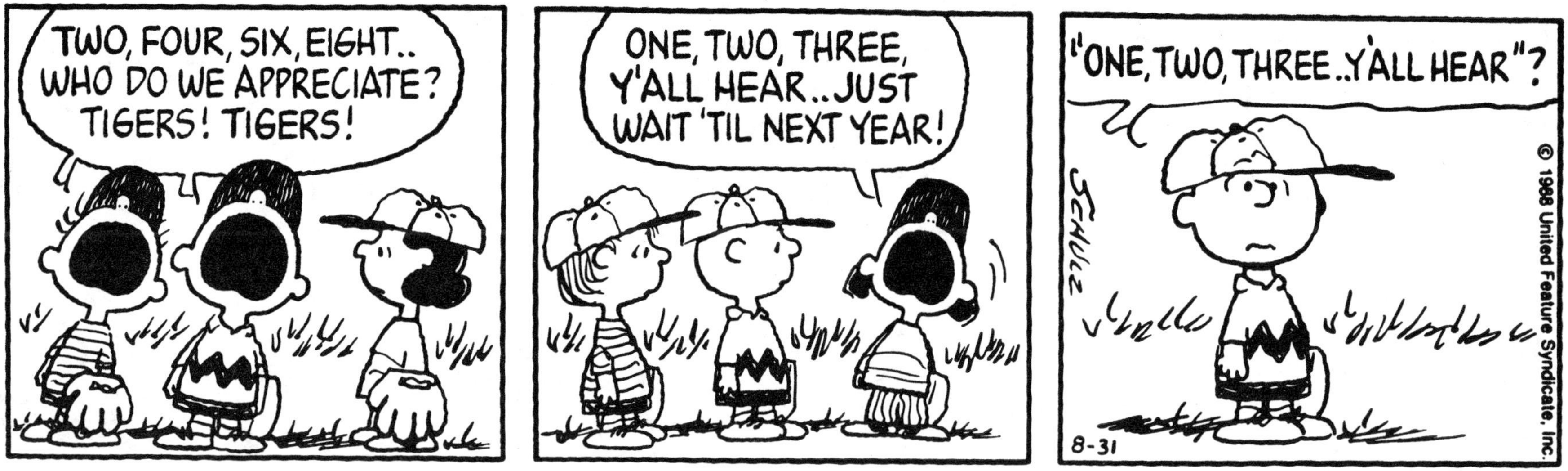
TWO, FOUR, SIX, EIGHT.. WHO DO WE APPRECIATE? TIGERS! TIGERS!
ONE, TWO, THREE, Y'ALL HEAR..JUST WAIT 'TIL NEXT YEAR!
"ONE, TWO, THREE..Y'ALL HEAR"?
SCHULZ
8-31
© 1988 United Feature Syndicate, Inc.

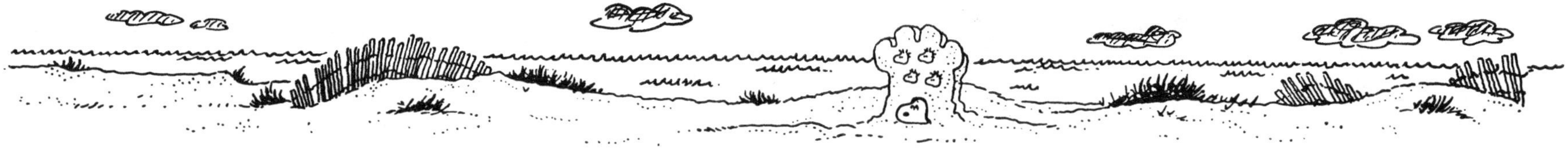

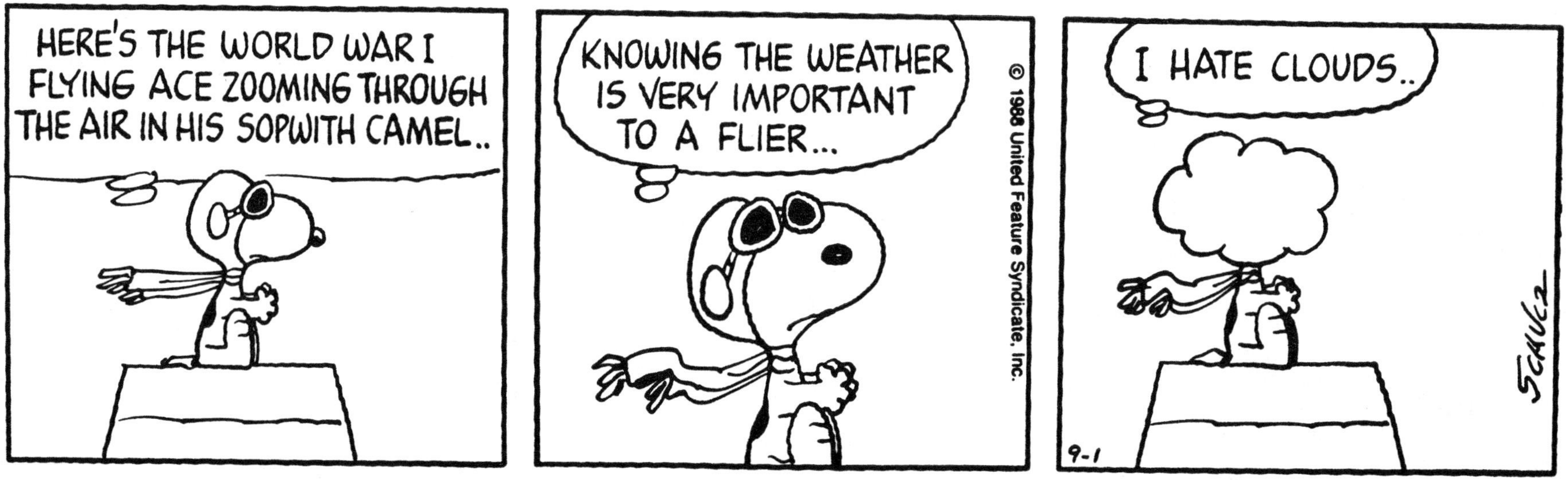
HERE'S THE WORLD WAR I FLYING ACE ZOOMING THROUGH THE AIR IN HIS SOPWITH CAMEL..
KNOWING THE WEATHER IS VERY IMPORTANT TO A FLIER...
© 1988 United Feature Syndicate, Inc.
I HATE CLOUDS..
SCHULZ
9-1

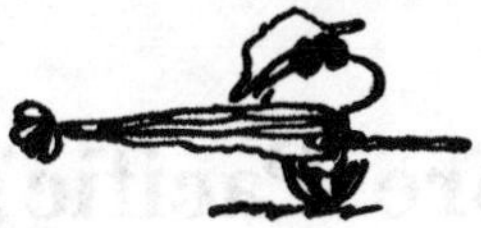

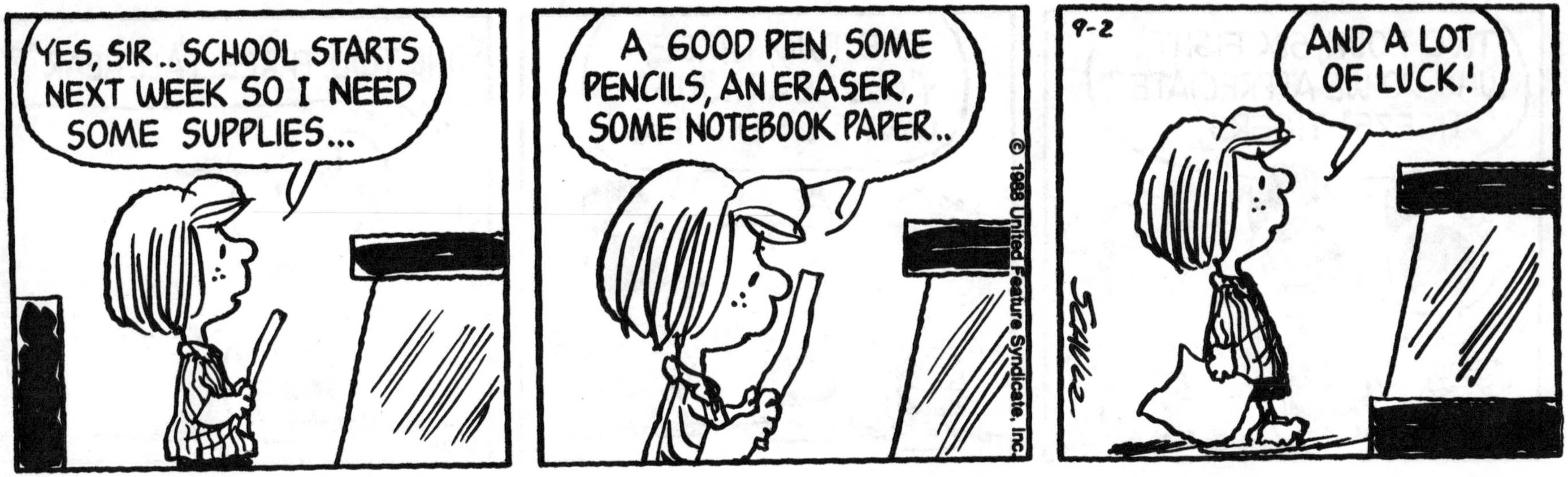
YES, SIR.. SCHOOL STARTS NEXT WEEK SO I NEED SOME SUPPLIES...
A GOOD PEN, SOME PENCILS, AN ERASER, SOME NOTEBOOK PAPER..
© 1988 United Feature Syndicate, Inc.
9-2
AND A LOT OF LUCK!
SCHULZ

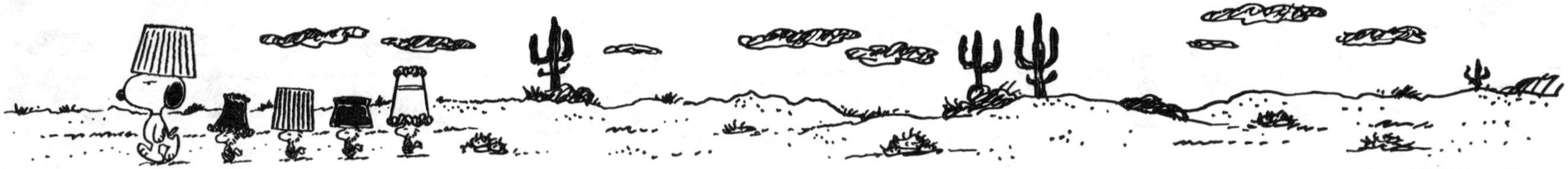

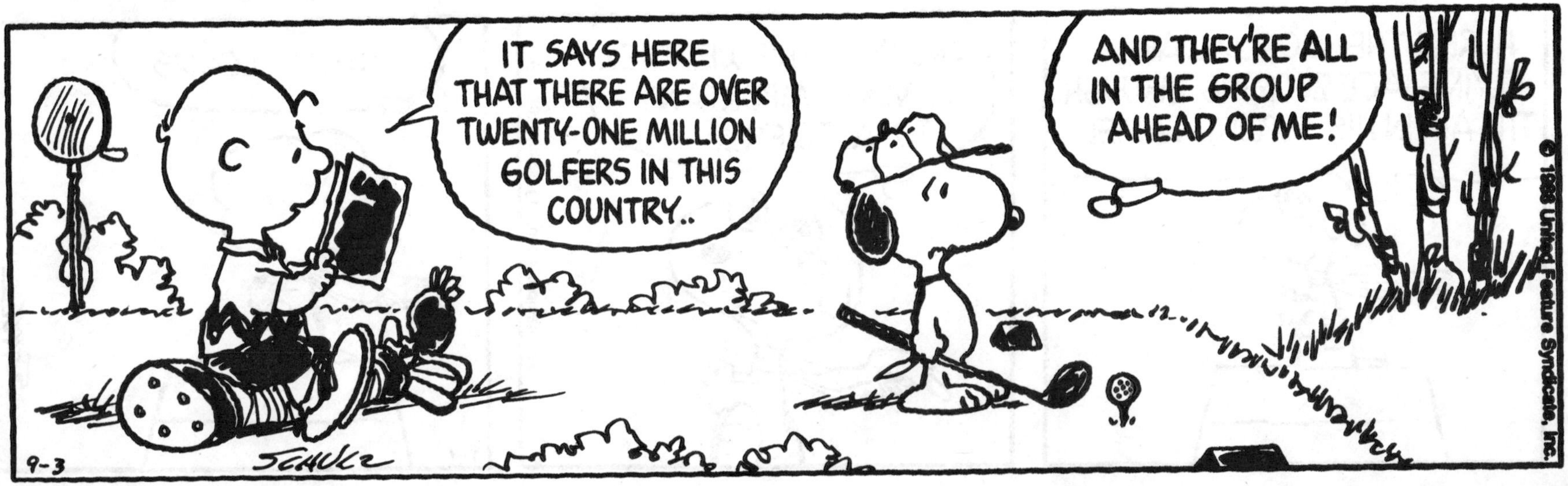
IT SAYS HERE THAT THERE ARE OVER TWENTY-ONE MILLION GOLFERS IN THIS COUNTRY..
AND THEY'RE ALL IN THE GROUP AHEAD OF ME!
© 1988 United Feature Syndicate, Inc.
9-3
SCHULZ

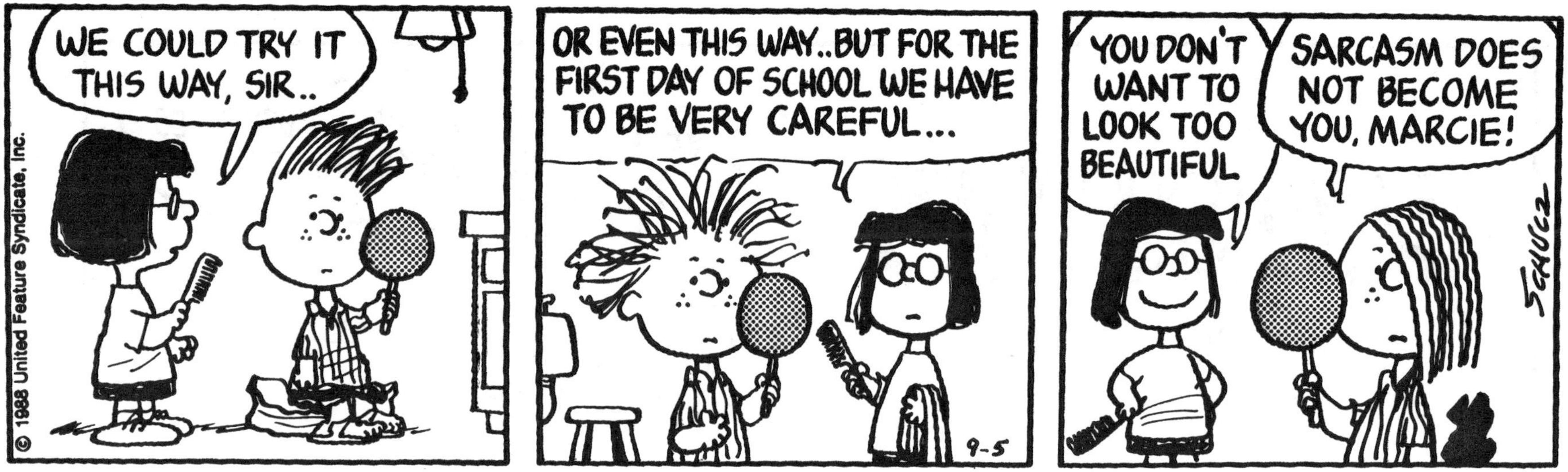
WE COULD TRY IT THIS WAY, SIR..
OR EVEN THIS WAY..BUT FOR THE FIRST DAY OF SCHOOL WE HAVE TO BE VERY CAREFUL...
YOU DON'T WANT TO LOOK TOO BEAUTIFUL
SARCASM DOES NOT BECOME YOU, MARCIE!
© 1988 United Feature Syndicate, Inc.
9-5
SCHULZ

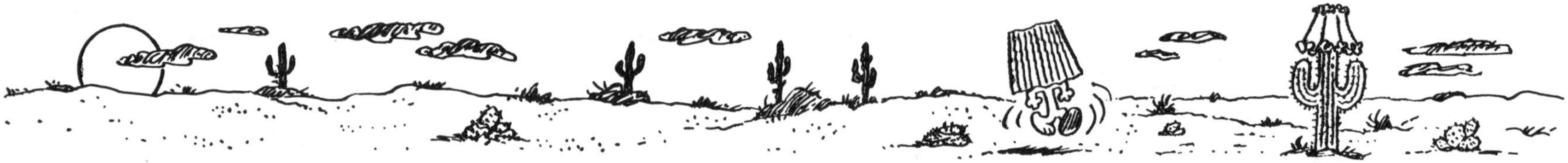

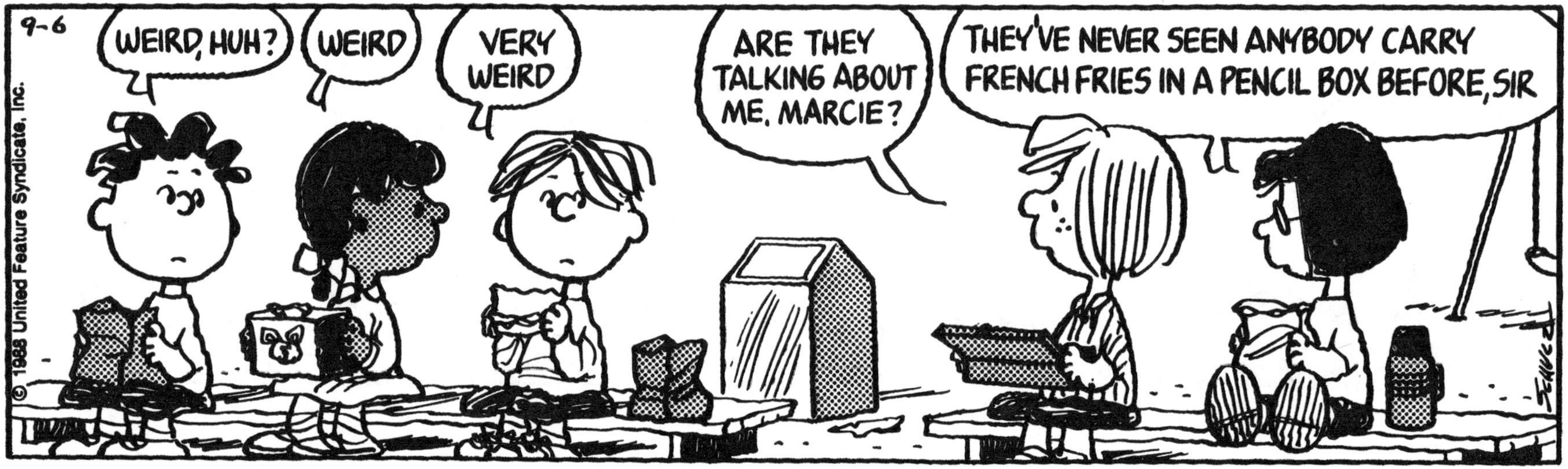
9-6
WEIRD, HUH?
WEIRD
VERY WEIRD
ARE THEY TALKING ABOUT ME, MARCIE?
THEY'VE NEVER SEEN ANYBODY CARRY FRENCH FRIES IN A PENCIL BOX BEFORE, SIR
© 1988 United Feature Syndicate, Inc.
SCHULZ

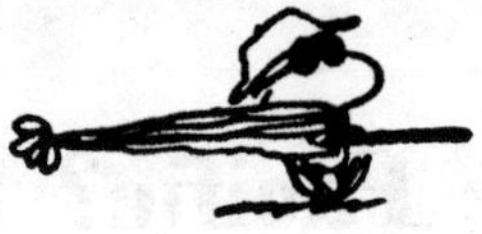

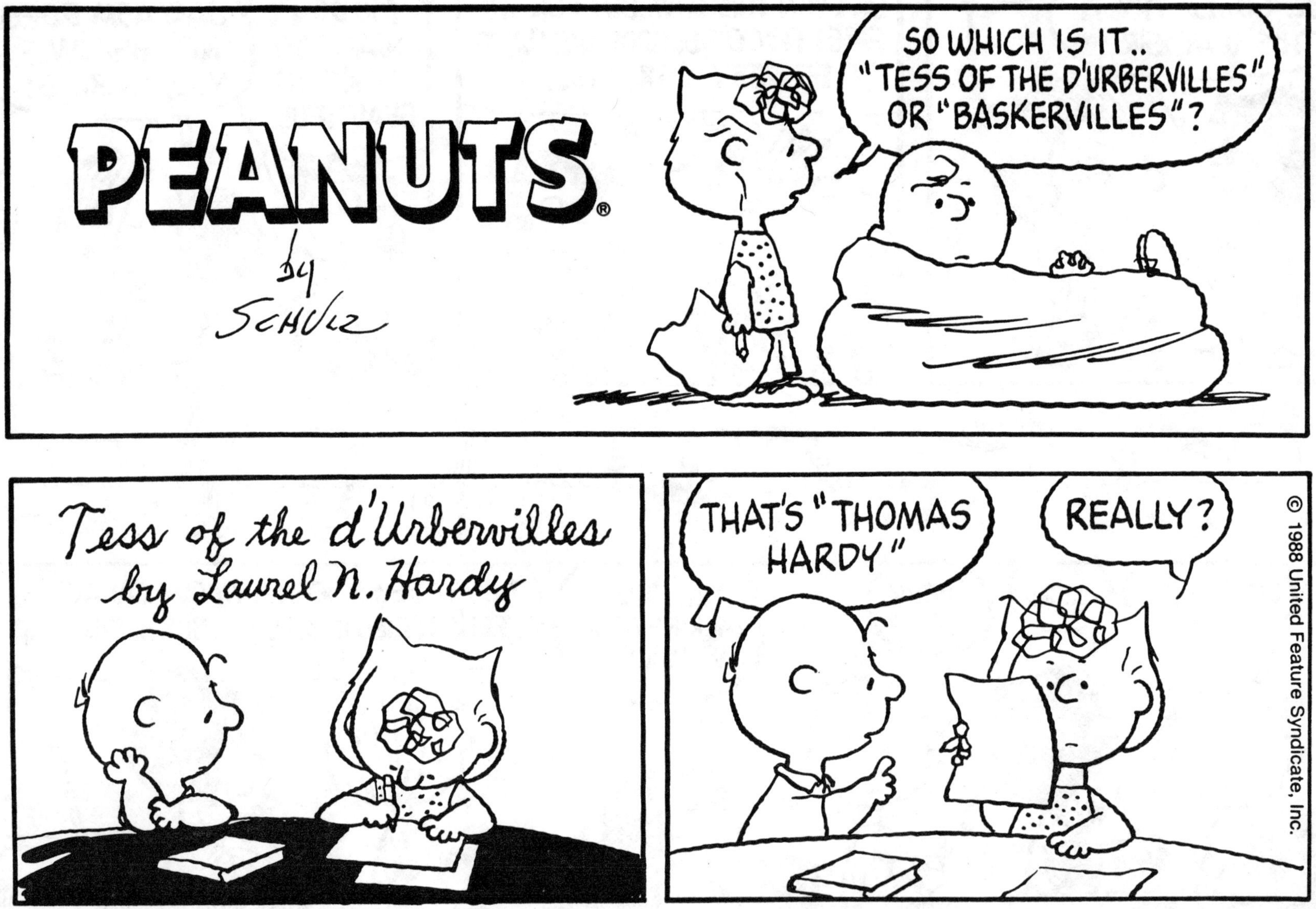
PEANUTS®
by SCHULZ
SO WHICH IS IT.. "TESS OF THE D'URBERVILLES" OR "BASKERVILLES"?
Tess of the d'Urbervilles by Laurel N. Hardy
THAT'S "THOMAS HARDY"
REALLY?

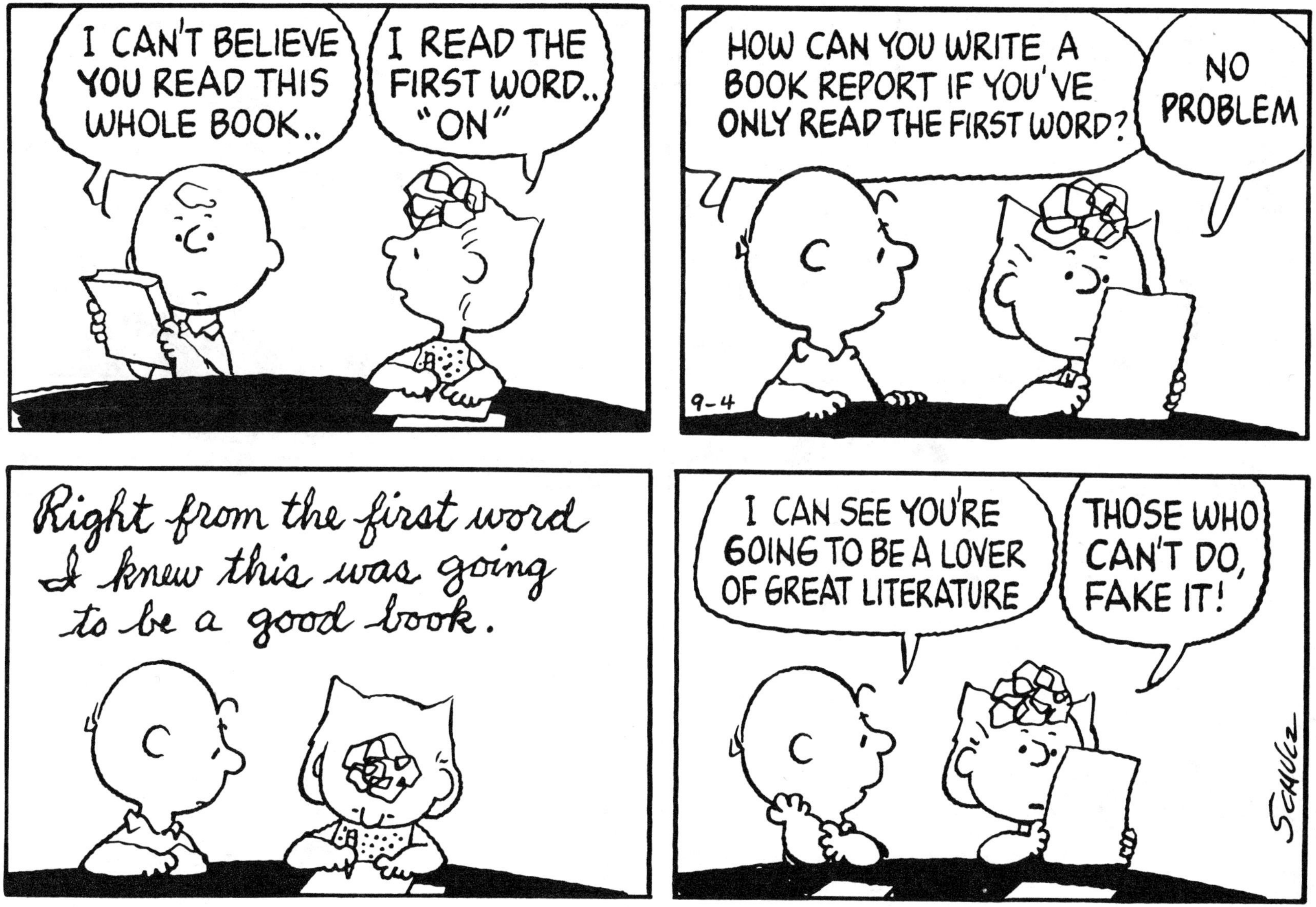
I CAN'T BELIEVE YOU READ THIS WHOLE BOOK..
I READ THE FIRST WORD.. "ON"
HOW CAN YOU WRITE A BOOK REPORT IF YOU'VE ONLY READ THE FIRST WORD?
NO PROBLEM
9-4
Right from the first word I knew this was going to be a good book.
I CAN SEE YOU'RE GOING TO BE A LOVER OF GREAT LITERATURE
THOSE WHO CAN'T DO, FAKE IT!
SCHULZ

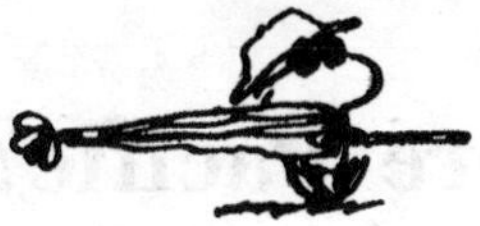

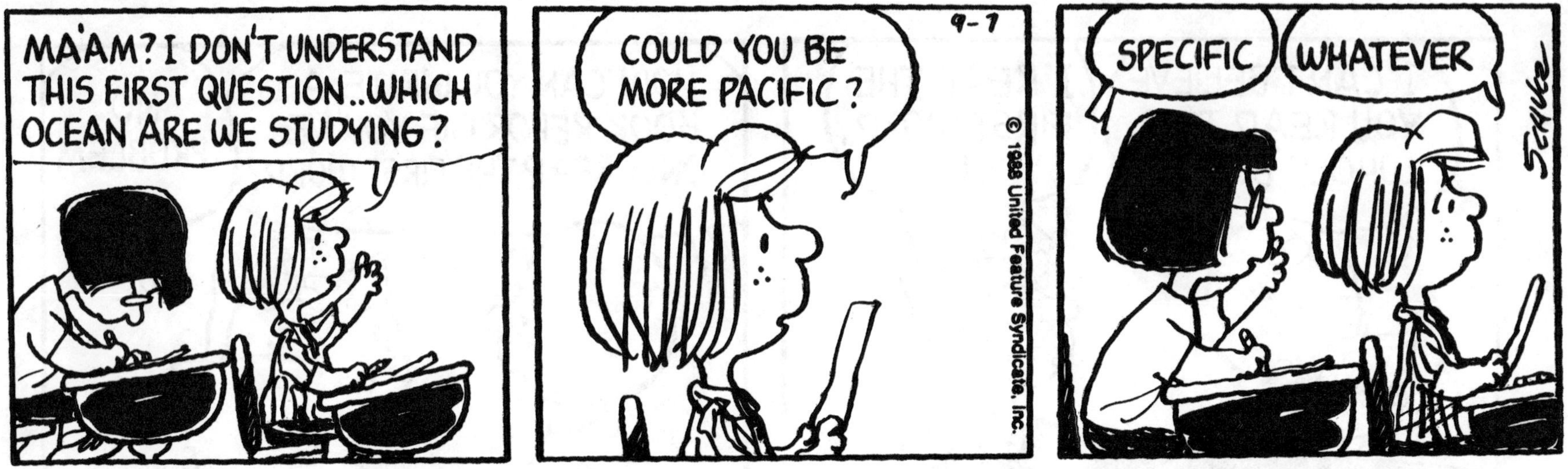
MA'AM? I DON'T UNDERSTAND THIS FIRST QUESTION..WHICH OCEAN ARE WE STUDYING?
9-7
COULD YOU BE MORE PACIFIC?
© 1988 United Feature Syndicate, Inc.
SPECIFIC
WHATEVER
SCHULZ

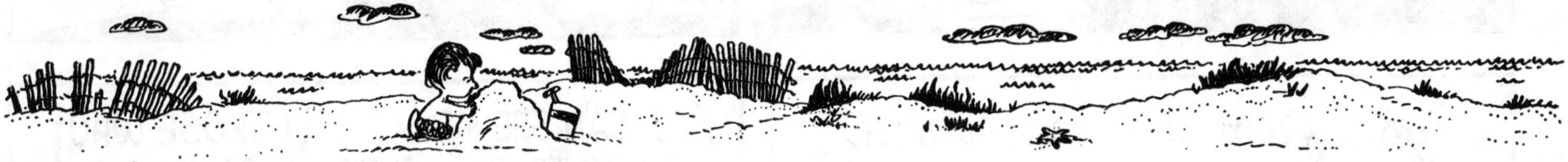

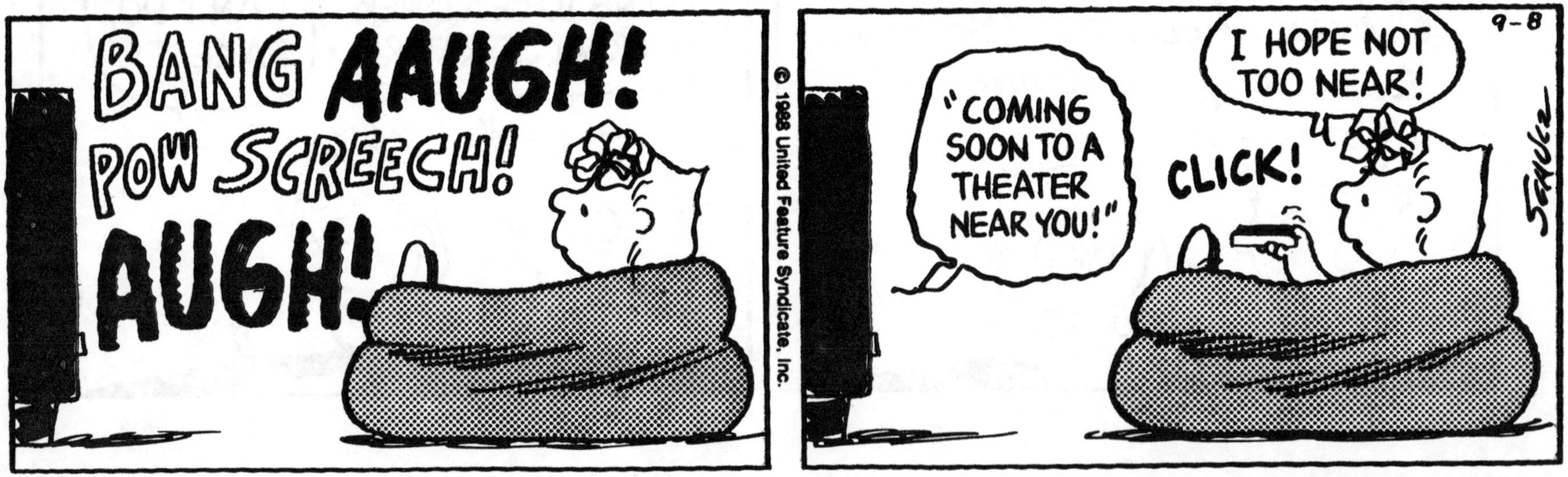
BANG AAUGH!
POW SCREECH!
AUGH!
© 1988 United Feature Syndicate, Inc.
9-8
"COMING SOON TO A THEATER NEAR YOU!"
CLICK!
I HOPE NOT TOO NEAR!
SCHULZ

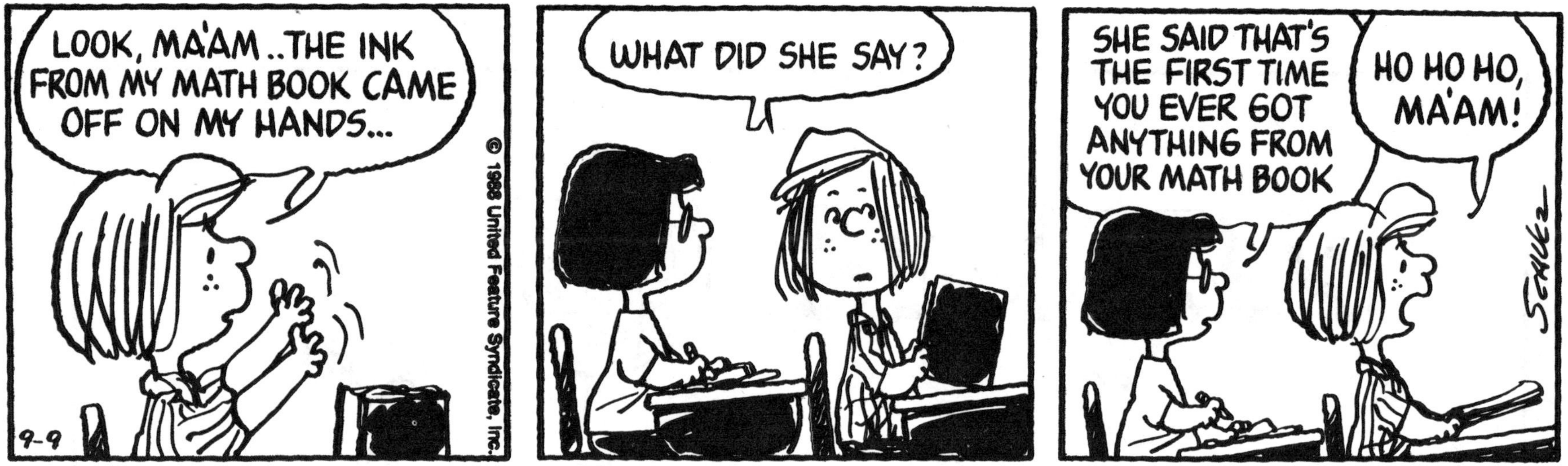
LOOK, MA'AM..THE INK FROM MY MATH BOOK CAME OFF ON MY HANDS...
WHAT DID SHE SAY?
SHE SAID THAT'S THE FIRST TIME YOU EVER GOT ANYTHING FROM YOUR MATH BOOK
HO HO HO, MA'AM!
9-9
© 1988 United Feature Syndicate, Inc.
SCHULZ

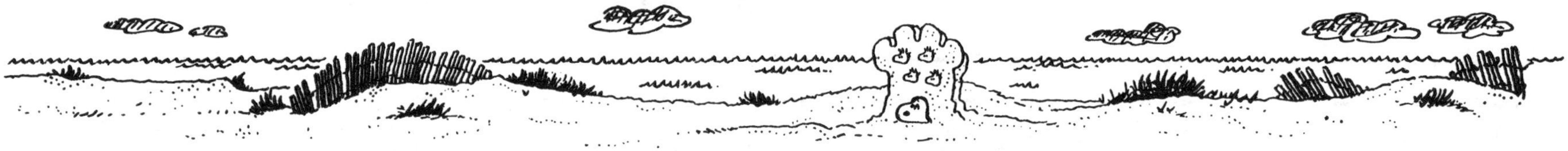

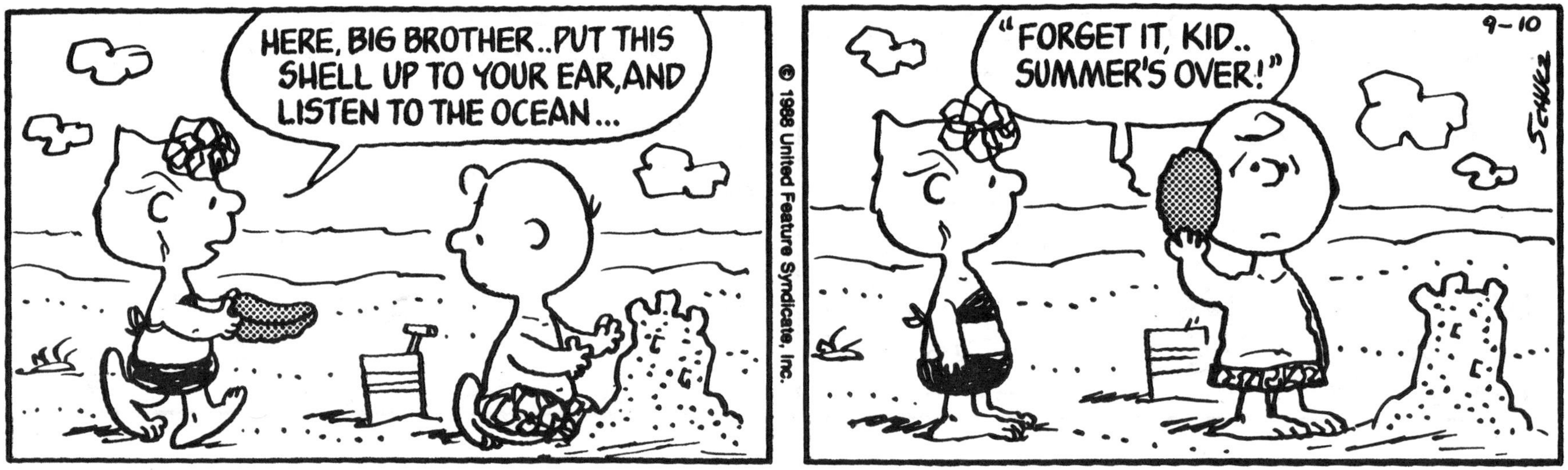
HERE, BIG BROTHER..PUT THIS SHELL UP TO YOUR EAR, AND LISTEN TO THE OCEAN...
"FORGET IT, KID.. SUMMER'S OVER!"
9-10
© 1988 United Feature Syndicate, Inc.
SCHULZ

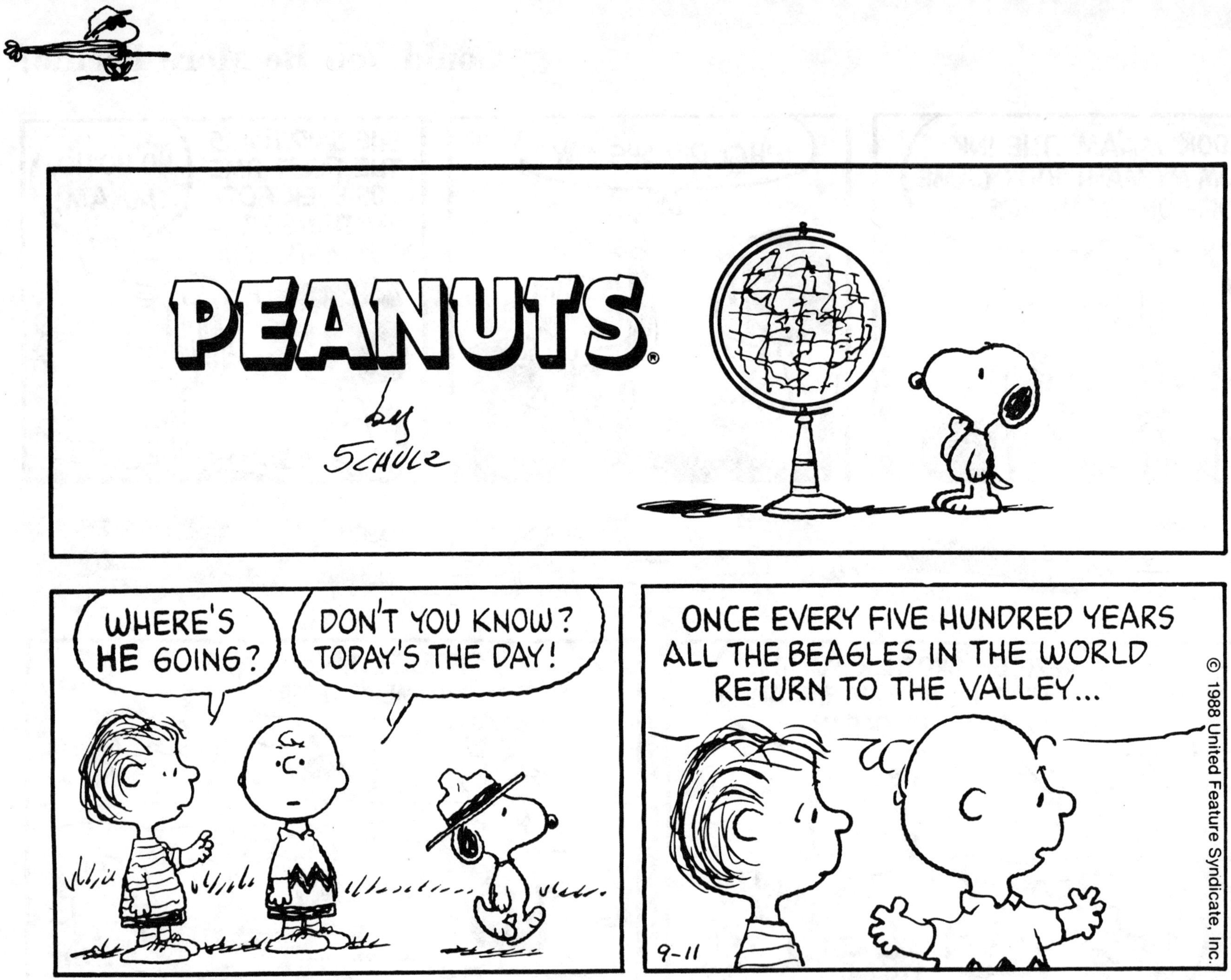

PEANUTS
by SCHULZ
WHERE'S HE GOING?
DON'T YOU KNOW? TODAY'S THE DAY!
ONCE EVERY FIVE HUNDRED YEARS ALL THE BEAGLES IN THE WORLD RETURN TO THE VALLEY...
9-11
© 1988 United Feature Syndicate, Inc.

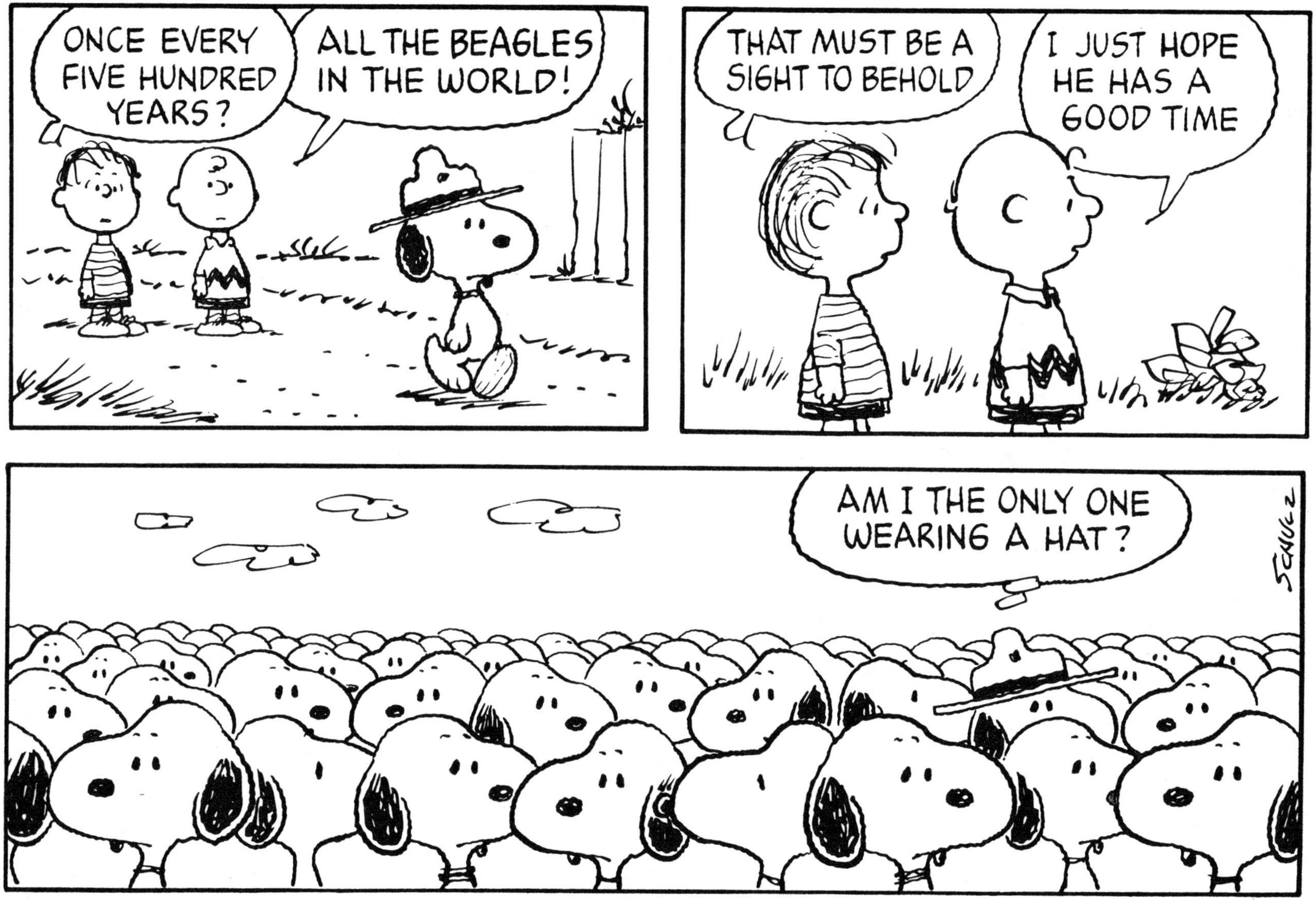
ONCE EVERY FIVE HUNDRED YEARS?
ALL THE BEAGLES IN THE WORLD!
THAT MUST BE A SIGHT TO BEHOLD
I JUST HOPE HE HAS A GOOD TIME
AM I THE ONLY ONE WEARING A HAT?
SCHULZ

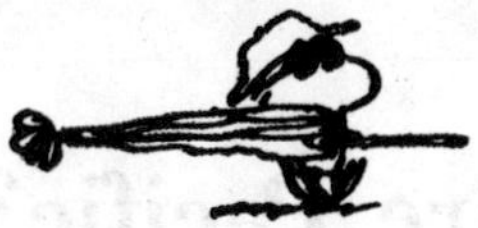

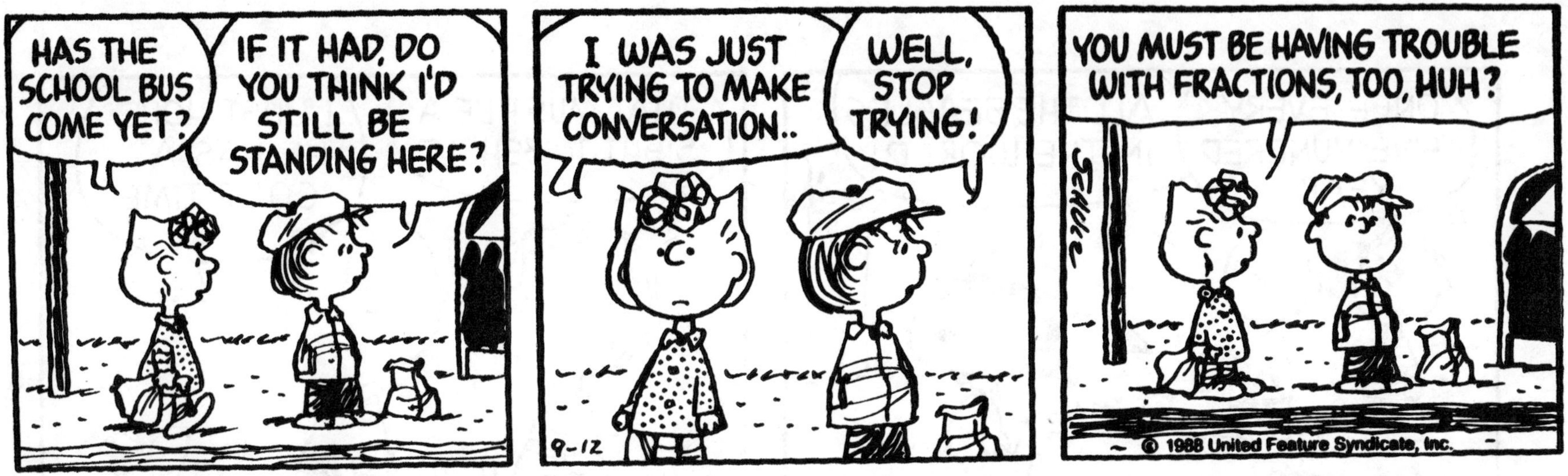

HAS THE SCHOOL BUS COME YET?
IF IT HAD, DO YOU THINK I'D STILL BE STANDING HERE?
I WAS JUST TRYING TO MAKE CONVERSATION..
WELL, STOP TRYING!
YOU MUST BE HAVING TROUBLE WITH FRACTIONS, TOO, HUH?
9-12
SCHULZ
© 1988 United Feature Syndicate, Inc.

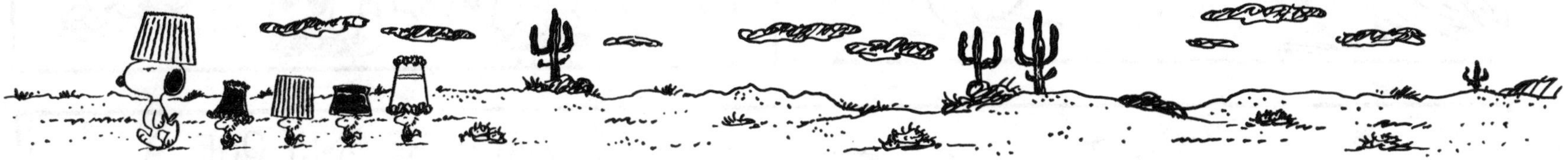

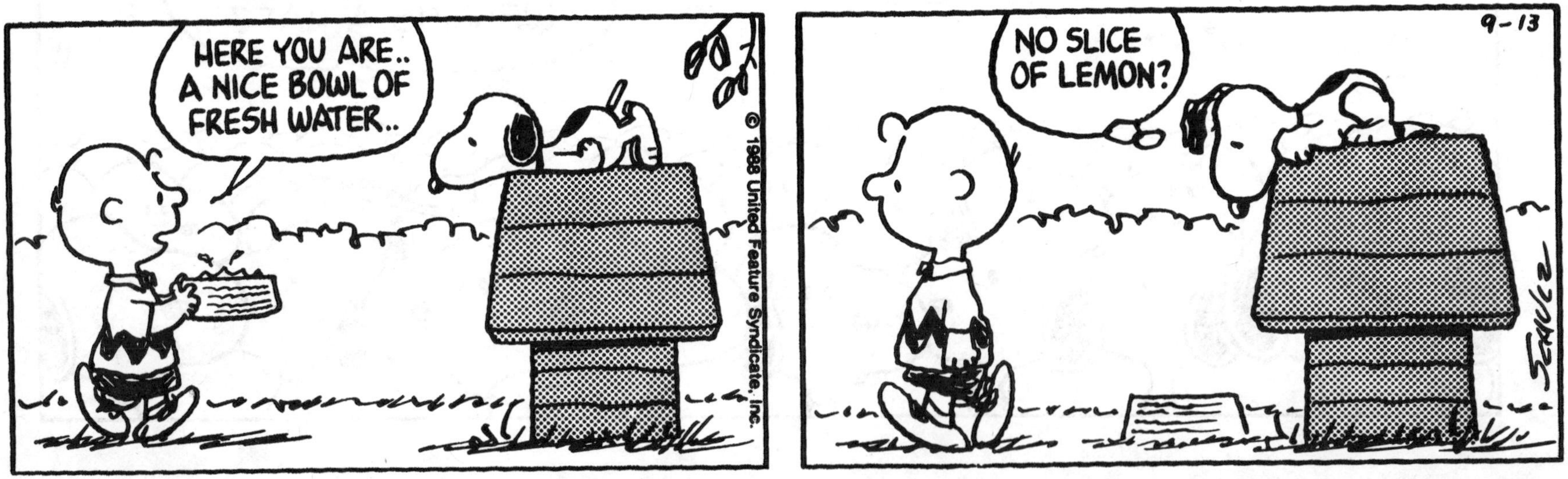

HERE YOU ARE.. A NICE BOWL OF FRESH WATER..
© 1988 United Feature Syndicate, Inc.
NO SLICE OF LEMON?
9-13
SCHULZ

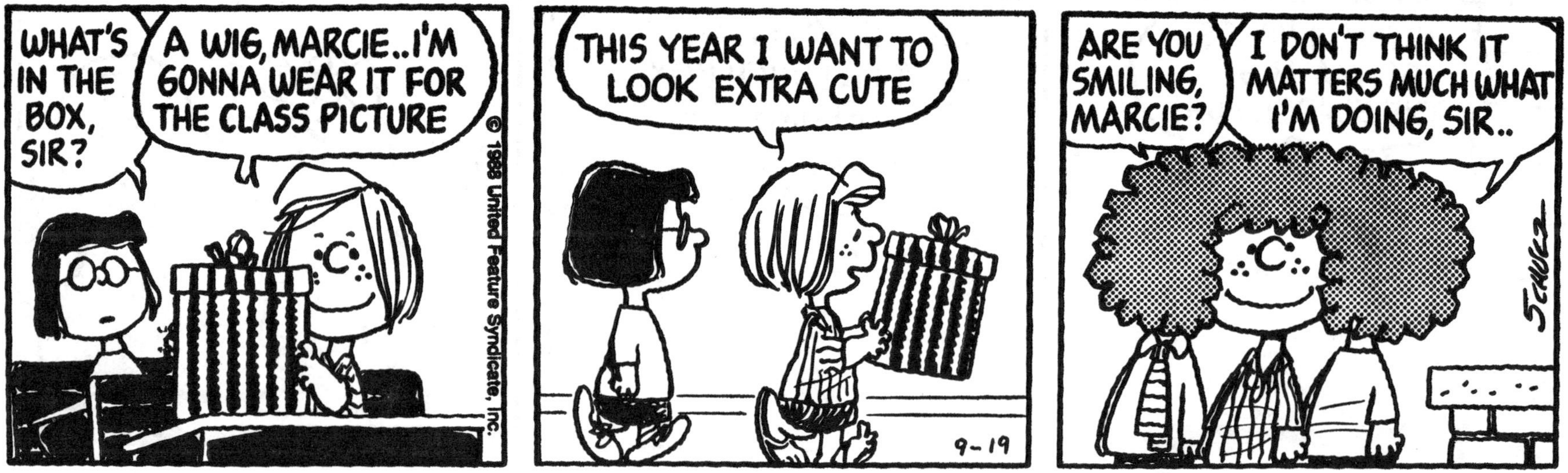
WHAT'S IN THE BOX, SIR?
A WIG, MARCIE..I'M GONNA WEAR IT FOR THE CLASS PICTURE
© 1988 United Feature Syndicate, Inc.
THIS YEAR I WANT TO LOOK EXTRA CUTE
9-19
ARE YOU SMILING, MARCIE?
I DON'T THINK IT MATTERS MUCH WHAT I'M DOING, SIR..
SCHULZ

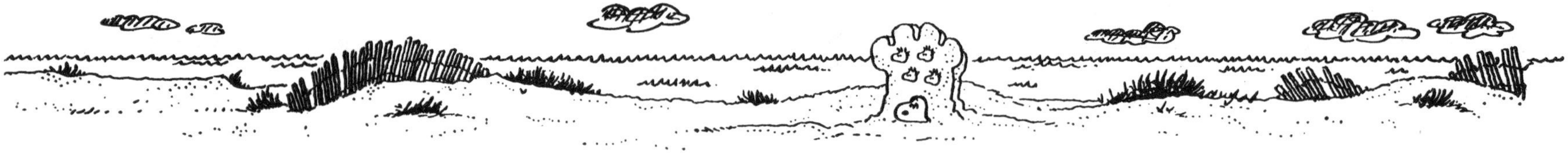

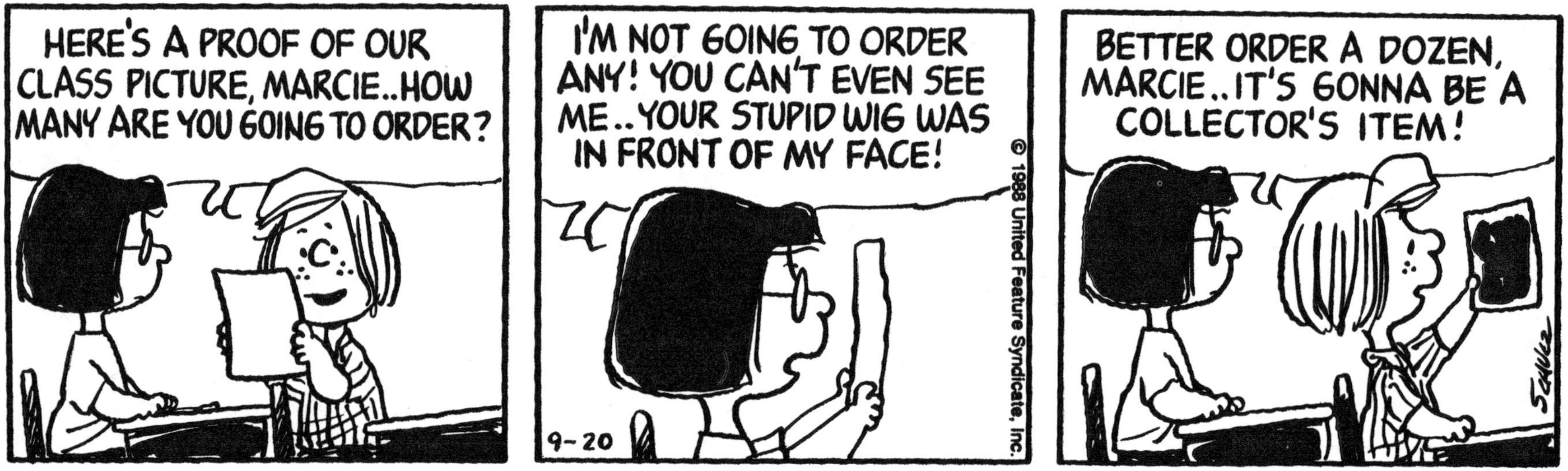
HERE'S A PROOF OF OUR CLASS PICTURE, MARCIE..HOW MANY ARE YOU GOING TO ORDER?
I'M NOT GOING TO ORDER ANY! YOU CAN'T EVEN SEE ME..YOUR STUPID WIG WAS IN FRONT OF MY FACE!
© 1988 United Feature Syndicate, Inc.
9-20
BETTER ORDER A DOZEN, MARCIE..IT'S GONNA BE A COLLECTOR'S ITEM!
SCHULZ

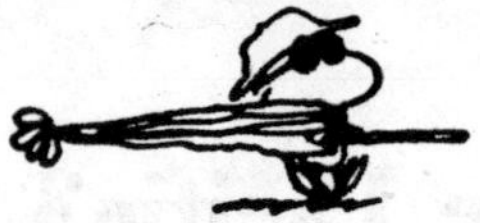

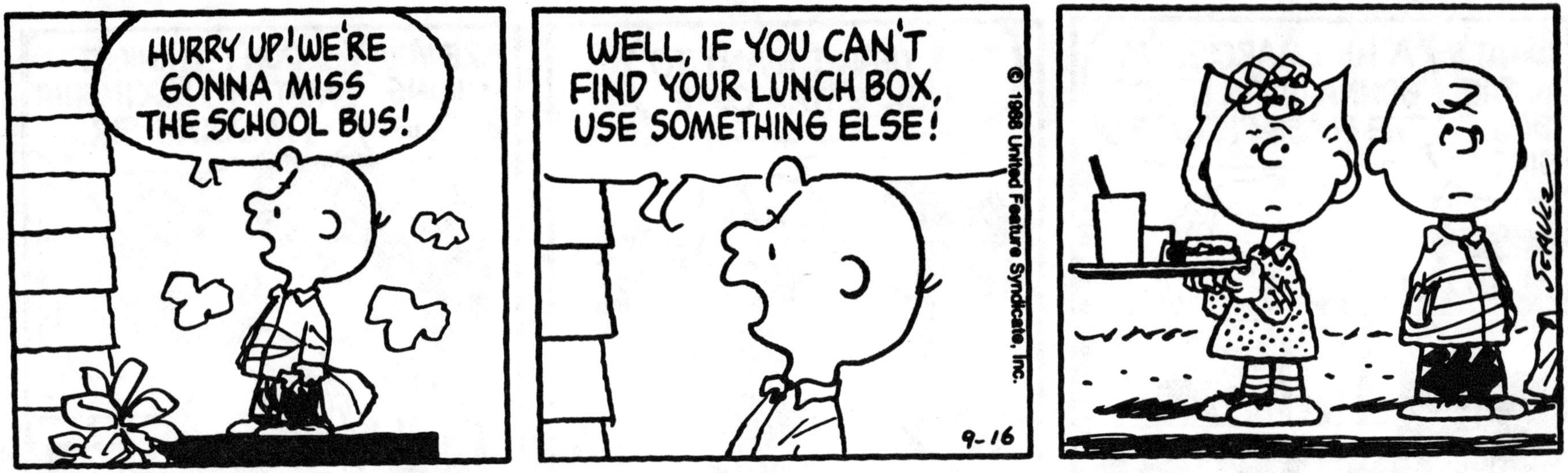
HURRY UP! WE'RE GONNA MISS THE SCHOOL BUS!
WELL, IF YOU CAN'T FIND YOUR LUNCH BOX, USE SOMETHING ELSE!
© 1988 United Feature Syndicate, Inc.
9-16
SCHULZ

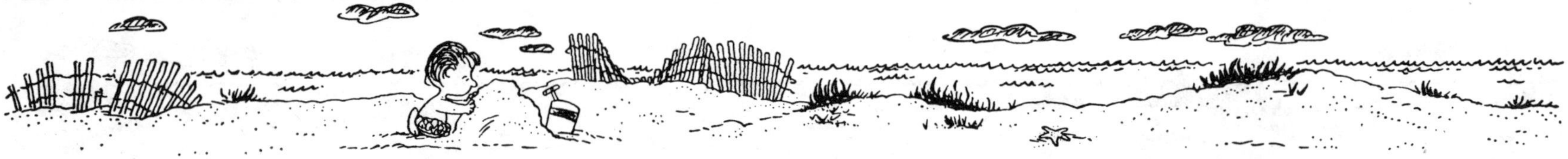

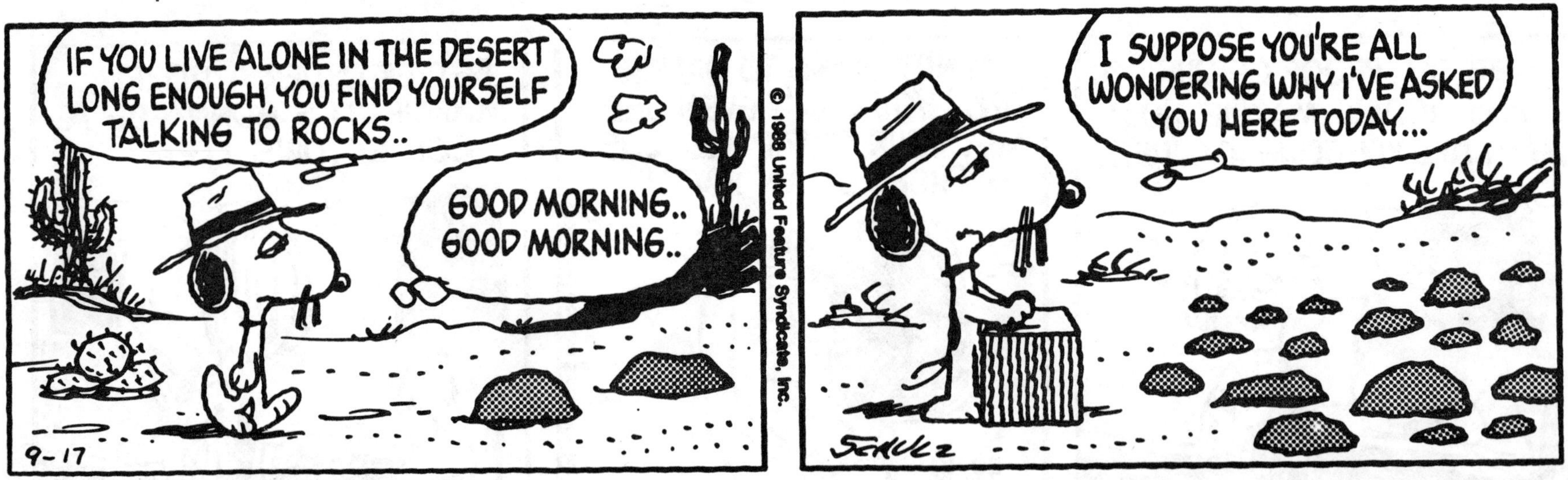
IF YOU LIVE ALONE IN THE DESERT LONG ENOUGH, YOU FIND YOURSELF TALKING TO ROCKS..
GOOD MORNING.. GOOD MORNING..
© 1988 United Feature Syndicate, Inc.
9-17
I SUPPOSE YOU'RE ALL WONDERING WHY I'VE ASKED YOU HERE TODAY...
SCHULZ

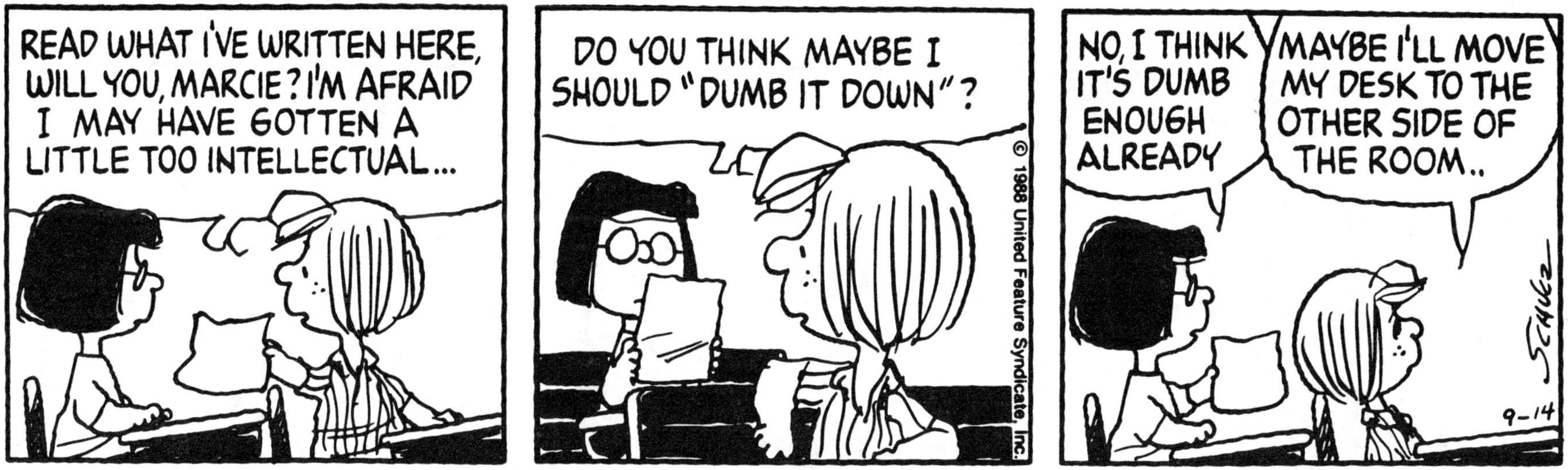
READ WHAT I'VE WRITTEN HERE, WILL YOU, MARCIE? I'M AFRAID I MAY HAVE GOTTEN A LITTLE TOO INTELLECTUAL...
DO YOU THINK MAYBE I SHOULD "DUMB IT DOWN"?
© 1988 United Feature Syndicate, Inc.
NO, I THINK IT'S DUMB ENOUGH ALREADY
MAYBE I'LL MOVE MY DESK TO THE OTHER SIDE OF THE ROOM..
SCHULZ
9-14

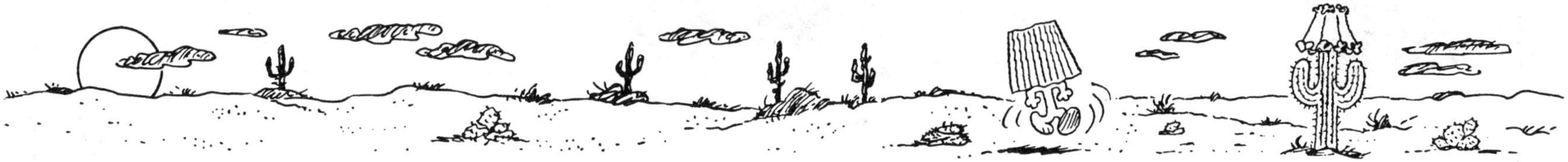

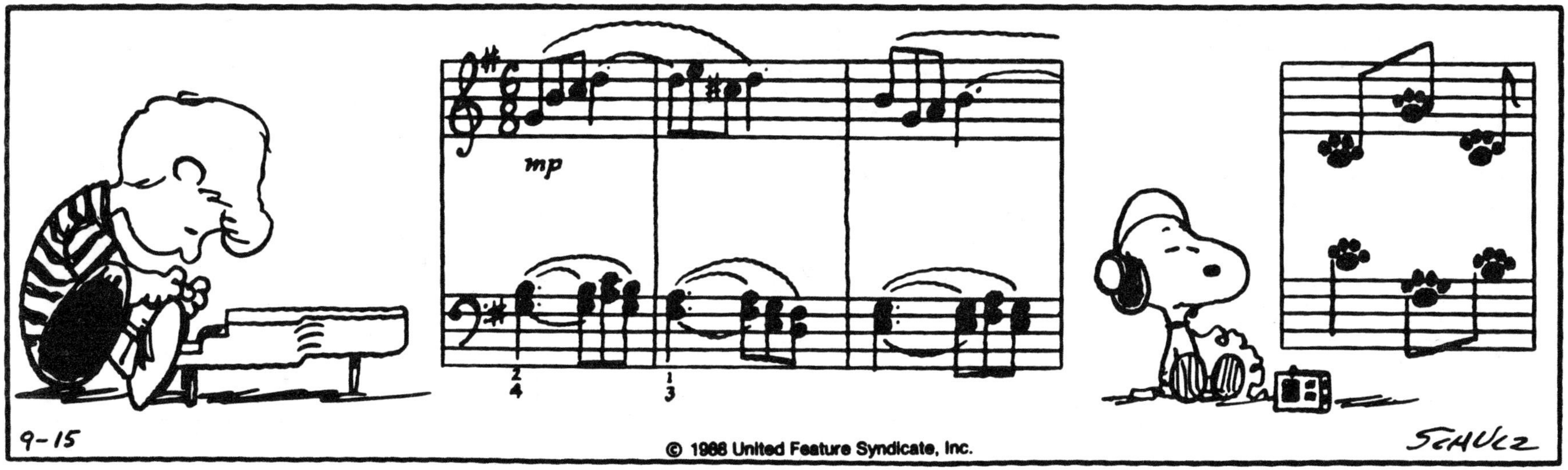
mp
9-15
© 1988 United Feature Syndicate, Inc.
SCHULZ

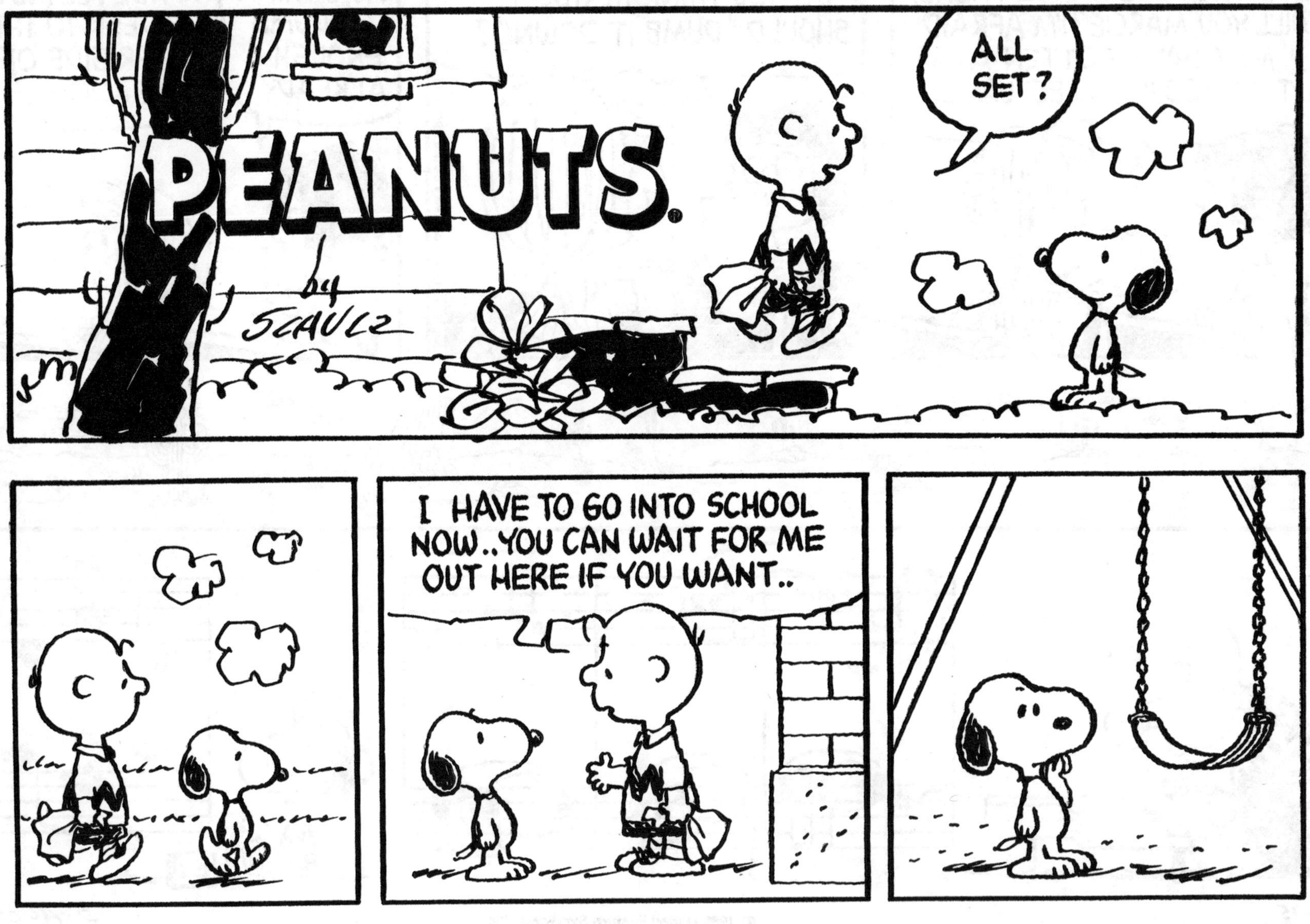
PEANUTS
by SCHULZ
ALL SET?
I HAVE TO GO INTO SCHOOL NOW..YOU CAN WAIT FOR ME OUT HERE IF YOU WANT..

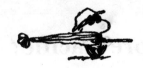

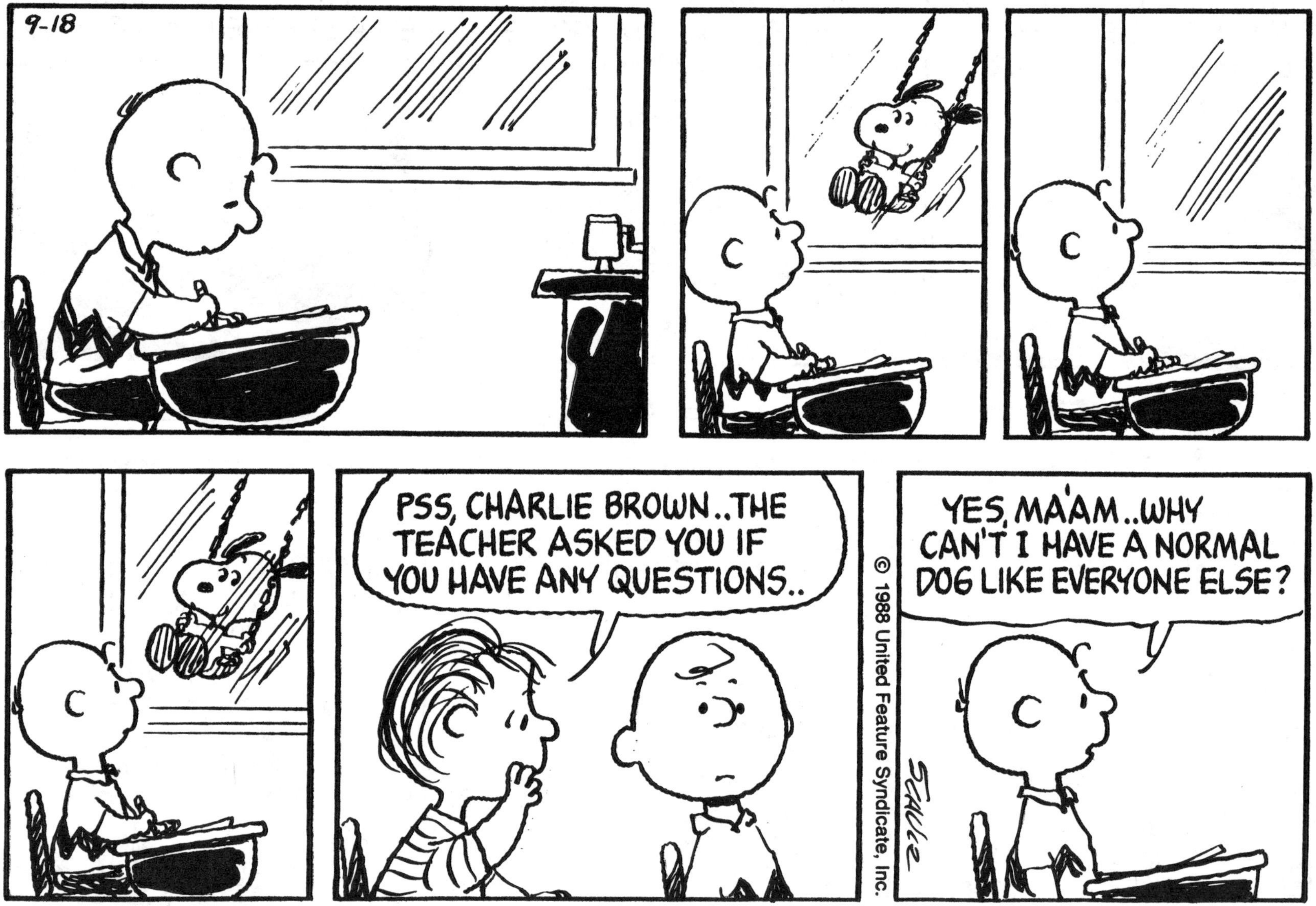
9-18
PSS, CHARLIE BROWN..THE TEACHER ASKED YOU IF YOU HAVE ANY QUESTIONS..
YES, MA'AM..WHY CAN'T I HAVE A NORMAL DOG LIKE EVERYONE ELSE?
© 1988 United Feature Syndicate, Inc.
SCHULZ

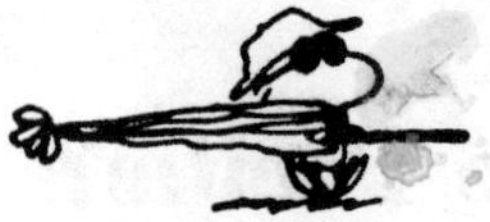

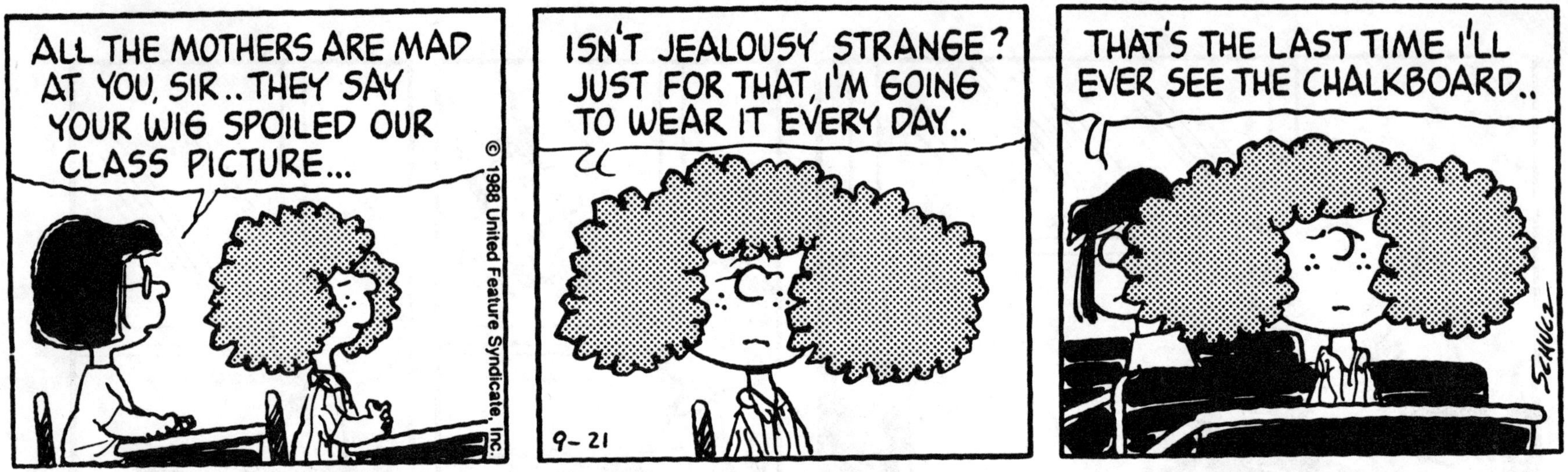
ALL THE MOTHERS ARE MAD AT YOU, SIR.. THEY SAY YOUR WIG SPOILED OUR CLASS PICTURE...
© 1988 United Feature Syndicate, Inc.
ISN'T JEALOUSY STRANGE? JUST FOR THAT, I'M GOING TO WEAR IT EVERY DAY..
9-21
THAT'S THE LAST TIME I'LL EVER SEE THE CHALKBOARD..
SCHULZ

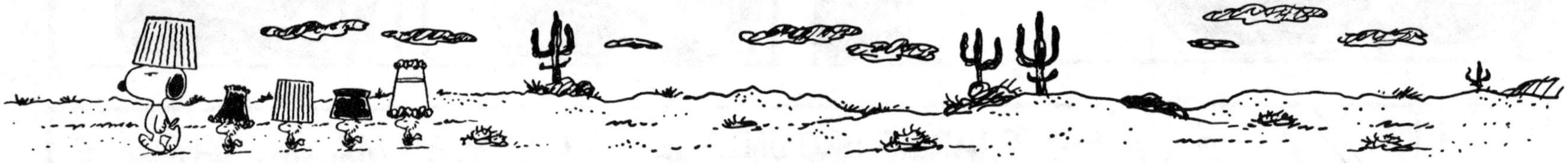

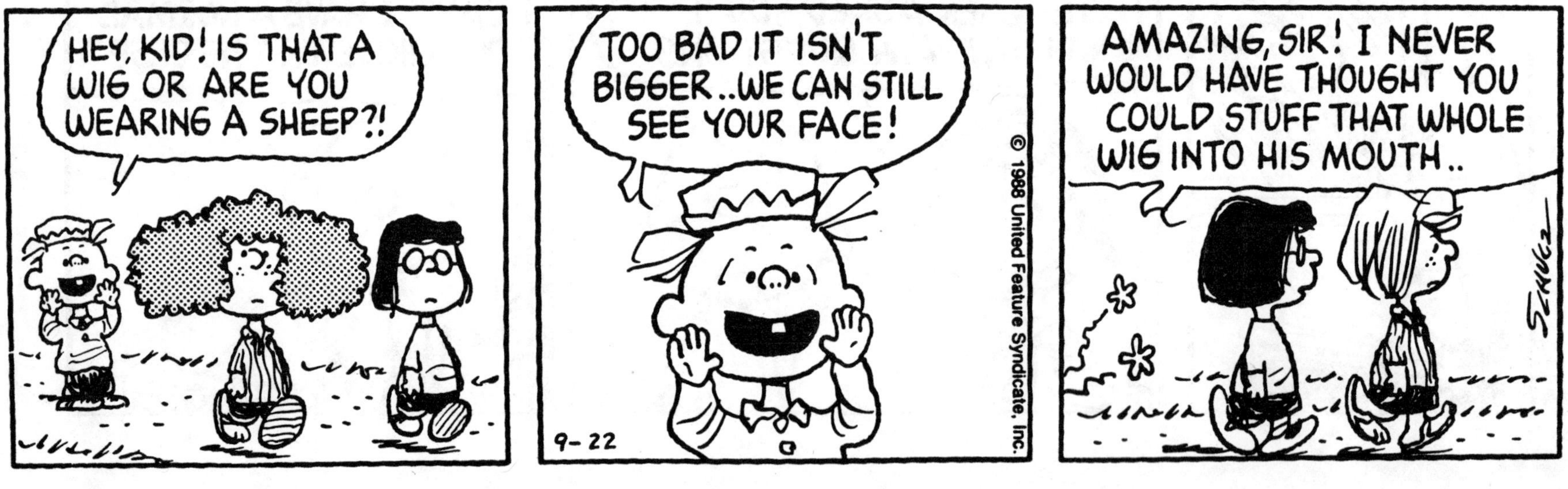
HEY, KID! IS THAT A WIG OR ARE YOU WEARING A SHEEP?!
TOO BAD IT ISN'T BIGGER..WE CAN STILL SEE YOUR FACE!
9-22
© 1988 United Feature Syndicate, Inc.
AMAZING, SIR! I NEVER WOULD HAVE THOUGHT YOU COULD STUFF THAT WHOLE WIG INTO HIS MOUTH..
SCHULZ

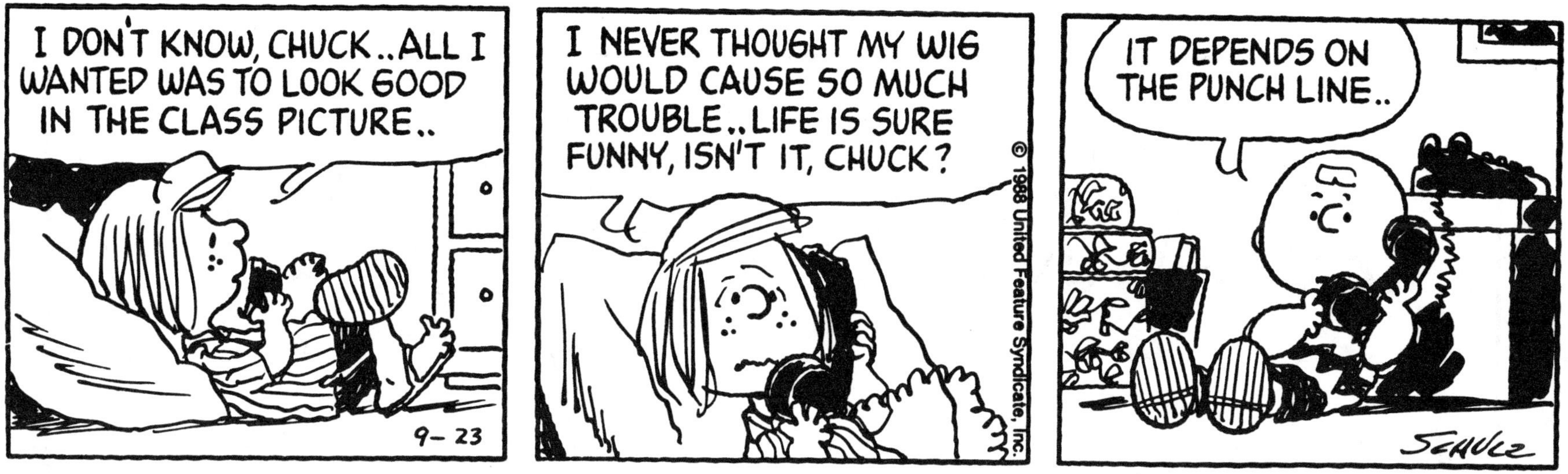
I DON'T KNOW, CHUCK..ALL I WANTED WAS TO LOOK GOOD IN THE CLASS PICTURE..
9-23
I NEVER THOUGHT MY WIG WOULD CAUSE SO MUCH TROUBLE..LIFE IS SURE FUNNY, ISN'T IT, CHUCK?
© 1988 United Feature Syndicate, Inc.
IT DEPENDS ON THE PUNCH LINE..

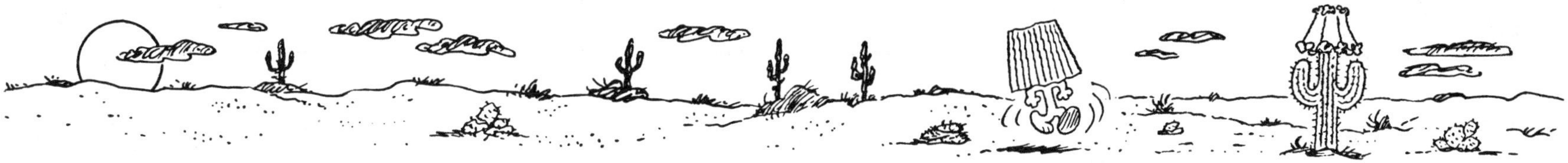

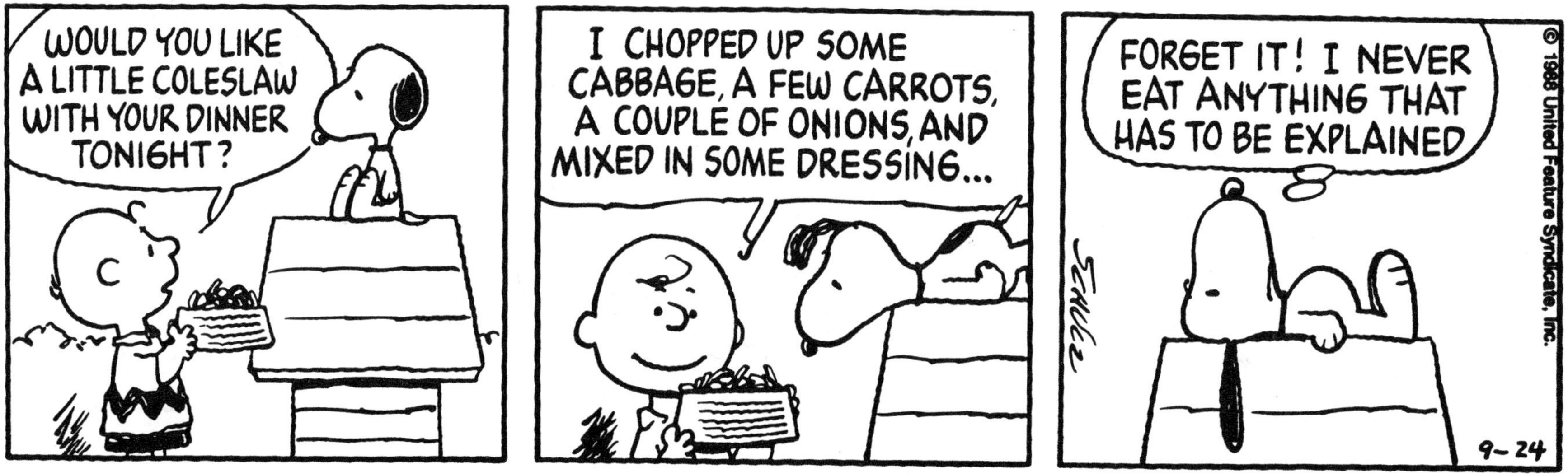
WOULD YOU LIKE A LITTLE COLESLAW WITH YOUR DINNER TONIGHT?
I CHOPPED UP SOME CABBAGE, A FEW CARROTS, A COUPLE OF ONIONS, AND MIXED IN SOME DRESSING...
FORGET IT! I NEVER EAT ANYTHING THAT HAS TO BE EXPLAINED
© 1988 United Feature Syndicate, Inc.
9-24

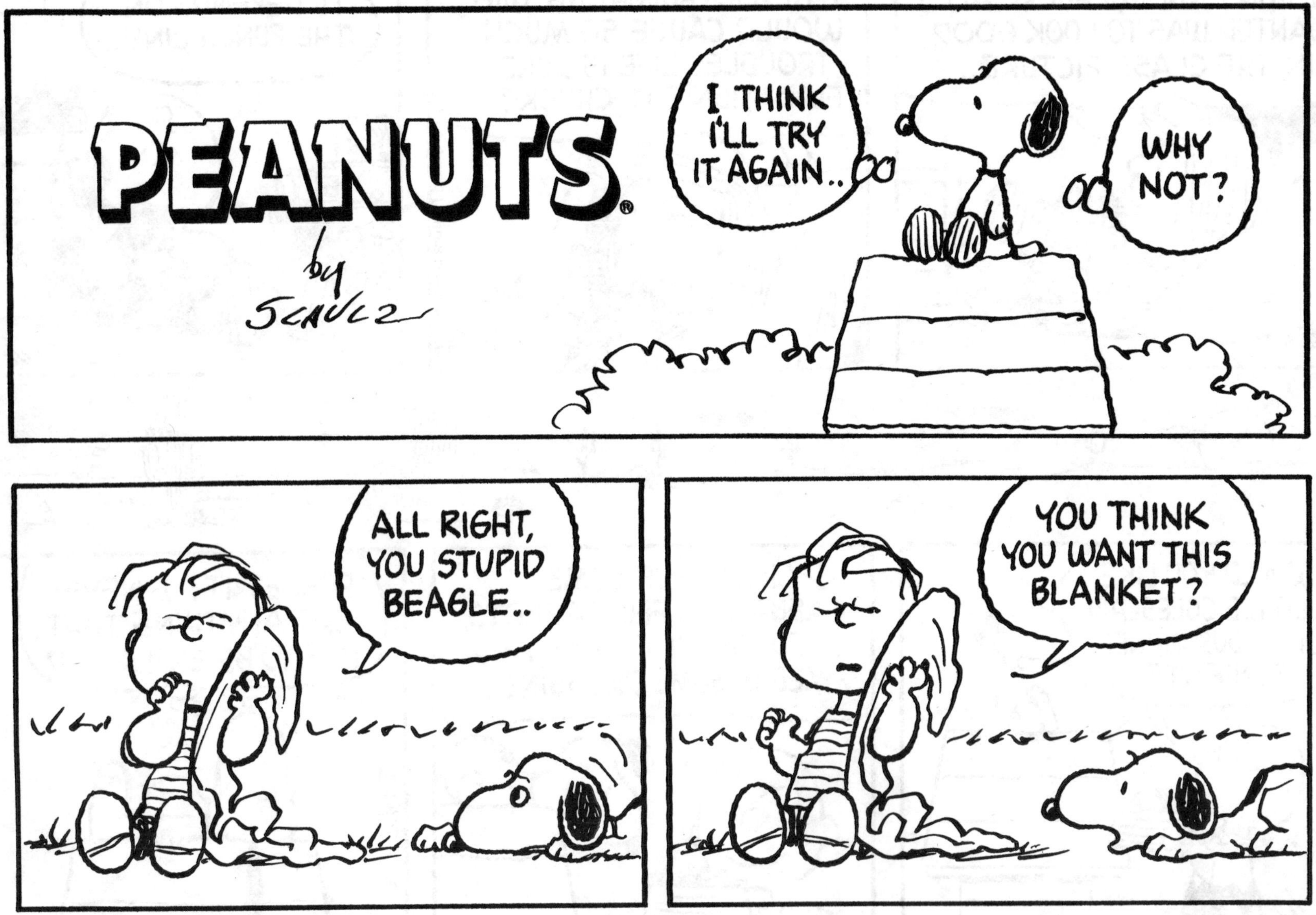
PEANUTS
by SCHULZ
I THINK I'LL TRY IT AGAIN..
WHY NOT?
ALL RIGHT, YOU STUPID BEAGLE..
YOU THINK YOU WANT THIS BLANKET?

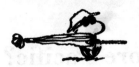

Could You Be More Pacific?

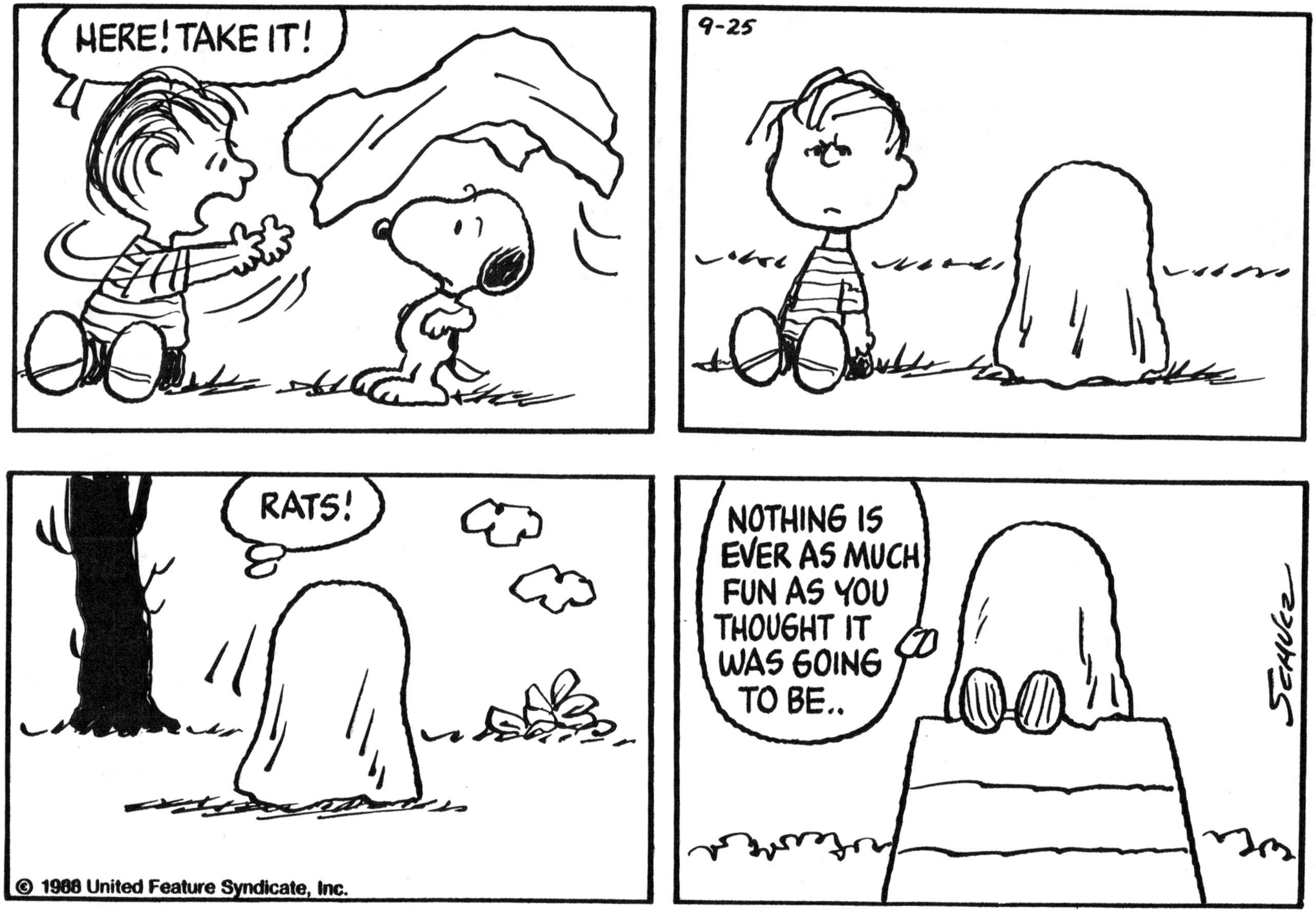
HERE! TAKE IT!
9-25
RATS!
NOTHING IS EVER AS MUCH FUN AS YOU THOUGHT IT WAS GOING TO BE..
SCHULZ
© 1988 United Feature Syndicate, Inc.

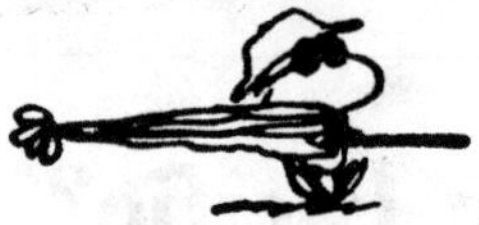

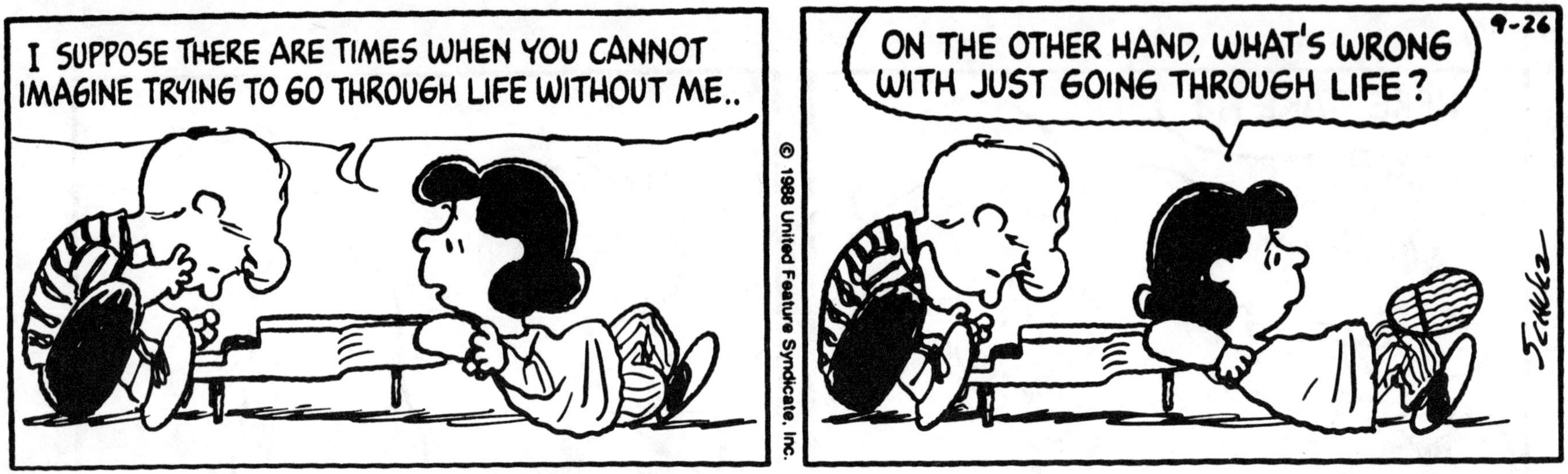
I SUPPOSE THERE ARE TIMES WHEN YOU CANNOT IMAGINE TRYING TO GO THROUGH LIFE WITHOUT ME..
© 1988 United Feature Syndicate, Inc.
9-26
ON THE OTHER HAND, WHAT'S WRONG WITH JUST GOING THROUGH LIFE?
SCHULZ

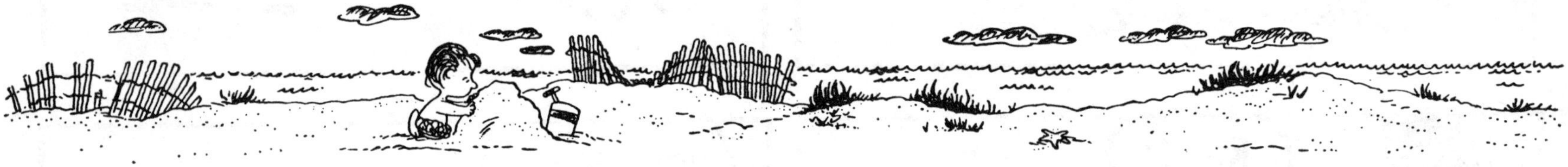

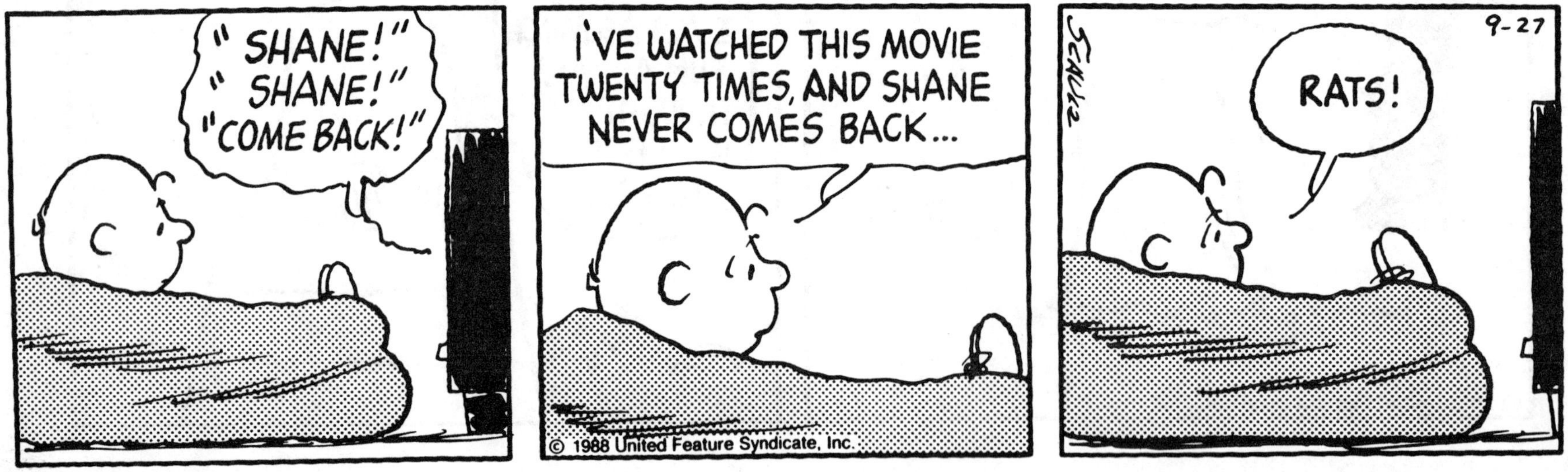
"SHANE!" "SHANE!" "COME BACK!"
I'VE WATCHED THIS MOVIE TWENTY TIMES, AND SHANE NEVER COMES BACK...
© 1988 United Feature Syndicate, Inc.
SCHULZ
9-27
RATS!

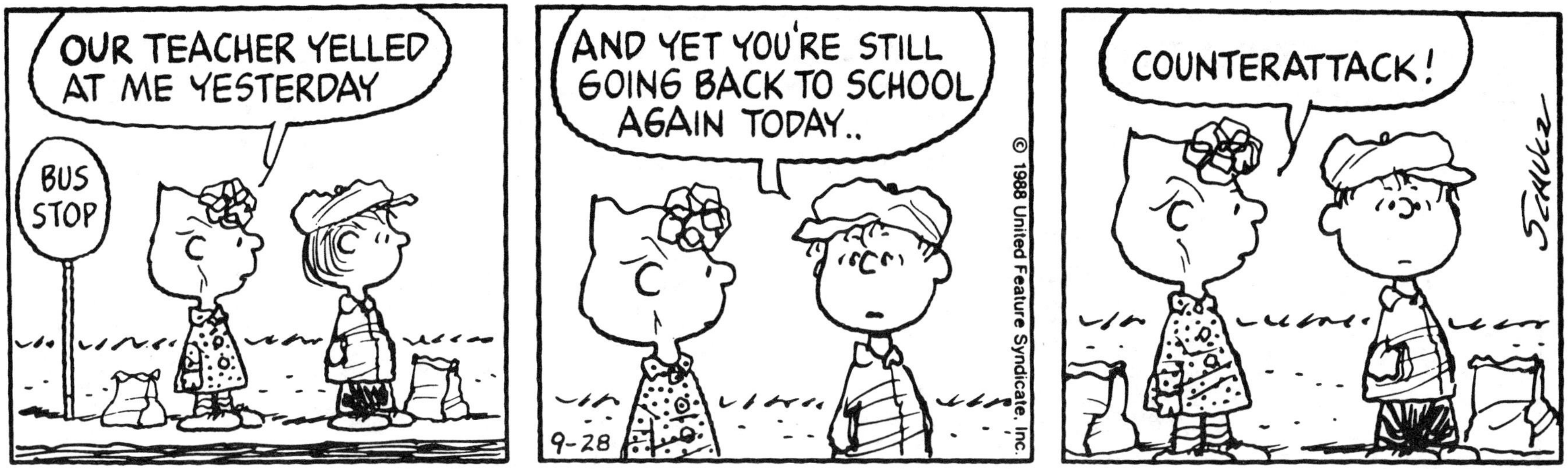
BUS STOP
OUR TEACHER YELLED AT ME YESTERDAY
AND YET YOU'RE STILL GOING BACK TO SCHOOL AGAIN TODAY..
9-28
© 1988 United Feature Syndicate, Inc.
COUNTERATTACK!
SCHULZ

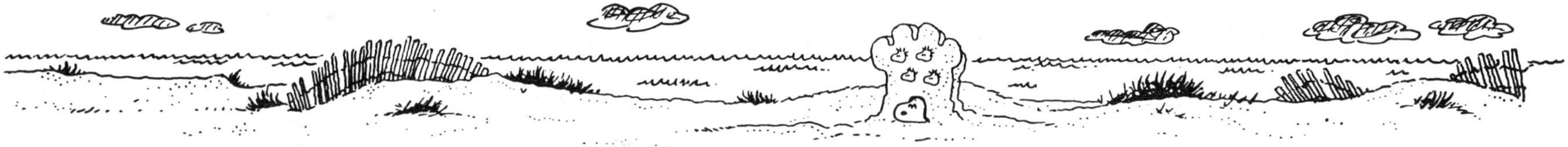

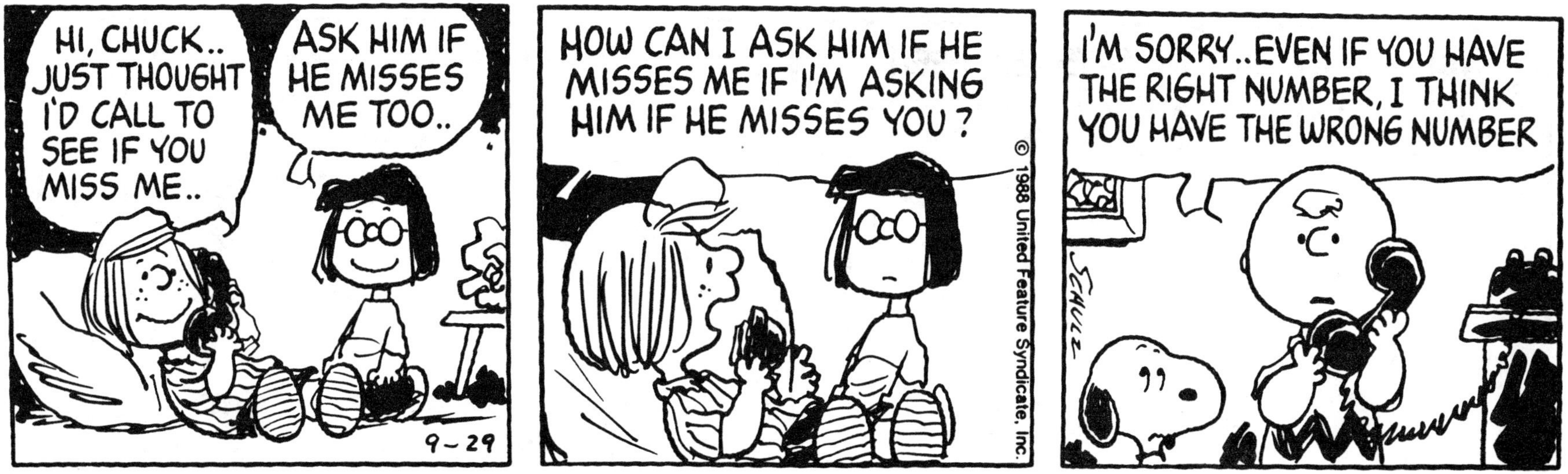
HI, CHUCK.. JUST THOUGHT I'D CALL TO SEE IF YOU MISS ME..
ASK HIM IF HE MISSES ME TOO..
9-29
HOW CAN I ASK HIM IF HE MISSES ME IF I'M ASKING HIM IF HE MISSES YOU?
© 1988 United Feature Syndicate, Inc.
I'M SORRY..EVEN IF YOU HAVE THE RIGHT NUMBER, I THINK YOU HAVE THE WRONG NUMBER
SCHULZ

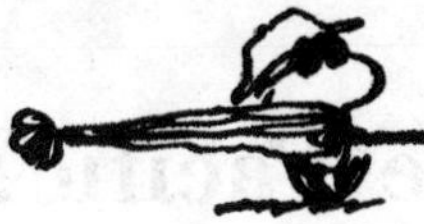

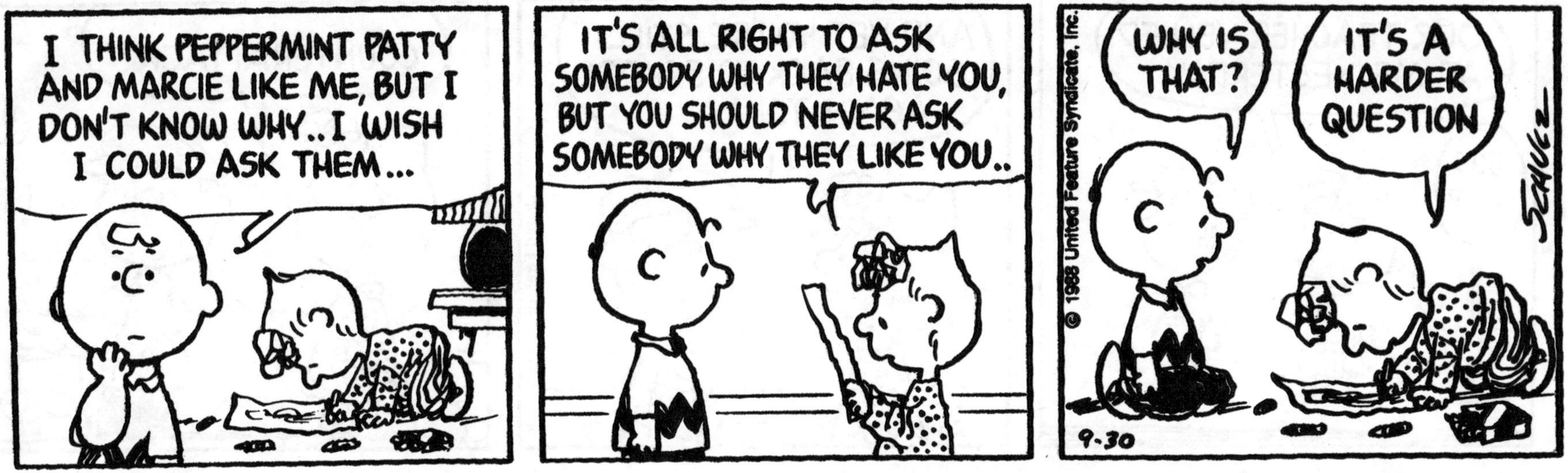
I THINK PEPPERMINT PATTY AND MARCIE LIKE ME, BUT I DON'T KNOW WHY.. I WISH I COULD ASK THEM...
IT'S ALL RIGHT TO ASK SOMEBODY WHY THEY HATE YOU, BUT YOU SHOULD NEVER ASK SOMEBODY WHY THEY LIKE YOU..
WHY IS THAT?
IT'S A HARDER QUESTION
© 1988 United Feature Syndicate, Inc.
9-30

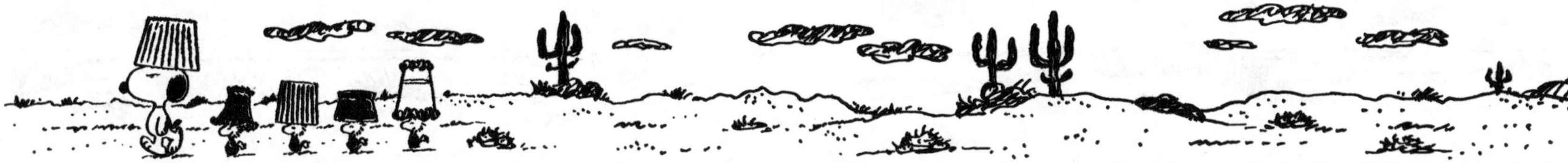

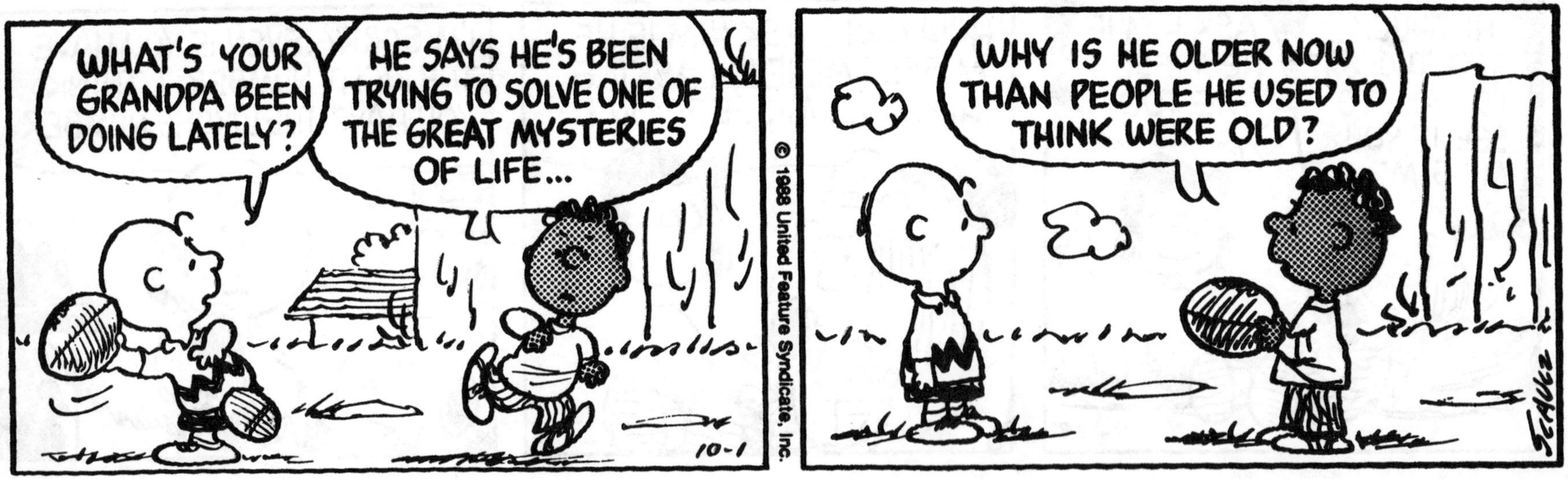
WHAT'S YOUR GRANDPA BEEN DOING LATELY?
HE SAYS HE'S BEEN TRYING TO SOLVE ONE OF THE GREAT MYSTERIES OF LIFE...
WHY IS HE OLDER NOW THAN PEOPLE HE USED TO THINK WERE OLD?
© 1988 United Feature Syndicate, Inc.
10-1

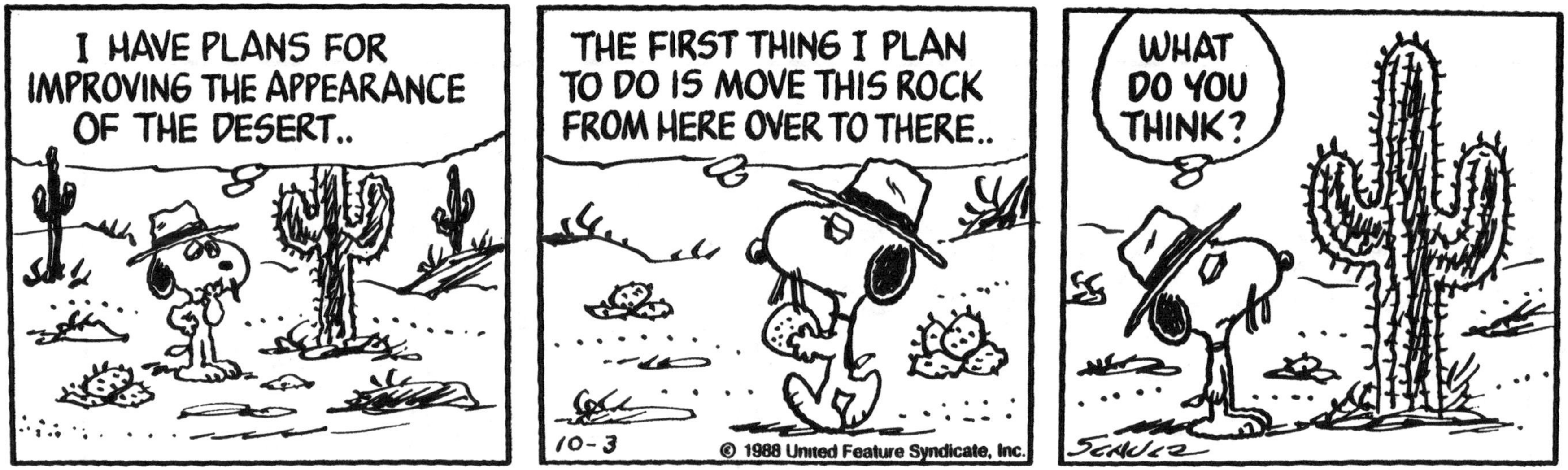
I HAVE PLANS FOR IMPROVING THE APPEARANCE OF THE DESERT..
THE FIRST THING I PLAN TO DO IS MOVE THIS ROCK FROM HERE OVER TO THERE..
WHAT DO YOU THINK?
10-3
© 1988 United Feature Syndicate, Inc.

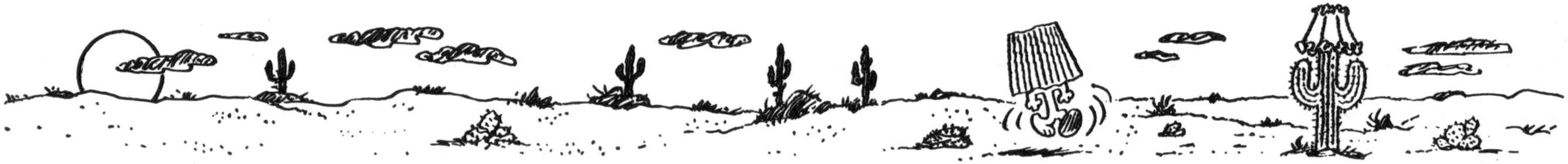

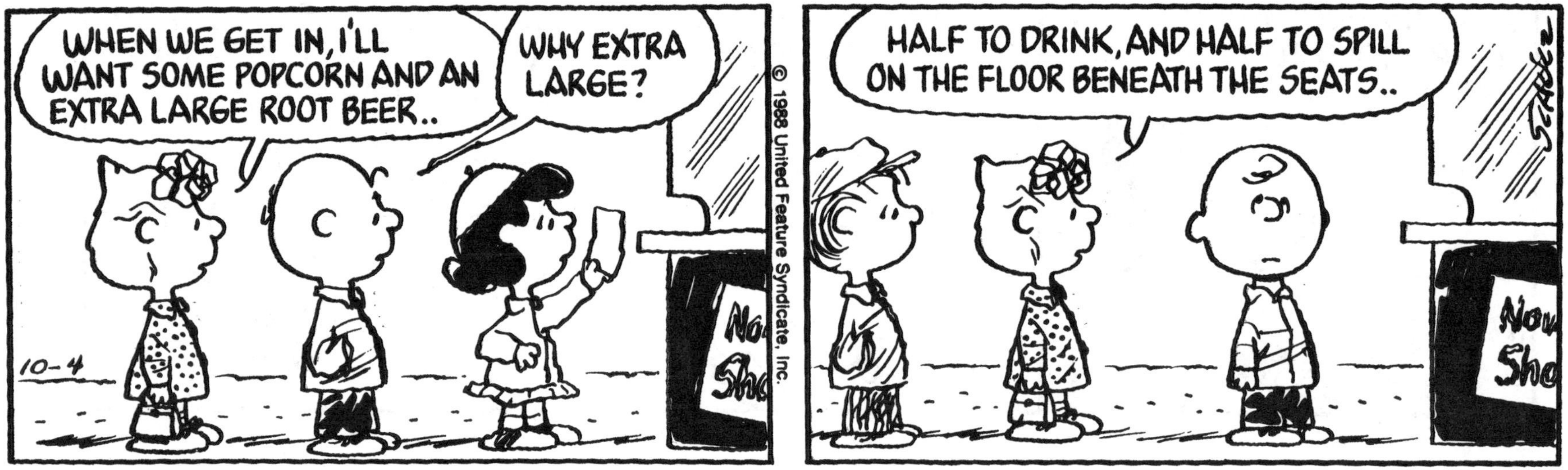
WHEN WE GET IN, I'LL WANT SOME POPCORN AND AN EXTRA LARGE ROOT BEER..
WHY EXTRA LARGE?
HALF TO DRINK, AND HALF TO SPILL ON THE FLOOR BENEATH THE SEATS..
10-4
© 1988 United Feature Syndicate, Inc.

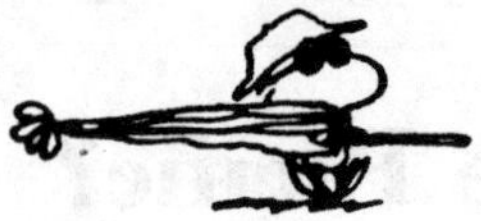

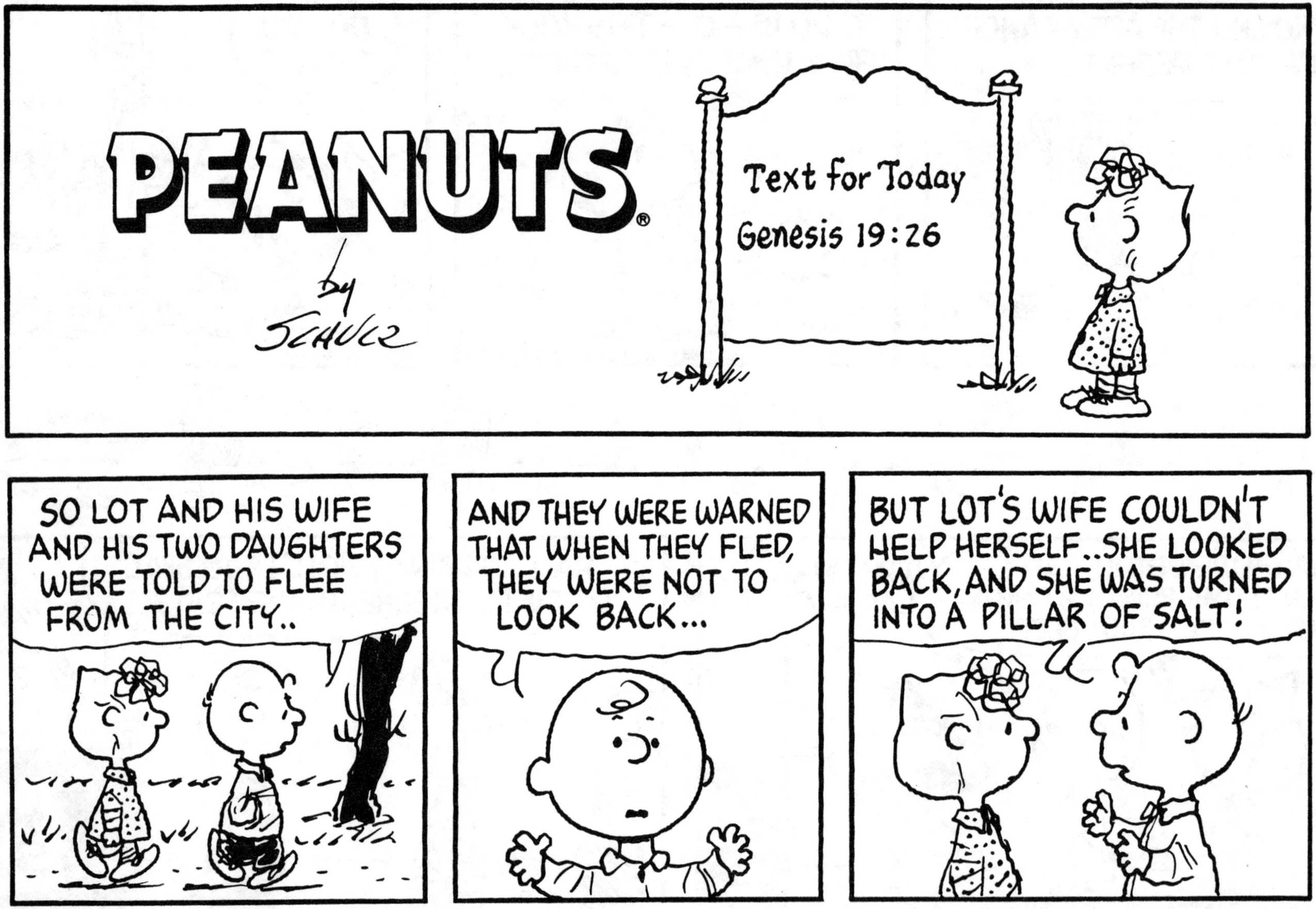
PEANUTS®
by SCHULZ
Text for Today
Genesis 19:26
SO LOT AND HIS WIFE AND HIS TWO DAUGHTERS WERE TOLD TO FLEE FROM THE CITY..
AND THEY WERE WARNED THAT WHEN THEY FLED, THEY WERE NOT TO LOOK BACK...
BUT LOT'S WIFE COULDN'T HELP HERSELF..SHE LOOKED BACK, AND SHE WAS TURNED INTO A PILLAR OF SALT!

Could You Be More Pacific?

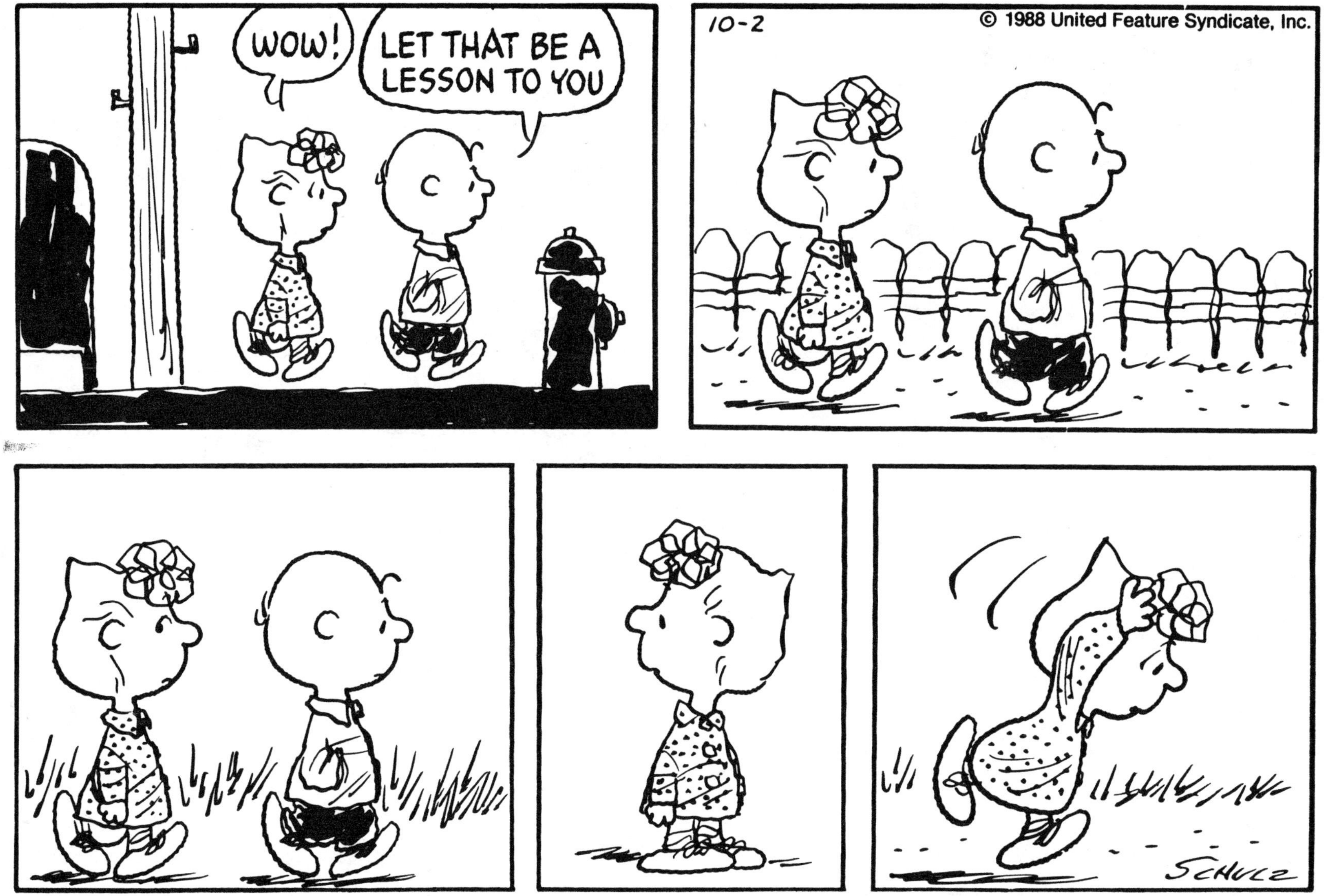
WOW!
LET THAT BE A LESSON TO YOU
10-2
© 1988 United Feature Syndicate, Inc.
SCHULZ

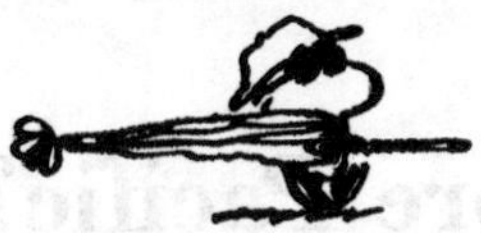

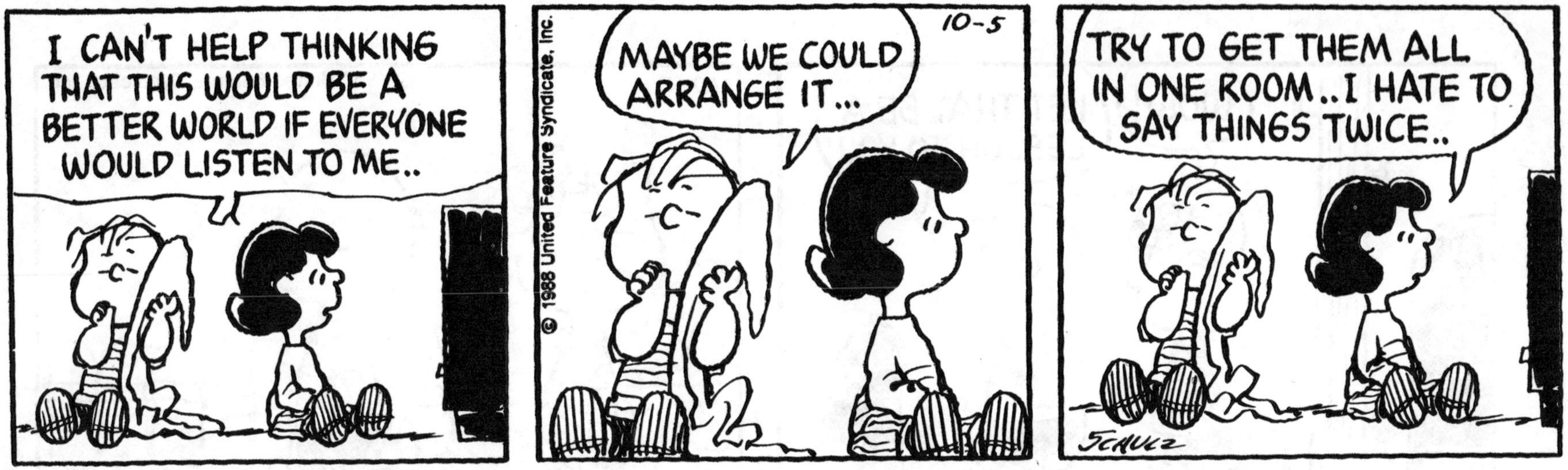

I CAN'T HELP THINKING THAT THIS WOULD BE A BETTER WORLD IF EVERYONE WOULD LISTEN TO ME..
© 1988 United Feature Syndicate, Inc.
10-5
MAYBE WE COULD ARRANGE IT...
TRY TO GET THEM ALL IN ONE ROOM..I HATE TO SAY THINGS TWICE..
SCHULZ

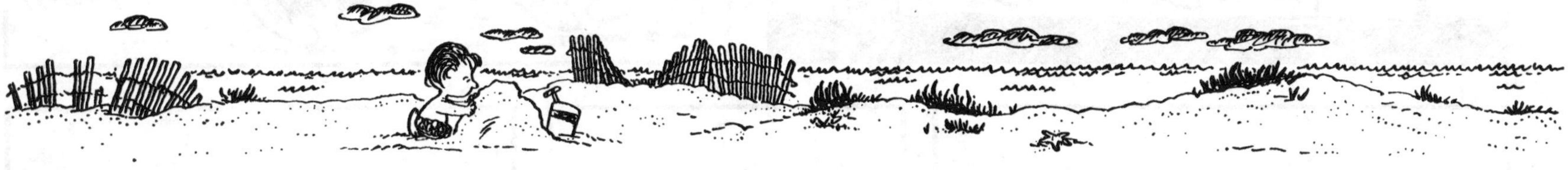

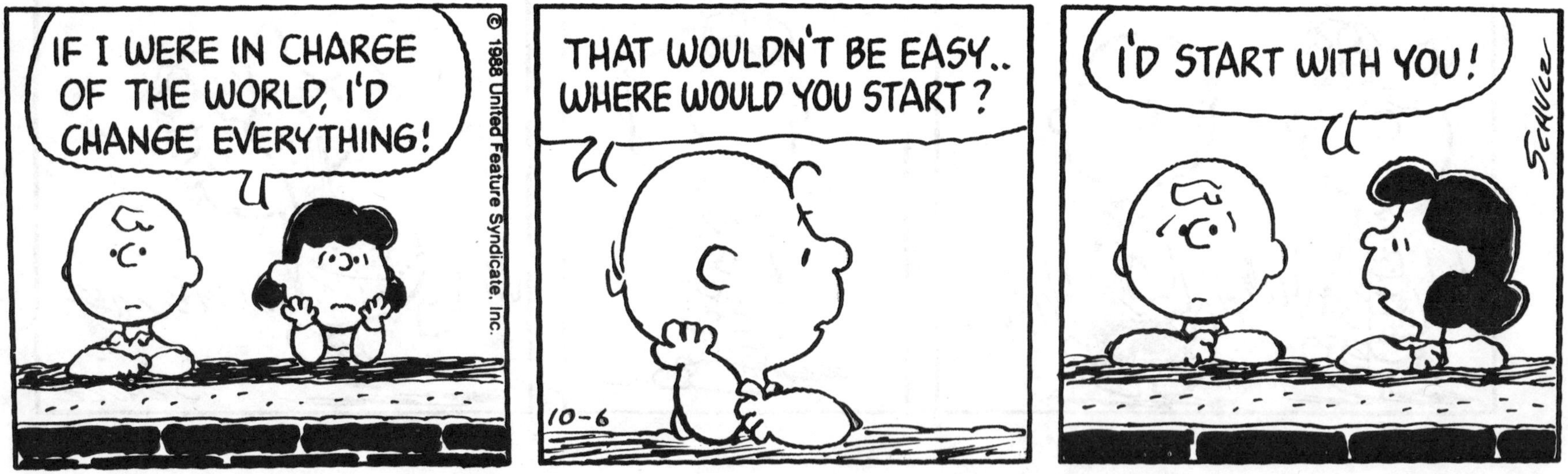

IF I WERE IN CHARGE OF THE WORLD, I'D CHANGE EVERYTHING!
© 1988 United Feature Syndicate, Inc.
THAT WOULDN'T BE EASY.. WHERE WOULD YOU START?
10-6
I'D START WITH YOU!
SCHULZ

Could You Be More Pacific?

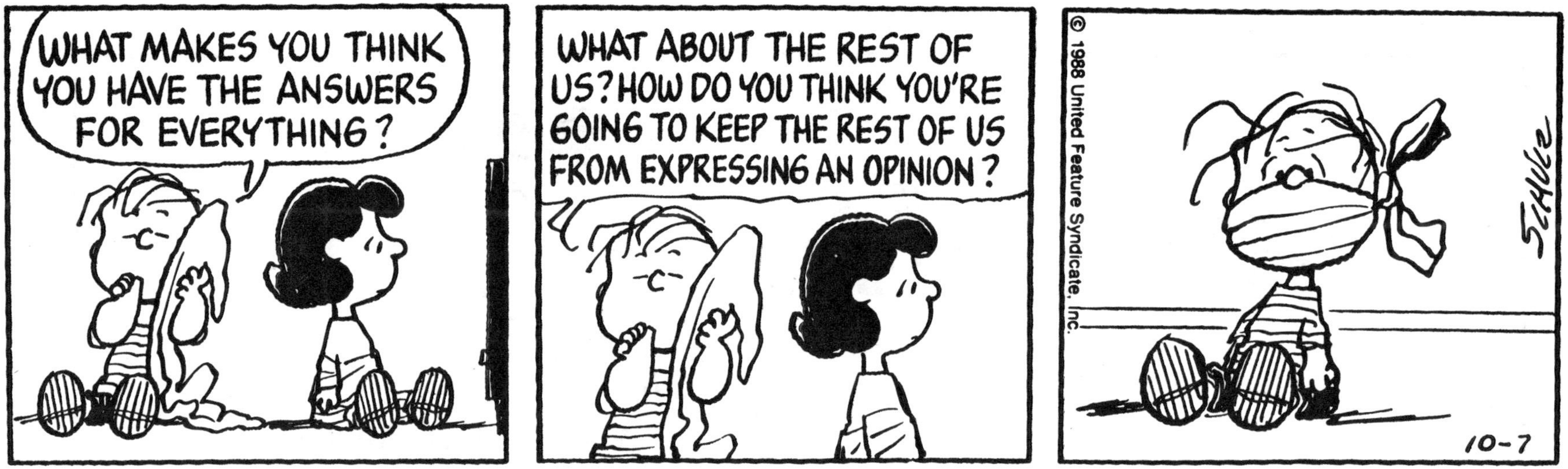
WHAT MAKES YOU THINK YOU HAVE THE ANSWERS FOR EVERYTHING?
WHAT ABOUT THE REST OF US? HOW DO YOU THINK YOU'RE GOING TO KEEP THE REST OF US FROM EXPRESSING AN OPINION?
© 1988 United Feature Syndicate, Inc.
SCHULZ
10-7

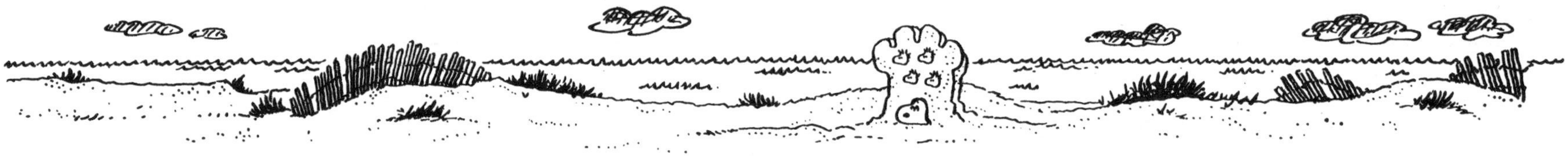

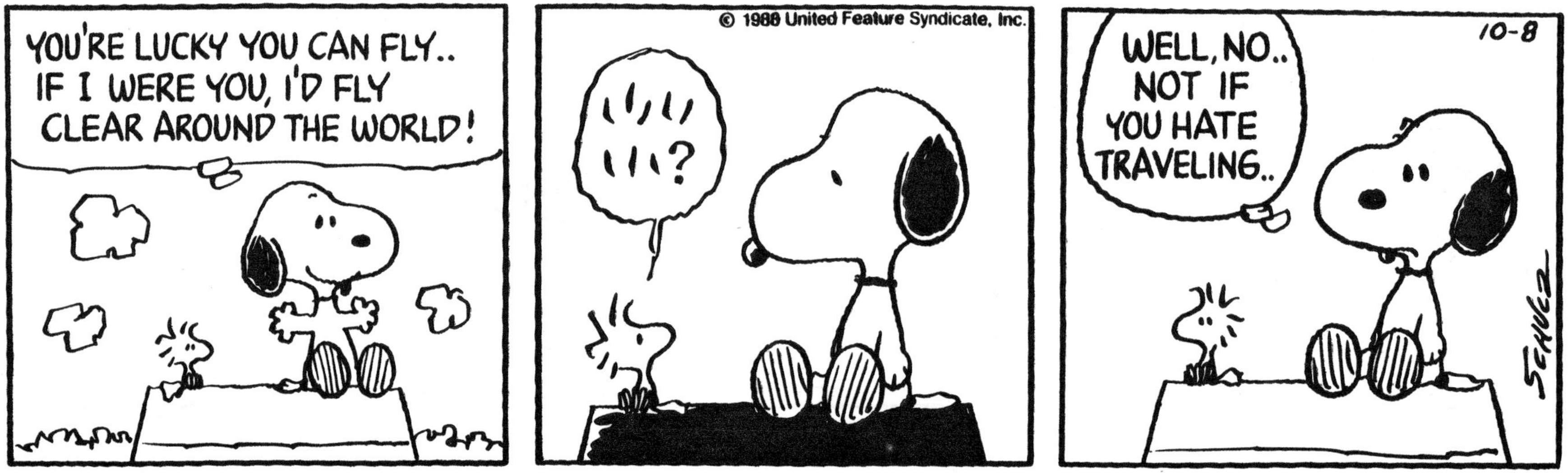
YOU'RE LUCKY YOU CAN FLY.. IF I WERE YOU, I'D FLY CLEAR AROUND THE WORLD!
© 1988 United Feature Syndicate, Inc.
!!!! !!!?
10-8
WELL, NO.. NOT IF YOU HATE TRAVELING..
SCHULZ

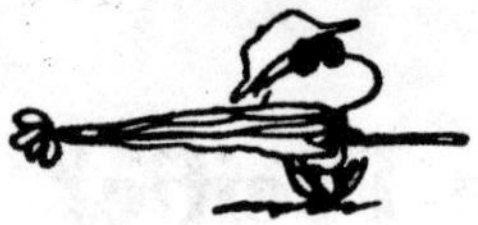

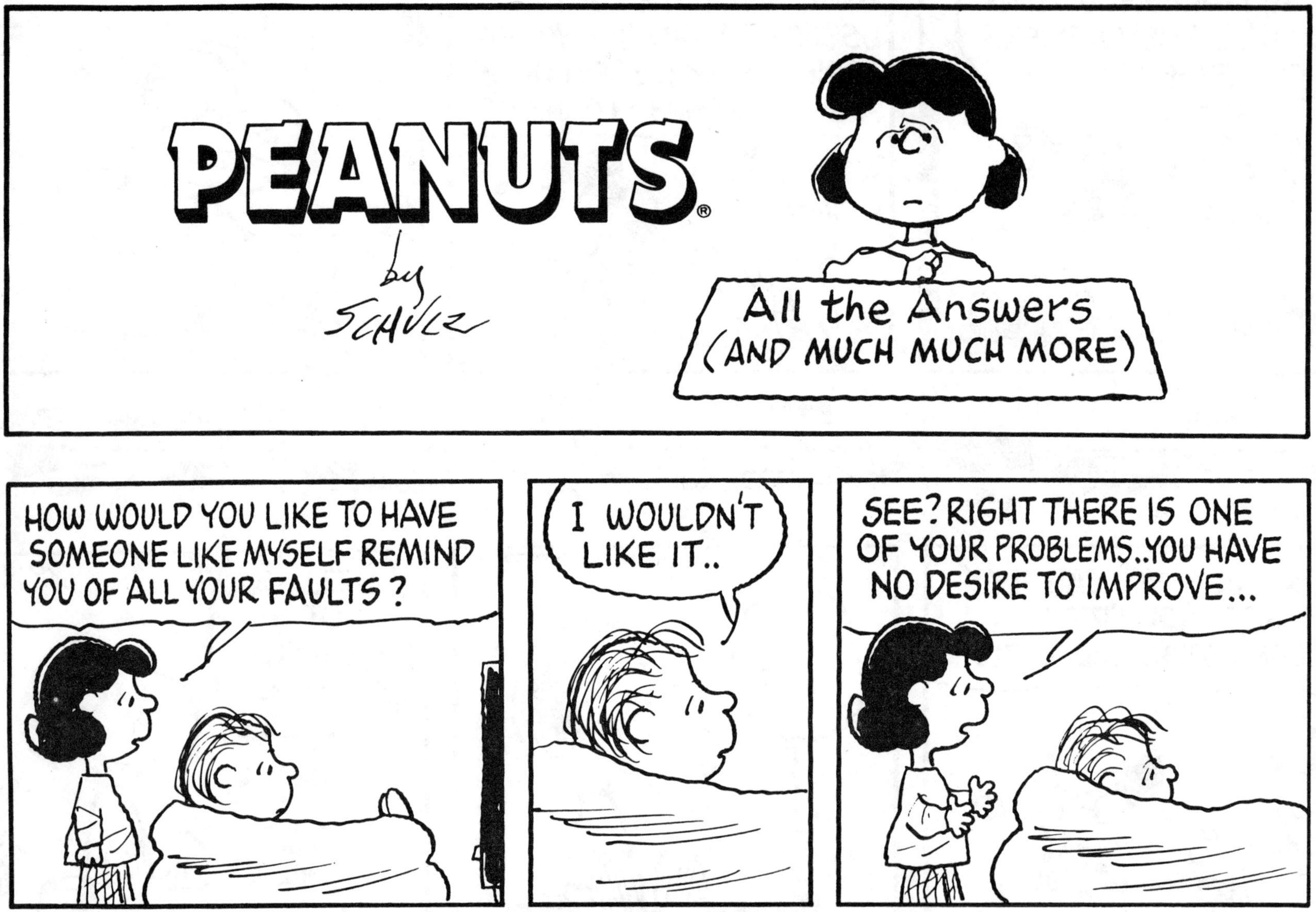
PEANUTS
by SCHULZ
All the Answers
(AND MUCH MUCH MORE)
HOW WOULD YOU LIKE TO HAVE SOMEONE LIKE MYSELF REMIND YOU OF ALL YOUR FAULTS?
I WOULDN'T LIKE IT..
SEE? RIGHT THERE IS ONE OF YOUR PROBLEMS..YOU HAVE NO DESIRE TO IMPROVE...

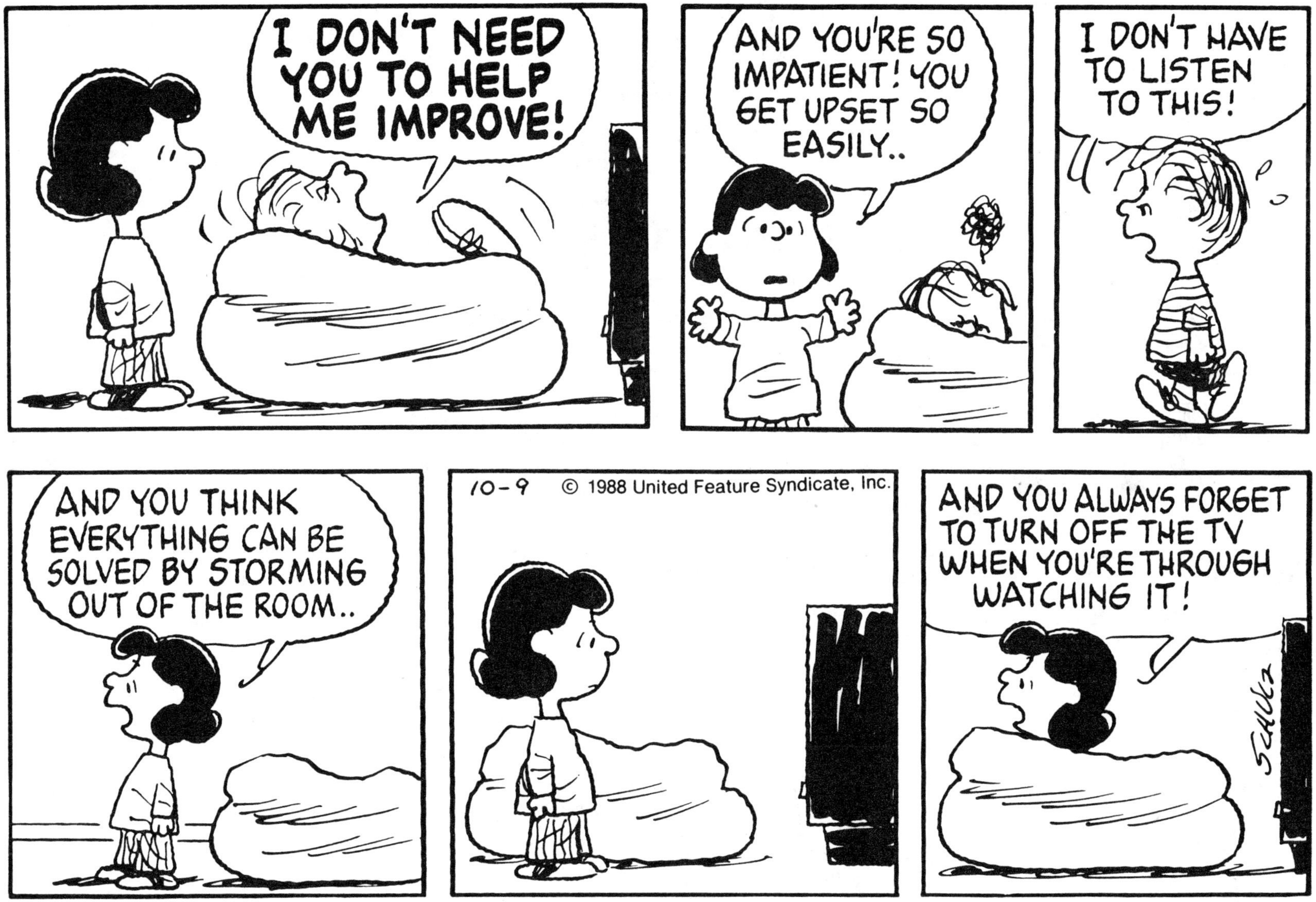
I DON'T NEED YOU TO HELP ME IMPROVE!
AND YOU'RE SO IMPATIENT! YOU GET UPSET SO EASILY..
I DON'T HAVE TO LISTEN TO THIS!
AND YOU THINK EVERYTHING CAN BE SOLVED BY STORMING OUT OF THE ROOM..
10-9 © 1988 United Feature Syndicate, Inc.
AND YOU ALWAYS FORGET TO TURN OFF THE TV WHEN YOU'RE THROUGH WATCHING IT!
SCHULZ

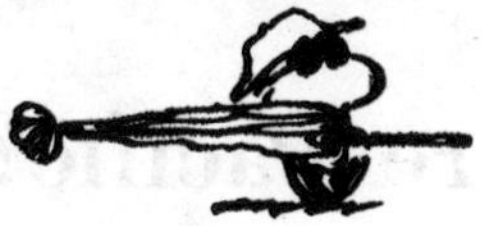

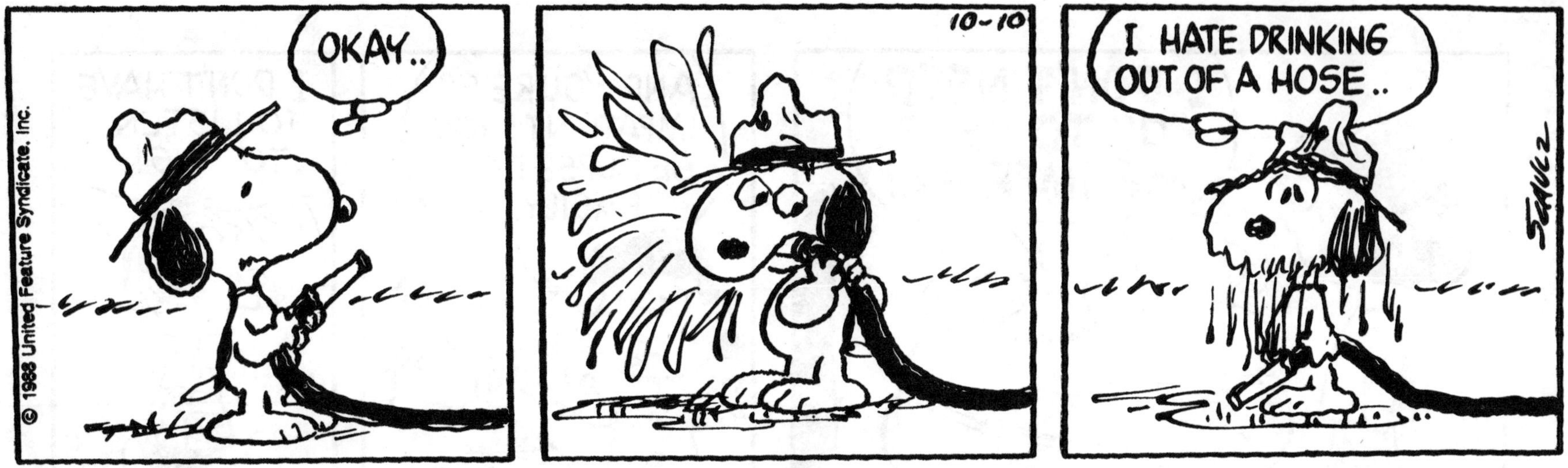
© 1988 United Feature Syndicate, Inc.
OKAY..
10-10
I HATE DRINKING OUT OF A HOSE..
SCHULZ

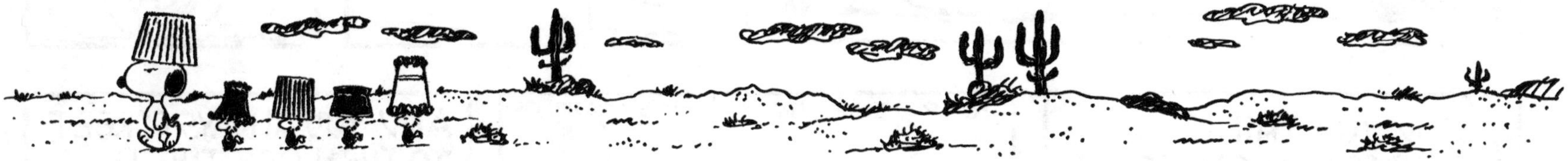

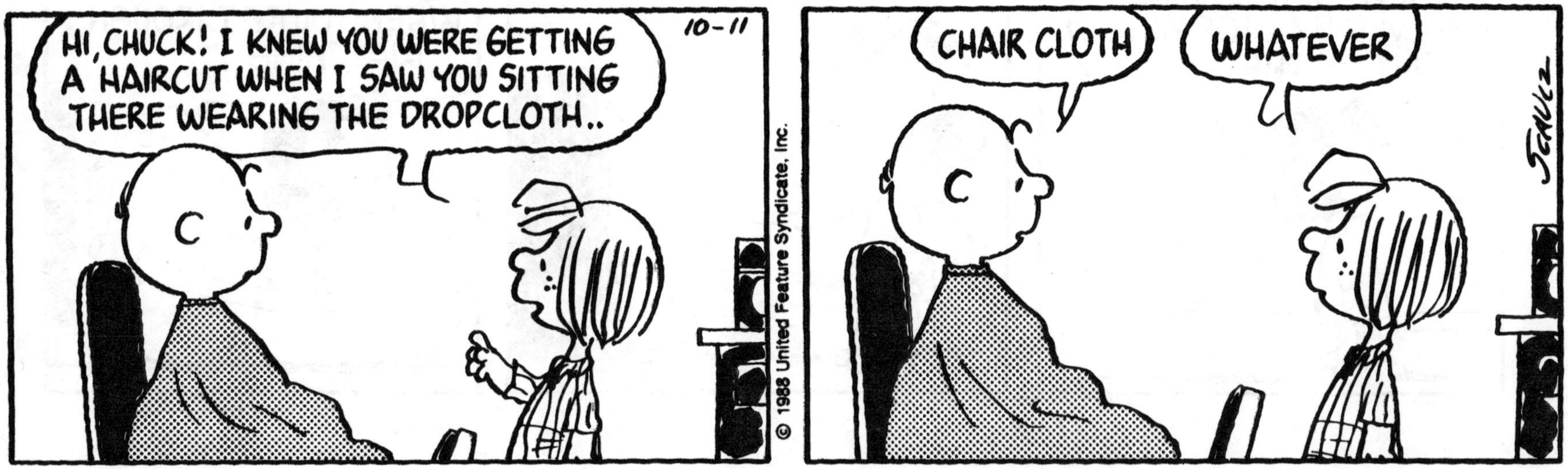
10-11
HI, CHUCK! I KNEW YOU WERE GETTING A HAIRCUT WHEN I SAW YOU SITTING THERE WEARING THE DROPCLOTH..
© 1988 United Feature Syndicate, Inc.
CHAIR CLOTH
WHATEVER
SCHULZ

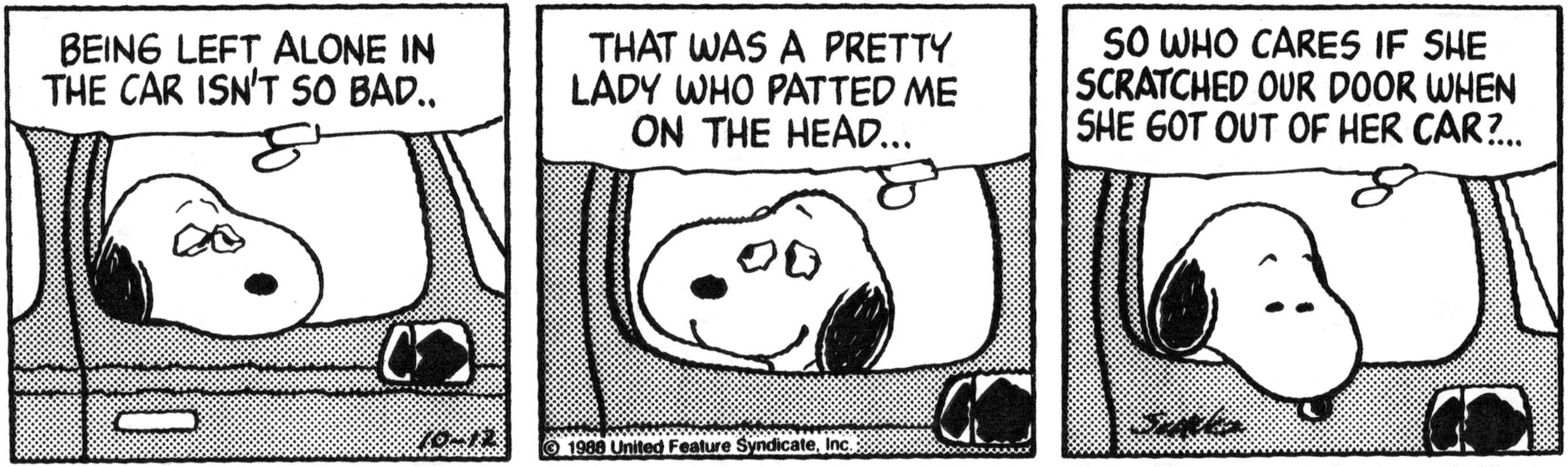
BEING LEFT ALONE IN THE CAR ISN'T SO BAD..
THAT WAS A PRETTY LADY WHO PATTED ME ON THE HEAD...
SO WHO CARES IF SHE SCRATCHED OUR DOOR WHEN SHE GOT OUT OF HER CAR?...
10-12
© 1988 United Feature Syndicate, Inc.

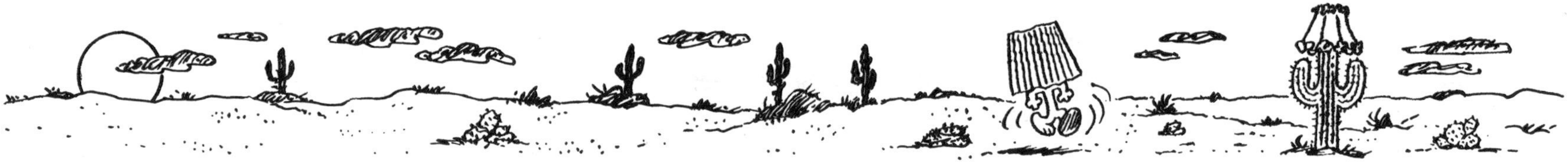

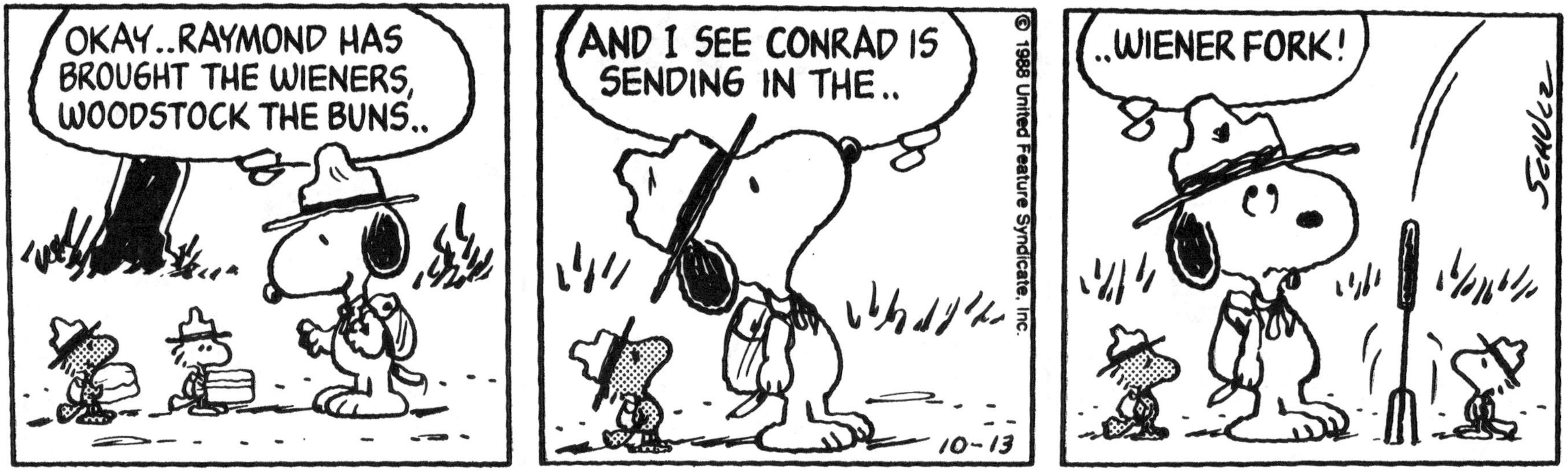
OKAY..RAYMOND HAS BROUGHT THE WIENERS, WOODSTOCK THE BUNS..
AND I SEE CONRAD IS SENDING IN THE..
..WIENER FORK!
© 1988 United Feature Syndicate, Inc.
10-13
SCHULZ

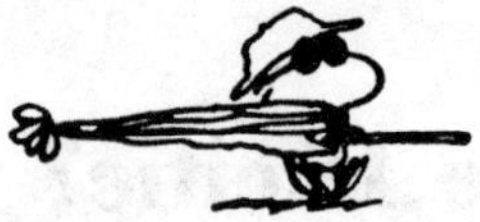

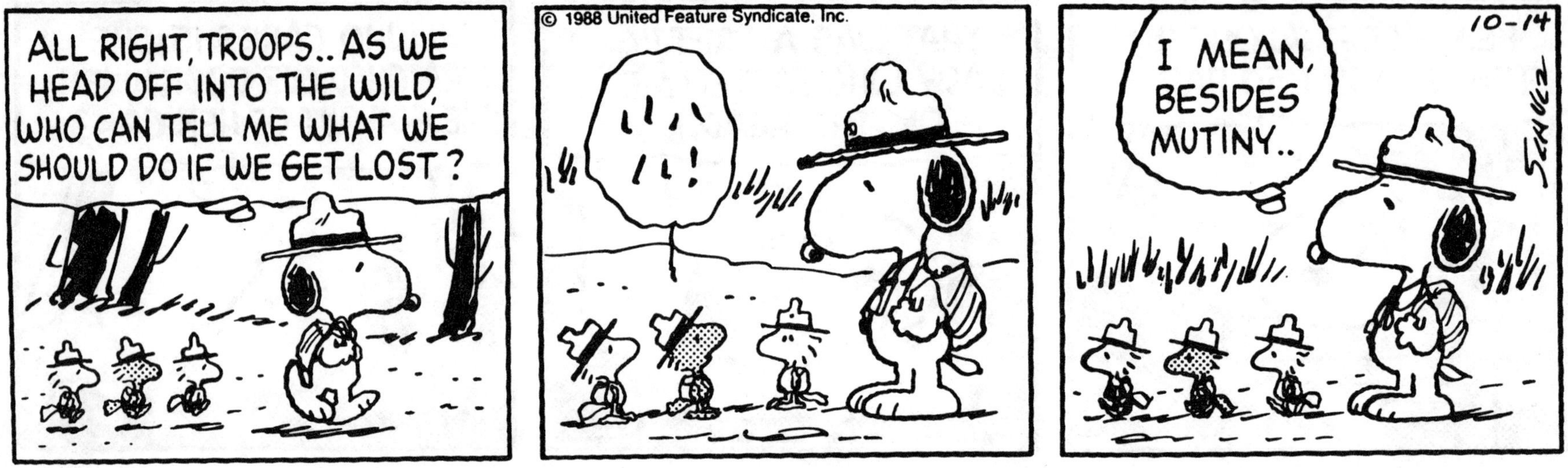
ALL RIGHT, TROOPS.. AS WE HEAD OFF INTO THE WILD, WHO CAN TELL ME WHAT WE SHOULD DO IF WE GET LOST?
© 1988 United Feature Syndicate, Inc.
I MEAN, BESIDES MUTINY..
10-14
SCHULZ

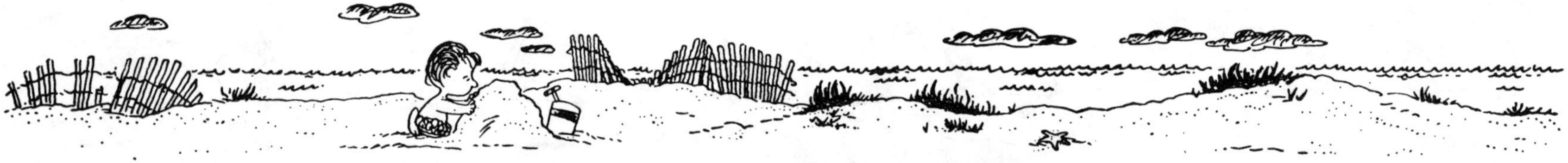

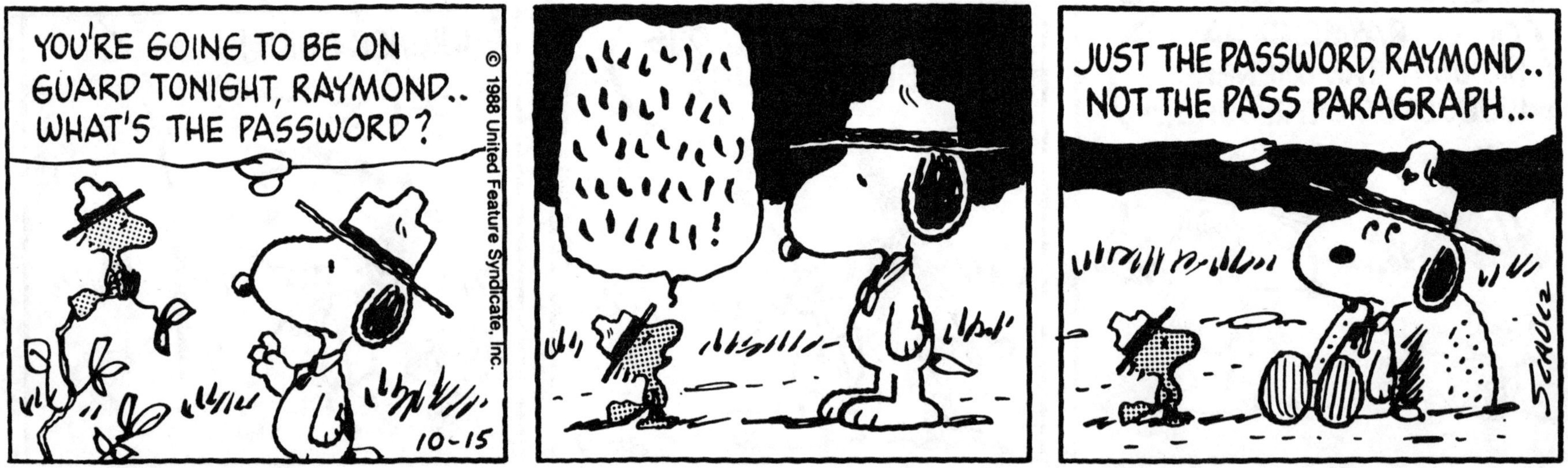
YOU'RE GOING TO BE ON GUARD TONIGHT, RAYMOND.. WHAT'S THE PASSWORD?
© 1988 United Feature Syndicate, Inc.
10-15
JUST THE PASSWORD, RAYMOND.. NOT THE PASS PARAGRAPH...
SCHULZ

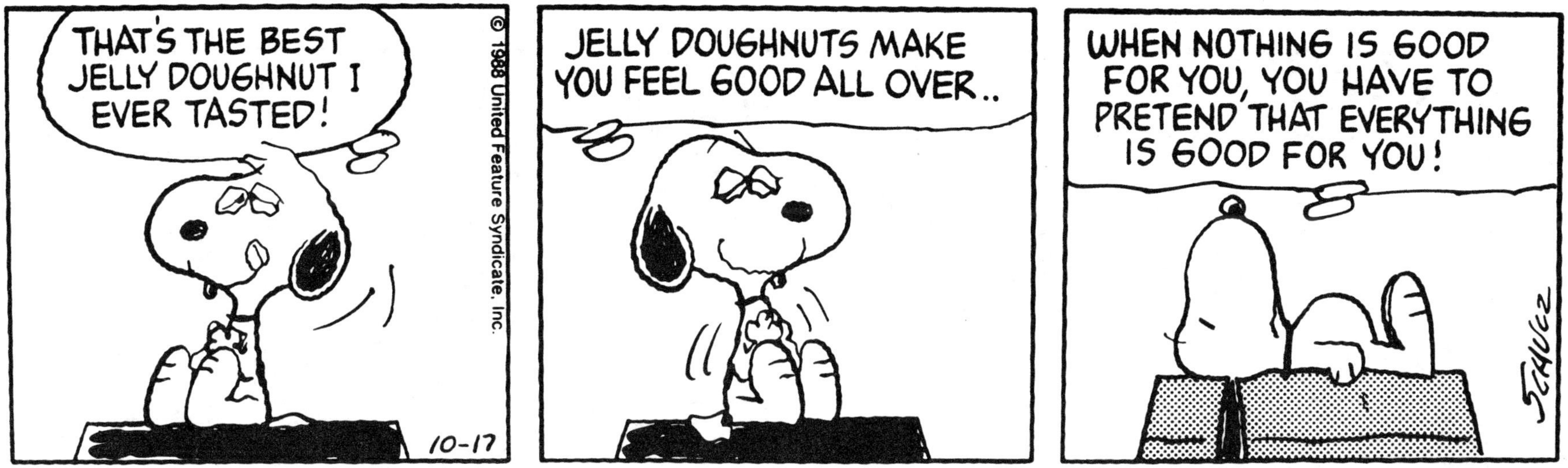
THAT'S THE BEST JELLY DOUGHNUT I EVER TASTED!
© 1988 United Feature Syndicate, Inc.
10-17
JELLY DOUGHNUTS MAKE YOU FEEL GOOD ALL OVER..
WHEN NOTHING IS GOOD FOR YOU, YOU HAVE TO PRETEND THAT EVERYTHING IS GOOD FOR YOU!
SCHULZ

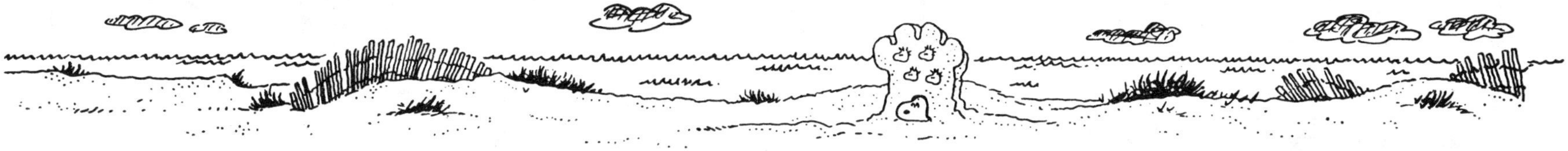

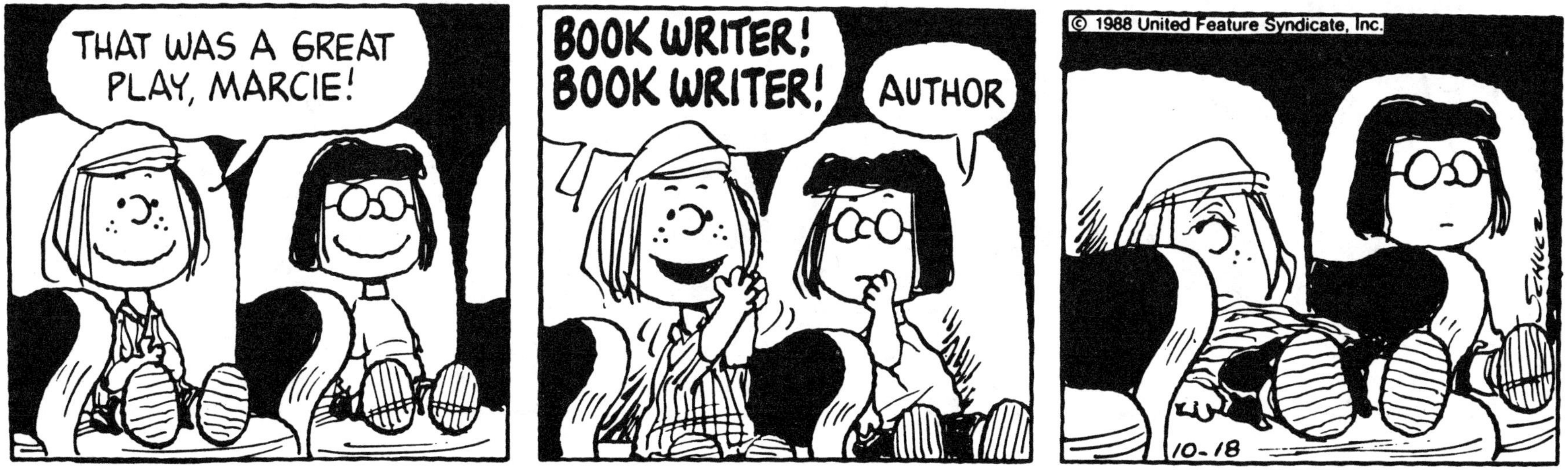
THAT WAS A GREAT PLAY, MARCIE!
BOOK WRITER! BOOK WRITER!
AUTHOR
© 1988 United Feature Syndicate, Inc.
SCHULZ
10-18

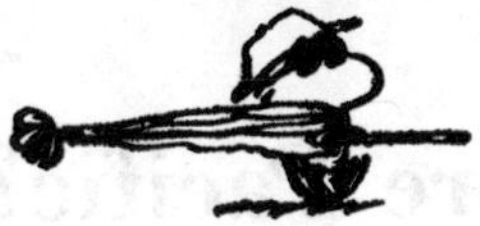

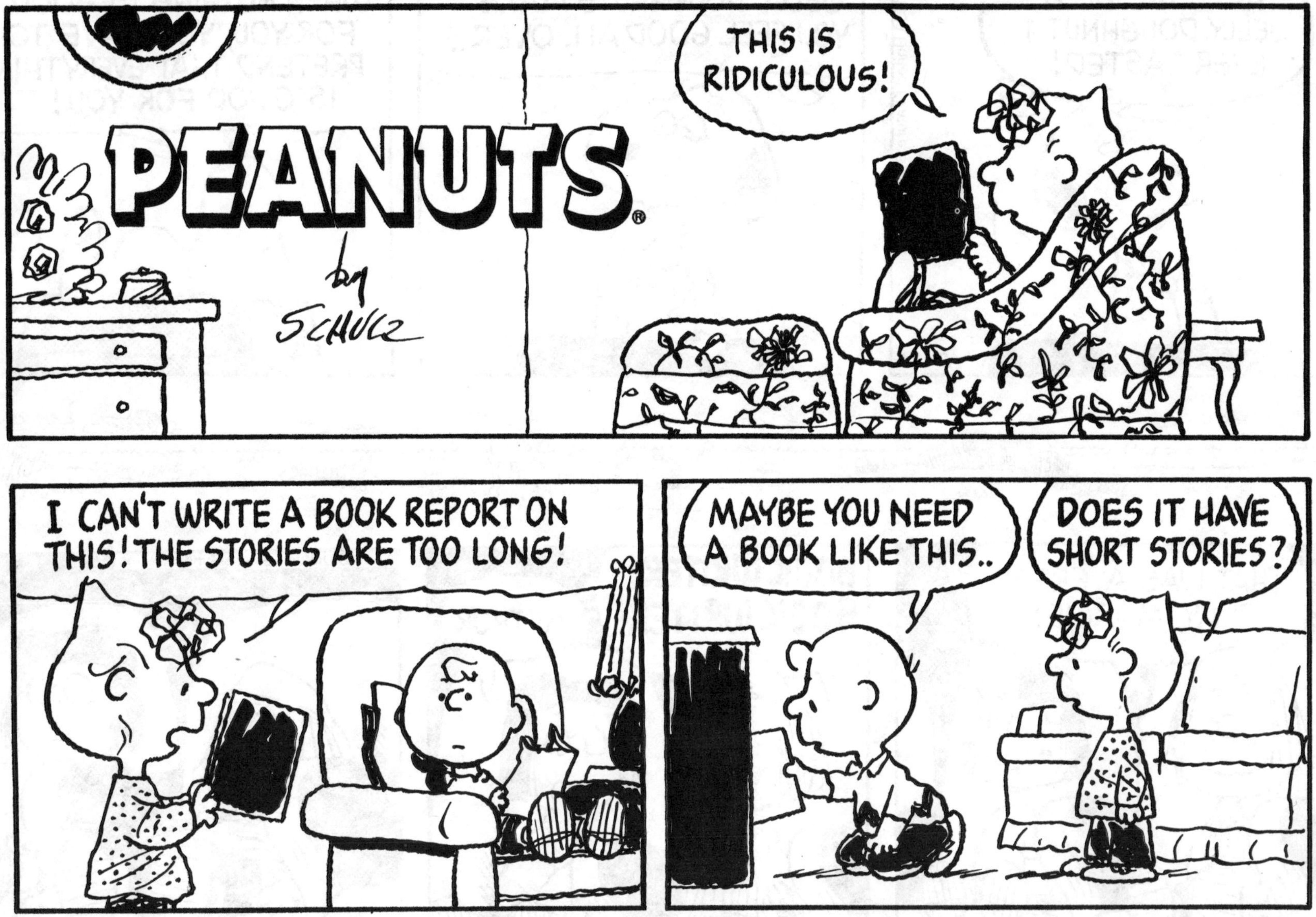
PEANUTS
by SCHULZ
THIS IS RIDICULOUS!
I CAN'T WRITE A BOOK REPORT ON THIS! THE STORIES ARE TOO LONG!
MAYBE YOU NEED A BOOK LIKE THIS..
DOES IT HAVE SHORT STORIES?

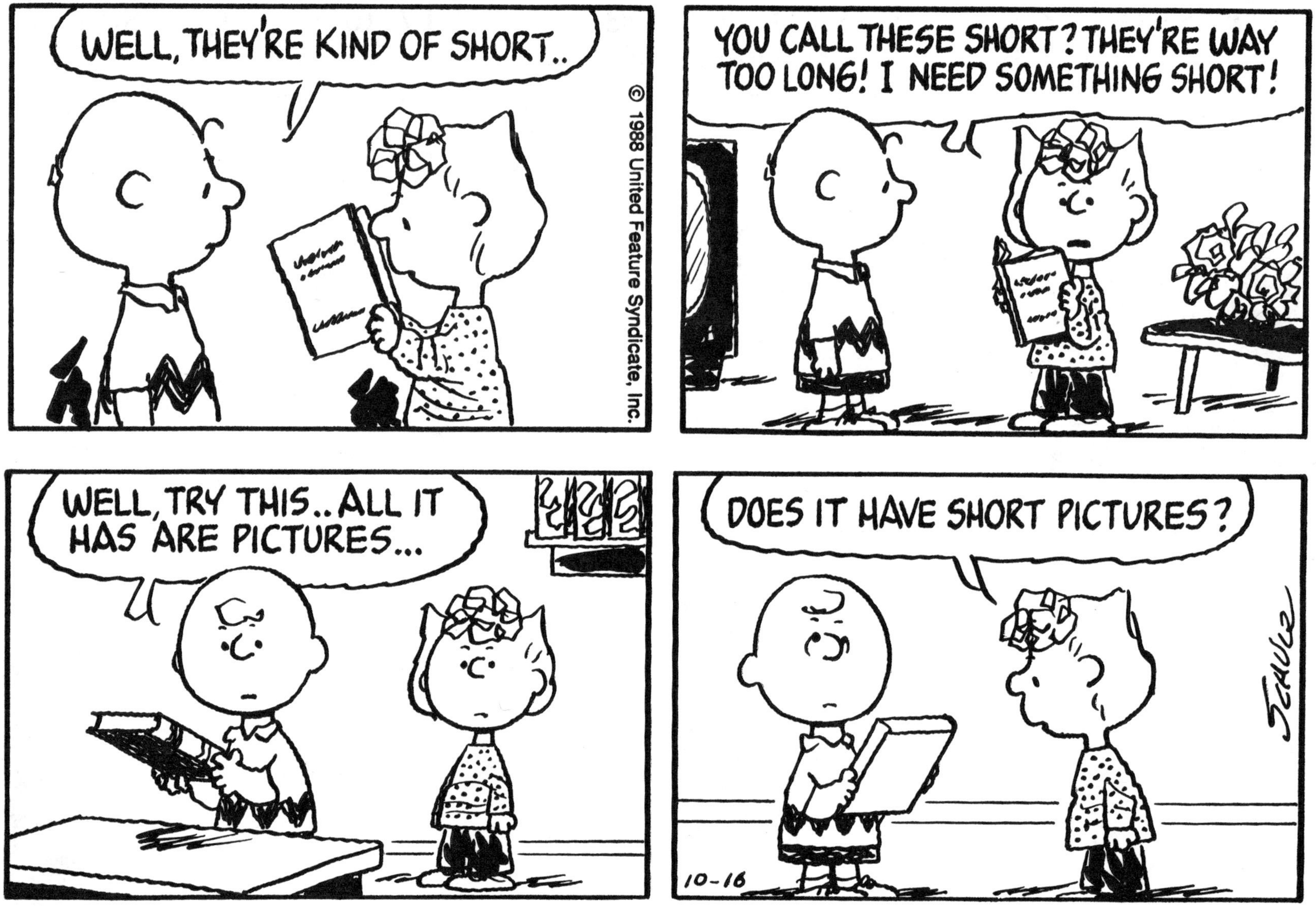
WELL, THEY'RE KIND OF SHORT..
© 1988 United Feature Syndicate, Inc.
YOU CALL THESE SHORT? THEY'RE WAY TOO LONG! I NEED SOMETHING SHORT!
WELL, TRY THIS.. ALL IT HAS ARE PICTURES...
DOES IT HAVE SHORT PICTURES?
SCHULZ
10-16

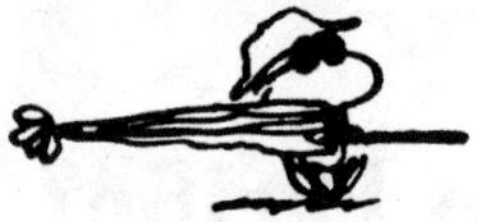

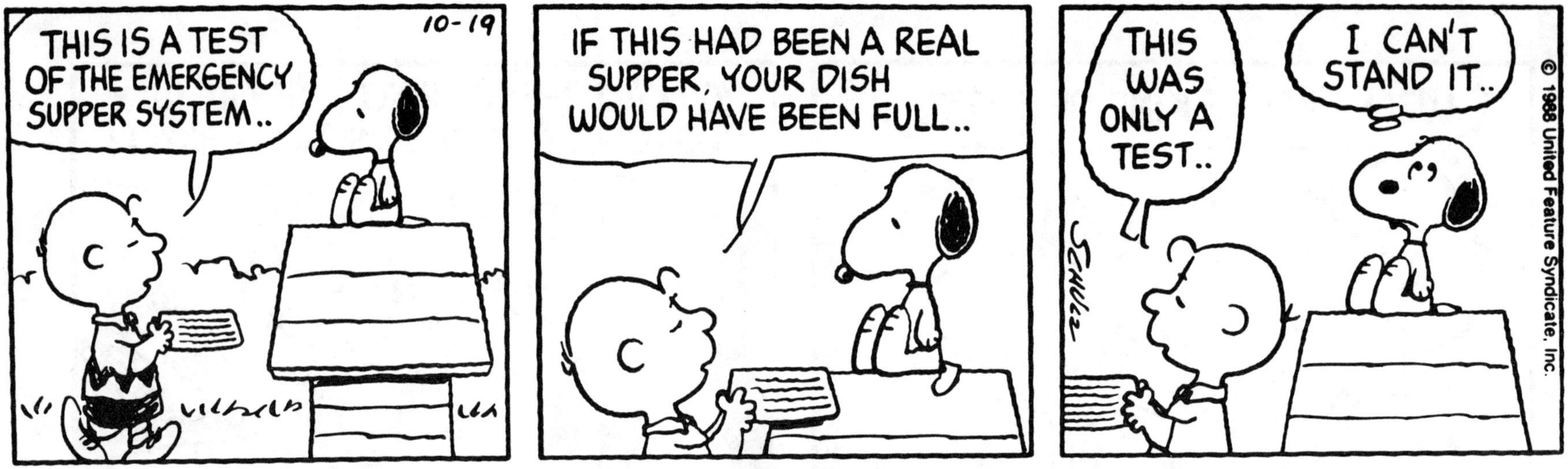
10-19
THIS IS A TEST OF THE EMERGENCY SUPPER SYSTEM..
IF THIS HAD BEEN A REAL SUPPER, YOUR DISH WOULD HAVE BEEN FULL..
THIS WAS ONLY A TEST..
I CAN'T STAND IT..
SCHULZ
© 1988 United Feature Syndicate, Inc.

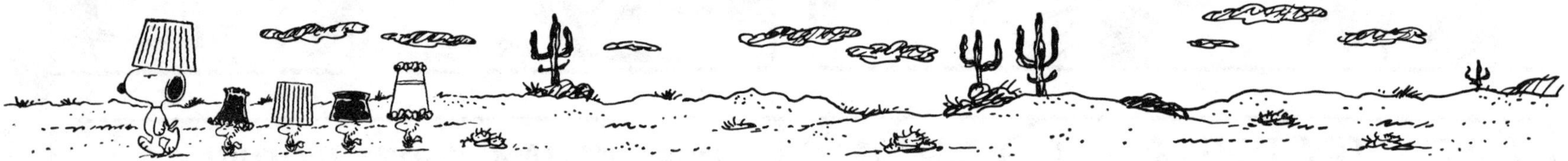

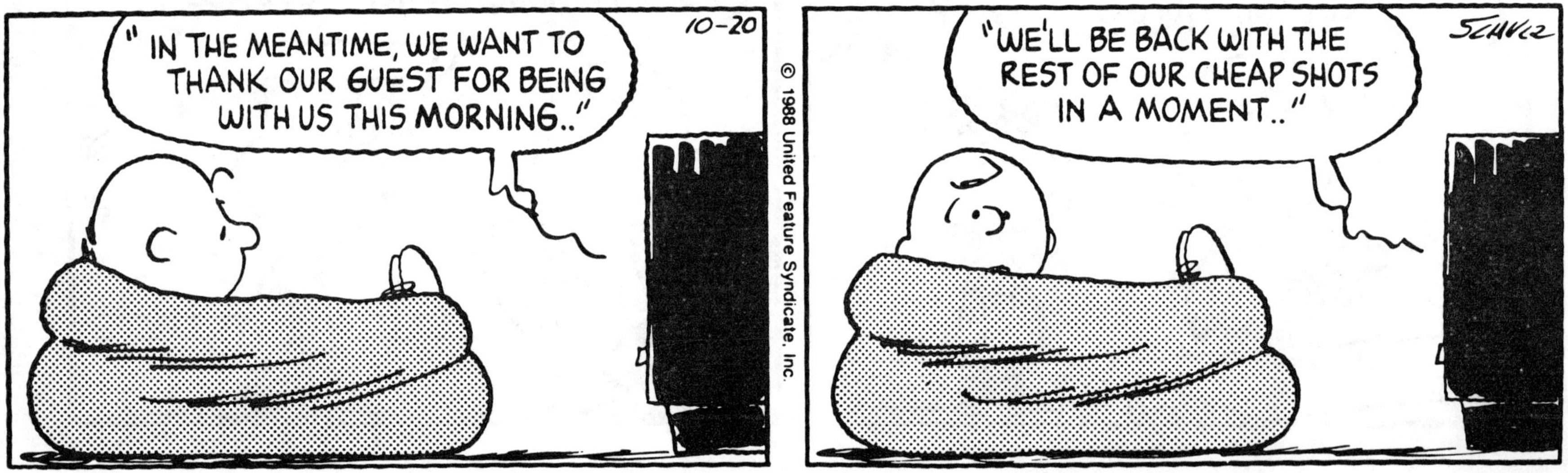
10-20
" IN THE MEANTIME, WE WANT TO THANK OUR GUEST FOR BEING WITH US THIS MORNING.."
© 1988 United Feature Syndicate, Inc.
SCHULZ
"WE'LL BE BACK WITH THE REST OF OUR CHEAP SHOTS IN A MOMENT.."

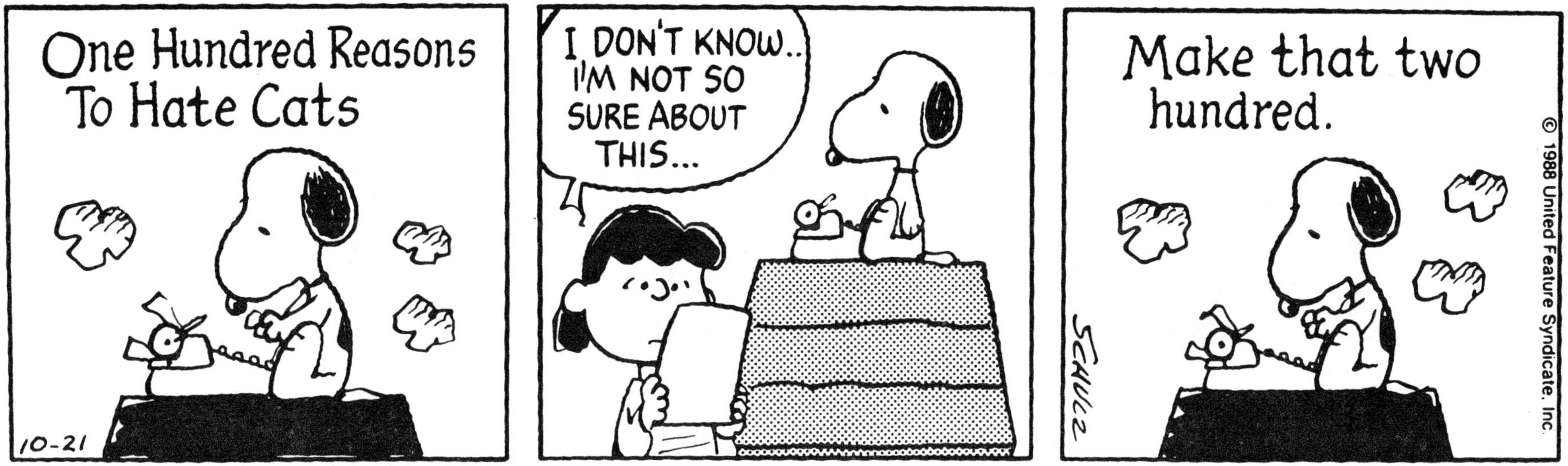
One Hundred Reasons To Hate Cats
10-21
I DON'T KNOW.. I'M NOT SO SURE ABOUT THIS...
Make that two hundred.
© 1988 United Feature Syndicate, Inc.

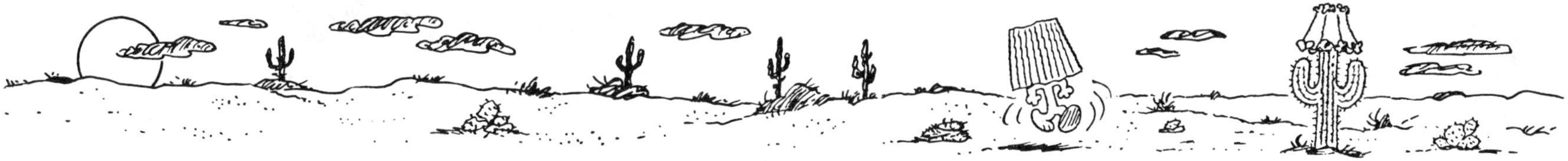

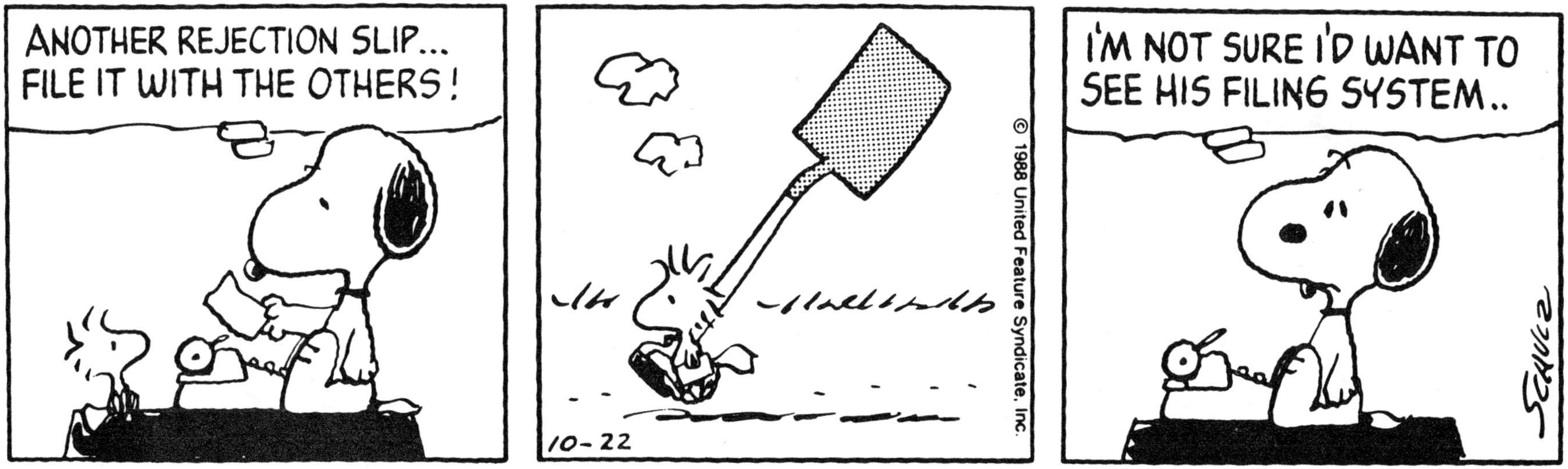
ANOTHER REJECTION SLIP... FILE IT WITH THE OTHERS!
10-22
© 1988 United Feature Syndicate, Inc.
I'M NOT SURE I'D WANT TO SEE HIS FILING SYSTEM..

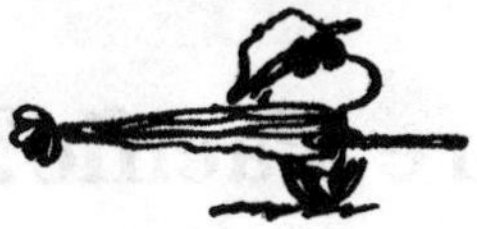

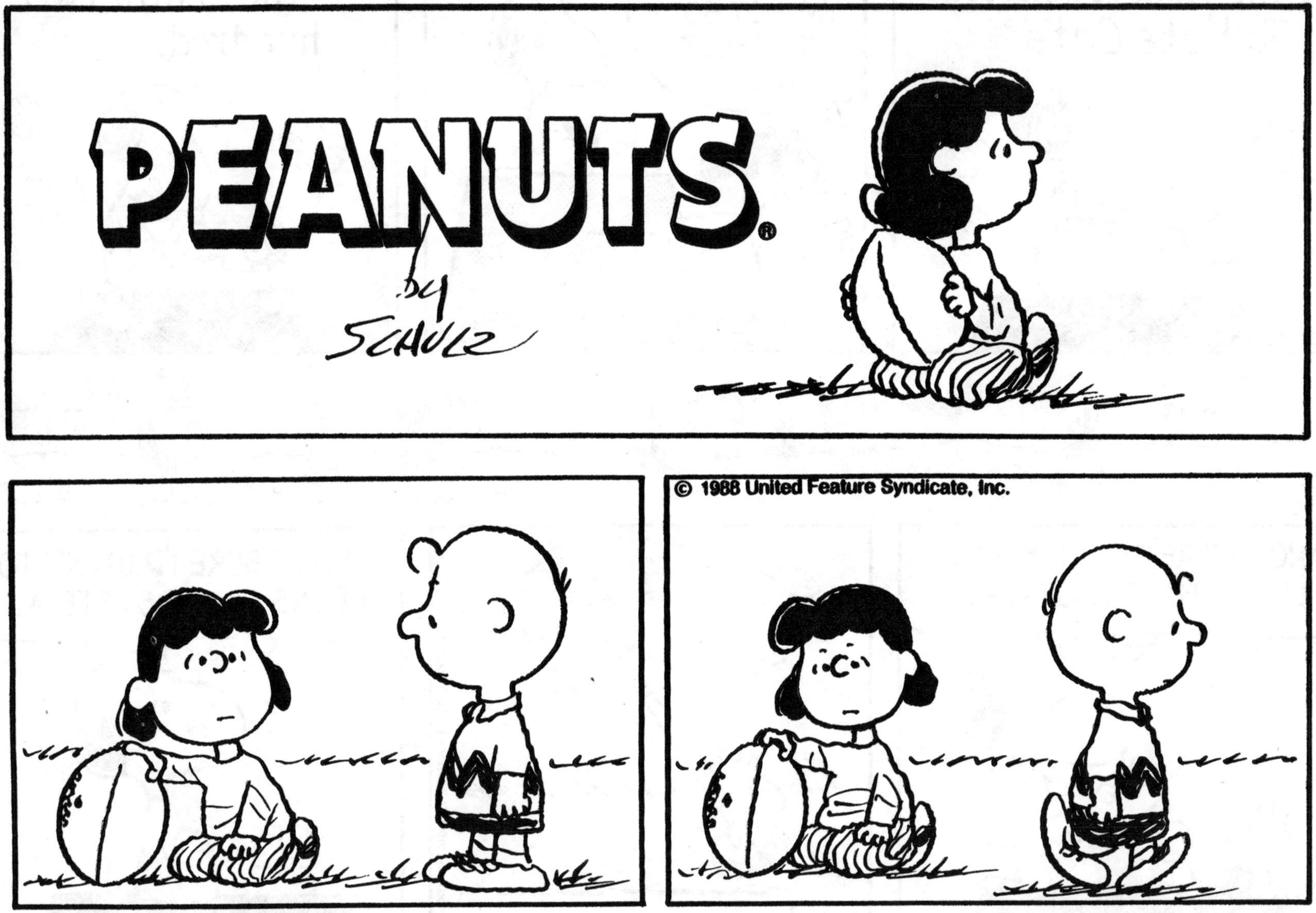
PEANUTS®
by SCHULZ
© 1988 United Feature Syndicate, Inc.

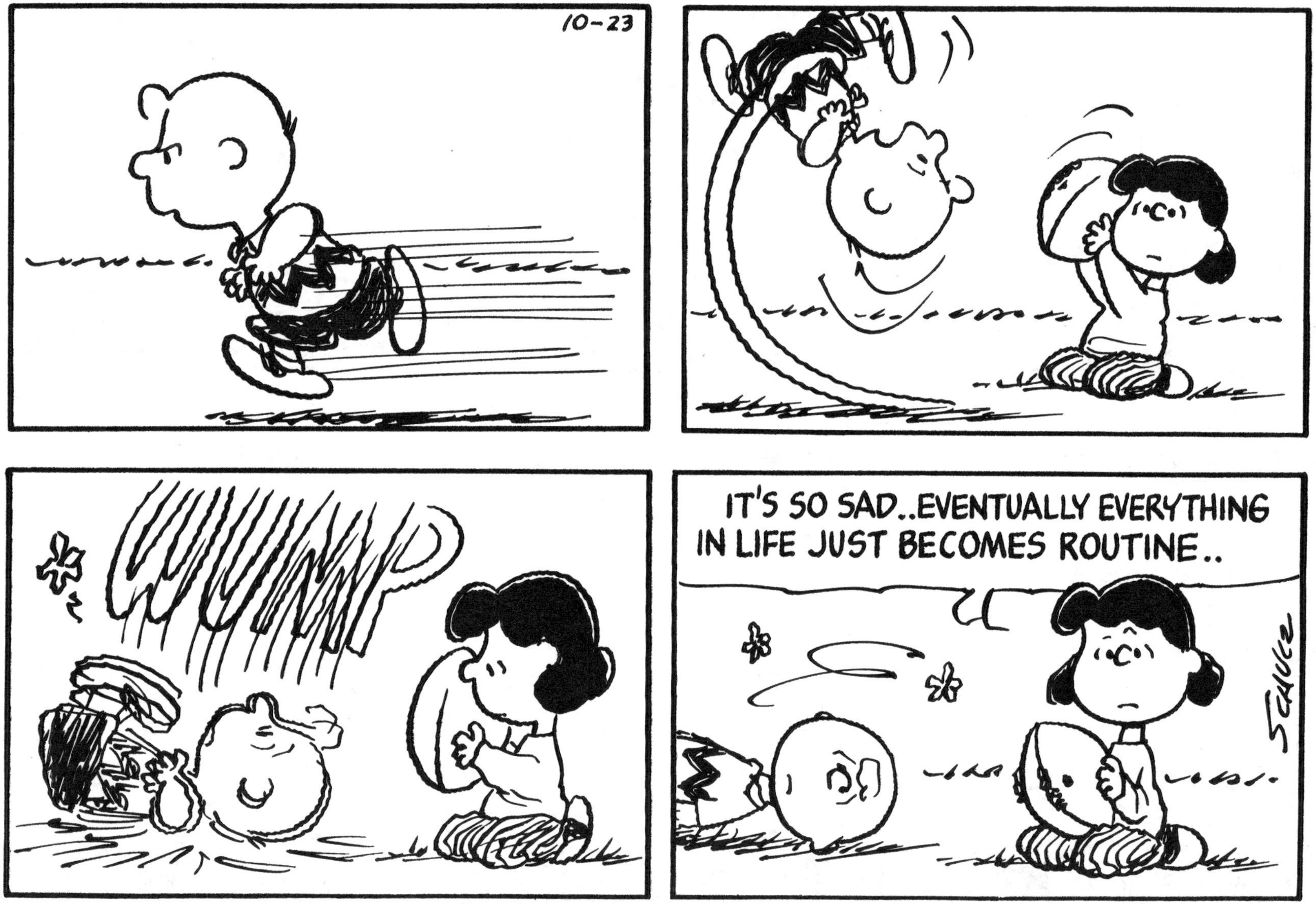
10-23
WUMP
IT'S SO SAD..EVENTUALLY EVERYTHING IN LIFE JUST BECOMES ROUTINE..
SCHULZ

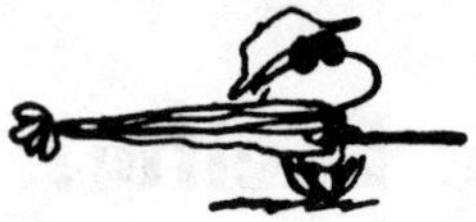

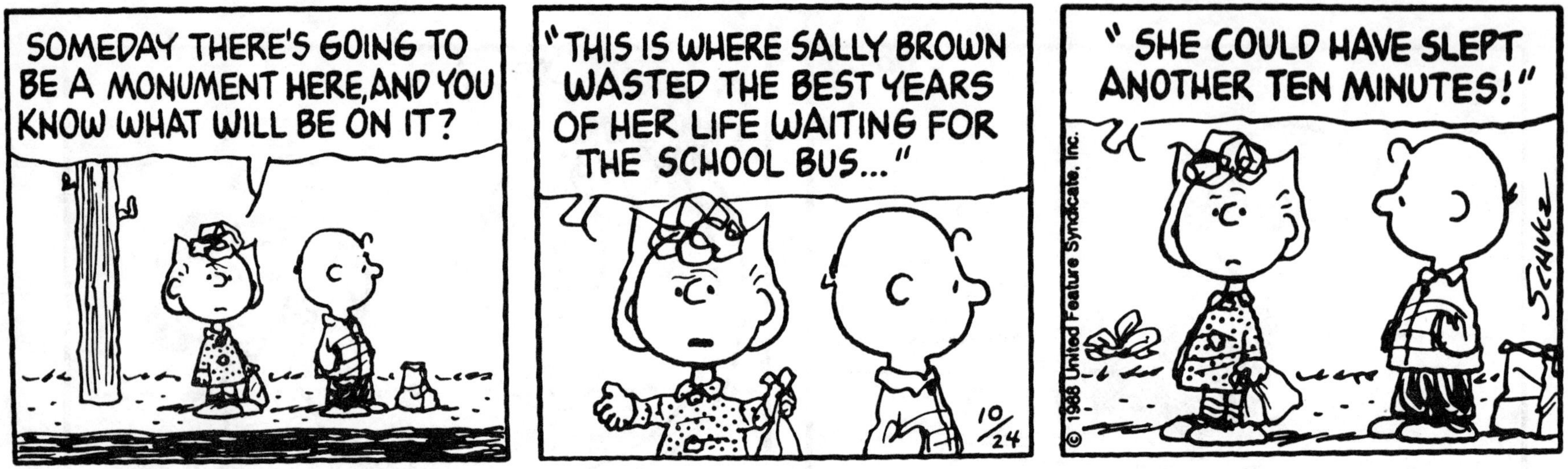

SOMEDAY THERE'S GOING TO BE A MONUMENT HERE, AND YOU KNOW WHAT WILL BE ON IT?
"THIS IS WHERE SALLY BROWN WASTED THE BEST YEARS OF HER LIFE WAITING FOR THE SCHOOL BUS..."
10/24
"SHE COULD HAVE SLEPT ANOTHER TEN MINUTES!"
© 1988 United Feature Syndicate, Inc.
SCHULZ

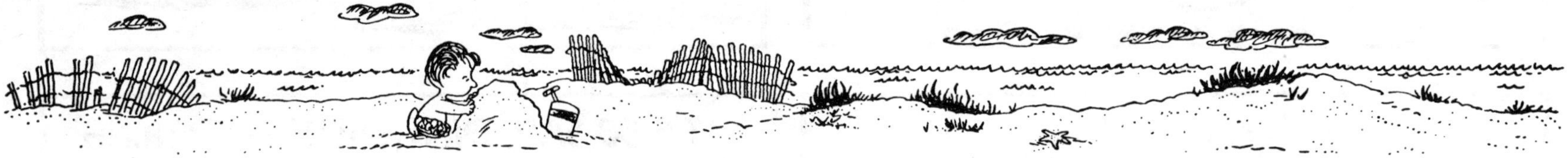

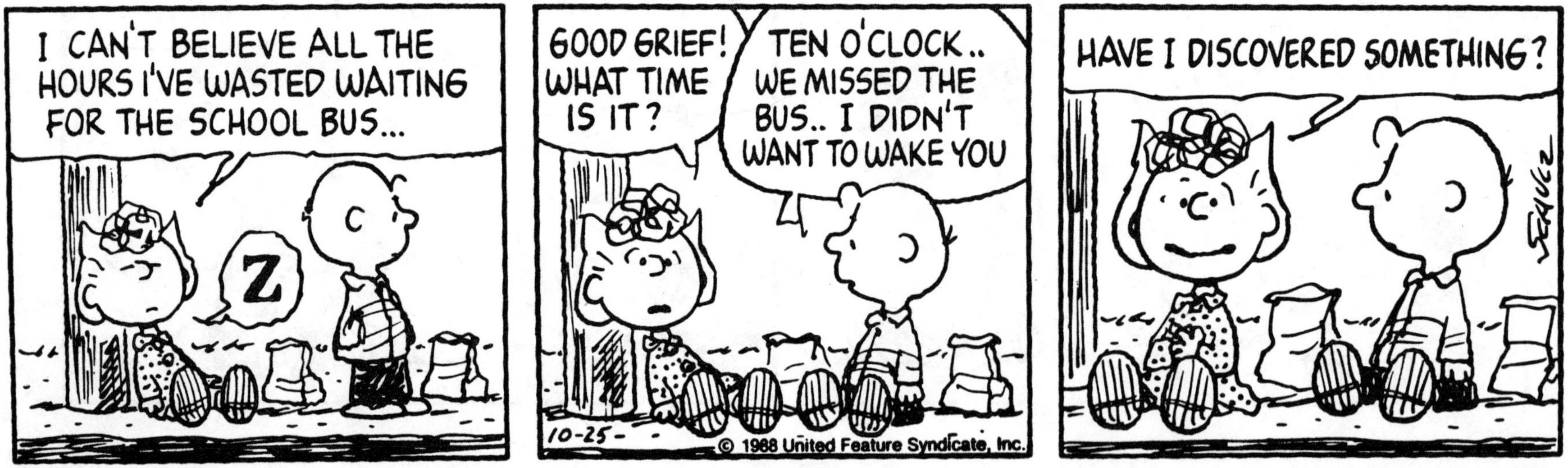

I CAN'T BELIEVE ALL THE HOURS I'VE WASTED WAITING FOR THE SCHOOL BUS...
Z
GOOD GRIEF! WHAT TIME IS IT?
TEN O'CLOCK.. WE MISSED THE BUS.. I DIDN'T WANT TO WAKE YOU
10-25
© 1988 United Feature Syndicate, Inc.
HAVE I DISCOVERED SOMETHING?
SCHULZ

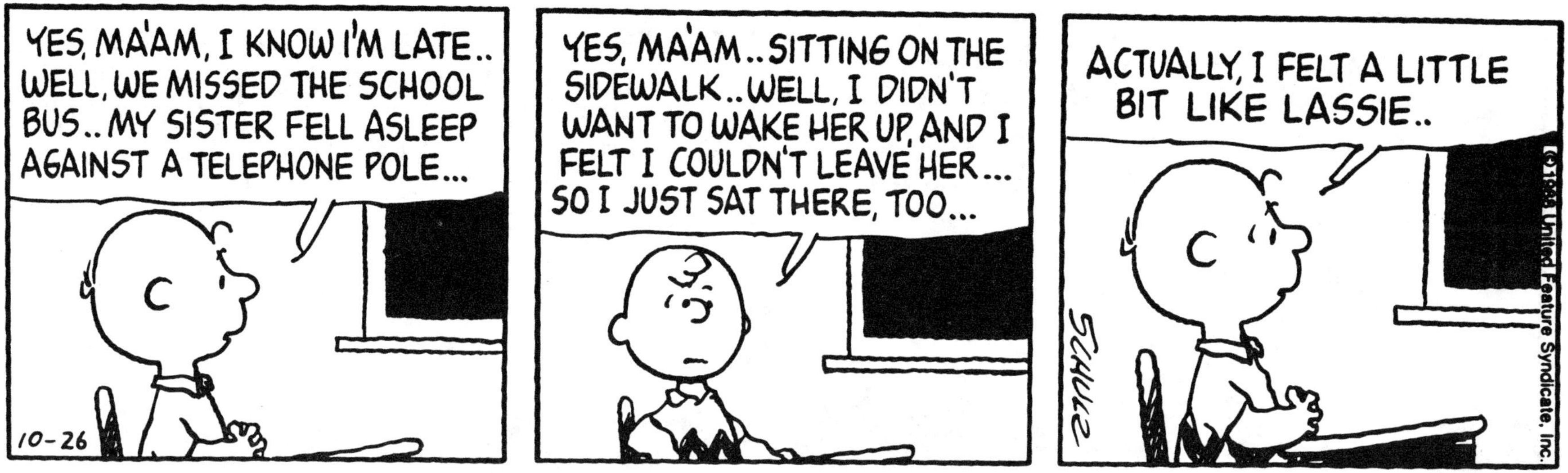
YES, MA'AM, I KNOW I'M LATE.. WELL, WE MISSED THE SCHOOL BUS.. MY SISTER FELL ASLEEP AGAINST A TELEPHONE POLE...
10-26
YES, MA'AM.. SITTING ON THE SIDEWALK.. WELL, I DIDN'T WANT TO WAKE HER UP, AND I FELT I COULDN'T LEAVE HER... SO I JUST SAT THERE, TOO...
ACTUALLY, I FELT A LITTLE BIT LIKE LASSIE..
SCHULZ
© 1988 United Feature Syndicate, Inc.

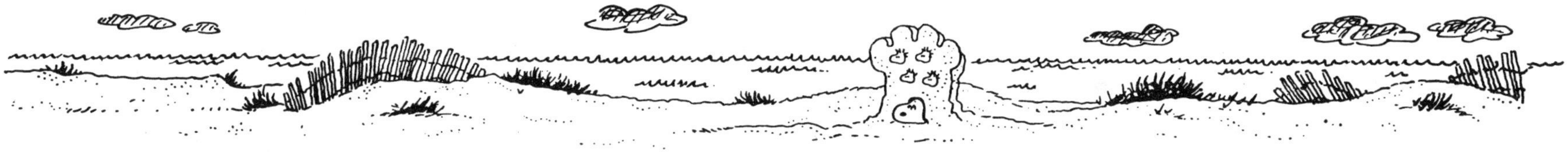

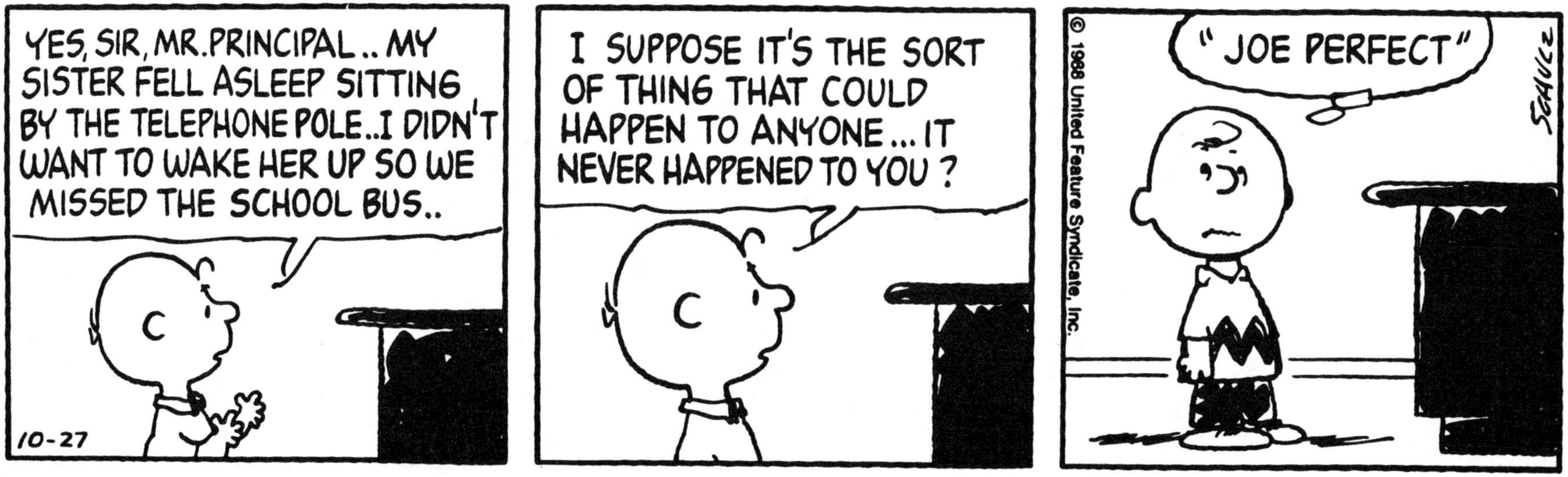
YES, SIR, MR. PRINCIPAL.. MY SISTER FELL ASLEEP SITTING BY THE TELEPHONE POLE..I DIDN'T WANT TO WAKE HER UP SO WE MISSED THE SCHOOL BUS..
10-27
I SUPPOSE IT'S THE SORT OF THING THAT COULD HAPPEN TO ANYONE... IT NEVER HAPPENED TO YOU ?
© 1988 United Feature Syndicate, Inc.
"JOE PERFECT"
SCHULZ

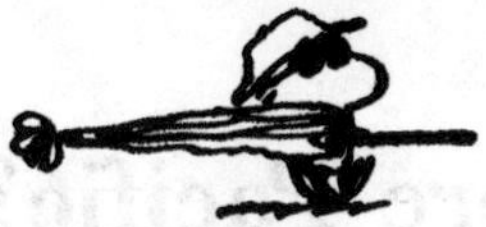

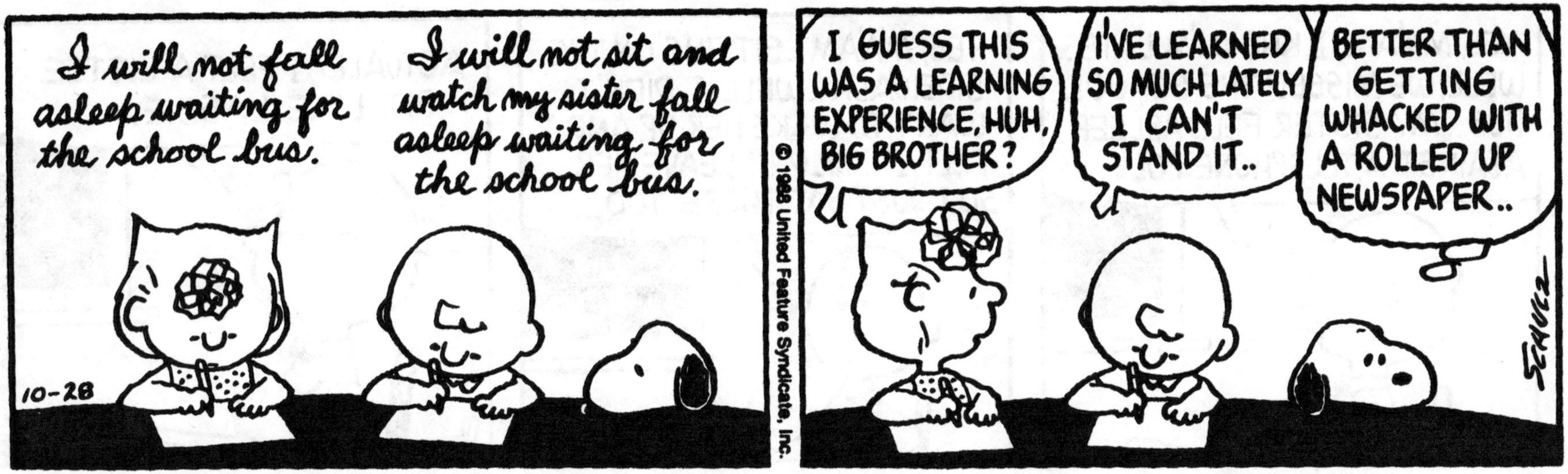
I will not fall asleep waiting for the school bus.
I will not sit and watch my sister fall asleep waiting for the school bus.
10-28
© 1988 United Feature Syndicate, Inc.
I GUESS THIS WAS A LEARNING EXPERIENCE, HUH, BIG BROTHER?
I'VE LEARNED SO MUCH LATELY I CAN'T STAND IT..
BETTER THAN GETTING WHACKED WITH A ROLLED UP NEWSPAPER..
SCHULZ

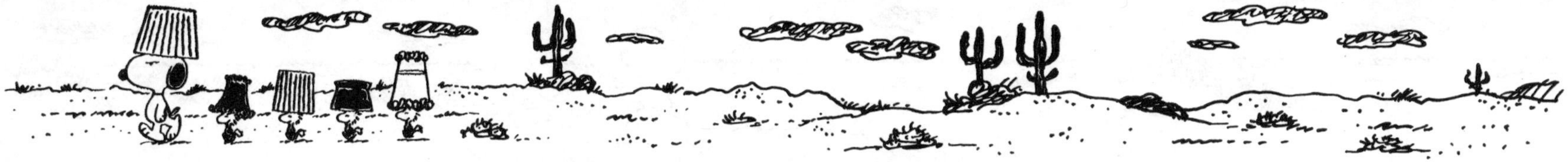

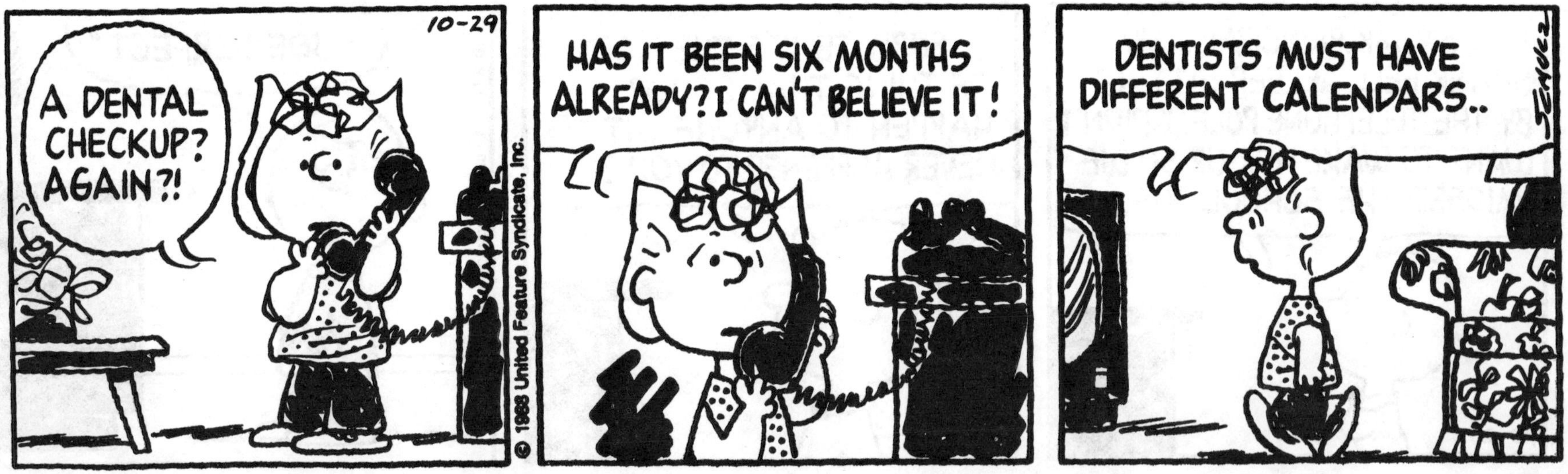
10-29
A DENTAL CHECKUP? AGAIN?!
© 1988 United Feature Syndicate, Inc.
HAS IT BEEN SIX MONTHS ALREADY? I CAN'T BELIEVE IT!
DENTISTS MUST HAVE DIFFERENT CALENDARS..
SCHULZ

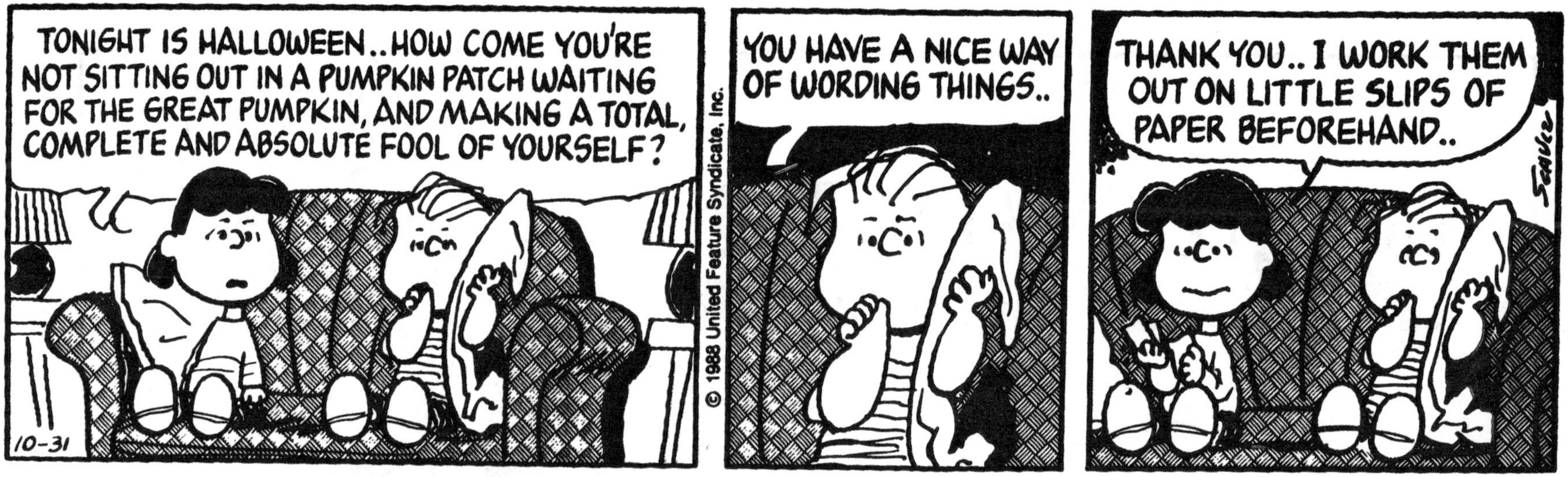
TONIGHT IS HALLOWEEN..HOW COME YOU'RE NOT SITTING OUT IN A PUMPKIN PATCH WAITING FOR THE GREAT PUMPKIN, AND MAKING A TOTAL, COMPLETE AND ABSOLUTE FOOL OF YOURSELF?
10-31
© 1988 United Feature Syndicate, Inc.
YOU HAVE A NICE WAY OF WORDING THINGS..
THANK YOU.. I WORK THEM OUT ON LITTLE SLIPS OF PAPER BEFOREHAND..
SCHULZ

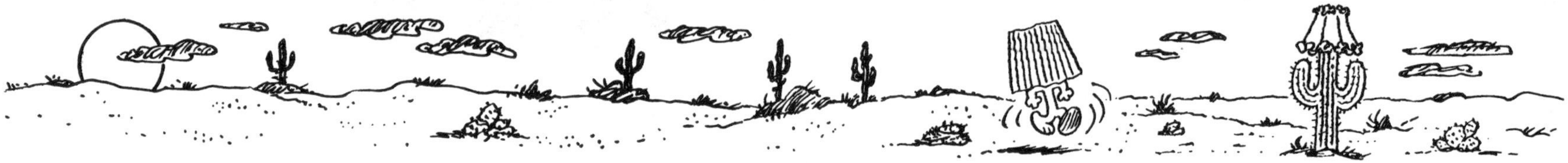

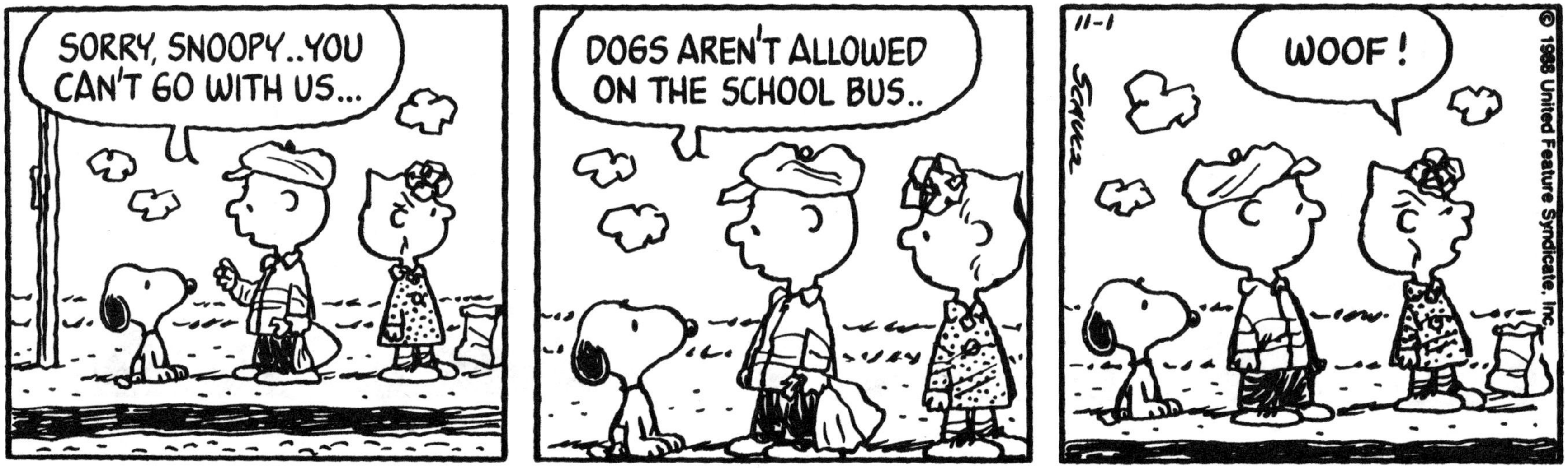
SORRY, SNOOPY..YOU CAN'T GO WITH US...
DOGS AREN'T ALLOWED ON THE SCHOOL BUS..
11-1
SCHULZ
WOOF!
© 1988 United Feature Syndicate, Inc.

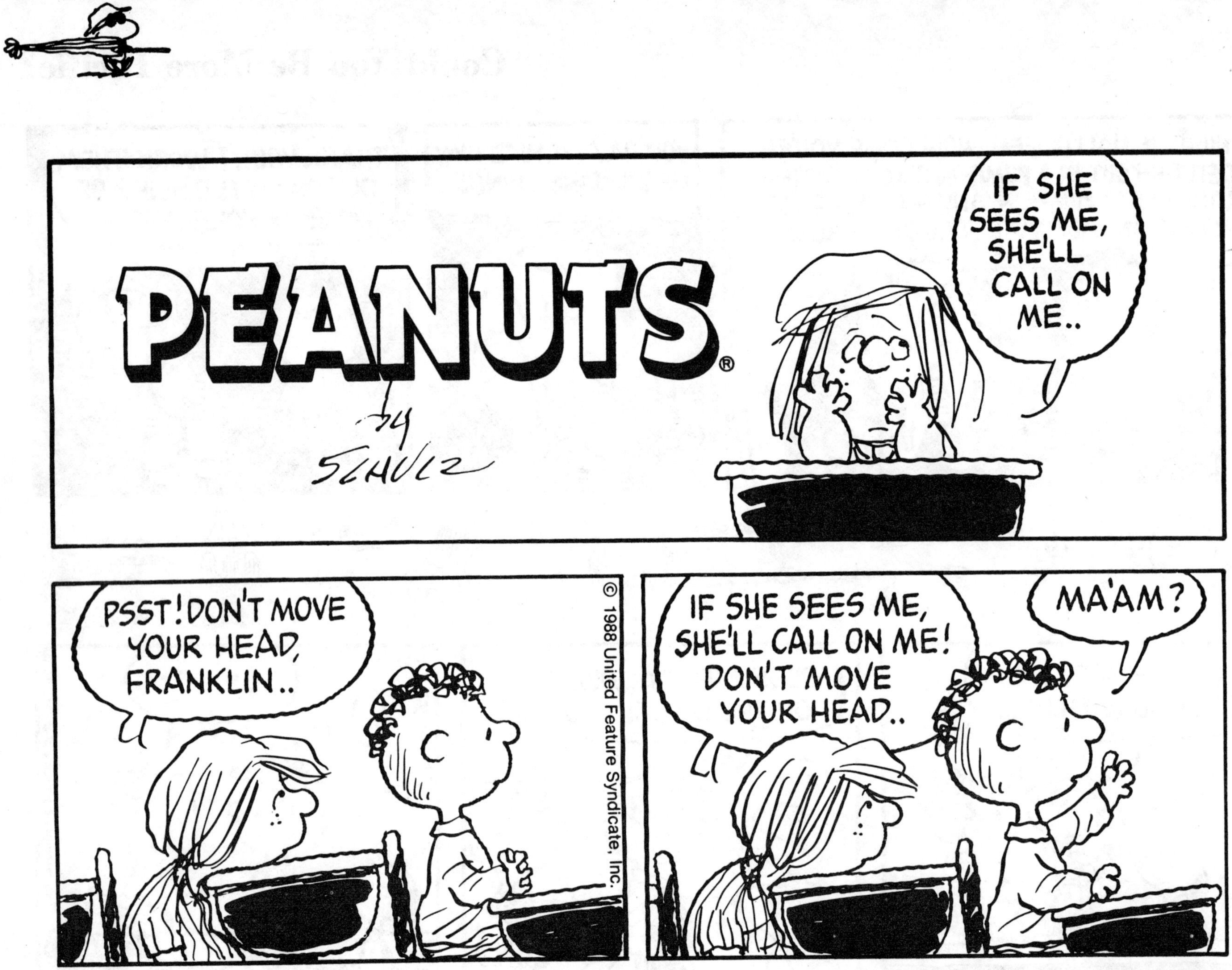
PEANUTS®
by SCHULZ
IF SHE SEES ME, SHE'LL CALL ON ME..
PSST! DON'T MOVE YOUR HEAD, FRANKLIN..
© 1988 United Feature Syndicate, Inc.
IF SHE SEES ME, SHE'LL CALL ON ME! DON'T MOVE YOUR HEAD..
MA'AM?

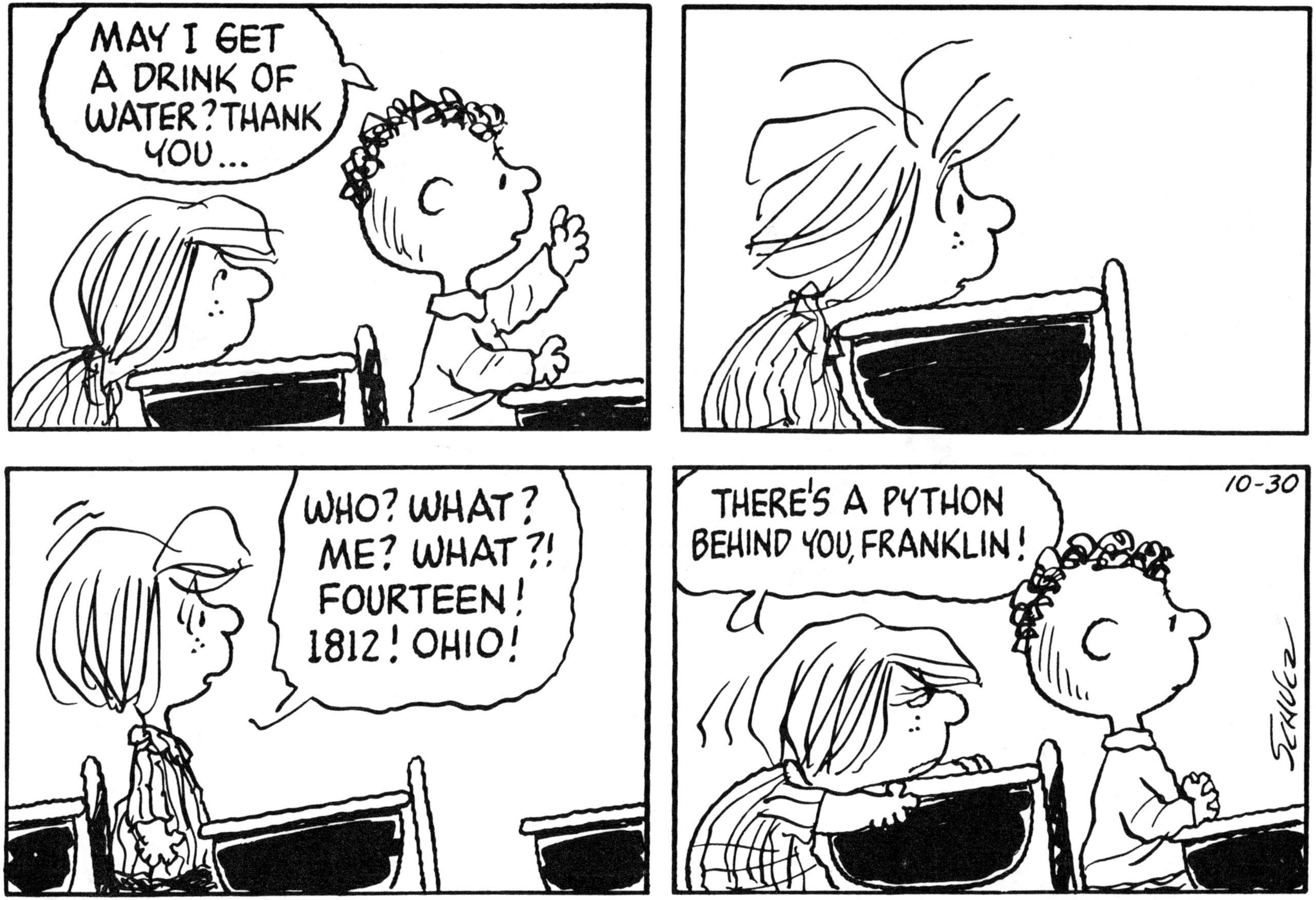
MAY I GET A DRINK OF WATER? THANK YOU...
WHO? WHAT? ME? WHAT?! FOURTEEN! 1812! OHIO!
10-30
THERE'S A PYTHON BEHIND YOU, FRANKLIN!
SCHULZ

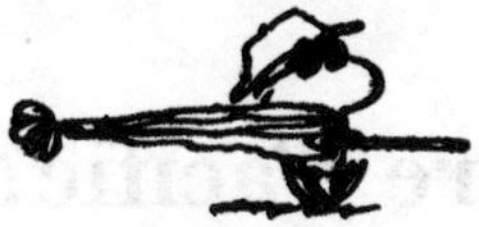

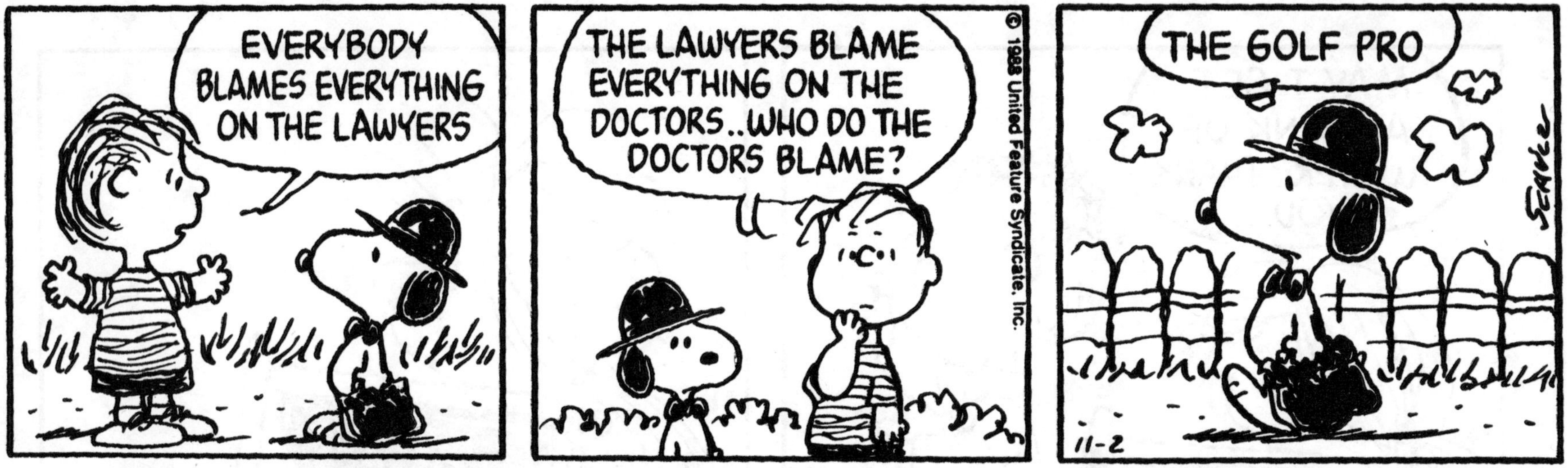
EVERYBODY BLAMES EVERYTHING ON THE LAWYERS
THE LAWYERS BLAME EVERYTHING ON THE DOCTORS..WHO DO THE DOCTORS BLAME?
© 1988 United Feature Syndicate, Inc.
THE GOLF PRO
11-2

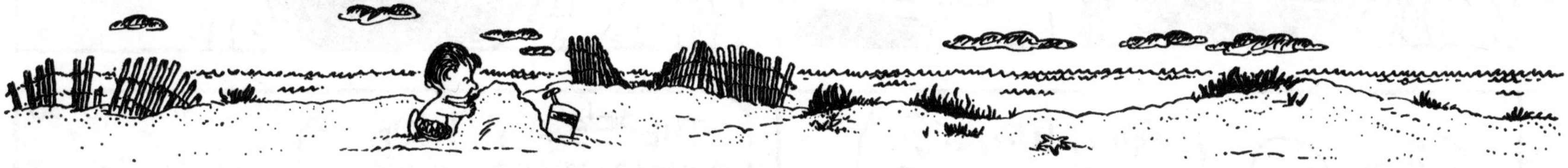

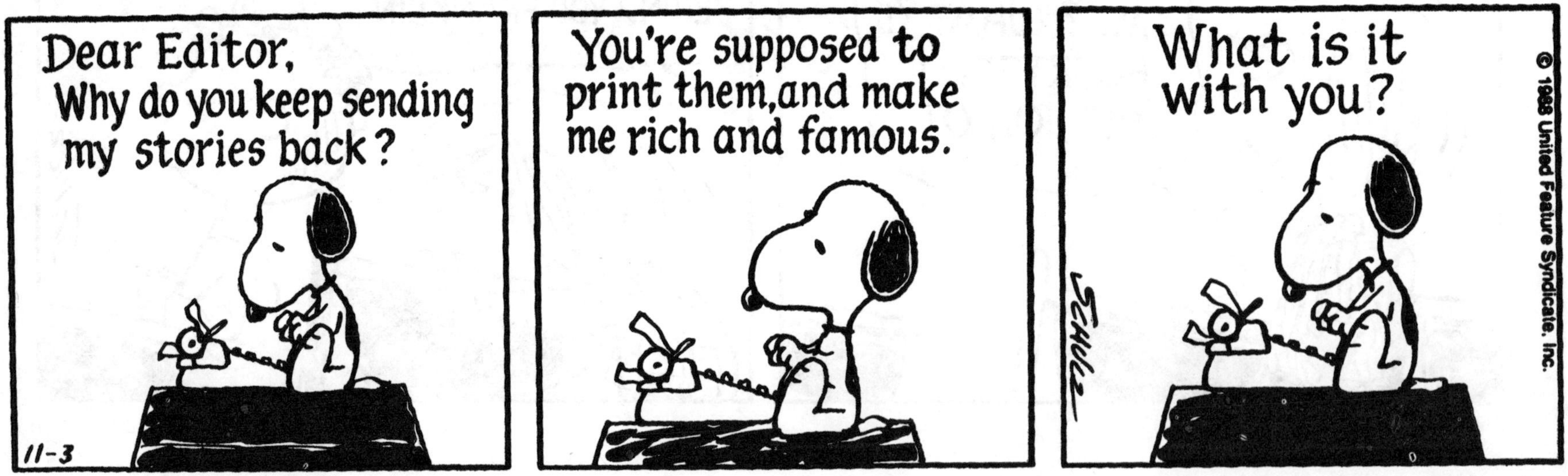
Dear Editor,
Why do you keep sending my stories back?
11-3
You're supposed to print them,and make me rich and famous.
What is it with you?
© 1988 United Feature Syndicate, Inc.

Could You Be More Pacific?

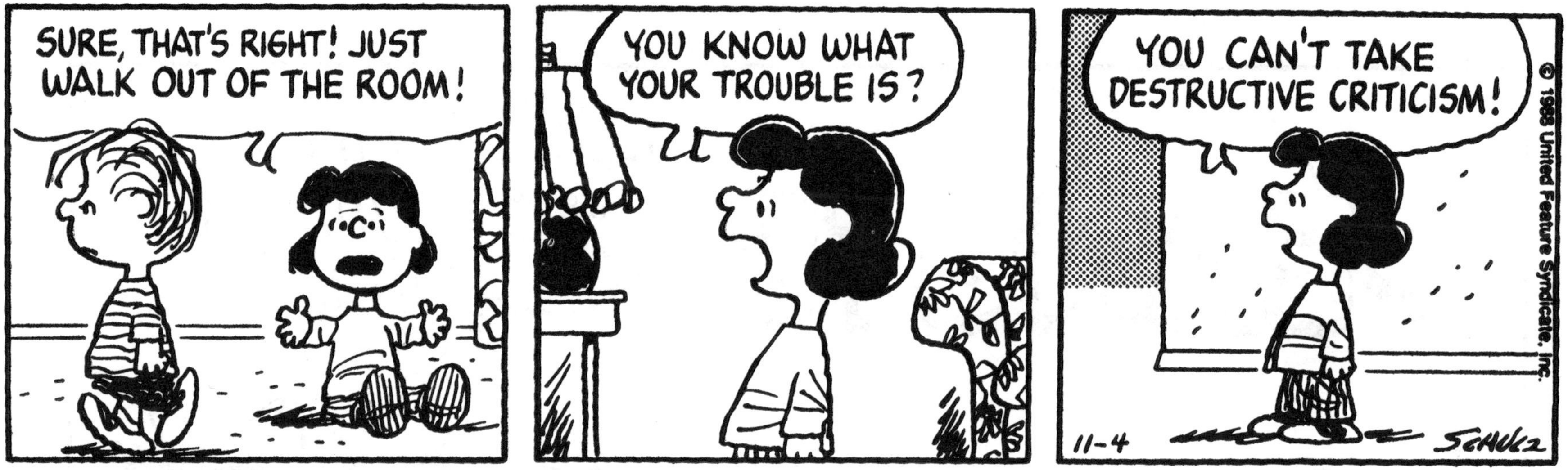
SURE, THAT'S RIGHT! JUST WALK OUT OF THE ROOM!
YOU KNOW WHAT YOUR TROUBLE IS?
YOU CAN'T TAKE DESTRUCTIVE CRITICISM!
© 1988 United Feature Syndicate, Inc.
11-4

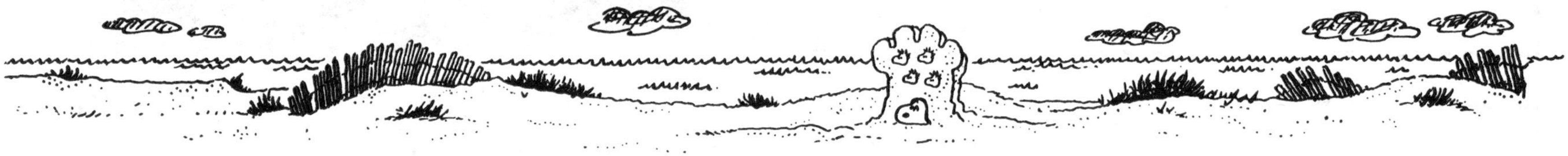

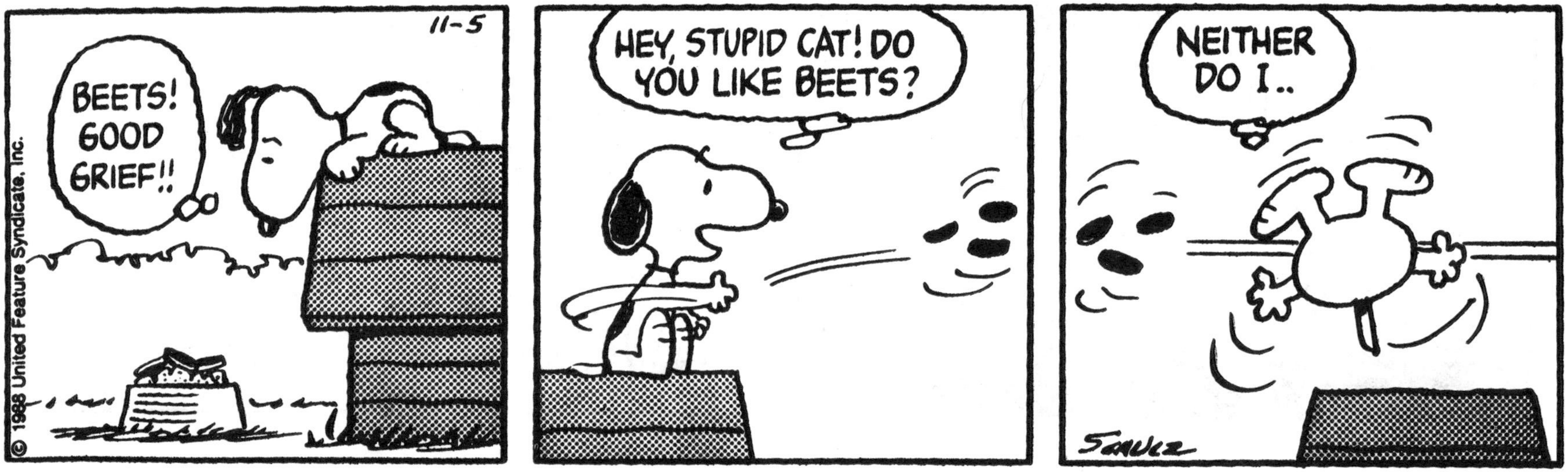
11-5
BEETS! GOOD GRIEF!!
HEY, STUPID CAT! DO YOU LIKE BEETS?
NEITHER DO I..
© 1988 United Feature Syndicate, Inc.

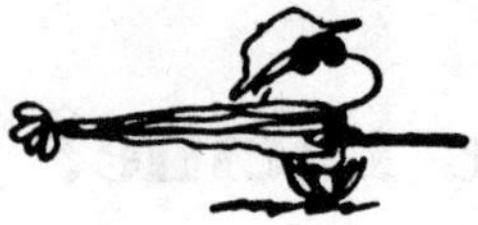

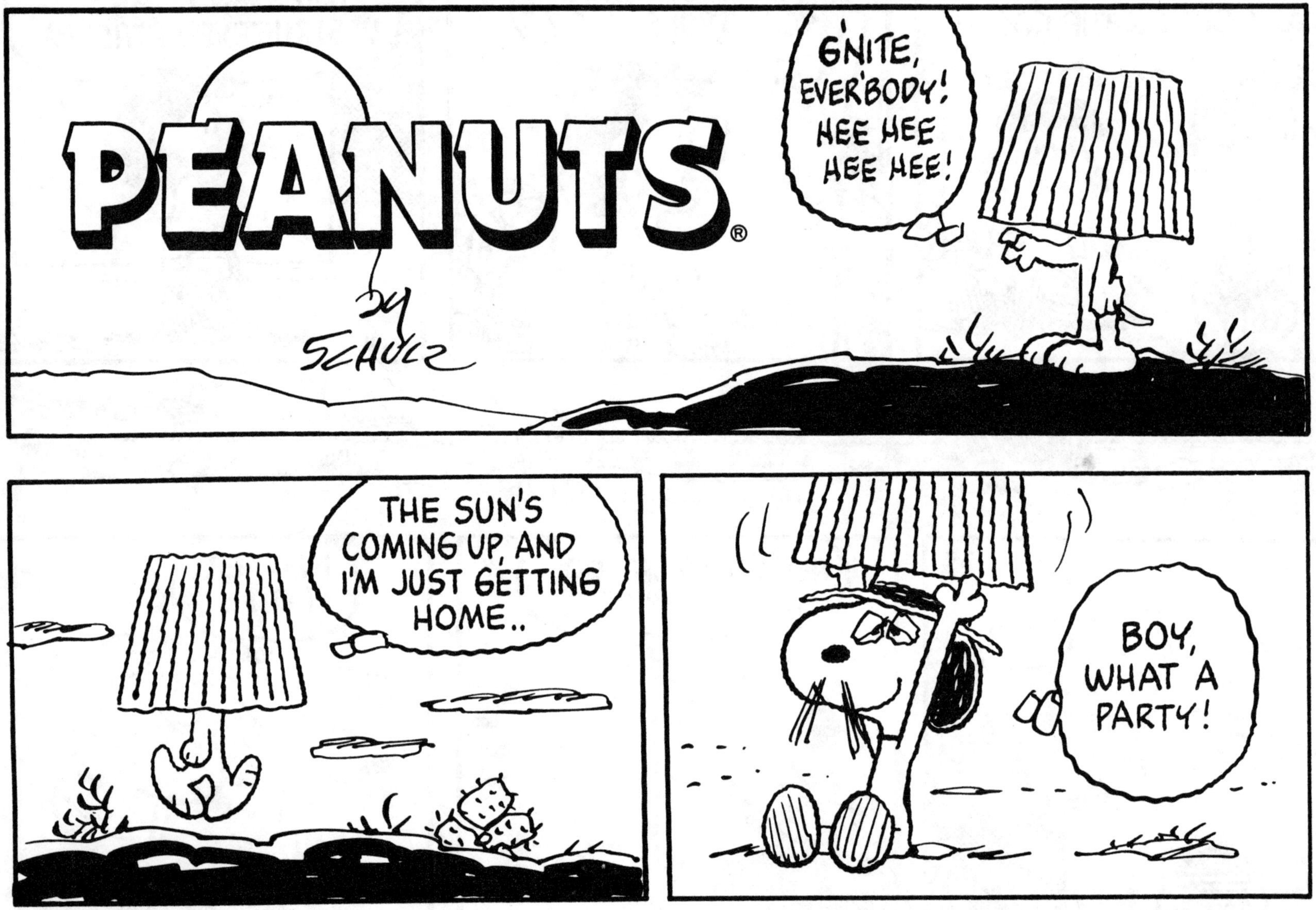
PEANUTS®
by SCHULZ
G'NITE, EVERBODY! HEE HEE HEE HEE!
THE SUN'S COMING UP, AND I'M JUST GETTING HOME..
BOY, WHAT A PARTY!

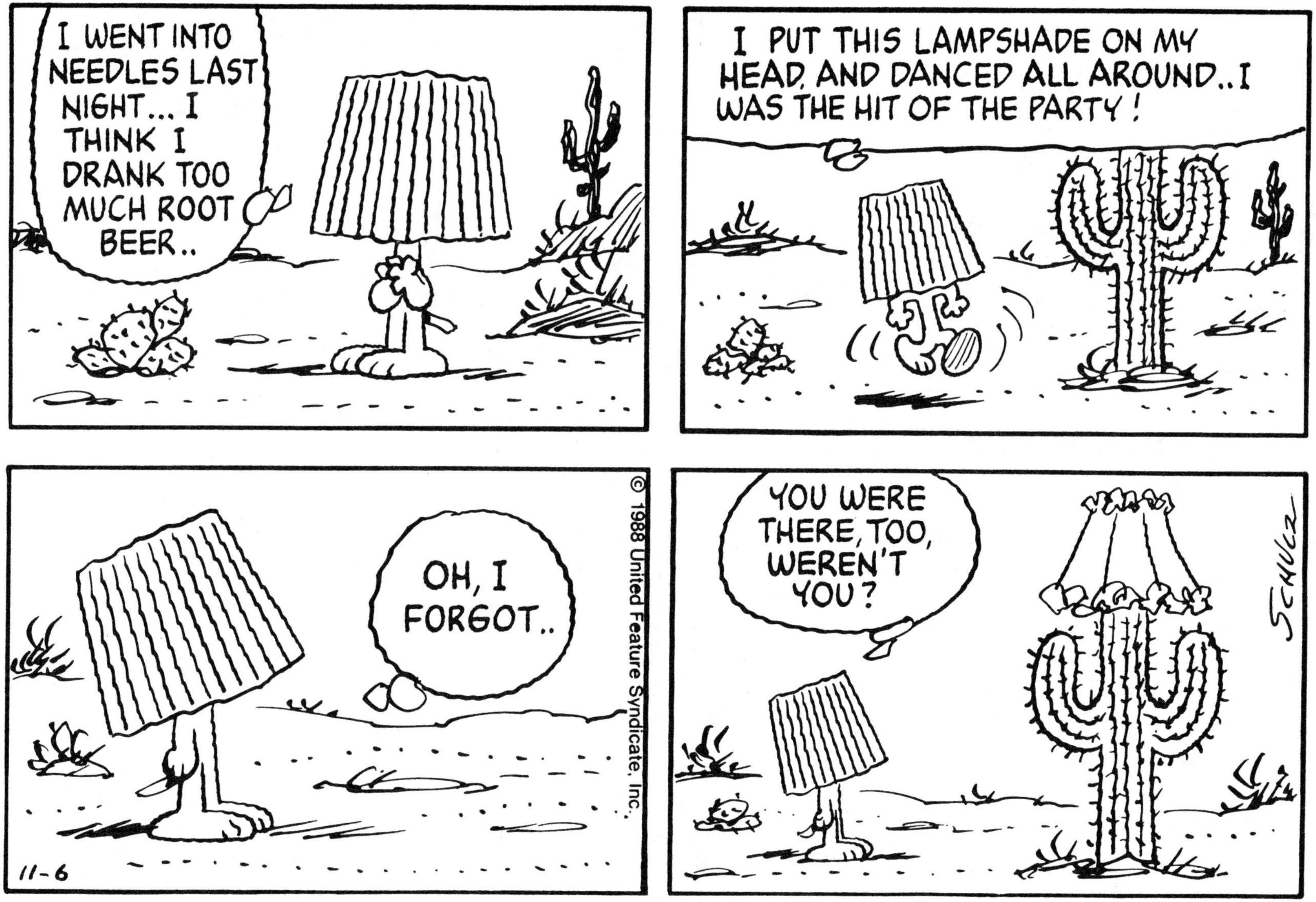
I WENT INTO NEEDLES LAST NIGHT... I THINK I DRANK TOO MUCH ROOT BEER..
I PUT THIS LAMPSHADE ON MY HEAD, AND DANCED ALL AROUND..I WAS THE HIT OF THE PARTY!
OH, I FORGOT..
© 1988 United Feature Syndicate, Inc.
11-6
YOU WERE THERE, TOO, WEREN'T YOU?
SCHULZ

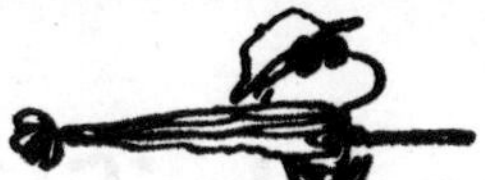

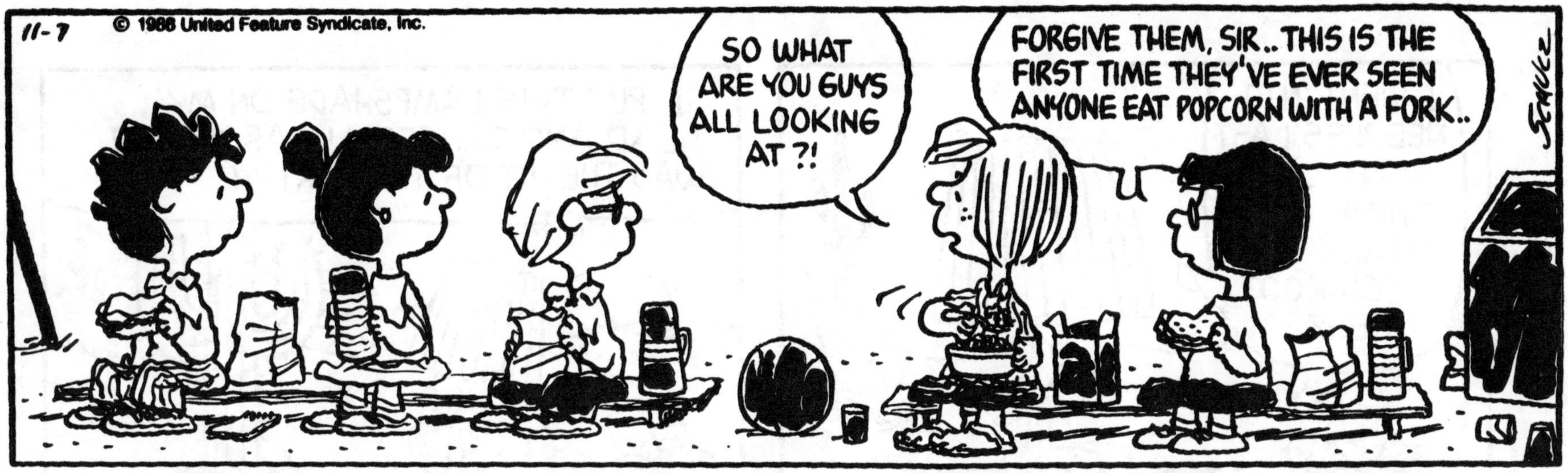
11-7
© 1988 United Feature Syndicate, Inc.
SO WHAT ARE YOU GUYS ALL LOOKING AT ?!
FORGIVE THEM, SIR.. THIS IS THE FIRST TIME THEY'VE EVER SEEN ANYONE EAT POPCORN WITH A FORK..
SCHULZ

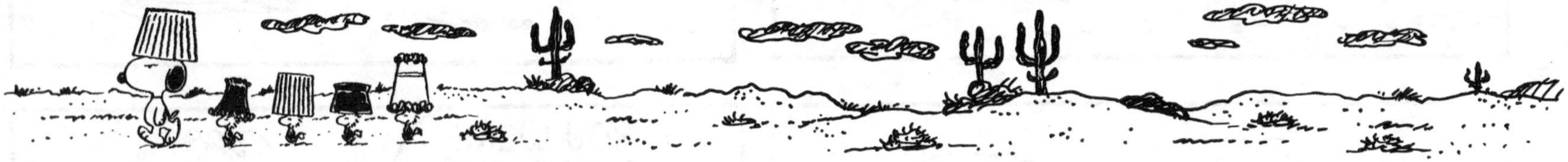

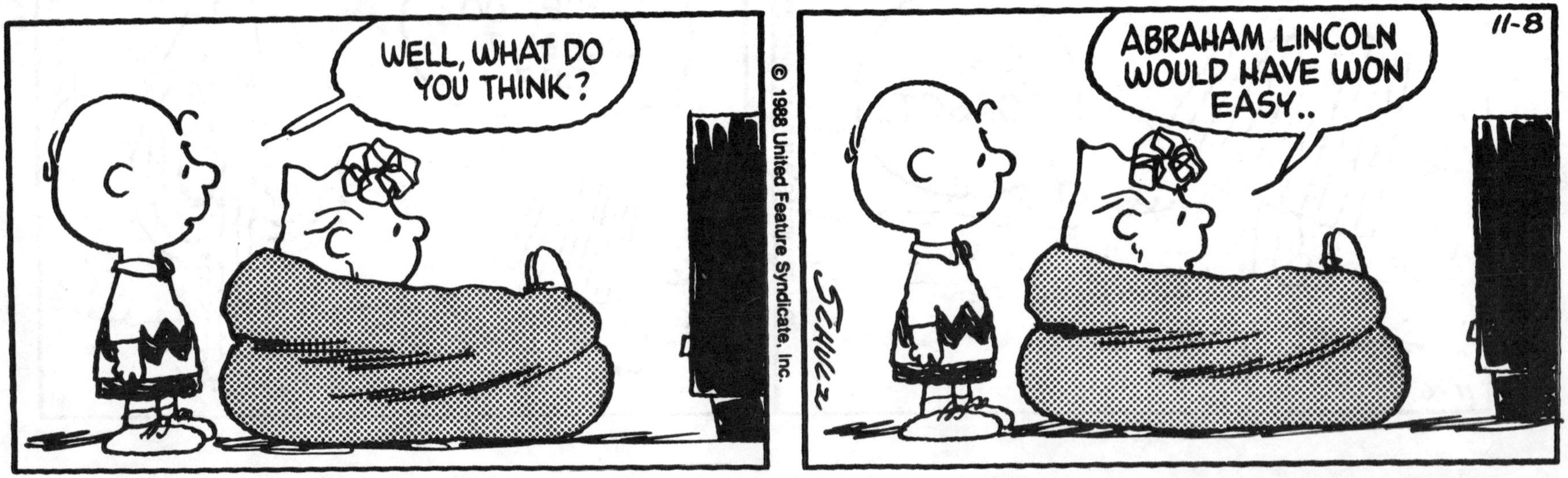
WELL, WHAT DO YOU THINK ?
© 1988 United Feature Syndicate, Inc.
SCHULZ
11-8
ABRAHAM LINCOLN WOULD HAVE WON EASY..

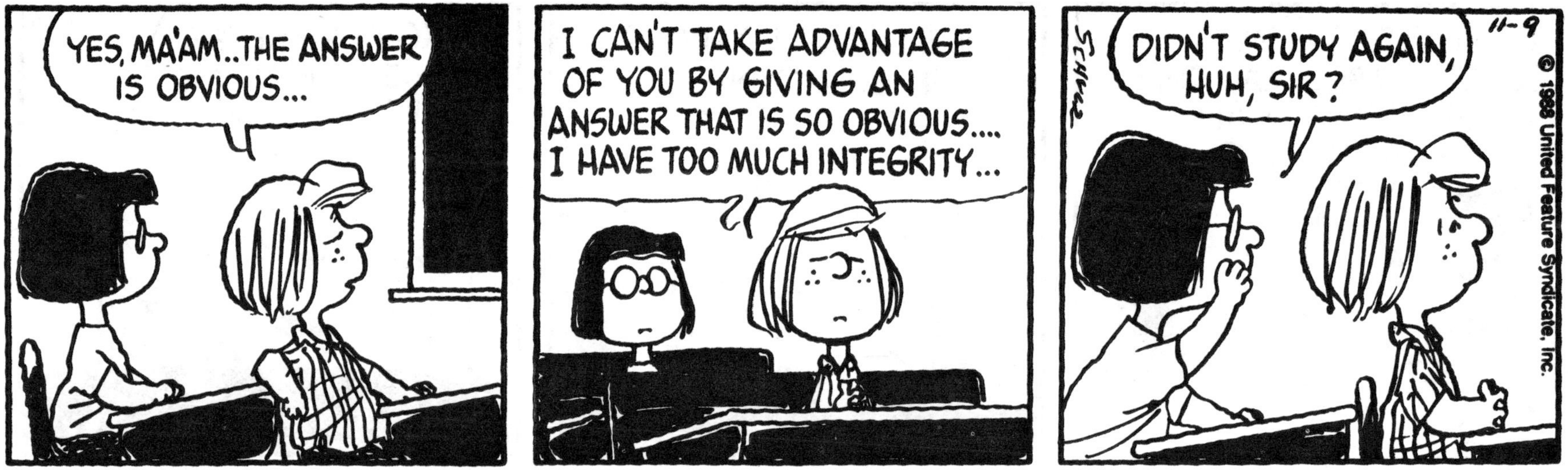
YES, MA'AM..THE ANSWER IS OBVIOUS...
I CAN'T TAKE ADVANTAGE OF YOU BY GIVING AN ANSWER THAT IS SO OBVIOUS.... I HAVE TOO MUCH INTEGRITY...
11-9
© 1988 United Feature Syndicate, Inc.
DIDN'T STUDY AGAIN, HUH, SIR?

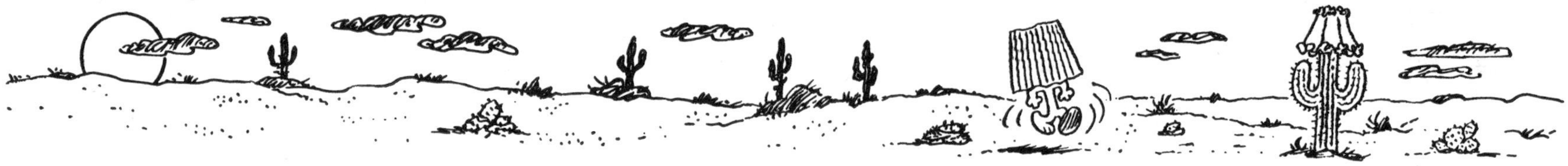

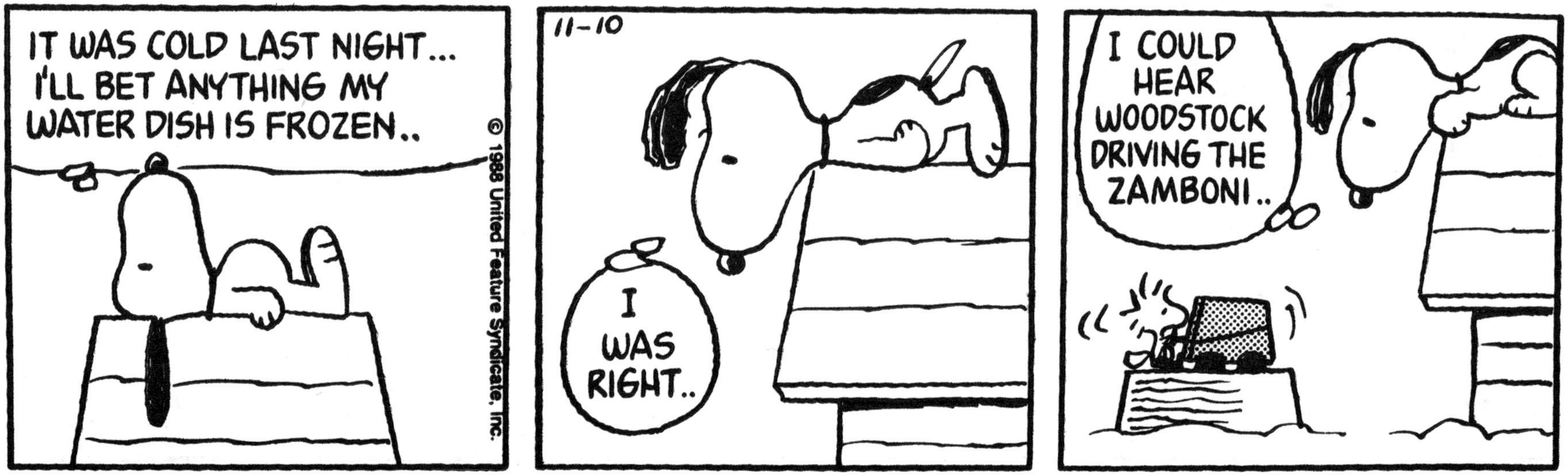
IT WAS COLD LAST NIGHT... I'LL BET ANYTHING MY WATER DISH IS FROZEN..
© 1988 United Feature Syndicate, Inc.
11-10
I WAS RIGHT..
I COULD HEAR WOODSTOCK DRIVING THE ZAMBONI..

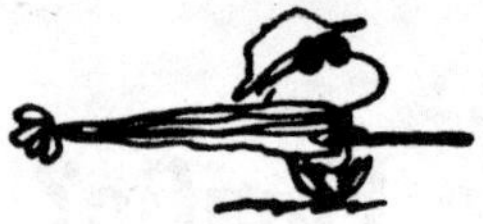

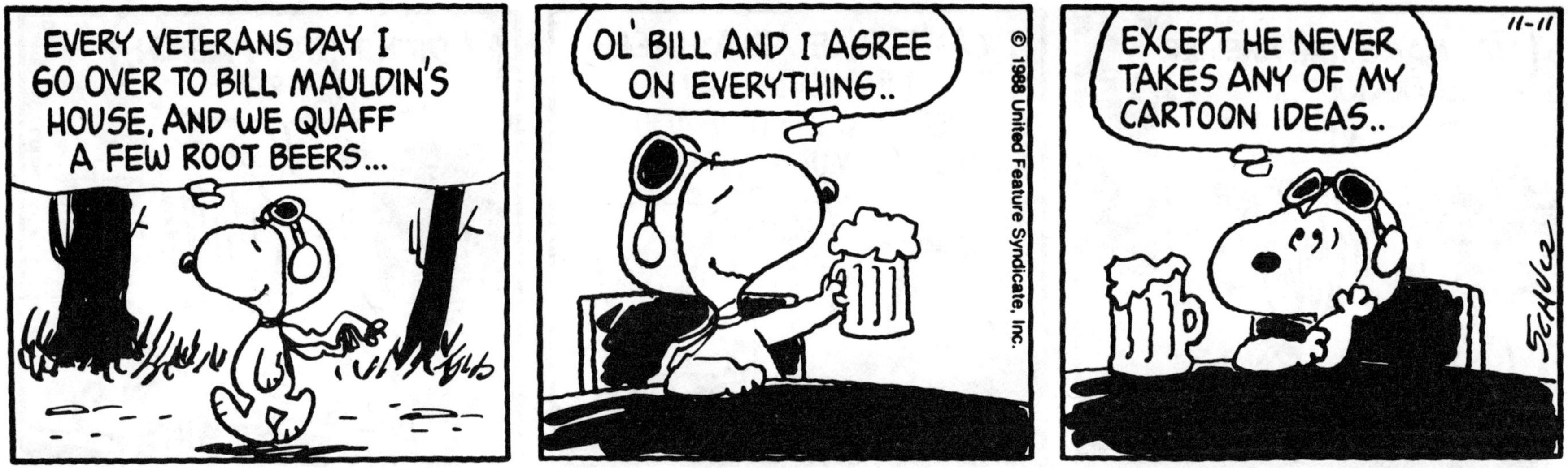
EVERY VETERANS DAY I GO OVER TO BILL MAULDIN'S HOUSE, AND WE QUAFF A FEW ROOT BEERS...
OL' BILL AND I AGREE ON EVERYTHING..
© 1988 United Feature Syndicate, Inc.
11-11
EXCEPT HE NEVER TAKES ANY OF MY CARTOON IDEAS..
SCHULZ

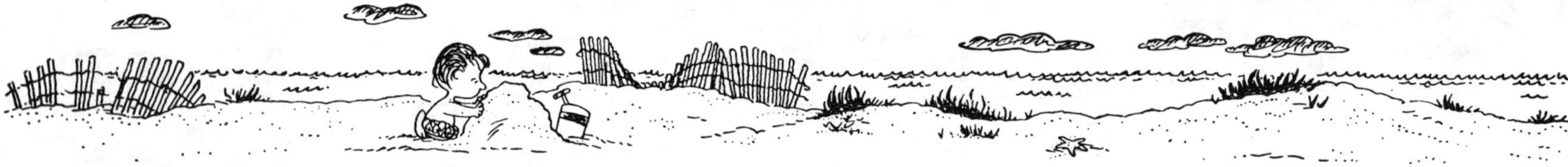

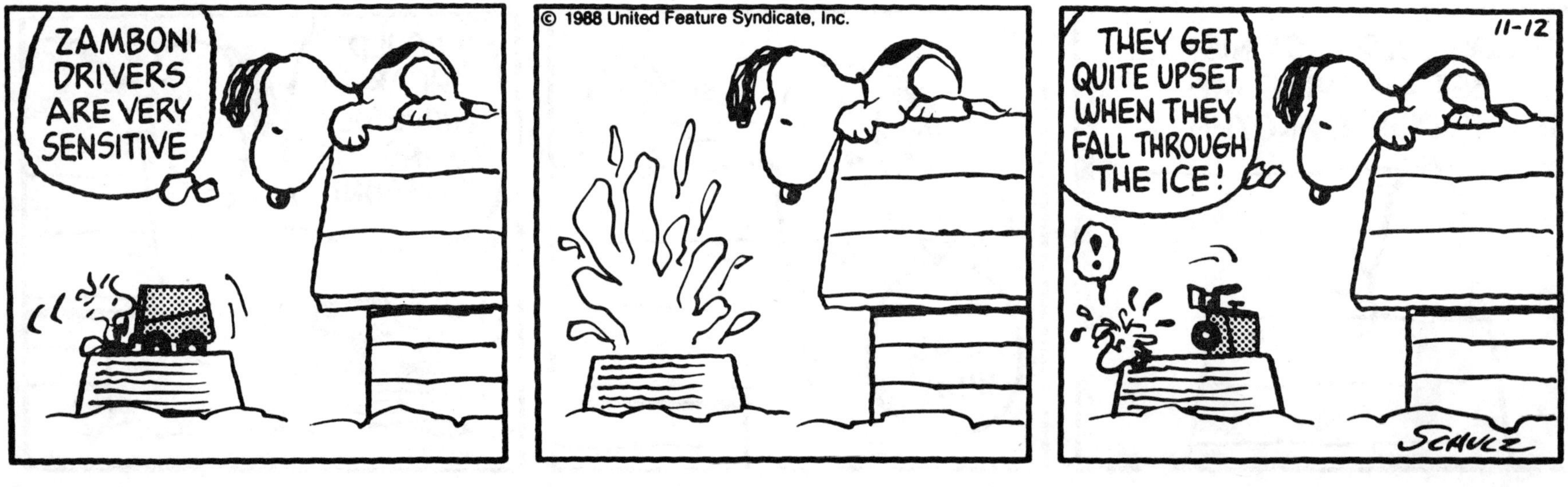
ZAMBONI DRIVERS ARE VERY SENSITIVE
© 1988 United Feature Syndicate, Inc.
11-12
THEY GET QUITE UPSET WHEN THEY FALL THROUGH THE ICE!
!
SCHULZ

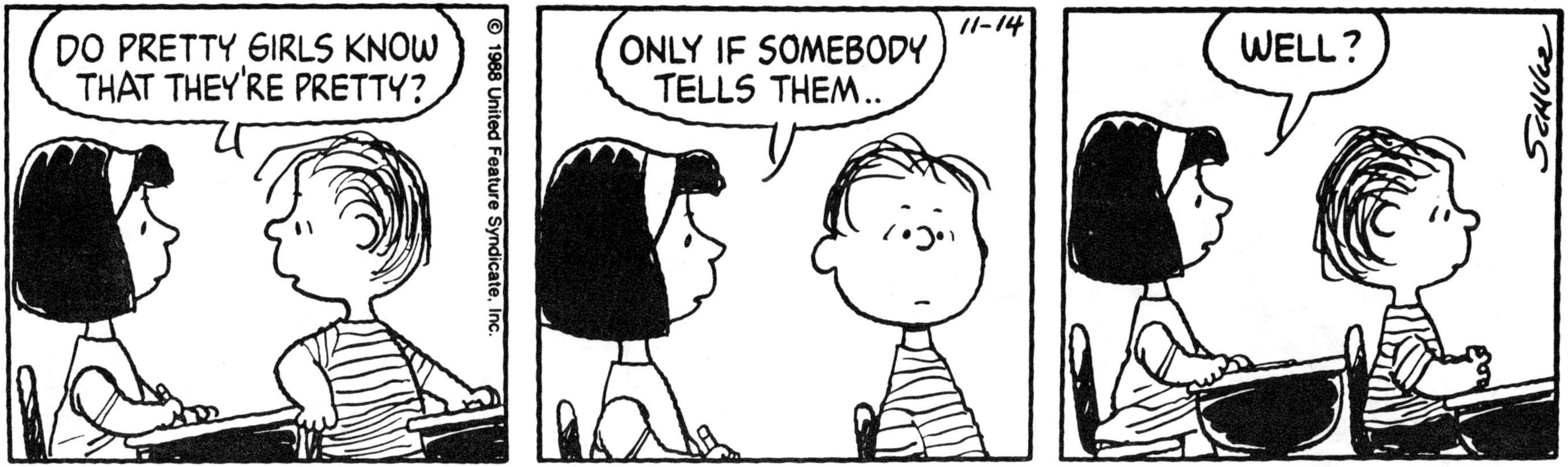
DO PRETTY GIRLS KNOW THAT THEY'RE PRETTY?
© 1988 United Feature Syndicate, Inc.
11-14
ONLY IF SOMEBODY TELLS THEM..
WELL?
SCHULZ

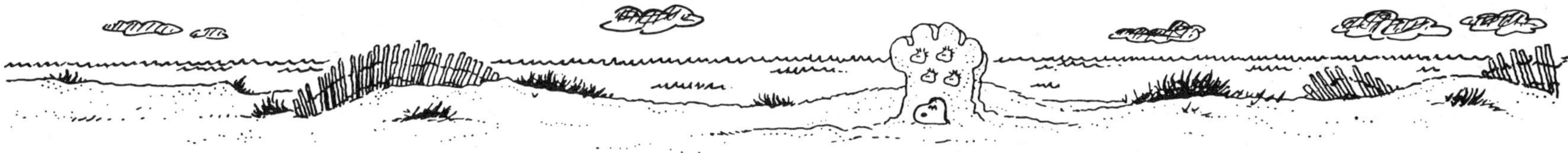

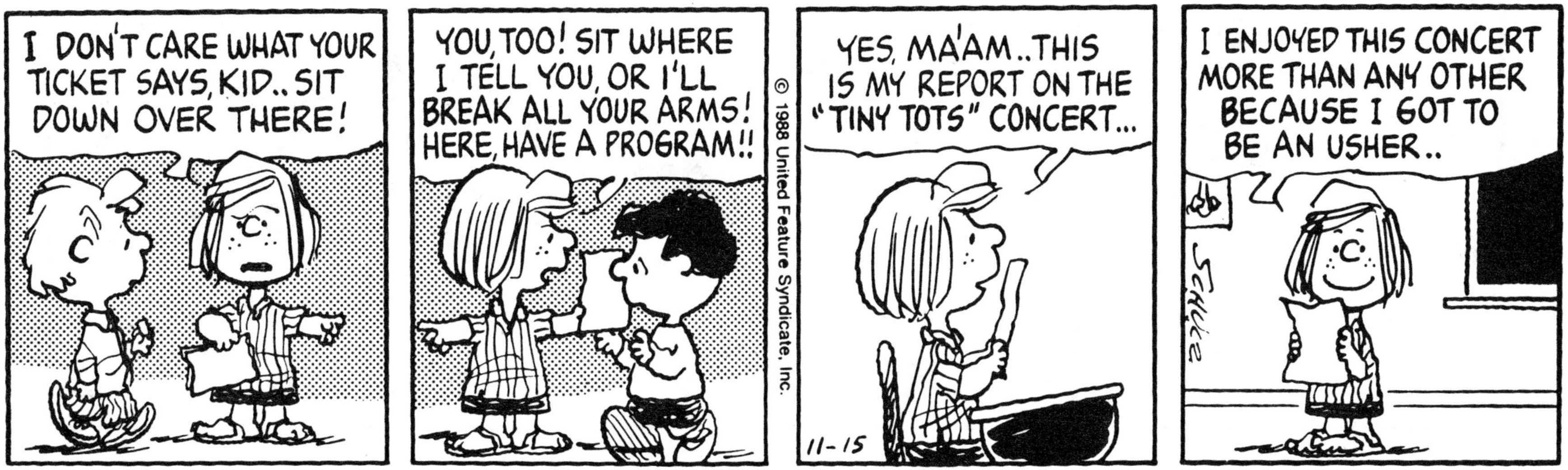
I DON'T CARE WHAT YOUR TICKET SAYS, KID.. SIT DOWN OVER THERE!
YOU, TOO! SIT WHERE I TELL YOU, OR I'LL BREAK ALL YOUR ARMS! HERE, HAVE A PROGRAM!!
© 1988 United Feature Syndicate, Inc.
YES, MA'AM.. THIS IS MY REPORT ON THE "TINY TOTS" CONCERT...
11-15
I ENJOYED THIS CONCERT MORE THAN ANY OTHER BECAUSE I GOT TO BE AN USHER..
SCHULZ

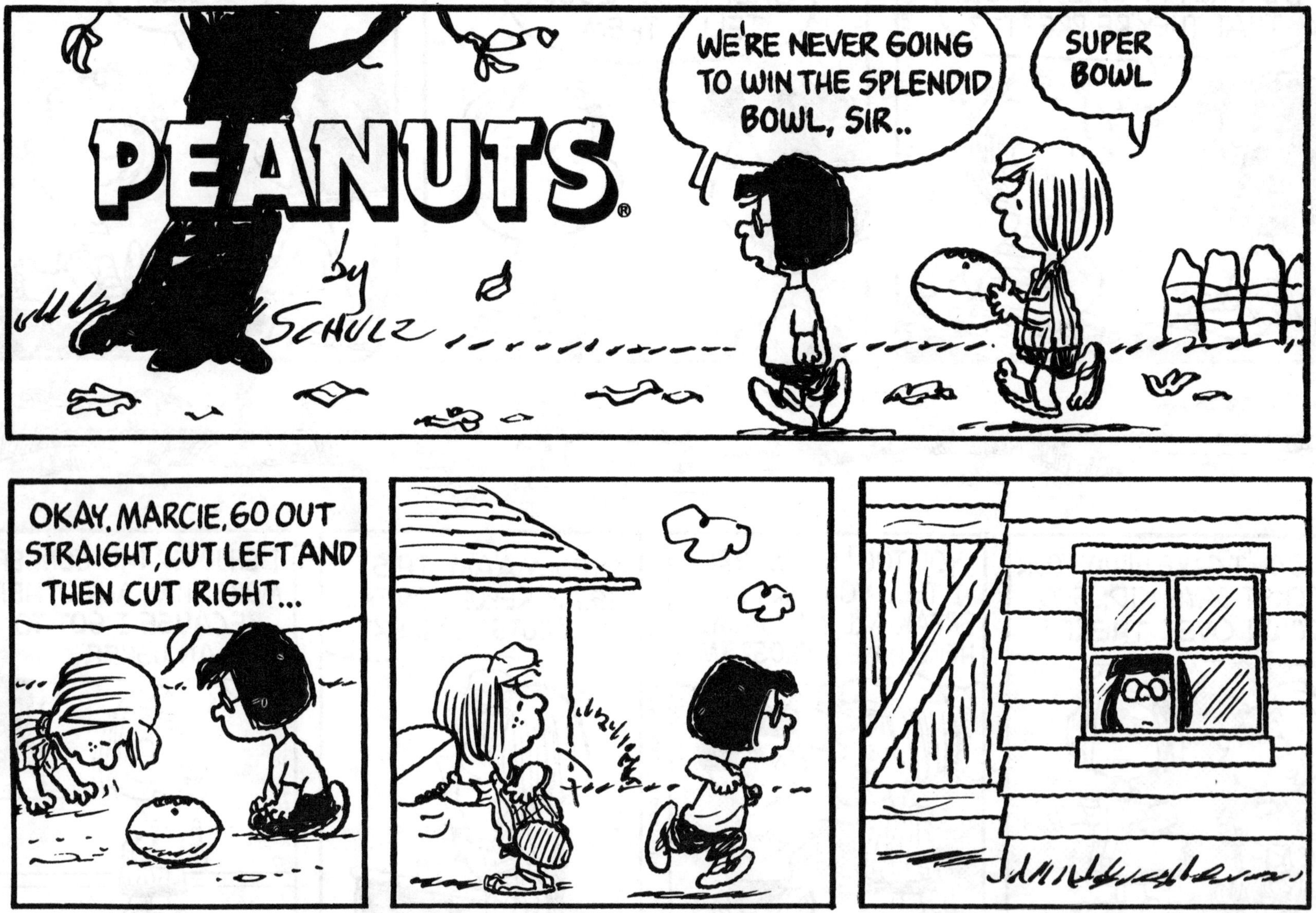
PEANUTS®
by SCHULZ
WE'RE NEVER GOING TO WIN THE SPLENDID BOWL, SIR..
SUPER BOWL
OKAY, MARCIE, GO OUT STRAIGHT, CUT LEFT AND THEN CUT RIGHT...

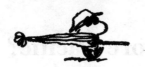

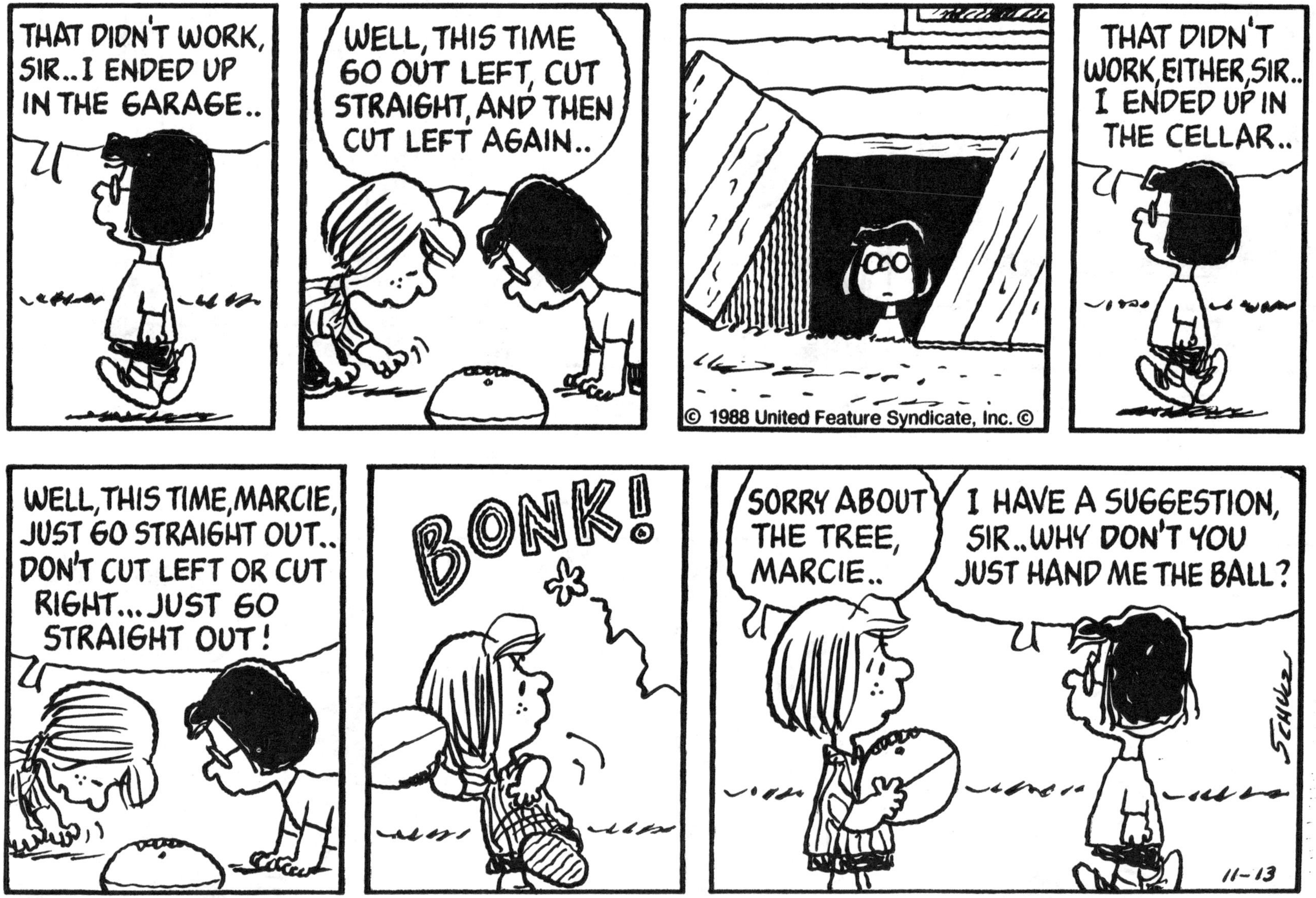
THAT DIDN'T WORK, SIR.. I ENDED UP IN THE GARAGE..
WELL, THIS TIME GO OUT LEFT, CUT STRAIGHT, AND THEN CUT LEFT AGAIN..
© 1988 United Feature Syndicate, Inc. ©
THAT DIDN'T WORK, EITHER, SIR.. I ENDED UP IN THE CELLAR..
WELL, THIS TIME, MARCIE, JUST GO STRAIGHT OUT.. DON'T CUT LEFT OR CUT RIGHT... JUST GO STRAIGHT OUT!
BONK!
SORRY ABOUT THE TREE, MARCIE..
I HAVE A SUGGESTION, SIR.. WHY DON'T YOU JUST HAND ME THE BALL?
SCHULZ
11-13

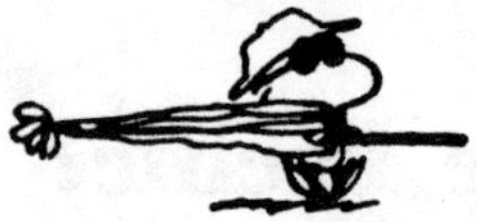

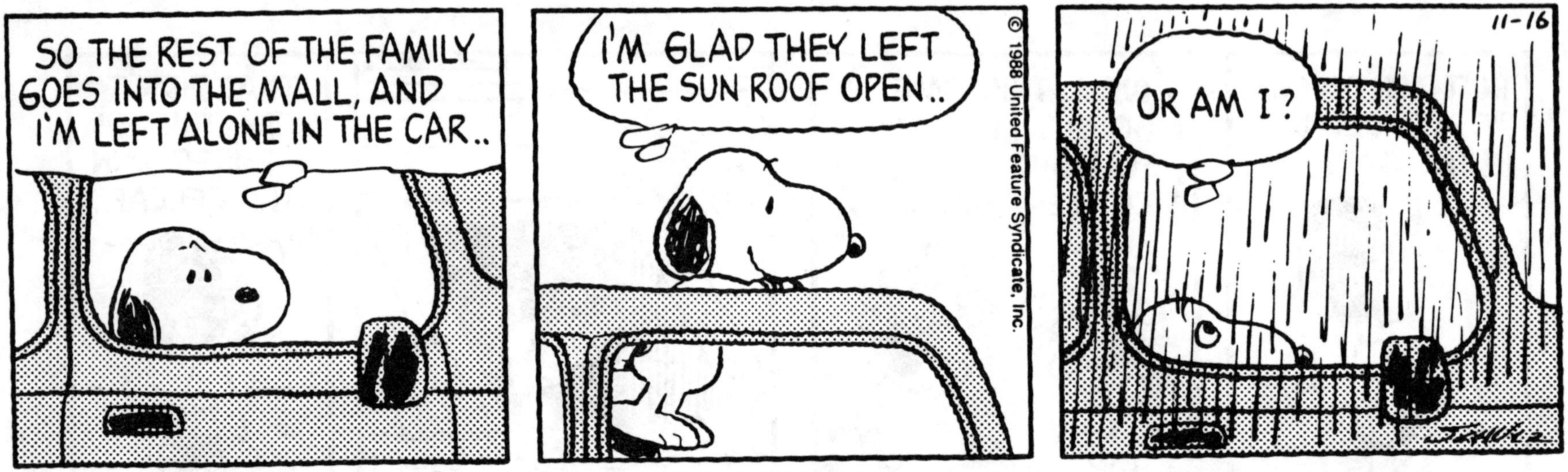
SO THE REST OF THE FAMILY GOES INTO THE MALL, AND I'M LEFT ALONE IN THE CAR..
I'M GLAD THEY LEFT THE SUN ROOF OPEN..
© 1988 United Feature Syndicate, Inc.
11-16
OR AM I?
SCHULZ

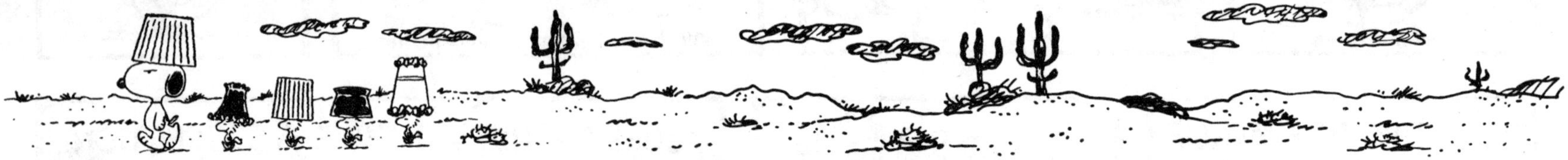

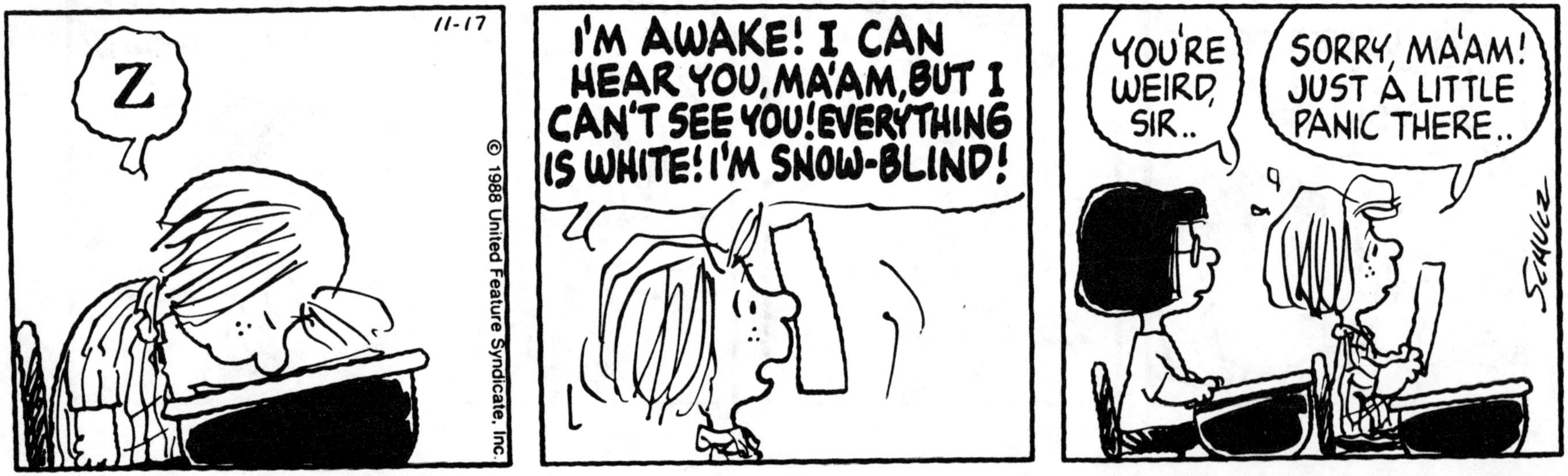
11-17
Z
© 1988 United Feature Syndicate, Inc.
I'M AWAKE! I CAN HEAR YOU, MA'AM, BUT I CAN'T SEE YOU! EVERYTHING IS WHITE! I'M SNOW-BLIND!
YOU'RE WEIRD, SIR..
SORRY, MA'AM! JUST A LITTLE PANIC THERE..
SCHULZ

Could You Be More Pacific?

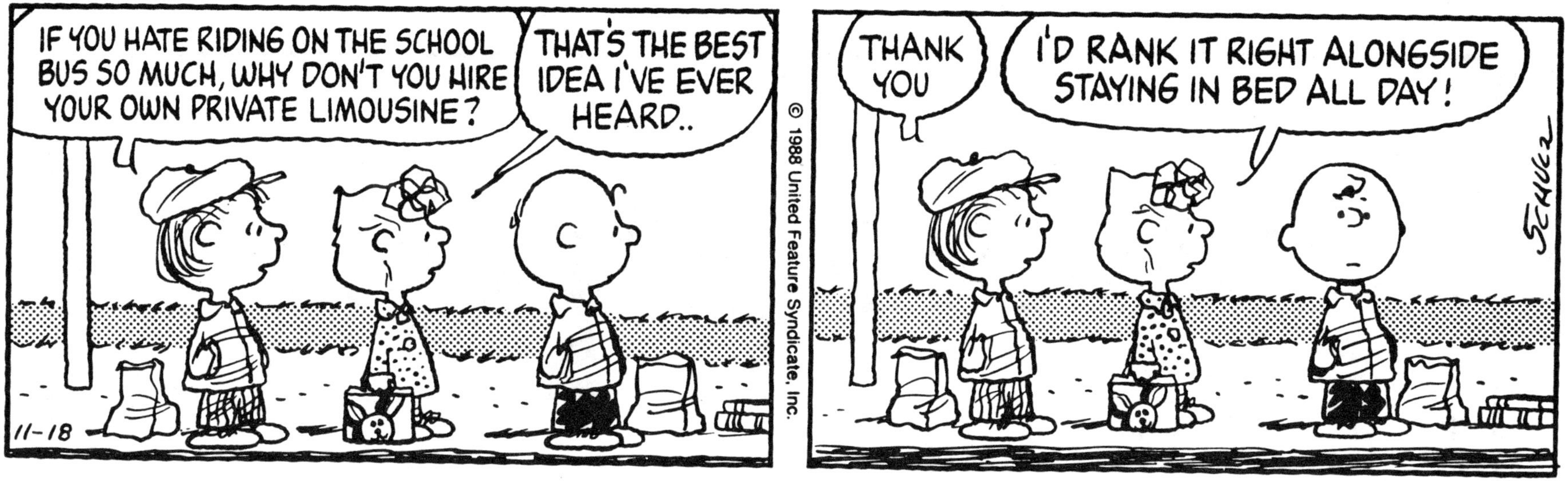
IF YOU HATE RIDING ON THE SCHOOL BUS SO MUCH, WHY DON'T YOU HIRE YOUR OWN PRIVATE LIMOUSINE?
THAT'S THE BEST IDEA I'VE EVER HEARD..
THANK YOU
I'D RANK IT RIGHT ALONGSIDE STAYING IN BED ALL DAY!
© 1988 United Feature Syndicate, Inc.
11-18
SCHULZ

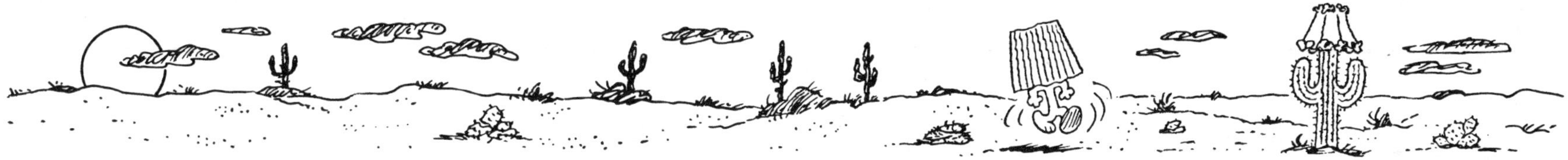

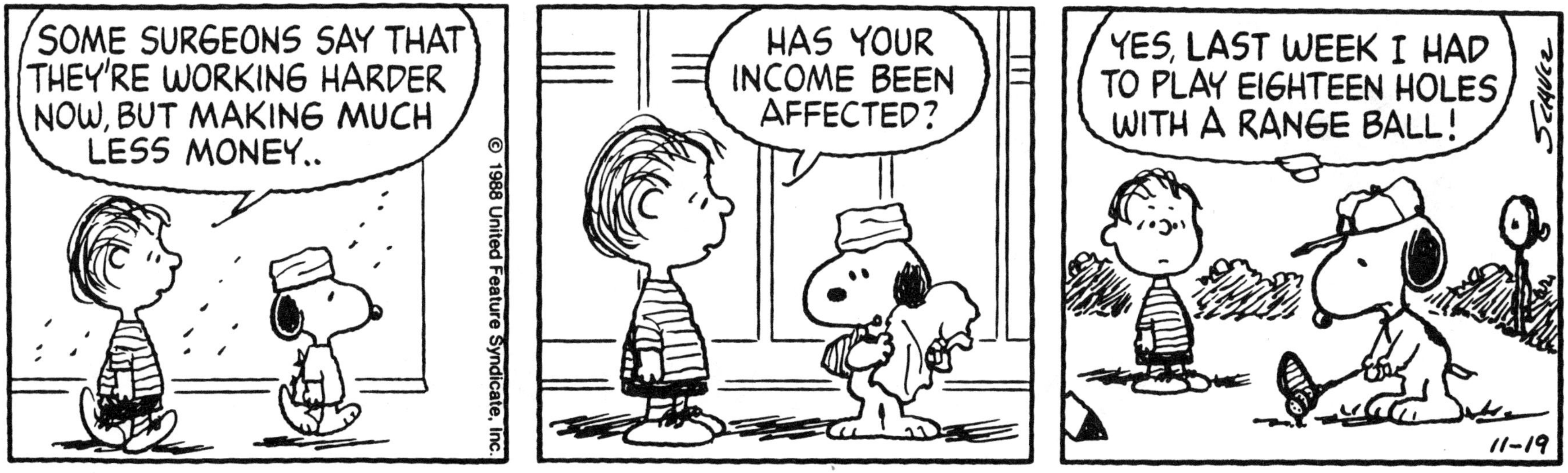
SOME SURGEONS SAY THAT THEY'RE WORKING HARDER NOW, BUT MAKING MUCH LESS MONEY..
HAS YOUR INCOME BEEN AFFECTED?
YES, LAST WEEK I HAD TO PLAY EIGHTEEN HOLES WITH A RANGE BALL!
© 1988 United Feature Syndicate, Inc.
SCHULZ
11-19

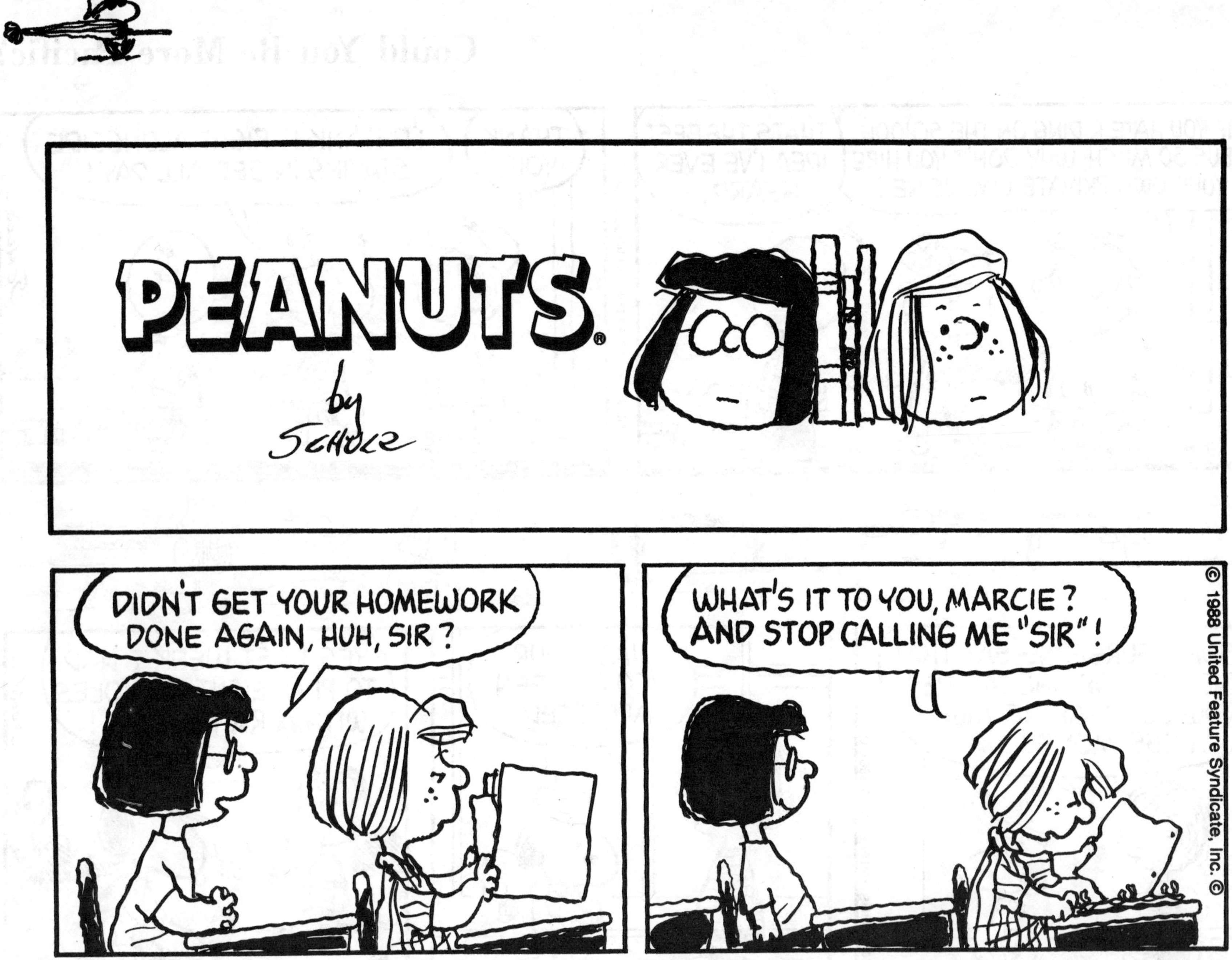
PEANUTS
by SCHULZ
DIDN'T GET YOUR HOMEWORK DONE AGAIN, HUH, SIR?
WHAT'S IT TO YOU, MARCIE? AND STOP CALLING ME "SIR"!
© 1988 United Feature Syndicate, Inc. ©

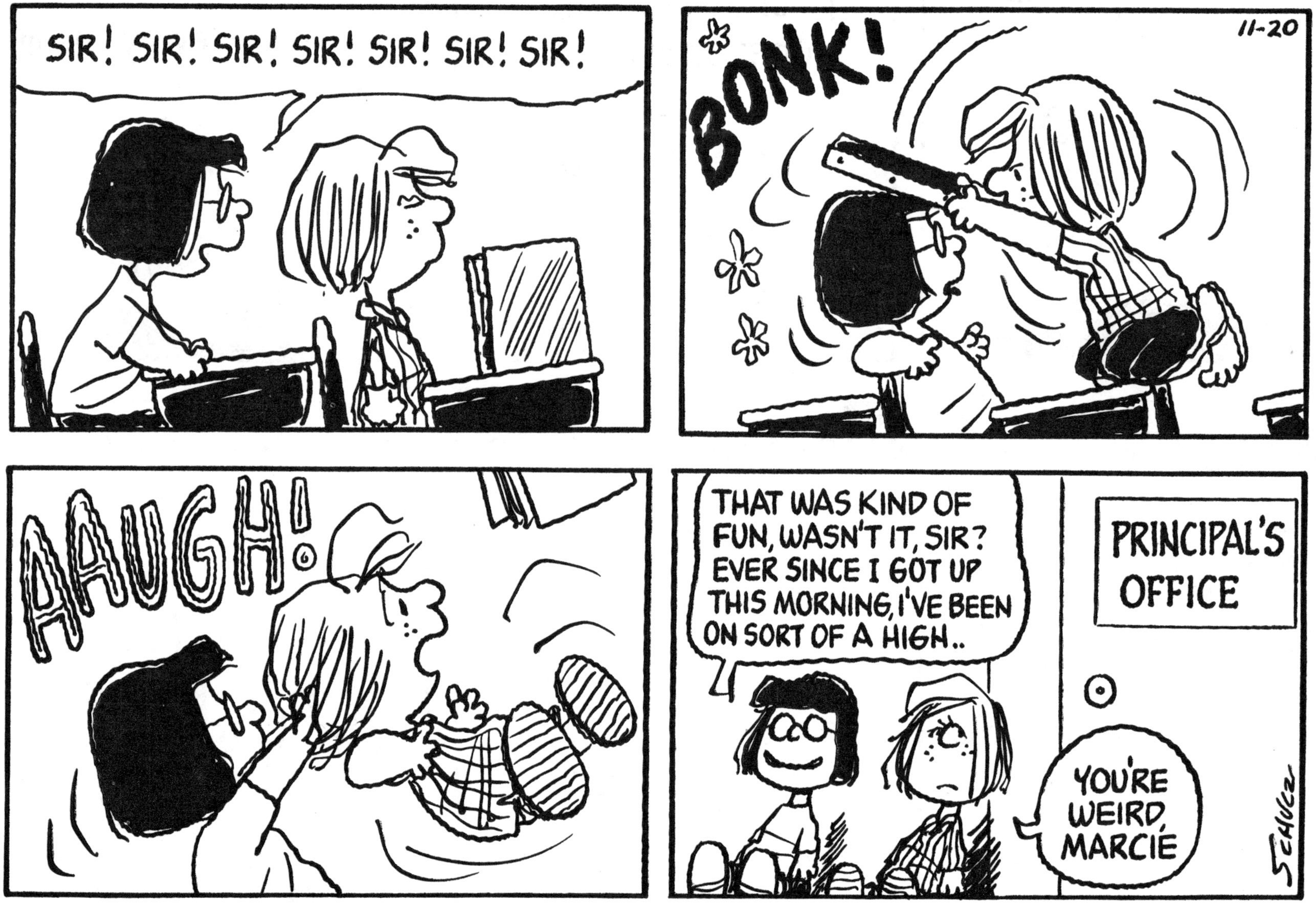
SIR! SIR! SIR! SIR! SIR! SIR! SIR!
11-20
BONK!
AAUGH!
THAT WAS KIND OF FUN, WASN'T IT, SIR? EVER SINCE I GOT UP THIS MORNING, I'VE BEEN ON SORT OF A HIGH..
PRINCIPAL'S OFFICE
YOU'RE WEIRD, MARCIE
SCHULZ

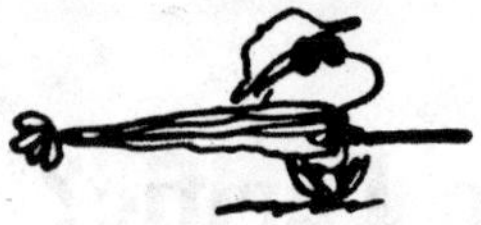

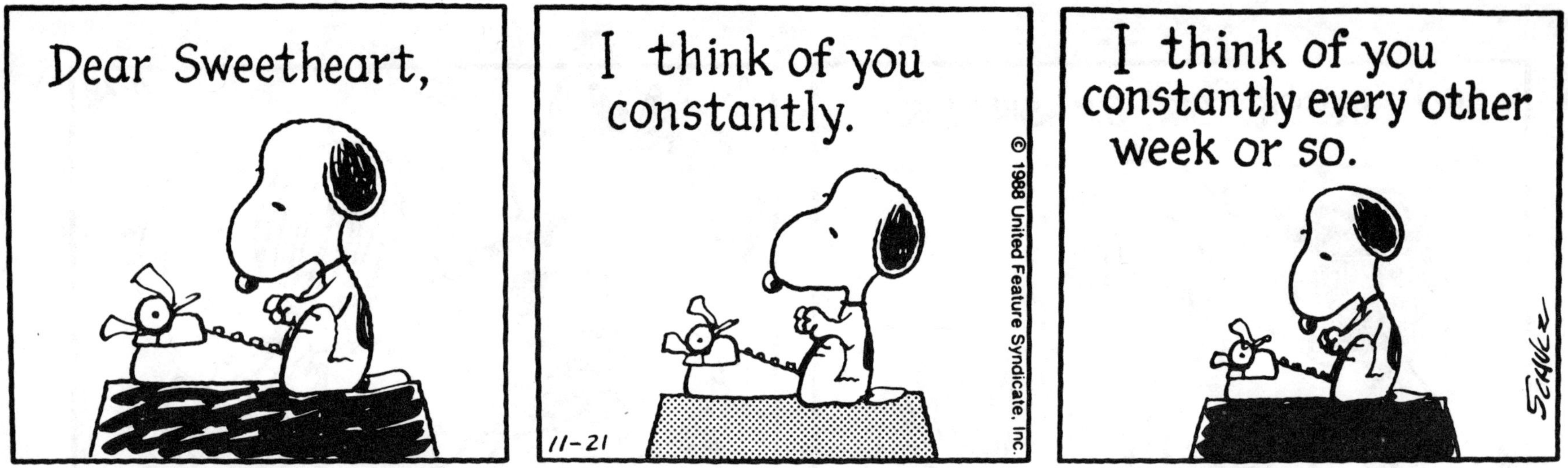
Dear Sweetheart,
I think of you constantly.
11-21
© 1988 United Feature Syndicate, Inc.
I think of you constantly every other week or so.
SCHULZ

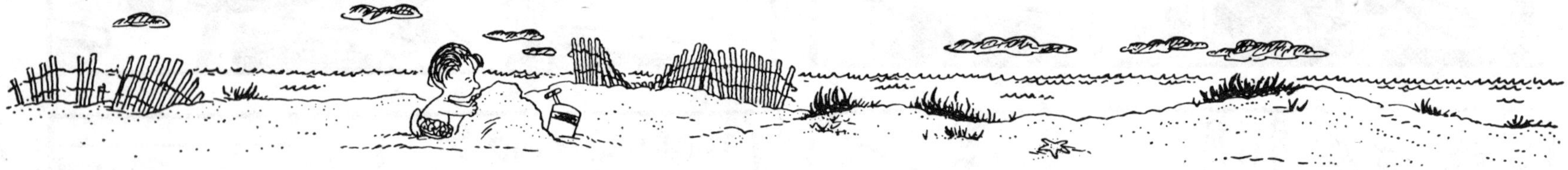

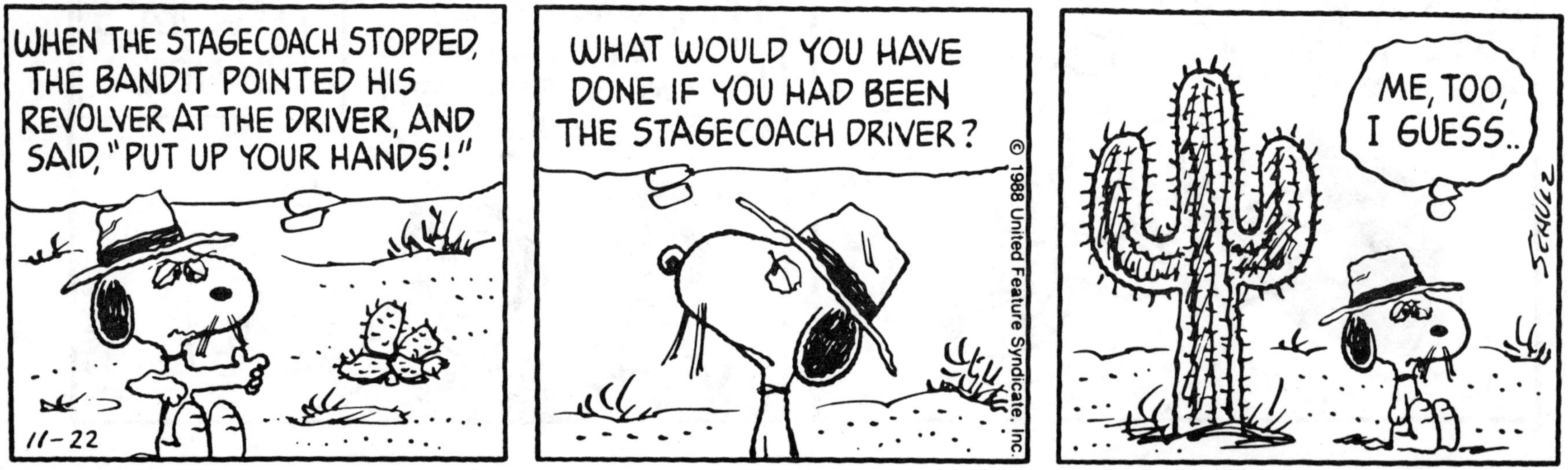
WHEN THE STAGECOACH STOPPED, THE BANDIT POINTED HIS REVOLVER AT THE DRIVER, AND SAID, "PUT UP YOUR HANDS!"
11-22
WHAT WOULD YOU HAVE DONE IF YOU HAD BEEN THE STAGECOACH DRIVER?
© 1988 United Feature Syndicate, Inc.
ME, TOO, I GUESS..
SCHULZ

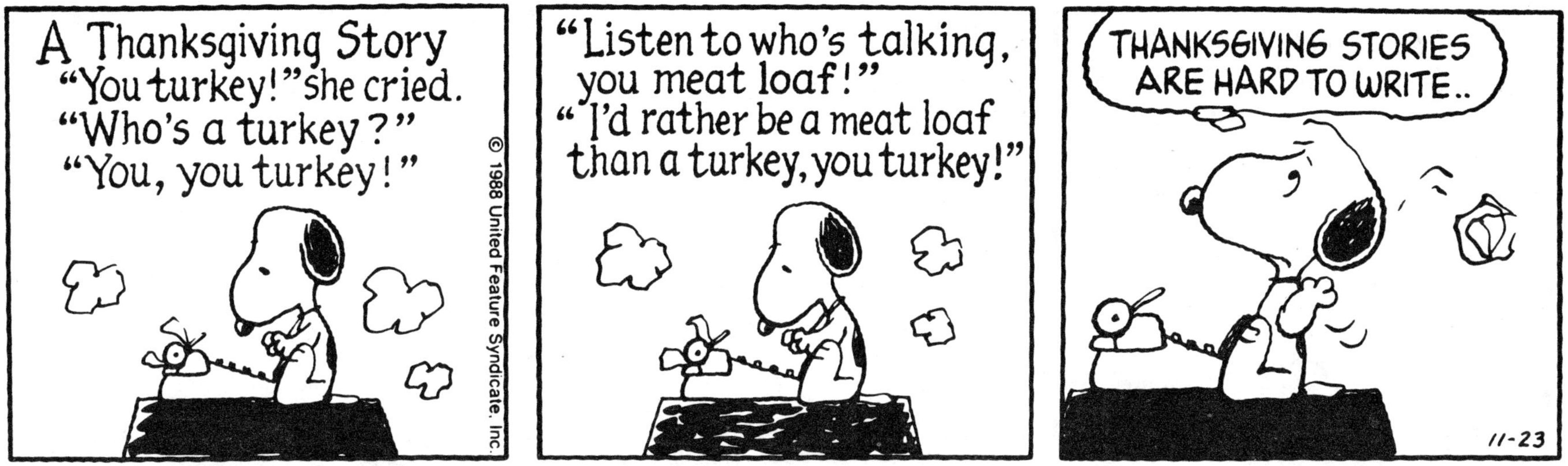
A Thanksgiving Story
"You turkey!" she cried.
"Who's a turkey?"
"You, you turkey!"
© 1988 United Feature Syndicate, Inc.
"Listen to who's talking, you meat loaf!"
"I'd rather be a meat loaf than a turkey, you turkey!"
THANKSGIVING STORIES ARE HARD TO WRITE..
11-23

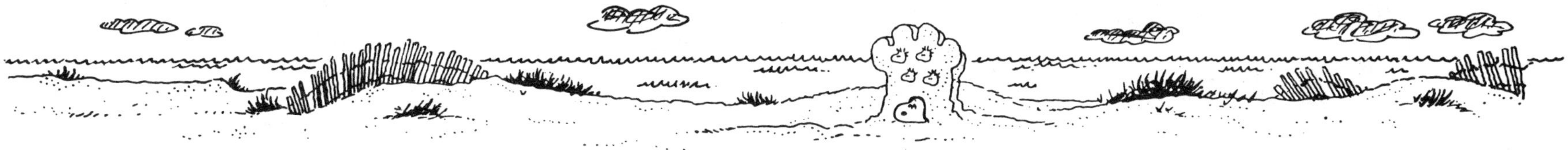

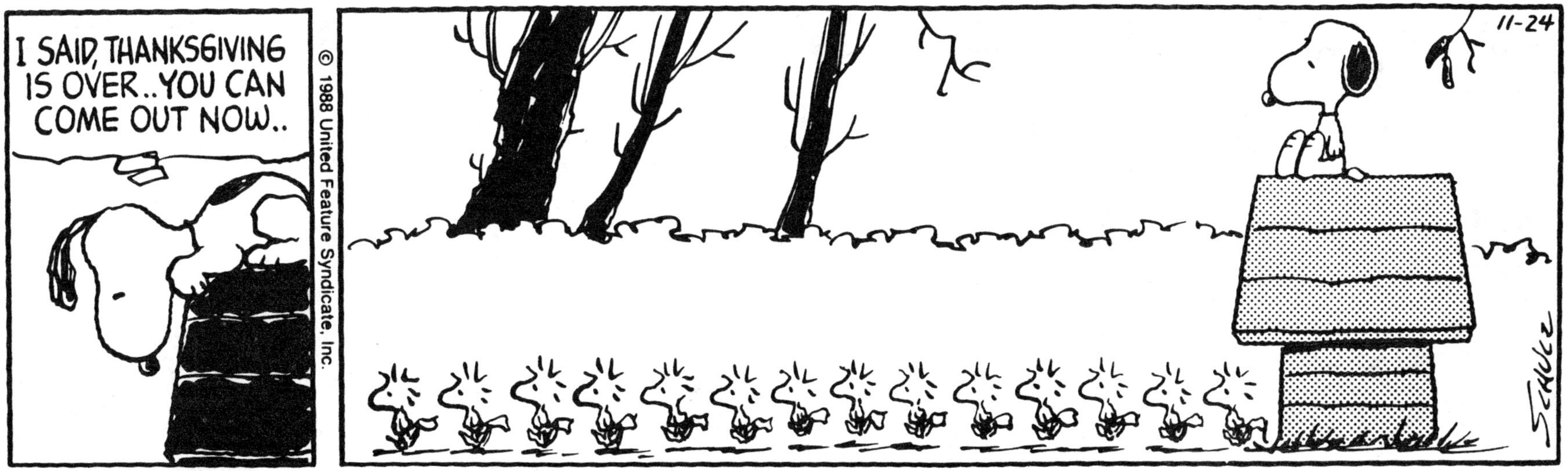
I SAID, THANKSGIVING IS OVER.. YOU CAN COME OUT NOW..
© 1988 United Feature Syndicate, Inc.
11-24
SCHULZ

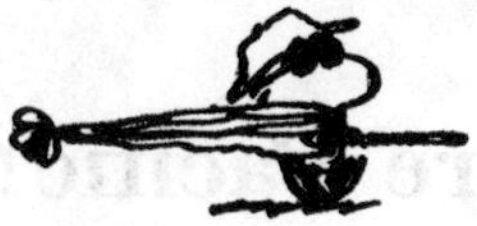

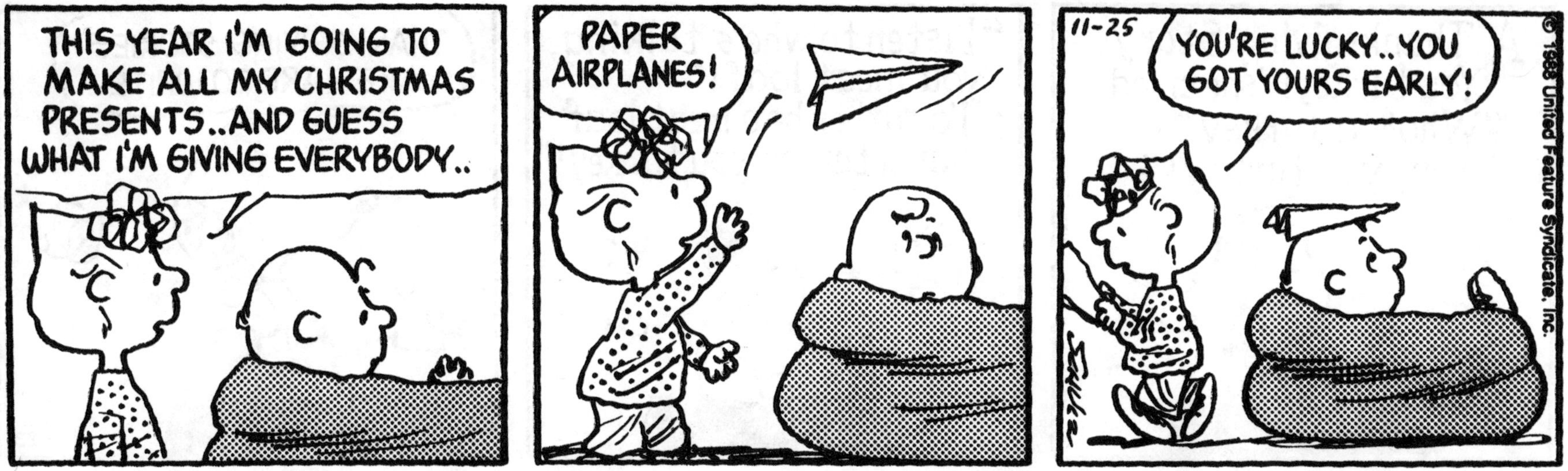

THIS YEAR I'M GOING TO MAKE ALL MY CHRISTMAS PRESENTS..AND GUESS WHAT I'M GIVING EVERYBODY..
PAPER AIRPLANES!
11-25
YOU'RE LUCKY..YOU GOT YOURS EARLY!
© 1988 United Feature Syndicate, Inc.
SCHULZ

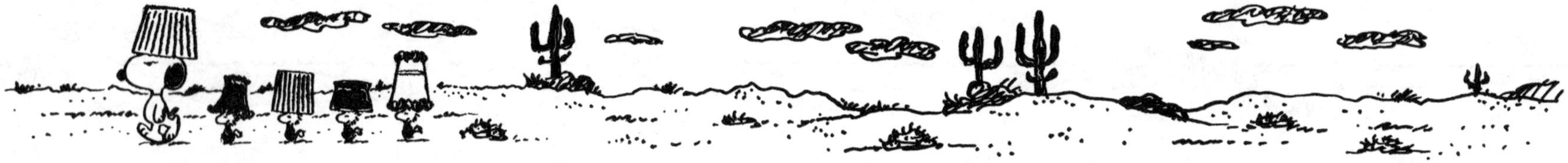

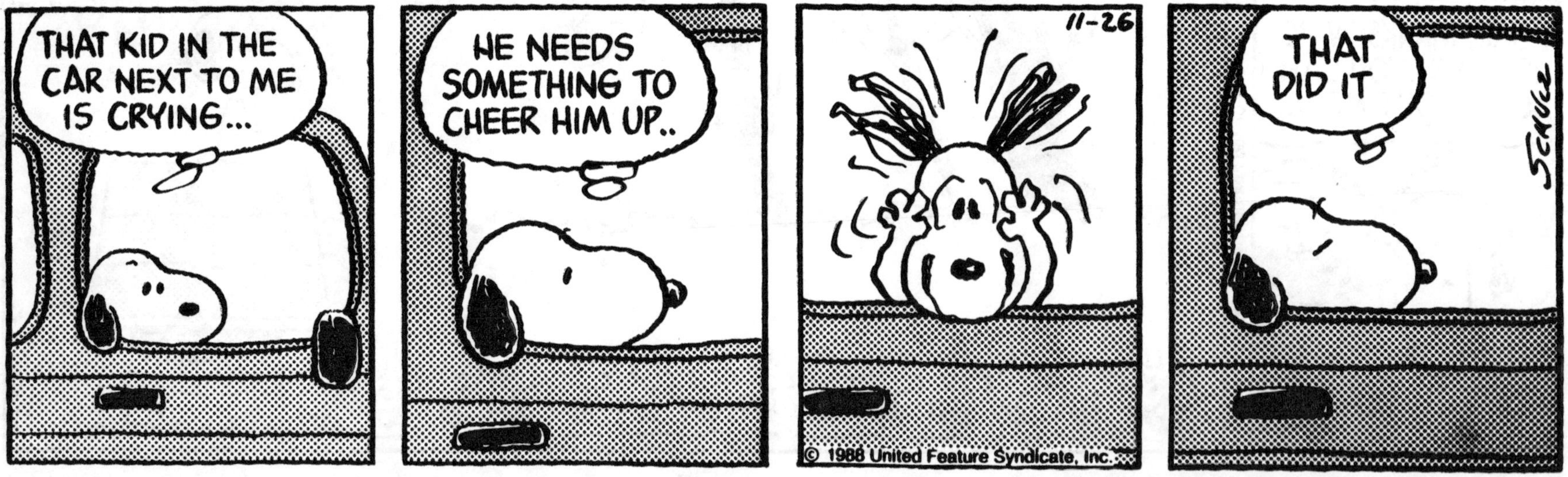

THAT KID IN THE CAR NEXT TO ME IS CRYING...
HE NEEDS SOMETHING TO CHEER HIM UP..
11-26
© 1988 United Feature Syndicate, Inc.
THAT DID IT
SCHULZ

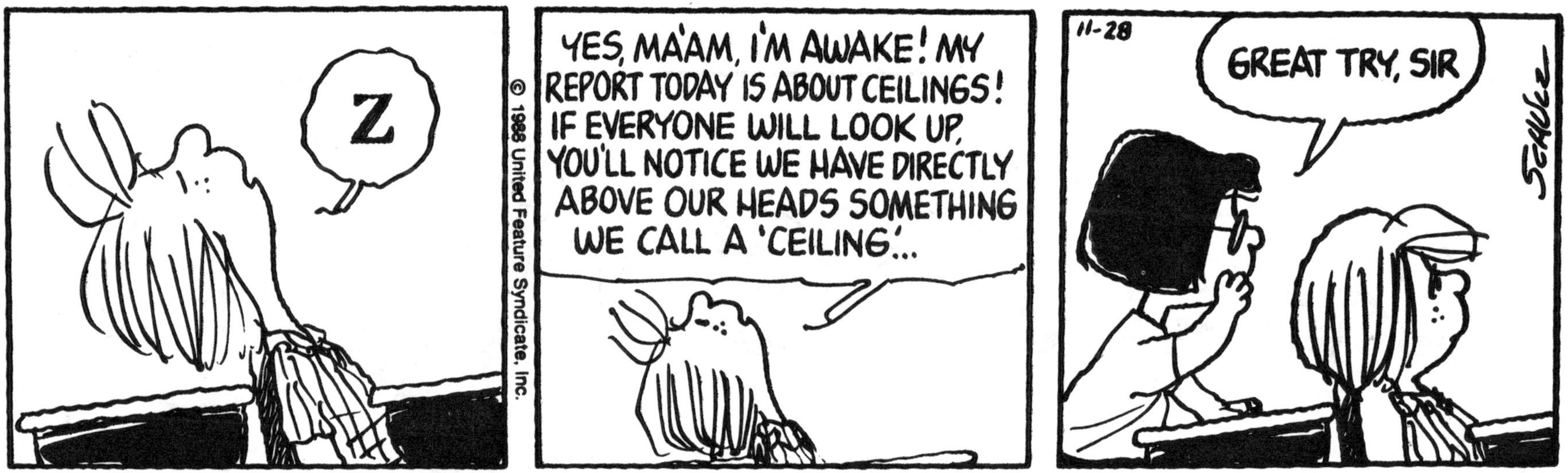
Z
© 1988 United Feature Syndicate, Inc.
YES, MA'AM, I'M AWAKE! MY REPORT TODAY IS ABOUT CEILINGS! IF EVERYONE WILL LOOK UP, YOU'LL NOTICE WE HAVE DIRECTLY ABOVE OUR HEADS SOMETHING WE CALL A 'CEILING'...
11-28
GREAT TRY, SIR
SCHULZ

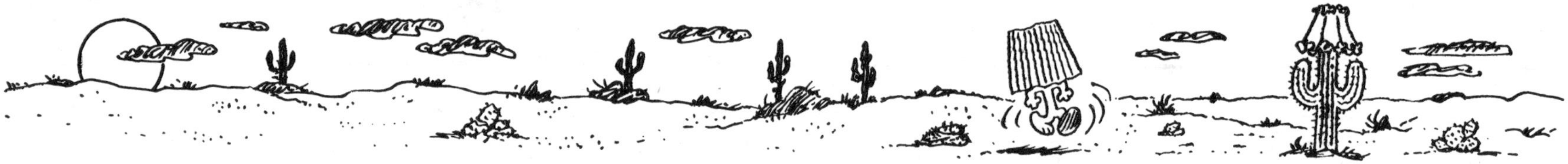

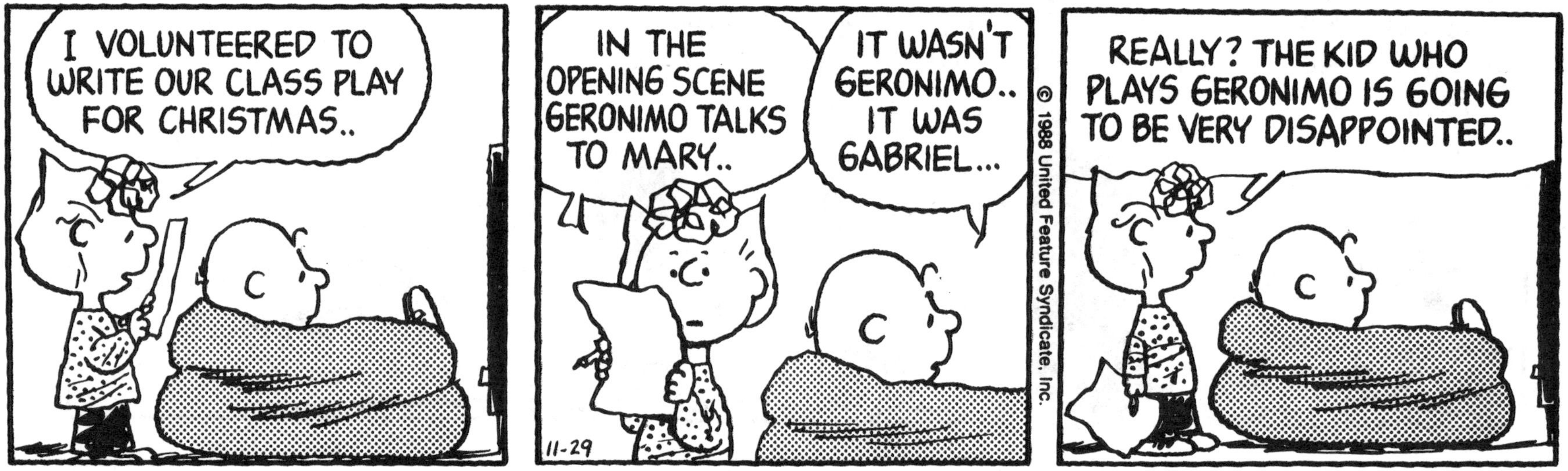
I VOLUNTEERED TO WRITE OUR CLASS PLAY FOR CHRISTMAS..
IN THE OPENING SCENE GERONIMO TALKS TO MARY..
IT WASN'T GERONIMO.. IT WAS GABRIEL...
11-29
© 1988 United Feature Syndicate, Inc.
REALLY? THE KID WHO PLAYS GERONIMO IS GOING TO BE VERY DISAPPOINTED..

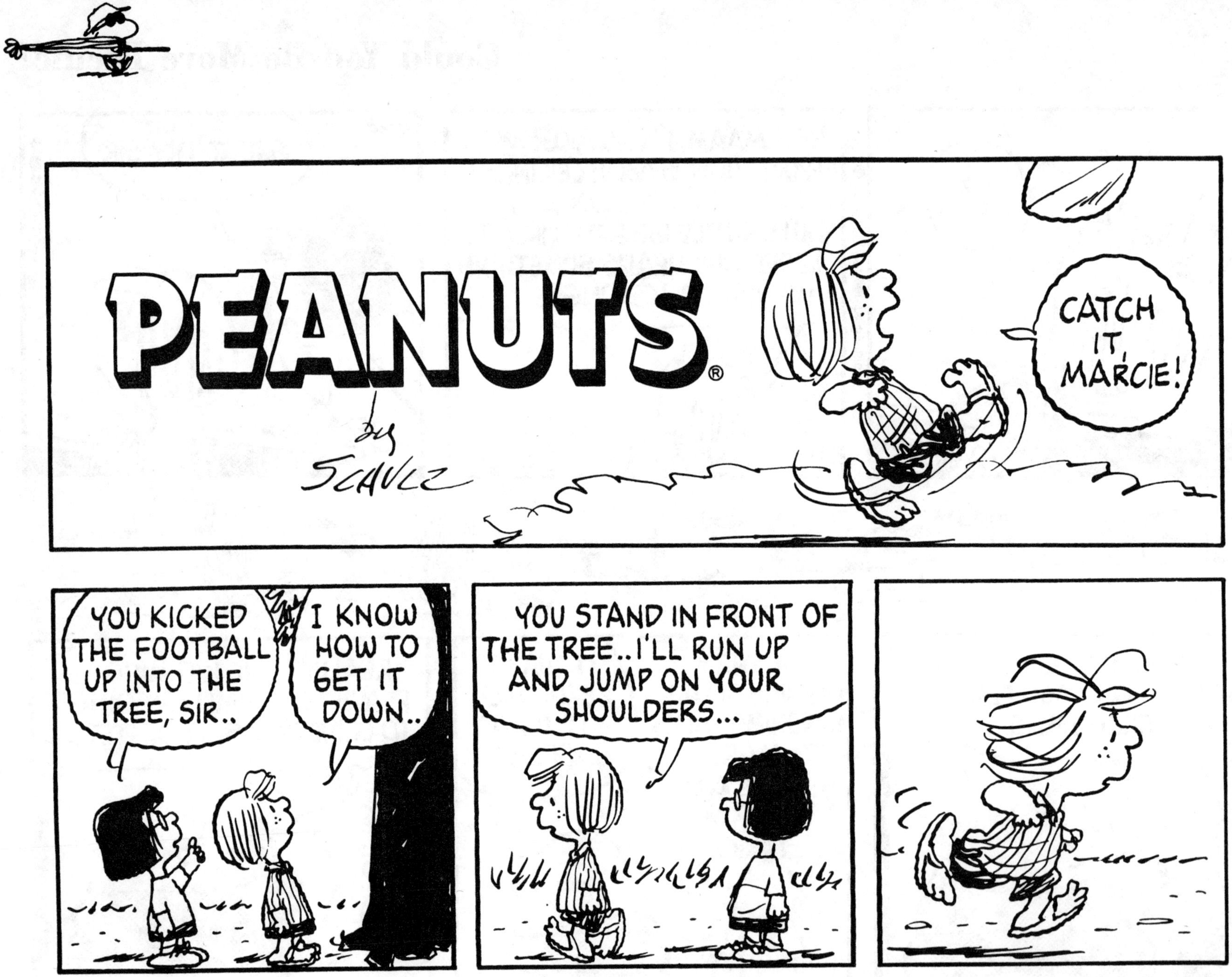
PEANUTS®
by SCHULZ
CATCH IT, MARCIE!
YOU KICKED THE FOOTBALL UP INTO THE TREE, SIR..
I KNOW HOW TO GET IT DOWN..
YOU STAND IN FRONT OF THE TREE..I'LL RUN UP AND JUMP ON YOUR SHOULDERS...

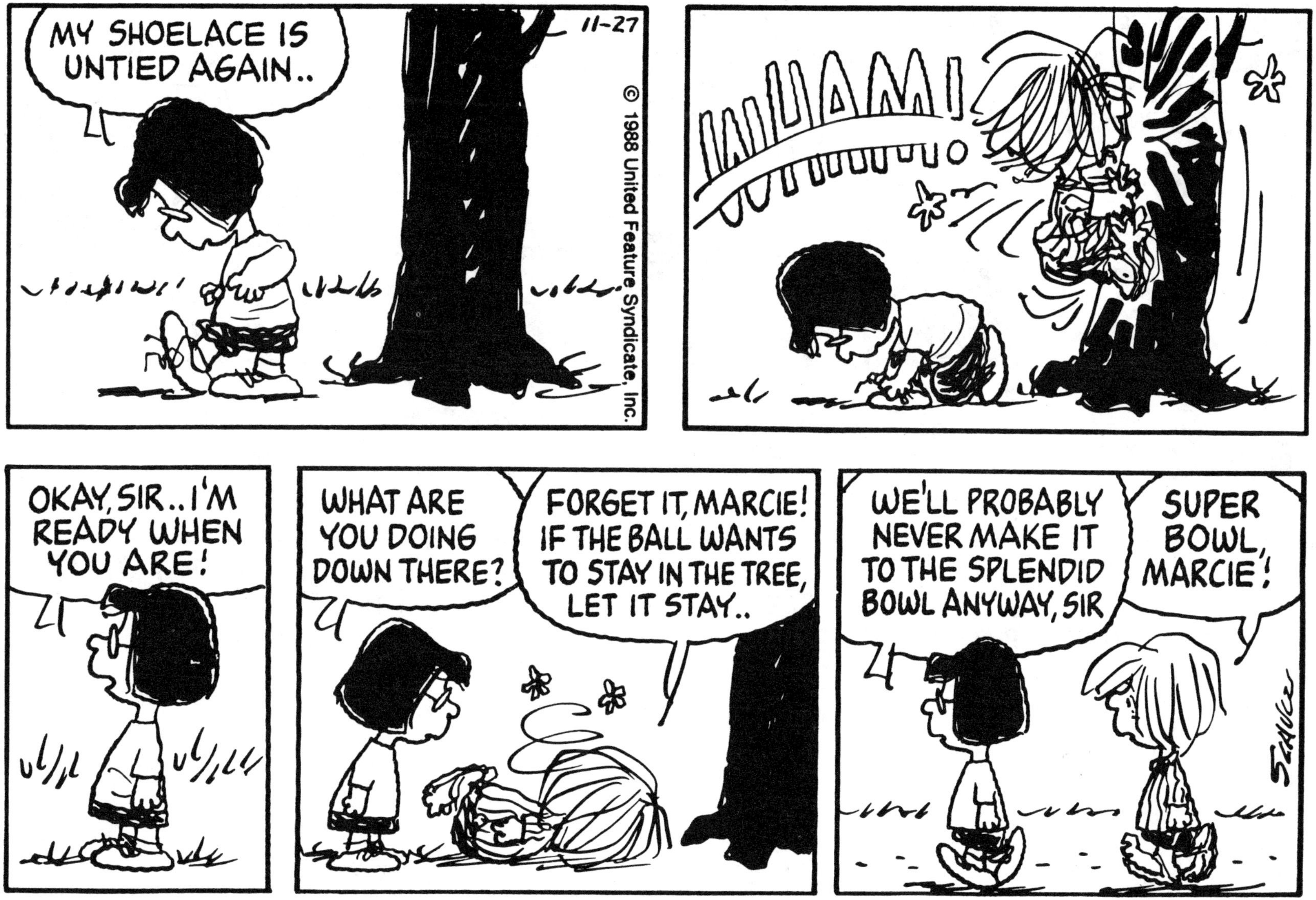
11-27
MY SHOELACE IS UNTIED AGAIN..
© 1988 United Feature Syndicate, Inc.
WHAM!
OKAY, SIR..I'M READY WHEN YOU ARE!
WHAT ARE YOU DOING DOWN THERE?
FORGET IT, MARCIE! IF THE BALL WANTS TO STAY IN THE TREE, LET IT STAY..
WE'LL PROBABLY NEVER MAKE IT TO THE SPLENDID BOWL ANYWAY, SIR
SUPER BOWL, MARCIE!
SCHULZ

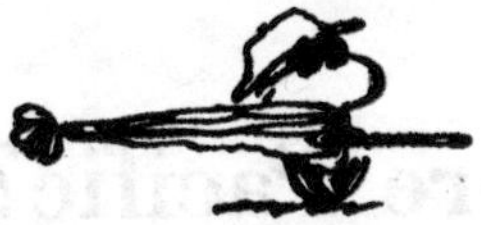

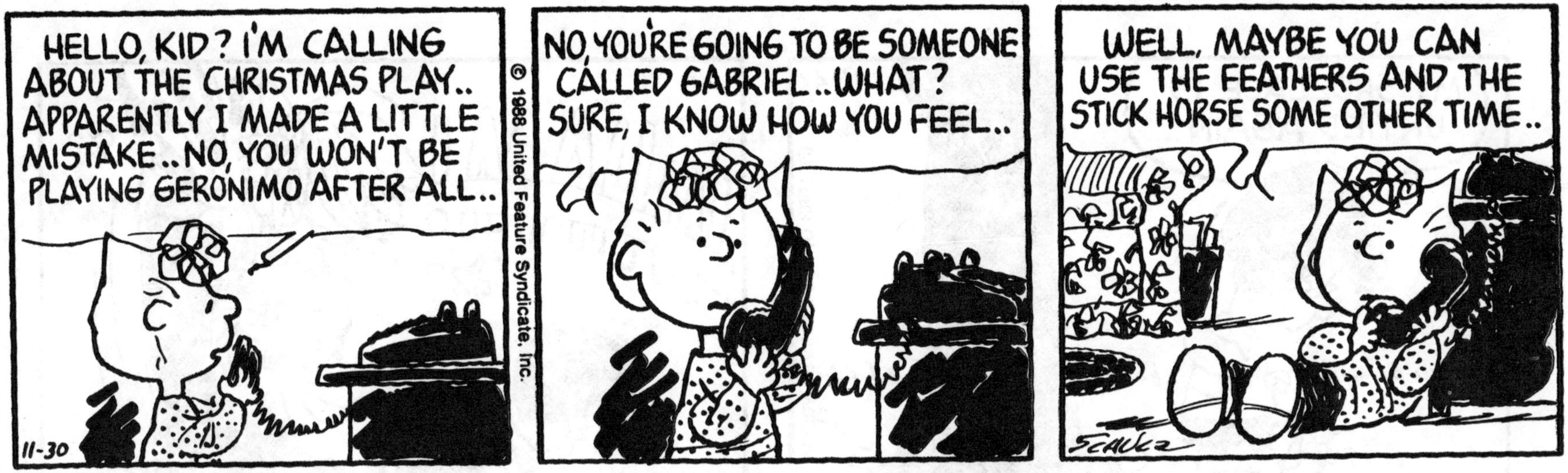
HELLO, KID? I'M CALLING ABOUT THE CHRISTMAS PLAY.. APPARENTLY I MADE A LITTLE MISTAKE..NO, YOU WON'T BE PLAYING GERONIMO AFTER ALL..
11-30
© 1988 United Feature Syndicate, Inc.
NO, YOU'RE GOING TO BE SOMEONE CALLED GABRIEL..WHAT? SURE, I KNOW HOW YOU FEEL..
WELL, MAYBE YOU CAN USE THE FEATHERS AND THE STICK HORSE SOME OTHER TIME..
SCHULZ

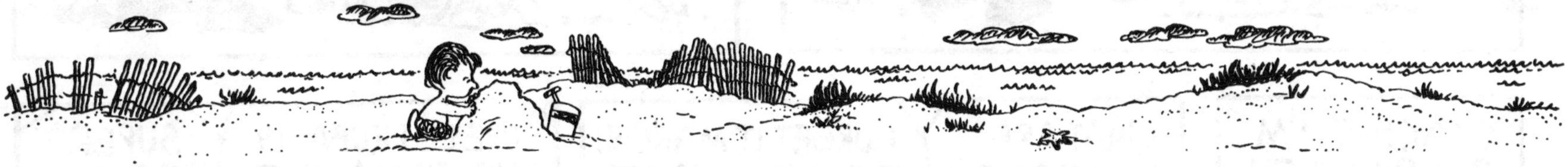

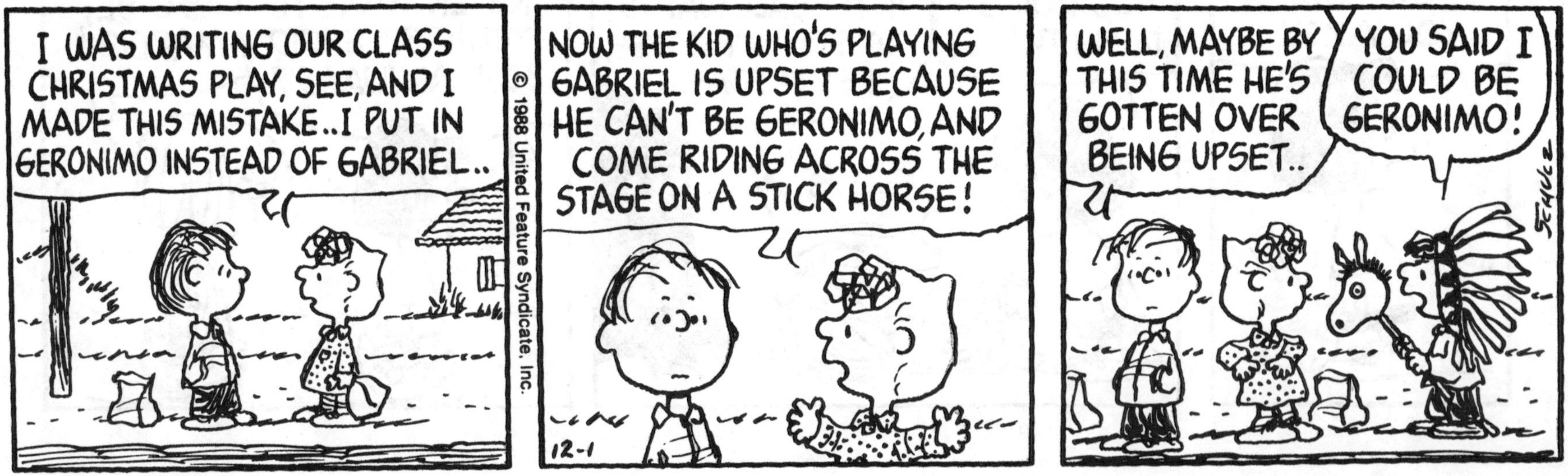
I WAS WRITING OUR CLASS CHRISTMAS PLAY, SEE, AND I MADE THIS MISTAKE..I PUT IN GERONIMO INSTEAD OF GABRIEL..
© 1988 United Feature Syndicate, Inc.
NOW THE KID WHO'S PLAYING GABRIEL IS UPSET BECAUSE HE CAN'T BE GERONIMO, AND COME RIDING ACROSS THE STAGE ON A STICK HORSE!
12-1
WELL, MAYBE BY THIS TIME HE'S GOTTEN OVER BEING UPSET..
YOU SAID I COULD BE GERONIMO!
SCHULZ

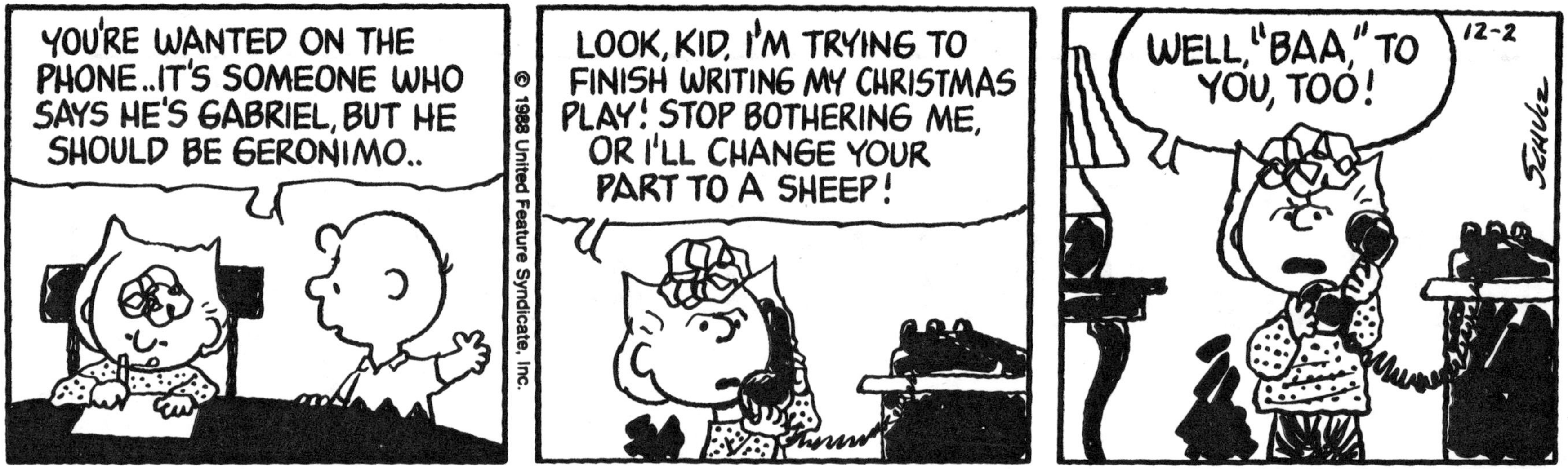
YOU'RE WANTED ON THE PHONE..IT'S SOMEONE WHO SAYS HE'S GABRIEL, BUT HE SHOULD BE GERONIMO..
© 1988 United Feature Syndicate, Inc.
LOOK, KID, I'M TRYING TO FINISH WRITING MY CHRISTMAS PLAY! STOP BOTHERING ME, OR I'LL CHANGE YOUR PART TO A SHEEP!
WELL, "BAA," TO YOU, TOO!
12-2
SCHULZ

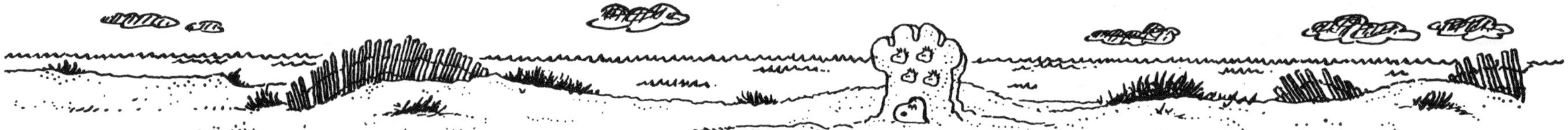

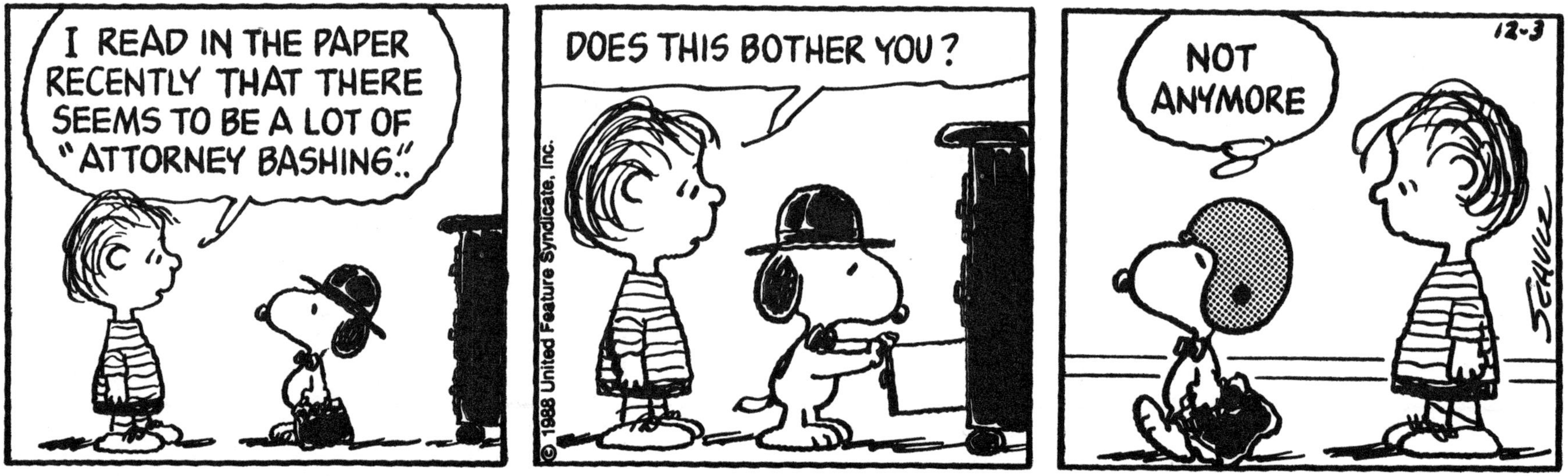
I READ IN THE PAPER RECENTLY THAT THERE SEEMS TO BE A LOT OF "ATTORNEY BASHING."
© 1988 United Feature Syndicate, Inc.
DOES THIS BOTHER YOU?
NOT ANYMORE
12-3
SCHULZ

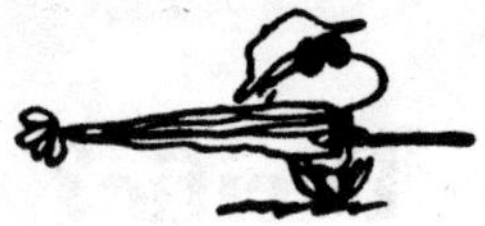

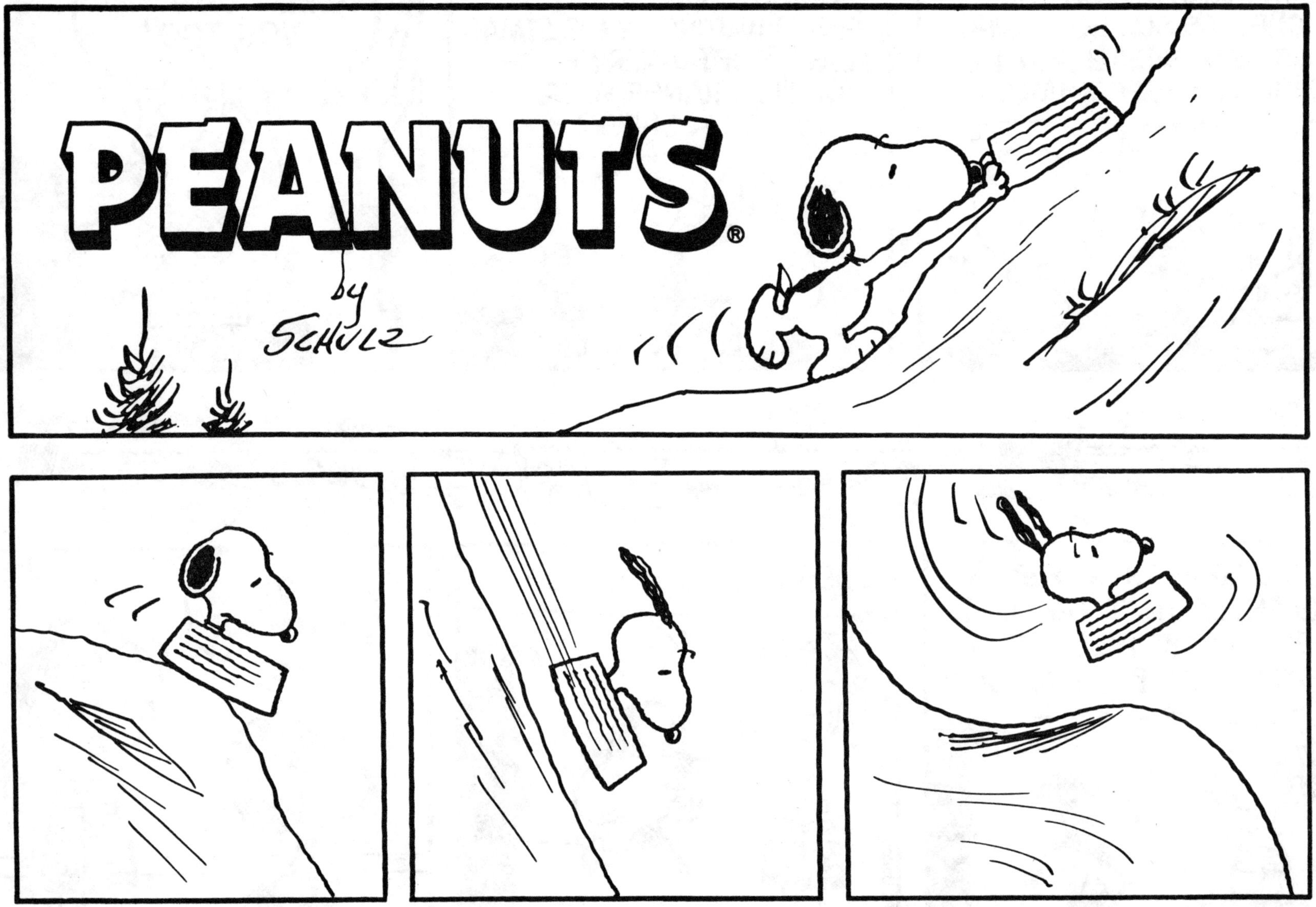
PEANUTS®
by SCHULZ

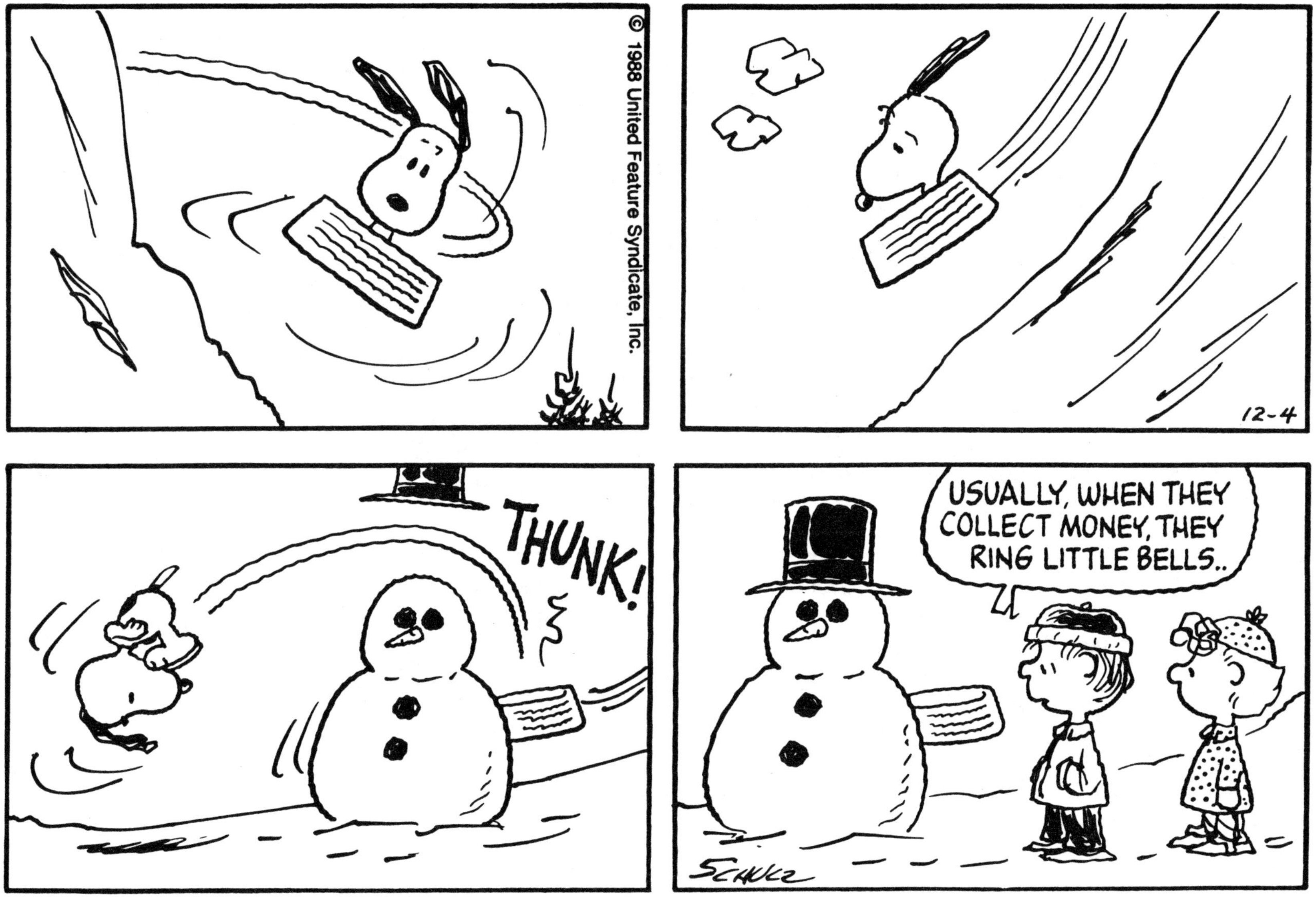
© 1988 United Feature Syndicate, Inc.
12-4
THUNK!
USUALLY, WHEN THEY COLLECT MONEY, THEY RING LITTLE BELLS..
SCHULZ

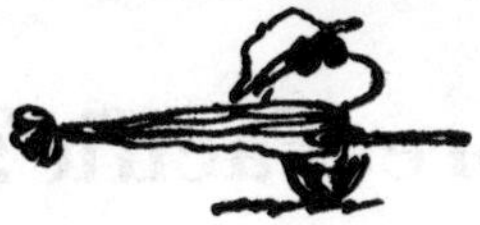

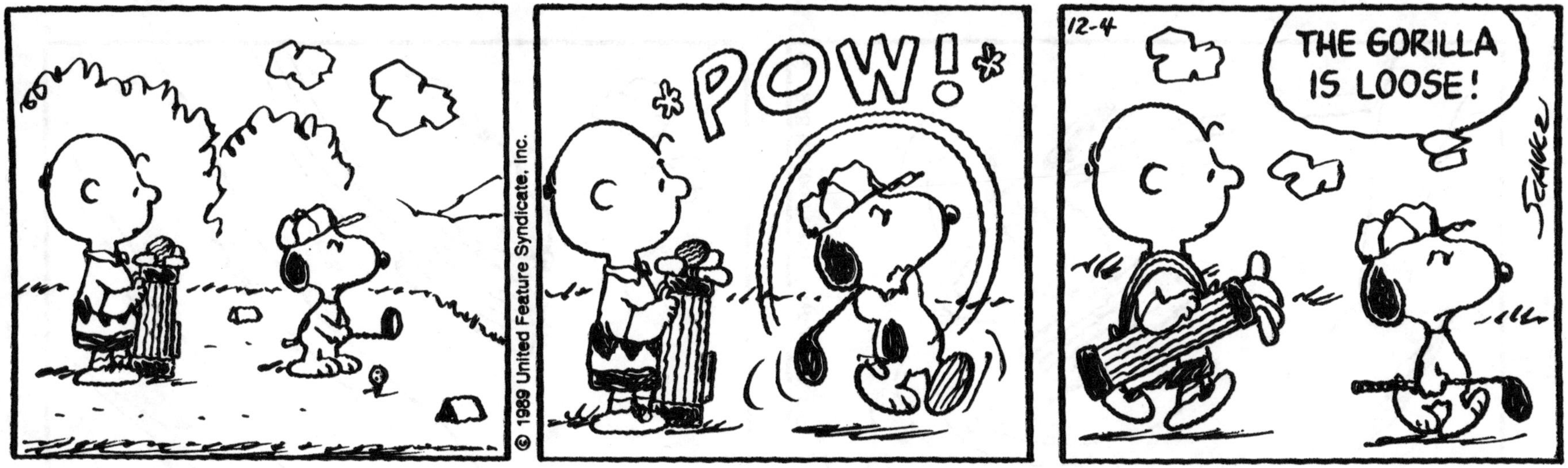
12-4
© 1989 United Feature Syndicate, Inc.
POW!
THE GORILLA IS LOOSE!
SCHULZ

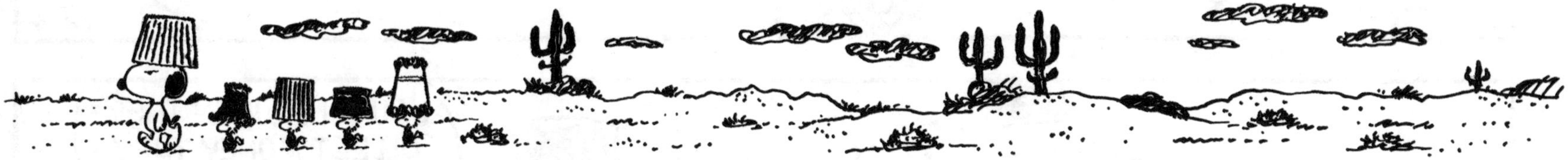

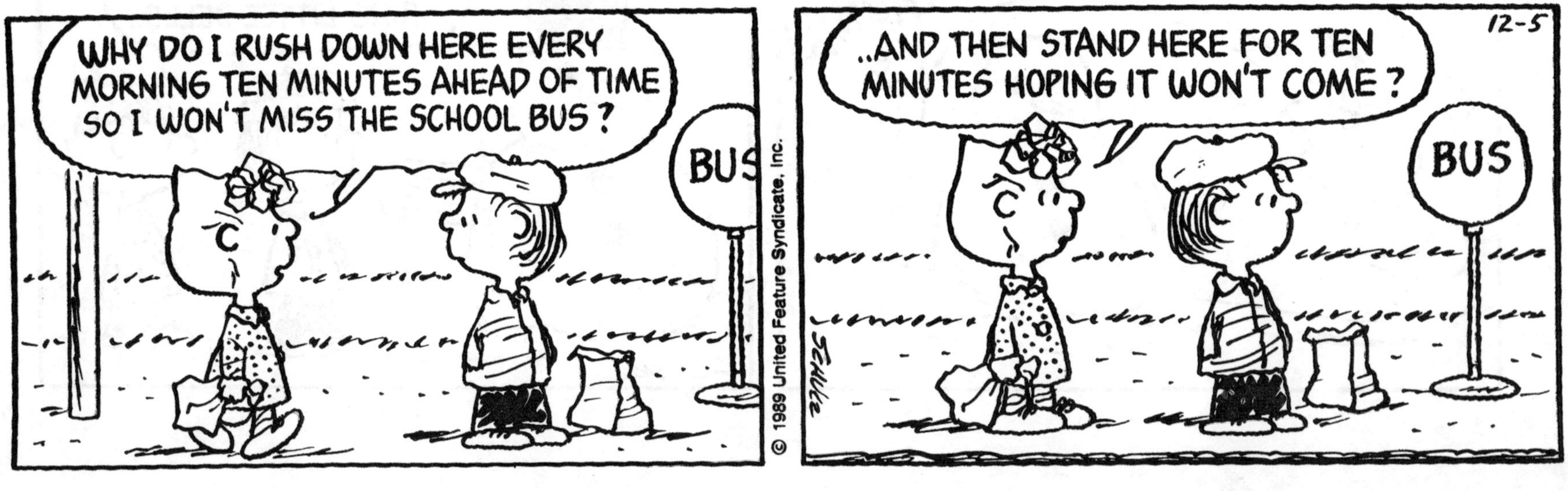
12-5
WHY DO I RUSH DOWN HERE EVERY MORNING TEN MINUTES AHEAD OF TIME SO I WON'T MISS THE SCHOOL BUS?
BUS
© 1989 United Feature Syndicate, Inc.
SCHULZ
..AND THEN STAND HERE FOR TEN MINUTES HOPING IT WON'T COME?
BUS

START YOUR OWN PEANUTS GALLERY

PEANUTS COLLECTOR SERIES

- ☐ (#1) DOGS DON'T EAT DESSERT **$5.95**
- ☐ (#2) YOU'RE ON THE WRONG FOOT AGAIN, CHARLIE BROWN **$5.95**
- ☐ (#3) BY SUPPER POSSESSED **$5.95**
- ☐ (#4) TALK IS CHEEP, CHARLIE BROWN **$5.95**
- ☐ (#5) IT DOESN'T TAKE MUCH TO ATTRACT A CROWD **$6.95**
- ☐ (#6) IF BEAGLES COULD FLY **$6.95**
- ☐ (#7) DON'T BE SAD, FLYING ACE **$6.95**
- ☐ (#8) COULD YOU BE MORE PACIFIC? **$6.95**
- ☐ BROTHERS & SISTERS: It's All Relative **$5.95**
- ☐ HAPPINESS IS A WARM PUPPY **$5.95**
- ☐ LOVE IS WALKING HAND IN HAND **$5.95**
- ☐ AN EDUCATED SLICE **$8.95**

PEANUTS JUVENILE BOOKS
(Full Color Oversized Hardcovers)

- ☐ CHARLIE BROWN This is Your Life **$7.95**
- ☐ SALLY School is My World **$7.95**
- ☐ SCHROEDER Music is My Life **$7.95**
- ☐ SNOOPY My Greatest Adventures **$7.95**

__ **TOTAL BOOKS** (Please add .50 per book for postage and handling.)

My check for $_____ is enclosed.

Ship to:

_____
NAME

_____
ADDRESS

_____
CITY STATE ZIP

Return to: Sales Dept., Pharos Books, 200 Park Avenue, New York, NY 10166.

Please allow 4-6 weeks for delivery.